LISTENING FOR A LIFE

A DIALOGIC ETHNOGRAPHY OF
Bessie Eldreth
THROUGH HER SONGS AND STORIES

LISTENING FOR A LIFE

A DIALOGIC ETHNOGRAPHY OF
Bessie Eldreth
THROUGH HER SONGS AND STORIES

Patricia Sawin

UTAH STATE UNIVERSITY PRESS
LOGAN, UTAH

Utah State University Press
Logan, Utah 84322-7800

Publication of this book was supported by a grant from the University Research Council at the University of North Carolina, Chapel Hill.

Manufactured in Canada
Printed on acid-free paper

Library of Congress Cataloging-in-Publication Data

Sawin, Patricia.
  Listening for a life : a dialogic ethnography of Bessie Eldreth through her songs and stories / Patricia Sawin.
     p. cm.
  Includes bibliographical references and index.
  ISBN 0-87421-582-X (pbk. : alk. paper)
1. Eldreth, Bessie Mae, 1913- 2. Eldreth, Bessie Mae, 1913—-Interviews. 3. Women folklorists—Appalachian Region—Biography. 4. Women storytellers—Appalachian Region—Biography. 5. Folk singers—Appalachian Region—Biography. 6. Folklore—Appalachian Region. 7. Folk music—Appalachian Region. 8. Appalachian Region—Social life and customs. I. Title.
  GR55.E53S397 2004
  398'.092—dc22

                              2004004974

For my parents, Marilynn and Lewis Sawin,

whose lives and stories I cherish and whose loving listening I

strive to emulate

Better go down upon your marrow-bones
And scrub a kitchen pavement, or break stones
Like an old pauper, in all kinds of weather;
For to articulate sweet sounds together
Is to work harder than all these, and yet
Be thought an idler by the noisy set
Of bankers, schoolmasters, and clergymen
The martyrs call the world.

—William Butler Yeats, "Adam's Curse"

But is it impossible to reveal, through a character's acts and through these acts alone, his ideological position and the ideological world at its heart, without representing his discourse?

It cannot be done, because it is impossible to represent an alien ideological world adequately without first permitting it to sound, without having first revealed the special discourse peculiar to it. After all, a really adequate discourse for portraying a world's unique ideology can only be that world's own discourse, although not that discourse in itself, but only in conjunction with the discourse of an author.

—M. M. Bakhtin, *The Dialogic Imagination*

Contents

Preface   ix

Transcription Conventions   xiii

1   *Introduction*
    Dialogism and Subjectivity   1

2   *"That was before I ever left home"*
    Complex Accounts of a Simple Childhood   28

3   *"If you had to work as hard as I did, it would kill you"*
    Work, Narrative, and Self-Definition   49

4   *"I said, 'Don't you do it'"*
    Tracing Development as an Empowered Speaker
    through Reported Speech in Narrative   68

5   *"He never did say anything about my dreams that would
    worry me after that"*
    Negotiating Gender and Power in Ghost Stories   98

6   *"I'm a bad one to go pulling jokes on people"*
    Practical Joking as a Problematic Vehicle
    for Oppositional Self-Definition   135

7   *"My singing is my life"*
    Repertoire and Performance   156

8   *Epilogue*   211

    Notes   214

    Works Cited   229

    Index   241

PREFACE

This is a book about a woman both remarkable and ordinary. It is simultaneously a book about the process, likewise both ordinary and remarkable, through which one person comes to know another. Bessie Eldreth and I first met in the summer of 1987, when she and her granddaughter, Jean Reid, were performing at the Smithsonian Institution's Festival of American Folklife on the mall in Washington, D.C. Members of a group from Ashe and Watauga Counties in northwestern North Carolina, they had been invited to represent the distinctive culture and speechways of a portion of the mountain South to some wider American culture of which, the festival setting implied, they were a crucial part yet from which they were somehow separated. Several impressions from that first meeting intrigued me and attracted me to the possibility of working with Eldreth. She was framed for me as a "traditional singer" of some sort, although at that point I did not stop to ask what that might mean. Folklorist Glenn Hinson, who presented her on stage, mentioned that she sang constantly around the house, which hinted at a specifically gendered performance practice. Further, when I introduced myself to Eldreth she responded with a flood of stories about salient personal experiences. The accounts themselves were compelling, and she was clearly a woman who had a story she wanted to share. In the intervening years Eldreth and I have spent many hours talking at her kitchen table and tape-recording her stories and her repertoire of close to two hundred songs. I have gone back again and again not only to Eldreth's house but also to those tapes, trying to grasp what our interactions meant and what she was trying to get across to me.

Increasingly, I realized that I needed to challenge the presuppositions with which I had framed Eldreth and our interactions. She is a remarkable and dedicated singer, but her repertoire and practice link her more to the national, commercial spread of early country music than to the ancient solo ballad tradition in which I had imagined her participating. I had, furthermore, assumed that the significant difference between us was one of culture and that she was valuable for a folklorist to study because of her participation in a distinctive Appalachian culture. However, I became more and more aware that, for Eldreth, the difference between us was an issue of class and specifically of the amount and kind of work we had had to do. I also gradually realized my error in supposing that I could understand her communications about herself without taking account of my role as the person to whom she was speaking. The dialogic approach that I eventually adopted recognizes that Eldreth, like all of us, talks and sings simultaneously to her immediate audience and to the ghosts of listeners past and future, both of whose understanding and response she anticipates. Once I learned to listen to Eldreth's songs and stories as multivocal communications, I realized that she had been trying to teach me what revisionist historians and folklorists were arguing in these same years—that Appalachia was a rhetorical construct more than a separate region and that the area was as internally class divided as any other part of the country. What makes Eldreth remarkable, then, is not some status as a representative of Appalachian culture (an ascription she both resists and capitalizes upon strategically). Rather she is remarkable for her perseverance and self-sacrifice, the work she did to support her children, her emotional survival despite minimal support from her husband. My goal is not, however, to paint her as flawless. In constructing a respectable self against the odds, Eldreth grasps at the resources available to her, which makes her complicit in reinforcing systems of racial and gender control upon which she relies. Over the years of working with Eldreth, I have grown (one might even say, grown up) as a person and a folklorist, learning above all that our disciplinary commitment to celebrate less-appreciated arts and artists need not blind us to the complexity of our subjects' lives. It has been a challenge and an honor to get to know Bessie Eldreth.

When I first asked Eldreth if I could come to North Carolina to talk with her and record her stories, she replied, "Child, you are as welcome as the water that runs." She has borne my questions with grace and humor, always encouraging me to come visit, and has been very patient waiting for her book. I cannot fully repay her willingness to let me write about her, but every sentence of this book and every hour of the time I have spent working on it is an attempt to show my gratitude.

I have been fortunate in getting to meet all of Eldreth's children and many of her grandchildren, and I appreciate their courtesy and tolerance of my involvement in their mother and grandmother's life. For their friendship and humor I am especially grateful to Roger Eldreth, Carl and Libby Eldreth, Stacey and Drew Eldreth (aged three and five when this study began) and their parents, Bob and Wanda Eldreth, and Lorene Greene and her husband Buster Greene and son Michael Wheatley. Patsy Reese kindly lent the photograph of Eldreth as a child with her siblings and mother. It has been a blessing to worship with the members of the Tabernacle Baptist Church over the years. Thanks especially to Johnny and Helen Moretz and A. C. and Glenna Hollars for the insights our conversations have given me into the changing life of church and community.

Mary Greene made this project possible in innumerable ways. A musician, scholar, and longtime neighbor of Eldreth's, Greene helped persuade me to embark on the work with Eldreth and was unfailingly generous in sharing her scholarly observations on mountain music and her personal reflections on grow-ing up in the area. She and her husband, Pat Baker, and their daughter Kathleen have kept me sane, challenged my assumptions, given me a place to sleep, fed me familiar food, and become cherished friends. I am grateful, too, to Greene's late mother, Cleo Greene, who found a graceful way to explain me to the communi-ty. In Boone while I was doing my initial fieldwork, Elizabeth Stevens and Hattie the golden retriever were wonderful housemates.

At Appalachian State University, Thomas McGowan provided support both practical and psychological for a fledgling scholar. Eric Olsen, former librarian of the Appalachian Collection at ASU, located earlier recordings of Eldreth, Reid, and Cratis Williams that proved extremely valuable. Along with McGowan, Cecilia Conway of ASU and Glenn Hinson, now my colleague at the University of North Carolina, Chapel Hill, have shared impressions from their work with Eldreth and encouraged mine. Conway and videographer Elva Bishop of UNC-TV persuaded me to collaborate on a video of Eldreth that helped me understand her rhetorical flexibility.

For the dissertation with which this project began, I was fortunate in having committee members as supportive as they were demanding. Richard Bauman encouraged me to create my own path, branching off from theoretical roads he laid out. Beverly Stoeltje has been an influential advocate of feminist principles and a forthright and encouraging critic. Michael Herzfeld challenged me to be exact in my thinking. Kenneth Pimple, Laura Marcus, Polly Adema, Hanna Griff, and Mary Beth Stein thought through early stages of the project with me. David Whisnant supplied material and intellectual support essential to the dis-sertation. The book in important ways reflects my process of fully grasping insights about the construction of "Appalachian culture" that he was prescient in articulating.

I gratefully acknowledge financial support for my fieldwork from the Indiana University Graduate School, the Berea College/Mellon Appalachian Studies Fellowship, and the Wenner-Gren Foundation for Anthropological Research. A summer research award at the University of Louisiana, Lafayette, and a junior faculty development grant and a faculty fellowship at the Institute for the Arts and Humanities (IAH) at the University of North Carolina, Chapel Hill, pro-vided crucial time to write. I acknowledge the constructive feedback of my fel-low fellows at the IAH, especially Jane Thrallkill and Trudier Harris, and the generosity of David E. Pardue, Jr., and Rebecca Pardue, who endowed the fel-lowship I received. A grant from the University Research Council at the University of North Carolina, Chapel Hill, made it possible to include color photographs.

Carl Lindahl read my entire dissertation and helped me begin the process of rethinking this project for a book. Marcia Gaudet was a beloved mentor and big sister in my transformation from student to faculty member. Connie Herndon and Katherine Roberts have shared their reflections on Appalachia and how to go about studying a region we all love. Mary Bucholtz and Margaret Brady provided encouragement that helped me believe there would be an audience for my work. Margaret Wiener and Yasmin Saikia read drafts of many chapters in a writing group that made the process of creating this manuscript much more joyful. They, along with Judith Farquhar and Dorothy Holland, offered insightful critiques that enabled me to see my focused project in light of larger trends and arguments. Marisol de la Cadena and Marc David gave me courage and knowledge to rethink the complexities of race. Louise Meintjes and Kathryn Burns engaged me in enlivening conversations that renewed my enthusiasm for the always shape-shifting project of cultural analysis. Leslie Rebecca Bloom has struggled along with me over the years to articulate a coherent feminist ethnographic practice; her intellectual and emotional sisterhood sustains me. Riki Saltzman has been my companion in folklore and my dear friend for more than twenty years; this project would never have come to fruition without her loving encouragement and inspiring example. Cathy Lynn Preston, Michael Preston, and James Lavita were instrumental in my choice of graduate study in folklore and have been fascinating interlocutors ever since. May they be pleased with what they have wrought.

Anita Puckett introduced me to the new Appalachian historiography that crucially reoriented my understanding of Eldreth's life. She, along with Amy Shuman and Elaine Lawless, read the entire manuscript and offered expert and exacting criticisms that have improved the work's precision and grounding. It has been a pleasure to bring out the book with Utah State University Press. I am especially grateful to my editor, John Alley, for his patience, faith in my project, and clarity of vision. Rebecca Marsh's graceful copy editing helped me make the prose flow. Kyle G. Sessions is responsible for the book's interior design, and Barbara Yale-Read for the cover, which approximate Eldreth's vision of a (relatively) "small, red book."

My parents, Marilynn and Lewis Sawin, instilled me with a love of learning and a fascination with the intricacies of artistic speech and have provided immeasurable encouragement as I pursued those issues in fields far from the literature they taught. Their love, inspiration, questions, and occasional impatience have kept me going. Bron Skinner has blessed me with his presence in my life, his music, his joyfulness, and his enlivening mix of pragmatism and spiritual idealism. I thank him for encouraging me to have confidence in myself and to enjoy the creative process.

Transcription Conventions

In transcribing Eldreth's stories and her conversations with me and other partners I have employed the following conventions to render oral communication into print.

.   A period indicates falling intonation and brief pause (as at the end of a declarative sentence).

?   A question mark indicates rising intonation (as at the end of an interrogative sentence), whether or not the phrase is a grammatical interrogative.

[that]   Brackets indicate words that the speaker did not actually say but that I have inserted to complete the sense or descriptions of accompanying nonverbal activity, such as laughter or hand motions.

[plate?]   Brackets with a question mark indicate a word or words that I cannot hear clearly on the tape. This is my best guess at making sense of what was said.

. . .   Ellipsis indicates a pause, especially within a sentence or phrase when the sense carries across the temporal disjuncture (for example, a pause as if searching for a name or particular word).

[. . .]   Bracketed ellipsis indicates an omission in my subsequent quotation of excerpts from a text.

| A vertical line indicates an abrupt break in sense or syntactical flow, which may be, but usually is not, marked by a short pause, as when Eldreth repeats a word, corrects or amplifies a phrase before she has completed it, or changes the topic or her approach to it in midsentence.

//oh//   Double slash marks indicate simultaneous or overlapping speech of two participants.

but—   A dash at the end of turn at talk indicates speaker breaking off because interrupted. (If the speaker takes up the same phrase after the interruption, the beginning of that turn at talk is marked with another dash.)

bu—   A dash following an incomplete word indicates a midword interruption.

italics   Italics indicate emphatic vocal stress.

In representing pronunciation I strive to enable readers to hear the sound and rhythm of Eldreth's voice, while being mindful to avoid stereotypical or negative representations of "Appalachian dialect." In instances where Eldreth's practice is consistent with broad patterns in informal American English—for example, the so-called dropped g at the end of progressive tenses or "till" rather than "until"—I simply employ standard spelling for all speakers. In instances where shortened forms have an impact on the flow of Eldreth's speech, however, I have chosen to represent contractions such as "'em" (them), "'bout" (about), and "'cause" (because). I retain distinctive regional grammatical constructions, such as "a-walking" and "hit" for "it" in emphatic positions when Eldreth employs them, and have represented occasional distinctive pronunciations, like "young'uns" and "Papaw," that would seem stilted or distorted if "corrected" toward some supposed standard. I similarly represent repetitions and false starts in Eldreth's storytelling, both because I want to capture the effect of an informal oral narration and because disfluencies are occasionally significant. I have silently excised listeners' frequent minimal responses in order to speed and facilitate reading but have included listeners' more explicit comments and questions where these are important to the sense of the passage or germane to the analysis offered. Since my analyses focus on the discourses and themes in the stories or on reported speech that is clearly demarcated and attributed to other speakers by Eldreth, I have presented the stories in paragraph form, using multiple paragraphs to indicate episodes or new phases (for example, the transition from exposition to evaluation) in longer accounts.

I

Introduction
Dialogism and Subjectivity

Bessie Eldreth and I have been talking, on and off, for the past fifteen years. She, actually, does most of the talking and sometimes sings. I do most of the listening. We have that particular, but not entirely artificial relationship that emerges between ethnographer and subject. The topic of our conversation has been almost entirely Eldreth herself: her ninety years, her life in the North Carolina mountains, her specific experiences as a woman, her large repertoire of old songs, and her interactions with family, neighbors, and, over the past twenty-five years, with folklorists and the new audiences for singing and telling stories to whom they have introduced her. The exposure and opportunities to talk that have characterized Eldreth's later life are an ironic inversion of her earlier experience. It is because she lived in a marginalized region and was often poor and dependent upon her own aesthetic resources that she is now celebrated as a "traditional Appalachian singer." It is because she was for so long silenced by her husband and the restraints of an unabashedly patriarchal society that the stories she tells about her life intrigue me as a feminist.

This book is my attempt to account as fully as possible for our conversations, to make sense of and make meaning from what transpired between us. In these conversations, Eldreth narrated a self, not simply describing an identity that fully preexisted our interaction, but speaking and singing herself into being, insofar as I am enabled to know her. Each individual story, like the overall self-narration to which it contributes, is constructed dialogically. Eldreth narrates herself in relation both to resilient social discourses that partially constrain definition of her gender, class, and region and to the anticipated responses of listeners past and present. While offering an account of Eldreth's life, this book is not a biography or a life history. It is, rather, an ethnography of subject formation that understands the creation of a self as a recursive and dialogic process.

The text thus unfolds at two levels simultaneously. At one level it functions as a portrait of Eldreth, derived primarily from her stories and songs and highlighting those aspects of her life and portions of her repertoire that she has most wished to share. At another level, however, it is an account of how Eldreth constitutes herself as a subject by means of the various communicative resources available to her and of how I as ethnographer construct her as the subject of ethnography. We can come to understand Eldreth, I argue, not by treating her stories simply as transparent carriers of meaning but rather by analyzing how she creates an identity through communicative interaction and how I, as her immediate partner in conversation, am implicated in any account that comes out of our interactions. My approach thus challenges the assumptions that underpin biography or life history, in that biography treats the subject as self-evidently significant, life history presents the subject as representative of a group, and both not only accept the subject as preformed and self-consistent but also obscure the process whereby various bits of information drawn from multiple sources and originally inflected by multiple voices are melded into "the story" of a person's life. The ethnography of subjectivity, in contrast, locates significance in exposing the process through which the subject creates her self through interaction and in interrogating the traces from which we can track that process.

Eldreth *is* a fascinating individual with striking stories to tell and a distinctive repertoire of songs. She can, indeed, tell us both what it was like to raise eleven children on a rented farm in the southern mountains during the Depression and what it was like to present herself as a person who had had that experience to an audience at the Festival of American Folklife on the national mall in Washington, D.C. In another sense, however, the story I can tell about Eldreth is interesting precisely because it defies and deconstructs conventional definitions of significance and typicality. She is neither a major historical actor nor a "representative Appalachian woman." She is a person doing what every person does, enacting a self. She can indeed provide information about the experience of a particular gender-class-region constellation, that of existing as a poor woman in that place that has been labeled Appalachia. If we think about her self-account in this light, however, we should recognize that our analysis runs counter to Eldreth's desire to stress her own uniqueness. At the same time, I acknowledge the irony that her particular version of the general process of self-creation came to my attention only because of the redressive attention that feminism and folklore pay to those who have been marginalized.

The stories and songs, enactments and performances through which Eldreth creates herself are wonderfully evocative in their artistry and particularity. One purpose of this book is certainly to make those available to a wider audience and thereby to further Eldreth's own project of laying claim to certain cherished identities: virtuous though beleaguered wife, loving mother, hard worker, humorous prankster, talented singer. My reciprocal project is to analyze her means of thus constructing a self, with the goal of tracing her process of subject formation in detail—her resources and models, the discourses in which she positions herself, the pressures she feels and her ways of responding to them, the influence and limits of my role as listener. To achieve this goal, I approach ethnography as an inherently dialogic process, a responsive interaction between subject and ethnographer. While striving to create a text that serves Eldreth's purposes as well as mine, I acknowledge that they are not identical and reject methodologies that mandate a coincidence and transparency that exceed and belie the nature of actual human communication. In the following pages I articulate a dialogic ethnography that enables me to find a secure and productive footing among the competing claims of multiple models of feminist and folkloristic ethnographic practice. A dialogic ethnography allays anxieties about the ethics of representation, promoting the ethnographer's joyful assumption of her inevitable interpretive responsibilities.

This approach in turn enables me to see and to represent more accurately the complexities and contradictions in Eldreth's character, which are of a kind that folklorists and feminist anthropologists—feeling bound to defend and celebrate their subjects—have rarely plumbed. Although over time she developed ways to resist or reject specific limitations placed on her because of her gender and class, Eldreth was never a conscious critic of the system that oppressed her. Consequently, she achieves positive self-ascription by indirect means and often at the cost of investing in positions that actually make her complicit in gender oppression or that take distressing advantage of racial privilege. Amid the current enthusiasm for studying social movements and activists who seek to understand and alleviate their own oppression, I focus on the much more common and problematic practice of a person who achieves only partial, temporary, and compromised release from hegemonic forces. In so doing I respond to the challenge articulated by José Limón, who critiques folklorists' tendency to see the world of the socially marginalized in wholly positive terms (1994), and by Donald Brenneis, who urges us to acknowledge our attraction to the easy-to-tell, heroic stories of resistance and to document "practices of domination, accommodation, and complicity" as a step toward "illuminat[ing] the complexity and moral ambiguity of those events through which relations of power are constituted" (1993:300–301).

A further clarification involves my abandonment of the notion that Eldreth could be considered an example of or participant in something we could call "Appalachian culture," however attached folklorists may be to that concept. The attention paid to Eldreth by new audiences over the last twenty-five years has been mostly articulated in these terms. To the extent that this attention has been a welcome recompense after years of being taken for granted and has conferred some material advantages, Eldreth has acquiesced. She thus benefits, however, from membership in a club she never joined and to the existence of which she remains indifferent if not hostile. Although she is devoted to her mountains, her religion, and her music, she rejects attempts to treat her as an example of Appalachian culture. The salient difference between herself and those from elsewhere, her self-accounts suggest, is one not of culture but of class, defined in terms of the kind and amount of work a person has to do. Her song repertoire bears witness to the region's connection with a wider "American" society, although it also reveals her own devotion to an image of an isolated and pastoral Appalachia that depends on nostalgic repression of memories of such connection. And while outsiders value her singing as a remnant of Appalachian culture, she justifies it as a form of practical and spiritual women's work. New audiences provide another resource for Eldreth's self-construction, another object of which to make efficient use, but she defines her subjectivity in terms of gender and labor and defies us to impose the construct of a regional culture that does not correspond to her experience.

THEORY: DIALOGISM AND GENDERED SUBJECTIVITY

The self, insofar as others perceive it and indeed to a considerable extent as we experience ourselves, is a product of social interaction (Mead 1934). There is no unified, essential identity, only a continual negotiation using terms that are themselves changed by that negotiation, a recursive but changeable enactment, a performance undertaken in the mode of belief (Bloom 1998; Butler 1990; Davies 1992; Walkerdine 1990; Weedon 1997). The subject authors herself by answering, producing herself through utterances that can exist only as responses to other utterances of other speakers, prior or anticipated (Holquist 1983). In order to engage in this interactive self-creation, one necessarily employs (and modifies) available models and resources—discourses, genres, ways of speaking, formulae, texts (and also, of course, nonverbal forms of enactment and communication, although because of the nature of my relationship with Eldreth, I have access to these mostly through the verbal dimension). It is through the use, nonuse, modification, and innovation of these collective resources that what we recognize as culture in turn emerges and evolves. In her self-performance Eldreth employs certain relatively formalized genres—including ghost stories and songs from the British traditional and early country music repertoires—that are strongly associated with the region in which she lives. She also makes distinctive use of widely available resources such as the reporting of words spoken in previous interactions, the capacity of joking to articulate masked critique, and the persuasive power of aesthetic performance. And she inevitably constructs a self rhetorically in relation not only to her current listeners but also to prior interlocutors and to the discourses that are the sedimented and internalized forms of social attitudes expressed in the past. As a dialogic ethnography of subjectivity, this work focuses on the means whereby Eldreth interactively produces her self, with chapters exploring a variety of discourses and expressive resources. The portrait of Eldreth, the account of what she presents herself *as*, emerges from the study of *how* she creates that self.

I ground this study theoretically by drawing together the feminist concept of gendered subjectivity as nonunitary and as constituted by recursive performance (Bloom 1998; Hollway 1984; Weedon 1997; Butler 1990) and the Bakhtinian model of the self as dialogically constituted (Bakhtin 1981; Holquist 1983). The two bodies of theory are fundamentally consistent because both spring from Derrida's rejection of the metaphysics of presence (Derrida 1976; Mannheim and Tedlock 1995:7; Weedon 1997:81). Language is not conceived of as representing a reality that exists elsewhere. The active, ongoing process of communicating creates the very structures that make "experience" meaningful and thus epistemologically possible. Whereas humanistic philosophy posited identity as a solid, definable entity preexisting social interaction, the theories of gender as performed and the self (and culture) as dialogic see the individual and culture as contingent and emergent constructions, fictions created in the course of interaction. Such constructions are stabilized and perpetuated by reenactment of previous patterns. They can, however, be transformed because of the existence of alternative resources that, although repressed or excluded, can be recovered and incorporated into the enactment (R. Williams 1977). The strength of pressures to repeat must not be underestimated, but both change and continuity are recognized as accomplishments (Butler 1990; Mannheim and Tedlock 1995:8–10). All structure emerges from action. Individual identity and culture are thus seen not only as produced by analogous processes but also as reciprocally producing the conditions for the emergence of the other, with actor and materials seen as mutually constituted and constituting.

Foucault and Bakhtin both locate the genesis of culture and subjectivity in "discourse," the network of actual utterances that supply the terms and define the conditions of possibility for subsequent expression (Foucault 1972; Bakhtin 1981). The fundamental unit of language is not the sentence, word, or phoneme but rather the utterance, an actual expressive statement, which Bakhtin further conceptualizes as a rejoinder in conversation. Both are poststructuralist in going beyond the Saussurean notion of the sign as meaningful because of its position in a system of signs rather than as a representation of reality to challenge the comprehensiveness and stability of the system and to locate meaning in concrete practices and manifestations of speaking. "Of course, discourses are composed of signs; but what they do is more than use these signs to designate things. It is this *more* that renders them irreducible to language" (Foucault 1972:49). "After all, language enters life through concrete utterances (which manifest language) and life enters language through concrete utterances as well" (Bakhtin 1986:63). In the work of both theorists and those who build upon them, the actual system of meanings in effect in any place or time is thus seen as neither complete nor legitimate but rather as hegemonic, supporting and supported by dominant interests. Yet there is a crucial difference of emphasis. Foucault, beginning with the project of explaining the powerful penetration of scientific discourses into social practice and conceptions of the self, draws attention toward the circulation of diffuse, abstract ideologies. Discourses in Foucault's sense involve "the delimitation of a field of objects, the definition of a legitimate perspective for the agent of knowledge, and the fixing of norms for the elaboration of concepts and theories" (1977:199). Bakhtin, fascinated with literature and especially with the novel's vibrant combination of the characteristic speaking styles of distinctive social groups, draws attention to the multiplicity of contending discourses (1981). Conceptualizing the utterance as primary (over the system of language) means that any act of expression is fundamentally a part of an ongoing dialogue.

> Any speaker is himself a respondent to a greater or lesser degree. He is not, after all, the first speaker, the one who disturbs the eternal silence of the universe. And he presupposes not only the existence of the language system he is using, but also the existence of preceding utterances—his own and others'—with which his given utterance enters into one kind of relation or another (builds on them, polemicizes with them, or simply presumes that they are already known to the listener). Any utterance is a link in a very complexly organized chain of other utterances. (Bakhtin 1986:69)

Bakhtin thus provides tools for tracing in more concrete form the sources from which determining discourses enter our talk and self-concept and the means available for engaging with and contesting as well as acquiescing to them.

The poststructuralist feminist theory that has elaborated the process by which gendered subjectivities come into being has drawn primarily upon Foucault (Weedon 1997:34). According to this model of "non-unitary subjectivity," the self is constantly reproduced through thought and talk (Hollway 1984:227). The terms of our self-conception and self-realization are established by discourses, invisibly coordinated and self-perpetuating assemblages of expressions that "produce permissible modes of being and thinking while disqualifying and even making others impossible" (Escobar 1995:5; Foucault 1972). People have some choice about how to position themselves within these discourses; they make that investment of self on the basis of the perceived advantages of that position over others (Hollway 1984:238). Subjectivity is thus neither consistent nor static for any individual (1984:228). Still, whatever the ostensible topic of talk, the position options tend to be different for men and women (1984:233, 236). For women, furthermore, the contradictions of a patriarchal society and the multiplicity of inconsistent roles, expectations, and experiences through which we form our subjectivities provide conflicting input (Harding 1987:7) that promotes correspondingly conflicted self-constructions. Given its reliance on the Foucaultian concept of discourse, study of the performance of gendered identity tends to emphasize analyzing texts to detect the semantic fields in which discussion can be couched, the subject positions speakers are allowed to assume, and the institutions that stabilize and promulgate these discursive fields (Davies and Harré 1990). Furthermore, because feminism conceptualizes the current system as a repressive gender hegemony, much work in this vein has focused on radical alternatives and means of enabling fundamental change.

An approach to discourse drawing on Bakhtin, in contrast, focuses attention on the historical dimension of language use and on the pragmatic communicative capacity of the live utterance. To be involved in discourse in Bakhtin's sense is to engage in dialogue, broadly conceived. To enter into dialogue is to interact not only with one's present interlocutor but also with all the previous speakers who have given meaning to the words one uses, as well as with those previous, internalized, and anticipated interlocutors in relation to whom we form our consciousness. Every utterance both responds to (multiple) past utterances and anticipates the reaction it will elicit. "When the listener perceives and understands the meaning . . . of speech, he simultaneously takes an active, responsive attitude toward it" (Bakhtin 1986:68). The utterance cannot be said to have been completed except in this responsive reception. A dialogic approach consequently emphasizes both the multivocality and inherent contradiction within any act of communication and the crucial role of the particular listener/interpreter. Such an approach focuses attention on the complexity of apparent continuity and on self-performance as interactive, not merely expressive.

My goal in this study is to bring the two approaches together, using the specificity of the Bakhtinian perspective to elucidate the concrete means by which subjectivity is constructed. In exploring Eldreth's creation of a gendered and classed sense of self, I necessarily consider how she positions herself relative to internalized societal discourses. I employ the dialogic perspective, however, for access to dimensions of rhetorical action that exceed the semantic and in order to explore as constructed the conservative as well as innovative facets of her subjectivity. Conceiving every utterance as a rejoinder, potentially at many levels, in an ongoing communicative interaction, dialogism recognizes semantic discourses as only one component of the existing or implicit utterances to which a text or statement responds. Any speaker has access (consciously and unconsciously) to an amazing variety of pragmatic resources. Eldreth prominently employs the capacities of genres (which in turn mobilize multiple lower-level resources), registers, degrees of fluency, conventions for reporting the (ostensible) speech of others, tones (for instance, parodic or serious), and specific preformed texts (in her case, songs). By directing attention to some of these levels of the utterance, we can observe with much greater detail and specificity what other utterances and voices a speaker is responding to and how she incorporates, processes, negotiates with, transforms, or rejects them. Even an apparently straightforward or conventional utterance, when closely analyzed, may reveal dimensions of multiaccentuality that suggest how many other voices and potentially new ideas mingle, acknowledged or unacknowledged, in the perpetual constitution of the speaker's subjectivity. At the same time, perceiving the subject as dialogically constituted counters the presentist excess of theories that describe the self purely as a performance. The self is not remade from scratch in every encounter but rather built up in layers of past interaction. The speaker may respond variably to past interlocutors and past selves, but the present perform-ance of self is inevitably shadowed by the ghosts of previous performances.

A dialogical approach offers numerous benefits to the study of gendered iden-tity. Because of the emphasis on the minutiae of multivocality contained within everyday communication, such an approach provides a more concrete idea of how existing discourses and practices might in effect be subtly challenged or trans-formed by small degrees. It likewise expands the range of materials and human subjects that can be studied. Analyses of gendered subjectivity have tended to look for major departures from conventional self-construction and hence to rely either on avant-garde literary or artistic works or on the introspection of highly self-conscious feminist intellectuals or of people whose self-identification in terms of sexuality, ethnicity, or disability impels explicit challenge to identity "norms." A focus on pragmatic manipulations of expressive resources allows us to consider the complex self-construction of those, like Eldreth, who may not consciously confront the social forces that constrain them or, at least, do not articulate their opposition in explicit terms. To perceive how change might be possible, we must understand the mixture of resistance and complicity that characterizes most lives.

To understand my approach to Eldreth's stories and songs, it is also crucial to distinguish two separable ways in which we recognize the dialogic nature of any particular utterance. On the one hand, we may become aware of the ways that a speaker incorporates prior utterances and expressive resources into her speech via quotation, allusion, the use of multiple languages or registers, and the mixing of genres and styles. In Bakhtin's memorable phrase, "Our speech . . . is filled with others' words, varying degrees of otherness or varying degrees of 'our-own-ness.'. . . These words of others carry with them their own expression, their own evaluative tone, which we assimilate, rework, and re-accentuate" (Bakhtin 1986:89; see also Holquist 1983). Literary scholars call this creative linguistic recycling intertextuality. Of Bakhtin's several labels, I gravitate toward het-eroglossia to stress the inclusion of another's word and the diversity of potential sources (Mannheim and Tedlock 1995:16; Todorov 1984). Eldreth does make use of a number of generic models: how to tell a ghost story or how to play a practi-cal joke, for example. For the most part, however, she avoids the kind of fluid heteroglossia (which Bakhtin sometimes calls "dialogic overtones" [1986:92]) whereby a discourse stylistically recognizable as typical of another speaker, text, or social group subtly infiltrates the speaker's own discourse. This is not, perhaps, surprising, given that for most of her life she spoke almost exclusively with peo-ple in a limited geographical region, who had education and accent similar to her own, and that she has a principled resistance to "putting on airs" by assimilating to the ways of those wealthier than herself. To the extent that she employs "other peoples' words," she rigorously attributes them to the original speaker, quoting "reported speech" directly so as to maximize both the distinction between her voice and that of the other speaker and the rhetorical usefulness of such remarks to her as the opinion of a separate authoritative speaker (Vološinov 1973:119–120; Bakhtin 1981:343–344).

On the other hand, utterances may respond to prior utterances and anticipate the responses they will evoke without necessarily revealing that by incorporating their distinguishable words or styles. In Bakhtin's view, speakers necessarily respond to multiple interlocutors, only some of whom are physically or temporally present. While addressing a specific person, a speaker does not forget unfinished conversations from the past, persistent social attitudes, possible future listeners who may hear the story secondhand, or perhaps the perfect understanding of God (Vološinov 1973).

> In reality, . . . any utterance, in addition to its own theme, always responds (in the broad sense of the word) in one form or another to others' utterances that precede it. The speaker is not Adam, and therefore the subject of his speech itself inevitably becomes the arena where his opinions meet those of his partners. . . . But the utterance is related not only to preceding, but also to subsequent links in the chain of speech communion. . . . From the very beginning, the utterance is constructed while taking into account possible responsive reactions, for whose sake, in essence, it is actually created. (Bakhtin 1986:94)

This kind of responsiveness to multiple possible listeners may be detectable through emotional or intellectual positioning—unexpected defensiveness, a response to attitudes the actual present listener has not articulated or does not hold, or apparent violations of Grice's maxim of conversational implicature (Nofsinger 1991:35–45). To the extent that Eldreth expressed attitudes that did not seem relevant to the tenor of our relationship or provided less information than I needed to make sense of the actions described, for example, I was able to recognize that she may have been talking (immediately) to me but that I was not actually her most important addressee. This is the kind of dialogism that occurs most often in Eldreth's speech and the interpretation of which is the greatest benefit of the dialogical approach I take to our ethnographic interaction.

METHODOLOGY: DIALOGISM AND ETHNOGRAPHY

> Once culture is seen as arising from a dialogical ground, then ethnography itself is revealed as an emergent cultural (or intercultural) phenomenon, produced, reproduced, and revised in dialogues between field-workers and natives. (Mannheim and Tedlock 1995:2)

Any work of ethnography is inherently dialogic. The text that is in one sense a single utterance produced by the author fundamentally incorporates and builds upon all that the ethnographer has heard and learned from her subjects. We may no longer believe that we, as anthropologists or folklorists, can fully succeed in seeing things from "the native's" point of view (Geertz 1973). Still, the goal of ethnography, in contrast to a more sociological inquiry, is precisely to acknowledge the humanity and uniqueness of those from whom we have sought to learn by giving some sense of how they talk about their own lives. As Mannheim and Tedlock observe,

> Even as the voice of objectification or interpretation narrows itself toward an authoritative monologue, it bespeaks, in the mind of an alert reader, the suppression of a multiplicity of other voices, whether they be those of natives, those of the writer in an earlier role as field-worker, or those of alternative interpretations or rival interpreters. (1995:3)

Indeed, the great challenge in writing ethnography is to establish a productive balance between the responsibility to offer a coherent account, which necessarily suppresses or gives short shrift to other voices, and the requirement to give adequate credit to one's interlocutors and to create a text that preserves some of the specificity of alternative and perhaps contesting voices. One of my aims in this text is precisely to make the dialogic production of the source materials and the text as much an object of analysis as the materials themselves.

From the beginning of our interaction I was interested in analyzing the material that I recorded from Eldreth in dialogic terms. Ironically, however, it took me a long time to widen the frame so as to apply that perspective to our relationship and to the process of composing this text as well. My current dedication to a dialogic approach has emerged in reaction to my previous efforts to deal with Eldreth in ways that did not work—specifically an attempt to focus so completely on her and to transmit her voice so perfectly that my own presence would not be evident. In order to appreciate what had actually gone on between Eldreth and me and thus what kind of material I really had to work with, I had first to recognize that some of what I initially believed was ethically or intellectually required of me was both impossible and destructive. Once I learned this lesson from the scholars who articulate the dialogic critique of ethnography, I realized that Eldreth had been trying, implicitly, to teach me much the same thing.

At the time that I began work with Eldreth in the late 1980s, anthropology was grappling with the problem of the relationship between what was said "in the field" and what shows up in the ethnographic text under the rubric of "representation" (Clifford 1983). Folklore, with its focus on songs and stories—that is, the aesthetically elaborated words of the subjects—approached the issue from the opposite direction, in terms of "natural context." Anthropologists were initially concerned with the tendency of ethnographic accounts to obliterate the personal and political concreteness of source voices while abstracting the content of what had been discussed as "data" for the ethnographer's argument (Clifford and

Marcus 1986). Folklorists, conversely, recognized that we had previously record-ed and reified subjects' words and detached them from the contexts in which they had been produced. The corrective would be to analyze the functions of the texts in their contexts of use, ignoring or correcting for the influence of the folk-lorist's presence (Paredes and Bauman 1972; Ben-Amos and Goldstein 1975; Bauman 1983a). Early feminist methodology placed further demands on the fem-inist ethnographer in order to correct for the tendency of previous, male-biased research to ignore women or treat them as objects rather than subjects. Feminist ethnography was supposed to "give voice" to silenced and disenfranchised women. Feminist researchers, women talking to women, should so accurately understand our subjects as to be able to design studies to respond to their needs (Harding 1987). All of these perspectives yearned for purity in the ethnograph-ic relationship—perfect communication and perfect transmission. All, however, were complicated by the further recognition that the kinds of purification appar-ently required to correct for earlier biases seemed unattainable. While earlier ethnography in a scientific mode unapologetically appropriated and amalgamat-ed what subjects said, postmodern scholars of representation argued that even those current authors who wished and claimed to convey their subjects' words could be accused of disingenuousness and bad faith, on the grounds that the enclosing context of the ethnographer's or historian's text would inevitably dis-tort and contaminate words presented as the subjects' own (Tyler 1986, 1987; Spivak 1988).

When I began working with Eldreth I thus imagined that it was both possible and mandatory to collect her performances of songs and stories in their natural contexts and to minimize or erase my influence on what was communicated between us. I also believed that I was duty bound as a feminist to produce an ethnographic text that gave her voice salience and also responded to her con-cerns and needs. This likewise seemed to require that I minimize my presence in the text. But I struggled with the contradictions. Perfect communication was unattainable in any case, and, to the extent that I came to the project with inter-ests not identical to Eldreth's, the effort to give priority to her goals would require me to suppress my own voice, which surely contravened feminist principles in another respect. Like others at the time, I wondered if it were truly possible to write ethnography while fulfilling my feminist responsibilities to the woman who was my subject (Stacey 1988) and agonized particularly over whether it was eth-ical to employ the words and experiences of a woman who would not call herself a feminist in order to build a feminist argument (Borland 1991; Lawless 1992). Certain feminist ethnographers, notably Ruth Behar (1993), responded to these concerns by producing texts in which the subject appears to speak for herself and the anthropologist's analysis is restricted to the margins. In order to produce a coherent, composite narrative in the subject's voice, however, the ethnographer must still engage in manipulations that are then smoothed over. I became increasingly convinced that such an approach would not do justice either to the richness of the communications between Eldreth and me or to the exploration of the construction of subjectivity in which I hoped to engage. My current approach is inspired rather by the confluence of liberatingly realistic perspectives drawn from authors whose theoretical backgrounds are quite divergent. Ofelia Schutte articulates an antiessentialist feminist philosophy. By arguing that we must never assume that shared gender can bridge the other experiential gaps (of sexuality, culture, and especially power and class) between women, she freed me from the unexamined assumption that I should, for starters, be able to understand Eldreth perfectly (Schutte 2000). Michael Jackson proposes "a radically empirical method [that] *includes* the experience of the observer and defines the experimental field as one of interactions and intersubjectivities" (1989:4). Sherry Ortner, lamenting a retreat from ethnographic "thickness" in recent work on political resistance, insists that "people not only resist political domination; they resist, or anyway evade, textual domination as well." Thus, assuming reasonably good faith on the part of the ethnographer, it is "grotesque to insist . . . that the [ethnographic] text is shaped by everything but the lived reality of the people whom the text claims to represent" (1995:188). Billie Jean Isbell takes a hard look at her own interactions with several generations of women in a Peruvian family and insists that in order to understand the subjects in whom we are interested we must understand the dialogues with and among them of which we *are* a part, though *only* a part (1995).

Conceiving ethnography as an inescapably dialogic project provides respite from the impossibilities and contradictions that initially plagued me, and here Bruce Mannheim and Dennis Tedlock articulate a model especially adapted to the detailed analysis of verbal material (1995). A dialogical ethnography rejects the communicative and ethical nihilism of the postmodern critique of ethnographic representation, reconceiving the problem at its epistemological root. The concern that the ethnographic account *mis*represents the ethnographic encounter is itself thus revealed as based upon "the notion that face-to-face dialogues are themselves instances of pure presence" (Mannheim and Tedlock 1995:7). From a Bakhtinian perspective, in contrast, it is clear "that any and all present discourse is already replete with echoes, allusions, paraphrases, and outright quotations of prior discourse" and that "one of the things language does best is to enable its speakers, in the very moment they are present to one another, to breach that presence" (1995:7–8). Seen in this light, the subject's utterance and the context in which it was communicated appear simultaneously less pure and more rich and evocative. A dialogic perspective on ethnography thus resolves both the contextual and representational impasses. Given that every utterance in its present manifestation alludes to its grounding in past contexts, it is impossible to privilege any single "authentic" context and pointless to regard the ethnographer's presence as contamination. Conversely, given that any speaker responds to both past and anticipated, as well as present, interlocutors, it is possible to read the influence of prior contexts and interlocutors out of utterances for which the ethnographer was the only apparent audience. A story, like an individual word, necessarily "tastes of the contexts in which it has lived its socially charged life" (Bakhtin 1981:293).[1] Furthermore, if we recognize context as not preexisting the discursive encounter but rather generated through the active "contextualization" that is part of a performance, we similarly see the relationship of ethnographer and subject as emergent (Bauman and Briggs 1990:68–69). The ethnographer's influence cannot be eliminated, but neither does it obliterate or take priority over other influences. The ethnographer's words, in turn, will be inflected by those of her subjects well beyond her conscious quotations and allusions. Trying to erase the ethnographer is mystifying and dishonest. Attempting entirely to disentangle the subject's and the ethnographer's purposes is impossible and counterproductive.

In reconsidering my conversations with Eldreth from a dialogic perspective I am heartened by the realization that whatever happened between us provides grist for the analytic mill. Approaches to interviewing that I would not now repeat and interactions that were confusing at the time contribute to my current sense of what I can say about Eldreth's self-construction, while in other respects the limitations of the material that I could record influence the shape of the project. I also realize with amusement and humility that Eldreth in important respects had a clearer, although implicit, idea than I did of what was going on between us and what could be accomplished.

When I began working with Eldreth I intended to focus, as the contextual paradigm dictated, on her performances of stories and songs in natural context. Much of the material upon which I draw for this analysis comes, however, from about a dozen particularly revealing interviews, intimate conversations that Eldreth and I conducted, with the tape recorder running, at her kitchen table or in her bedroom. My reliance on these sources in part reflects the practical limits of research on people's social interactions. Eldreth was not involved in as many or as many different kinds of performances during the course of my fieldwork as I had hoped. Running the tape recorder when family and friends were visiting Eldreth, even with permission from all involved, would have constituted a sort of eavesdropping that I was uncomfortable initiating. Although I had imagined the private conversations largely as sources of background data, the stories she told me captivated my attention. A feminist analysis could not ignore these vignettes of stress, drama, affirmation, and conflict. Even though I was at first concerned about including these materials (since they clearly did not involve stories told "in natural context"), I now regard the taped interviews as complex negotiations in which Eldreth and I, without being explicitly aware of what we were doing, worked out what it was going to be possible for me to learn about her and to accomplish in the book about her.

To put it another way, I thought I was "collecting folklore," while Eldreth intuitively grasped that we were setting up situations in which she would have the opportunity to share extensive portions of her life story. Charlotte Linde

defines "life story" as "consist[ing] of all the stories . . . told by an individual during the course of his/her lifetime that . . . have as their primary evaluation a point
about the speaker . . . [and] have extended reportability" (1993:20). The life story
is thus inevitably "temporally discontinuous" and not only any single telling but
any series of tellings will be necessarily incomplete (1993:25). The better we are
acquainted with a person, the more portions of her life story we know, and vice
versa. The temporal ordering of fragments and the conceptual coherence of any
listener's version of a speaker's life story "must also be understood as a cooperative achievement" (1993:12). There were ways in which Eldreth and I talked
past each other because of having different notions of how to conduct a conversation, but the cooperative construction of a life story was a discursive activity
we actually shared, though, ironically, she knew it and I did not. Edward Ives
points out that the folkloristic notion of some other context being a more appropriate setting for the telling of oral history than the oral history interview is suspect (1988). Without reinvesting in the notion of "natural context," I believe it
is possible to argue that Eldreth's and my kitchen table conversations were certainly a no less—and possibly even a more—suitable context for the creation and
sharing of parts of her life story than the supposed prior settings with family and
friends into which I felt bound to project them. In recognizing my responsibility
to generate some coherence and to share my version of Eldreth's life story with
readers, I also of course follow the foundational example of Roger Abrahams's
work with Almeda Riddle (Riddle 1970). My commitment to a dialogic ethnography that considers my role in the elicitation of the material and my interest in
the construction of Eldreth's narratives keep me, however, from imposing the
degree of coherence that enabled Abrahams to subordinate Riddle's life story as
an explanation of her song repertoire.

I am especially amused in retrospect by the efforts I made to avoid influencing Eldreth. When we sat down to talk I often tried to be nondirective, intending to create a situation in which, theoretically, she could say whatever she wanted. It is, of course, almost impossible to engage in purposeless talk (Wolfson
1976); and in trying to leave the floor open for Eldreth, I effectively left her to
guess at or extract my purposes. Going over the tapes of our conversations, I
notice how often she ended up prompting me to prompt her, asking, "Have you
got anything in mind? Anything you want to ask me?"[2] She was, in effect, showing me that what I thought I had to have—"natural" material completely
buffered from my influence—was impossible to obtain but that she could provide
me with material that would suit both our purposes if I would take responsibility
for eliciting it by simply holding up my end of the conversation.[3]

In my interactions with Eldreth I also never characterized either myself or the
project as explicitly feminist, fearing either that I might "contaminate" my subject, inducing her to tell me what I wanted to hear, or that I might alienate her.
I did my best to remain neutral, expressing interest in the stories she told me but
not evaluating reported actions and especially not offering a feminist or class-based

analysis, even when I later went home and cried over the tragedies and injustices she had experienced. Fortunately, I also taped a couple of conversations in which other less reticent feminist ethnographers joined me in interviewing Eldreth. The comparison enabled me both to see how she responded to their encouragement to express critical opinions and also subsequently to recognize the effect of my interests on Eldreth even though I tried to conceal them. The very fact of Eldreth's and my coming together to talk made gender a topic of mutual discussion. I could not help but ask about and pay particular attention to her reflections on her experience as a gendered subject. She, in turn, took advantage of the particular discursive space created by my questioning in order, in part, to explore facets of her experience that she had not often been given an opportunity to talk about. Whether we say that Eldreth responded to my implicit invitation or that I picked up on implications in Eldreth's discourse that a listener not interested in gender would not have noticed, once the two of us started talking to each other, there was no way that a critical evaluation of gender could *not* be central.

While in certain respects I thus inevitably influenced Eldreth even though I tried not to, in other respects my turning control of our interactions over to Eldreth did allow her to shape the direction the project would take, although sometimes in paradoxical ways. The impossibility (not to say effrontery) of my attempting to study her lifetime of performance in a few months or years was not immediately apparent to me. Eldreth, however, seems to have realized that she was going to have to fill me in on all the years that I could not go back in time to observe, and she made sure to tell me stories about prior instances of singing and storytelling as well as many other aspects of her life. That, of course, is what any narrator does in sharing portions of her life story with a new acquaintance. Some of these accounts may have been told, for the first or only time, to me. It is also important to remember, however, that by the time I started working with her, Eldreth had been singing for and being interviewed by folklorists and folklore students for more than a decade. The dozens of stories Eldreth told me about performances, interviews, and filmings served several purposes I was not aware of until later, one of which was probably to affirm by past example that she was worthy of attention from someone like me (another folklorist) and another of which may well have been to clue me in to my place in the long line of interviewers with whom she had already talked. Eldreth certainly found it congenial to talk at length about her experiences. It seems entirely possible that she had learned from prior interviewers that it was appropriate to tell an extended series of stories entirely about herself, that is, she learned how to act like the interviewee. It struck me that whenever I tried to insert a story of my own, that is, to respond to her story in a more conversational mode, she would treat it as an interruption and go back to another of her accounts without acknowledging any connection. This may indicate a distinctive sense of how to use stories in conversation or could reflect a pressing need to focus attention on herself after many years of being unappreciated. I suspect, however, that since I left it to her to define the parameters of our interaction, Eldreth was imposing the most likely model, one she had been encouraged to adopt by other interviewers and one I implicitly approved because of my interest in her. Thus, her response to my inserted story was an appropriate rejection of a frame break.[4]

Left largely to her own devices, Eldreth also, logically enough, often provided me with accounts that were clearly well-crafted and oft-repeated versions of her experiences—that is, precisely the sort of previously told stories I thought I wanted. Some contain metareferences to the reactions of earlier audiences. Her tendency to name places and people unknown to me without offering or seeming to sense the need for an explanation (in contrast to Bauman's analysis of the way storyteller Ed Bell "[went] into more detail" for audiences unfamiliar with the setting of his stories [1986:78]) also hints that she was retelling accounts originally developed for a different and probably local audience. Most often, however, I know that these are stories Eldreth tells repeatedly in much the same form because when I have tried to get her to comment either on the events narrated or on some aspect of the narrative itself, she has simply told the story over again. In one respect, this suggests a way in which the purposes of an eloquent speaker and an ethnographer of speaking almost inevitably coincide. The kinds of aesthetically marked or eminently quotable stretches of speech in which analysts tend to be interested are already relatively "entextualized," spoken in the first instance in anticipation of being removed from the original context and repeatedly reused and reinserted into others (Bauman and Briggs 1990). In another respect, however, Eldreth's insistence upon repeating rather than commenting on her stories hints at a resistance to my efforts to make sense of her self-account in my own terms for my own purposes. As Paul Willis reflects, regarding the similar practice of a working-class man he interviewed extensively:

> My interpretation is grappling with aspects of the structural-historical formation of persons in a specific site. But Percy will have none of my specific interpretation. Faced with my reductive interpretation, he just tells the story again. The whole tale is the irreducible meaning for him, not any moral, homology, or connection to be drawn from it. (2001:195–196)

Thus, I attempt to approach Eldreth's stories as Willis does Percy's: "How does my 'rightness' relate to [her] 'rightness'? First, not in displacing or denying it. . . . What I propose should be seen as an *addition* to, not a substitution for, what [Eldreth] says" (2001:205).

In a much more pedestrian pragmatic vein, the fact that Eldreth was willing and able to repeat her stories in essentially the same form proved convenient in those frequent instances where she told me a significant story when we did not have the tape recorder running. As readers will observe from the conversational remarks with which many story transcriptions begin, quite a few of the versions available for analysis are repetitions for the recorder. It is also important to remember that a story's repeatability does not provide absolute assurance as to its origin or the situation in which it was previously or ordinarily told. I know Eldreth gave me (some) stories originally shaped in other contexts, but I cannot be sure if she first (or ever) told them to family and friends or only began formulating such self-accounts when other ethnographers constituted her as an object of interest.

Eldreth also turned many of our interviews into singing sessions, making sure that we got her entire repertoire of close to two hundred songs down on tape. While I regretted not being able to capture more performances "in context," she understood these inherited texts as already multiply de- and recontextualized and thus prioritized the song and her singing of it as an entextualized object. Eldreth's treating the song text and the high quality performance as more important than the context of a rendition makes sense. It corresponds to commonsense notions of a song as a performance piece, to the entire history of recorded music available for replay at the listener's convenience, and to the probable approach of earlier folklorists who had been interested in finding out what old songs Eldreth knew. At the same time, however, she realized that we could capture the song as text by one means (her singing it for the recorder) and the singing context by another (her telling me stories of singing for people in the past), and she actually provided me with both, just not simultaneously.

A dialogic approach to ethnography liberates the ethnographer from the impossible quest for perfect representation or natural context. It also reminds us, however, of the inevitable limitations imposed on an ethnographic project by the constraints of conversational interaction, particularly between two people who come to the interaction with somewhat different notions of what is going on and how to proceed. Eldreth's tendency to retell a story rather than comment upon it highlights the fact that I can analyze the accounts she shared but cannot get behind them to know what *really* happened or what she *really* felt (although people to whom I talk about her often press me for such information). Perhaps a different interviewer might have induced or enabled Eldreth to engage more reflexively with her self-accounts; perhaps I could have, had I been more confident or determined. Still, eventually we run up against the realization that we are not allowed to see directly into others' souls and that, for Eldreth as for everyone, her performed self is the only self that others can know. In formulating these stories, I believe Eldreth has completed the processing of her experiences in which she is willing to engage.[5] I may be able to understand more about her subject formation through analysis—such is the premise of this book—but her unwillingness to elaborate upon or analyze the texts she has created draws the limit beyond which the task falls to me and the insights are necessarily derived.

My reliance upon Eldreth's self-account also means that I am in many respects restricted to consideration of matters of significance to her. In conversation and in her stories she tends to focus on concrete instances and known persons. For

Eldreth, as for the residents of a nearby mountain community whose speech practices have been extensively studied, "nearly all quotidian discourse . . . is about events, personalities, activities, things, and behaviors empirically accessible to interlocutors" (Puckett 2000:30).[6] I can bring her into dialogue with certain scholarly discourses about the region. However, there are many matters historical, political, and economic that probably impinged upon her life and that it would be valuable to have insight into but that she does not talk about. She avidly quotes the words of friends and family members and shapes her self-image in response to local discourses and attitudes she ascribes to outsiders whom she has met. She does not, however, evidently incorporate and respond to official, governmental, or medical discourses or voices (contrast Hill 1995). Eldreth reads only local newspapers and, when looking at them or at television news, seems to pay attention almost exclusively to local human interest stories. She is not involved in politics; and in interaction with articulators of other authoritative discourses—for instance, doctors—she tends to reinterpret their remarks in her own terms rather than allow herself to be drawn into their discursive field. This is another reason that I detect in Eldreth's talk little heteroglossia—the subtle shading of remarks in one register or style with the voice of a speaker of a different style—except in her singing, where listeners know by other means that the words are not strictly her own. While the focus of our discussions upon Eldreth herself may have excluded certain kinds of talk in which she engages with other interlocutors, I believe that the historical/political framing simply does not fall within her domestic and personal discursive range. To me, in any case, Eldreth *is* the subject enacted in our conversations; that subject is thus constituted by the range of discourses and techniques she employed with me.

The book I have been able to write about Eldreth thus emerged from my sense of the inherent dialogism of both her self-construction and our interaction. I recognize that Bakhtin's observation—"Our speech is filled to overflowing with other people's words, transmitted with highly varied degrees of accuracy and impartiality" (1981:337)—applies equally to Eldreth and to me. While I have tried to be as accurate as possible and to take account of her goals and wishes, I acknowledge my responsibility as a transmitter who could not help but inflect the product with my own voice. In practice, this meant that I decided usually to set Eldreth's stories and songs, highly entextualized portions of our interaction, as texts quoted verbatim, objects for analysis that could be cut out of the contexts in which they had been conveyed. At the same time, however, I have commented on their functions in both present and past contexts, recognizing their grounding in both and privileging neither. I have also acknowledged the necessity of selecting only some of the stories and songs Eldreth shared with me, summarizing a few more, and leaving out many others, even when it pained me to eliminate them. In thus resisting the impulse to include more and more of what she told me, I recognize not only that I cannot serve as a frictionless conduit for Eldreth's voice but also that our mutual purpose of creating a portrait of her is better served by my exercising an editorial prerogative. Her process of telling personal stories to an endlessly and artificially receptive listener and mine of creating a coherent and readable ethnographic text are different and require different treatment of common material. I recognize that in selecting only some of Eldreth's many stories and songs for analysis, I inevitably act as does every interlocutor, processing most of what we hear into propositional information and reproducing verbatim only an occasional especially artistic or authoritative remark. The ethnographic expedient of making mechanical recordings of conversations with our subjects effectively disables the failsafe of partial memory, making the process of choice and elimination conscious and often full of regret rather than automatic. Like Eldreth, however, in order to tell a coherent story—even that of Eldreth's own self-fashioning—I must exclude, summarize, and comment, as well as quote.

My ethnographic approach—as researcher and as writer—differs in ways that require explanation from the innovative approaches that two other feminist ethnographers with goals similar to mine have employed: Elaine Lawless's reciprocal ethnography (1991) and Kathleen Stewart's new ethnography (1996). Reciprocal ethnography "means that [ethnographer and subject] need to sit down together and begin a dialogue about what they each have written and presented and record their responses to this gathering of information" (Lawless 2000:201). It involves sharing transcripts of stories and versions of interpretations with one's subjects, learning from their corrections and disagreements. When it works, reciprocal ethnography is a tremendously powerful method for putting the subject's and ethnographer's words and ideas on equal footing. It is not, however, always possible. I continue to wonder if Eldreth's apparent disinterest in talking *about* what she had previously told me, except by retelling the same stories, was a barrier I could have found a way around with more persistence or more nerve. As Lawless notes, "no one said it was easy" (2000:197). Still, if we take seriously the concept of differing discursive styles, we must acknowledge that not every ethnographic subject will be willing to engage with our texts or even our entextualized versions of their words in a way that seems so automatic within the world of academic hyperliteracy. We do have to try to interrogate our own fear and reluctance, but there is no point in beating ourselves up if subjects are not interested in the project despite our good faith efforts. Though reciprocal ethnography entails juxtaposing the ethnographer's own analyses with those of her respondents, I would argue that it also at some level rests on the assumption that our subjects could tell us everything that needs to be said or known, if only our collection technique were perfect enough—if only, to reuse a term, we could become frictionless conduits. Dialogic ethnography, in contrast, allows the ethnographer not to feel guilty for assuming an interpretive responsibility from which, I would argue, we cannot escape in any case. Putting myself inside the dialogic frame with Eldreth reveals how much can be learned from imperfect material; and all material is imperfect. In effect, I approach my own fieldwork in the spirit of Bauman's analysis of the successive recontextualizations of Schoolcraft's early nineteenth-century collection of Native American tales, which culminated in Longfellow's *Hiawatha* (Bauman 1993b), demonstrating how prior contexts can be recovered from their influence on the text itself. But this is not only a way of salvaging meaning from texts collected with bad or antiquated technique. Similar questions ultimately apply to any material, no matter how engaged and reflexive the ethnographer.

Stewart, in her postmodern ethnography of a West Virginia coal-camp town, elects to bring her own analysis and her subjects' words into equalizing juxtaposition by creating heteroglossic sentences in which local wording is partially set off with italics or quotation marks but mingles with and is allowed to speak for itself within the analytical discourse: "Those who fail to recognize and engage precise, local *ways* are called *shameless*." "People who seem so nice and 'keep things up so nice' might turn around and treat their mommy and daddy like dogs" (1996:123). Acknowledging the great effectiveness of this technique for supporting her argument about the ways her subjects generate their subjectivity in complex "back-talk" with each other and against hostile and objectifying outside discourses, I have not followed her lead for several reasons. First, Eldreth seems to me to have been more constrained by and compliant with controlling discourses for much of her life. Stewart's inventive style presumably captures the energetic flavor of talk in the community she studied, but things are a lot quieter and more repressed at Eldreth's house. Second, many Appalachian readers have evidently perceived Stewart's heteroglossia as parody rather than as her intended display of equality and respect (Fine 1999). Heteroglossic cleverness may not be read as we would like it to be by those whose sensitivity has been raised by a history of being mocked. And finally, in order to talk about the dialogic nature of the texts Eldreth produced during our interactions, to trace the connections generated by talk between two parties, I needed to keep our contributions perceptually separate.

This book has, nevertheless, been significantly shaped by what I believe are Eldreth's own priorities and by the ways in which she required me to revise my presuppositions and my original framing of her. She welcomed and encouraged the attention she received from those of us who regarded her primarily as a singer, but she insisted on depicting other facets of her life, especially how hard she has worked. She likewise humored those of us who identified her as a participant in an "Appalachian culture." I gradually learned, however, that she did not employ that category, let alone apply it to herself, that she resisted attempts to depict her as an example of that culture rather than simply as herself, and that she regarded class rather than culture as the prime difference between herself and her new audiences. Scholars of the region have argued for some decades that the resilient notion of Appalachia as a distinct region has predominantly been bolstered by successive generations of people from outside, intent upon demonstrating that the poverty of mountain residents could be attributed to inherent inferiori-ty—biological or social (Batteau 1990; Whisnant 1983). As early as 1980, Allen Batteau argued categorically, "What cultural distinctiveness Appalachia has . . . is either an adaptation to past forms of exploitation which were more clearly based in class relationships, or else is the romanticized projection of the exploit-ing class itself" (1980:29). Folklorists, however, have listened to the lesson but often assumed we were exempt, since our goal in celebrating a "traditional" Appalachian culture was to honor and celebrate those whom others denigrated (J. A. Williams 2002:356–357). I had to learn, from my dialogic rereading of the stories Eldreth shared, just how little sense the "Appalachian" label made to her. Only then could I fully grasp Lila Abu-Lughod's exhortation that feminist anthropologists must create "ethnographies of the particular" in order to "write against" a reified concept of culture that enforces hierarchical separations between self and other (1991:138, 149) or Amy Shuman's call for folklorists to "dismantle local culture" and to recognize that the designation or delimitation of a "local" is never politically neutral (1993: 345).

Certain chapters of the book focus on issues that are more evident and more interesting to me than to Eldreth— for example, the changes I observed over the course of her life in her reported pattern of speech interactions with men and with women. Other chapters, however, convey what I gather Eldreth herself most wished me to share with a wider audience, notably her stories on her work life and on the defining experiences of her childhood. The chapters on ghost sto-ries and singing reflect the convergence of my interest in her as a verbal artist with her interest in having her well-crafted stories and cherished repertoire of songs recorded and attributed to her. The chapter on Eldreth's practical joking reflects the greatest strain between our nonidentical purposes. She loves to pro-mote an image of herself as a harmless jokester, while I have difficulty finding the humor in joking that strikes me as cruel in general and am particularly disturbed by her tendency to target children and her use of blackface disguise. Once sub-ject and ethnographer are engaged in dialogue, however, there is no absolute boundary between their purposes. What is said and known is generated by both through cooperation and conflict. I admittedly create the larger text that frames Eldreth's stories. While she "speaks" copiously in the following pages, I cannot deny the effects of my selection and shaping on what readers "hear." I neverthe-less have faith that, in this thoroughly dialogized text, her self-depiction will necessarily exceed and escape my control. I also intend that my effort to analyze Eldreth's means of self-fashioning will support her goal of creating a self that oth-ers, near and far, direct and mediated through this book, will understand and admire. As Bakhtin argues, an utterance does not fully exist until it receives an active response from a listener (1986). This book is my way of actively listening and responding to Eldreth.

BESSIE ELDRETH: A BRIEF CHRONOLOGY

While I resist the tendency to reduce Eldreth's expressive self-construction to an enforcedly univocal biography, I nevertheless acknowledge that part of what we as listeners do with the personal anecdotes told us by an individual in whom we are interested is to organize the incidents chronologically in order to form some picture of a life trajectory. Eldreth, significantly, never showed an inclination to do this for herself with me. Even when I asked her to try to start at the beginning and give me an overview of her life, the details of a particular anecdote and its thematic or emotional ties to other incidents or songs soon pulled her away from a sequential historical narration. I found, however, that in order simply to manage the welter of details and to trace developments and changes over the course of her life, I needed to construct such a chronology (in effect, to approximate the internal personal history—what Linde calls the "inner life story" accessible only to introspection [1993:11]—that is so evident to Eldreth that she has no need to articulate it). I expect that readers will similarly find it easier to make sense of the facets of Eldreth's self-construction explored in individual chapters if given a basic structure to which to attach them, even though such a monologic history is woefully dry.

Bessie Mae Killens was born October 22, 1913, in Ashe County in the Blue Ridge Mountains in the far northwestern corner of North Carolina. She has lived in Ashe County and neighboring Watauga County for practically all of her life. Home for her is this part of the mountains, a rural area in which farming and timbering have been the principal occupations and which has recently become a favored area for vacation homes. She was the third child and third daughter in a family that eventually included thirteen children. A younger brother, Joe, was her favorite childhood companion. As a teenager she most often worked and played with her older sister, Clyde. Her mother, Flora Milam Killens (born 1893), came from a family that was well established in that area. Eldreth's Milam grandparents were relatively prosperous farmers who owned a substantial tract of bottom land. Her father, Romey Killens (born 1883), had moved into the area from Surrey County (two counties to the east of Ashe) as a young man with his mother and siblings after his father's death. His father had made his living as a "musicianer," and the younger Killens was also a skillful fiddle and banjo player. Eldreth's parents married in 1908, when her father was twenty-five, and her mother, fifteen. When asked about her ethnic background, Eldreth reports that her father "told us we were Irish."

Ashe County, North Carolina, was home base for Eldreth's parents, and the family maintained strong ties to that area and to relatives living there. Her parents saved money to buy a small farm in the rural area called Buffalo but sold it after a few years and moved to Pennsylvania at the urging of friends who preceded them there. Eldreth's father had no luck finding good work, however, and they came back south. Throughout the rest of her childhood, her father alternated between farming rented land and wage labor, including a stint at a "dye plant" in Damascus, Virginia, and the family moved frequently. Eldreth remained close to her parents throughout their lives and was mourning the recent loss of her mother when we began our interviews in 1987.

On April 27, 1930, at age sixteen, Bessie Killens married Ed Eldreth, whose brother had recently married her sister Maud. Bessie and Ed had eleven children: Lorene, Clyde, Fred, Grace, Betty, Virginia, Carl, Roger, Bob, Denver, and Patsy—the eldest born when Bessie Eldreth was seventeen, the youngest when she was forty-three. The Eldreths remained married for forty-seven years, until Ed's death, although Eldreth now describes herself as largely "dissatisfied" with her marriage and professes not to have loved her husband. Ed Eldreth was evidently not a very dedicated worker or responsible husband and father, and in 1945 he was partly disabled in a sawmill accident that injured one of his hands. Under these circumstances, much of the support of the family fell to Eldreth herself, who did housework and fieldwork for neighbors, besides taking care of her own children. The family continued to live mostly in the areas of Ashe County where Eldreth had grown up—near Creston, on "Three Top," and later in Todd, although in the late 1950s and early 1960s they lived briefly in Lenoir (an hour's drive south today), where Ed Eldreth had work in a furniture factory. The Eldreths lived in a series of houses that they rented or that were made available to them by family members. One of these was washed away in a flood in 1940; two others burned down.

The 1970s brought several major changes in Eldreth's life. In 1972 she purchased a plot of land in Watauga County with money she had gradually saved from her own labors. Several of her sons built her a simple but comfortable ranch-style house, which has afforded her greater security than she ever experienced before. In 1976 her husband died, and she became free for the first time in decades to do as she pleased. She has not been solitary, however. All of her children have taken up residence within about an hour's drive, working in factories or in construction or for the building and maintenance departments of Appalachian State University (ASU) in Boone. Her son Roger, who never married, has lived with her. Her son Carl and his family built a house just down the hill on her land. After her own children had grown, she took care of many of her grandchildren, sometimes a dozen at a time.

Eldreth always loved to sing around the house and in church, as well as to teach songs and tell stories to her grandchildren. In the 1970s one of her granddaughters, Jean Reid, was noticed by a teacher who was interested in traditional mountain music, and thence Reid came to the attention of the folklorists and scholars of Appalachian culture at ASU. She was invited to perform publicly in the context of the upsurge of interest in local cultures associated with the United States Bicentennial. Eldreth initially went along to keep her granddaughter company, then began singing with her, and eventually began performing on her own after Reid went to nursing school. I met Eldreth in 1987 when she and Reid were performing at the Festival of American Folklife in Washington, D.C.,[7] as part of a group from Ashe and Watauga Counties intended to represent the distinctiveness of mountain speech. Over the past twenty-five years Eldreth has performed regularly for local festivals, including a festival on Grandfather Mountain in honor of fellow Watauga County resident Doc Watson in 2000. She has also been featured in numerous educational programs at ASU, including an annual Elderhostel on Appalachian music and a summer workshop for K-12 music teachers. She has traveled to perform in Charlotte and Durham, North Carolina, Jonesboro, Tennessee, and New York City, as well as Washington, D.C., and has been filmed twice—by actress Stella Stevens (for an unreleased documentary on "The American Heroine") and by a group of which I was a member.[8] In 1994 she was recognized for her singing by the North Carolina Folklore Society (see Sawin 1994), and in 1998 she was honored with a North Carolina Folk Heritage Award. These opportunities and recognitions have not made major changes in the rhythm of Eldreth's everyday life, and she gives family responsibilities priority over invitations to perform. She has, however, received a measure of local fame and has been brought into ongoing contact with groups of relatively educated and (in her analysis) "rich" people, who pay an extraordinary kind and amount of attention to her.

The period in which I got to know Eldreth represented a high point of sorts in terms both of the extent of her travel for public performances and of the focus on her home as a gathering place for the extended family of which she as mother and grandmother was head. In the years since, age has taken its inevitable toll. Although she is amazingly active, cleans her house, cooks several meals a day, attends church regularly, and visits neighbors, Eldreth no longer grows a big garden every summer. Many of her children are retired and suffer from disease and disability brought on by years of intense physical labor. One of her sons died after a long illness through which she nursed him, and another son and her eldest daughter are fighting cancer as I write. It is now grandchildren and their children whom I am likely to meet in her living room on a Sunday visit. At ninety, however, and despite the tremendous amount of work and sorrow she has experienced, Eldreth proclaims herself a "happy person."

Facets of Identity Construction

Each of the following chapters explores one facet of Eldreth's construction of self through her stories and songs. The chapters are, in one sense, intentionally inconsistent in that I have eschewed any attempt to divide either her life or her repertoire into consistent, comparable chunks within a single dimension. Instead, I rely upon multiple criteria—temporal, thematic, technical, generic— to group segments of her repertoire so as to highlight the many different ways in which she enacts herself.

Chapter 2 begins this account by focusing on the childhood about which Eldreth talks so fondly. I argue that the salience of this period in Eldreth's accounts reflects a hard-used woman's reluctance to privilege the subsequent period of her marriage in a similar way. Interestingly, however, her stories of childhood paint what seem to be two contradictory images—one of pastoral stability and one of repeated disruption and economic desperation—although Eldreth herself does not seem to sense a disparity. Eldreth's self-presentation challenges the view (promoted by early Appalachian studies activists) of the region as an agrarian paradise of yeoman farmers prior to industrial exploitation at the end of the nineteenth century. Her presentation is consistent with a more recent historical treatment that traces the coexistence of substantial wealth disparities and resource extraction for export to the beginning of regional development. Still, romanticized images of the moral person created by a tight-knit community have their discursive utility for Eldreth as well.

Chapter 3 highlights the theme of work. Eldreth frequently told me stories about specific kinds of work that she had done, commenting explicitly on how hard she had worked in comparison to other people. In reviewing our conversations I was increasingly persuaded that this was the most important message that she wanted to get across to me and to potential readers of this book. My analysis brings out the multiple levels of discursive self-positioning in even these apparently simple and monovocal accounts. Her obsession with depicting herself as hardworking, I argue, is a response both to older local discourses that connect morality with work and to her impression of her contemporary audiences as "rich" and not hardworking.

In chapter 4 I turn to Eldreth's use of reported speech in her stories, noting changes over time and differences in the ways that men and women (reportedly) spoke to her. While acknowledging that "reported speech" is a fiction rather than an accurate account of exactly what was said on a particular occasion, I suggest that Eldreth's reports may reflect typical pragmatic patterns of verbal interaction. While men offer authoritative (usually positive) evaluations, women compete and talk past each other. In discursive terms, this means that reporting other men's supportive commentary enables Eldreth to depict her taciturn husband's lack of care and responsibility via his contrasting silence. In practical terms, it means that a change in women's talk over the course of the life cycle from competitive to supportive appears to have been crucial in enabling her eventually to talk back to her unsupportive husband. In recent years audience members and folklorists have also become quotable interlocutors, and I explore such outsiders' discursive utility to her and the ways in which her stories thus model the kind of response she encourages new listeners to give.

Internalized discourses and dialogically incorporated voices are ghosts of a sort, lingering presences, not detectable directly, yet made manifest in the actions of those who are aware of them. Eldreth also perceives more literal ghosts, however, and chapter 5 explores her stories of encounters with ghosts and

premonitions. Ghosts seem to emanate from stress and imbalance in sexual relationships; they are experienced especially by young couples negotiating their relative influence and are explained as having been produced by immoral and violent actions, especially those of women abrogating their assigned roles as wives
and mothers. Discursively, Eldreth's own insecurity drives her to take advantage
of these "bad women" in order to portray herself by contrast as obedient and
blameless. In a subset of stories about premonitions, however, supernatural forces
back her up, providing rare opportunities for her to challenge her husband's dominance and assert her claim to valid knowledge and perception.

Chapter 6 focuses on Eldreth's practice of playing practical jokes on neighbors
and family members. Her expressed intention is simply to add a little levity and
surprise to a life largely shaped by hard work and serious moral concerns. I, however, see joking as both powerful and problematic. Spontaneous jokes, like pretending to drop a plate full of food that she is handing to someone, appear to
have served Eldreth as a form of coded resistance, allowing her to escape momentarily from the pressures of the role as perfect wife, devoted mother, and blameless Christian she otherwise strove to inhabit. She long ago gave up the more
elaborated planned jokes that seriously frightened children and relied upon denigrating, stereotypical blackface impersonations. Given that she still unselfconsciously tells stories about these events, however, her portrait must include a
recognition of her willingness to exploit others in order to combat her own mar-
ginality. Simultaneously I struggle with the way in which hearing these stories
makes me as listener uncomfortably complicit in her assumption of white privilege.

With chapter 7 I turn at last to Eldreth's singing, the practice that piqued my
initial interest in her and one that reinforces impressions revealed by her stories.
Her repertoire of songs—early country favorites, nineteenth-century sentimental songs, popular hymns, and a handful of American traditional ballads—makes
it clear that the Appalachia of Eldreth's youth was scarcely isolated from the
American cultural mainstream. Her practice of learning songs by ear and preserving the texts in handwritten songbooks further suggests that she is now perceived as a "traditional" singer in part because of the availability of the kind of
schooling that was once considered the death knell for oral tradition. Still, her
assumption of the supposedly traditional role of a solitary ballad singer is less a
retention than an innovation occasioned because radio and recordings displaced
opportunities for communal secular performance. Eldreth's practice as a singer,
on the other hand, responds largely to gender expectations. Unable to learn an
instrument, because the time required was considered incompatible with
women's endless domestic labor, Eldreth channeled her musical interests into
singing. Singing proved an acceptable form of artistic expression for a woman
because it could be defined as a form of work in the service of one's family (lull-
abies) and one's religious community (offering solos in church). In her recent
interactions with folklorists, however, Eldreth at last seizes the opportunity to

perform in an unhedged way and consequently resists presenters' attempts to frame her musical performance as a cultural example.

In working with Bessie Eldreth I have gone through a learning process. Because I initially framed her as a producer of an objectified "folklore," I set out to collect stories and songs from her "in natural context." In the course of this futile attempt, however, I initiated a form of interaction that gave Eldreth considerable control. I simultaneously opened myself up to being educated about how she wanted to represent herself to me and others. The result is this text, which expounds the central themes of her identity while exploring the discursive and dialogic means that she has employed to construct herself relative to available discourses and interlocutors. For most of her life, Eldreth has had to shape her identity by coded and deniable means, fighting against criticism and prejudice. Later contact with folklorists offered many new opportunities, yet framed her in ways that, as I had to learn, were not entirely congenial. I hope she will judge that I have been a sympathetic listener and an apt learner.

2

"That was before I ever left home"
Complex Accounts of a Simple Childhood

In a quiet country village stood a maple on the hill.

—Gussie L. Davis

Six o'clock. It's quitting time.

—Bessie Eldreth, "first song," composed at age 3 or 4

Bessie Eldreth loves to talk about her childhood. Whatever the ostensible topic or purpose of a conversation, we seem always to come around to discussion of her early memories and of her interactions with parents, grandparents, siblings, and teachers. My account of her will begin, then, at this beginning to which Eldreth so insistently directed my attention, the foundation of what I as a new listener evidently needed to know in order to understand her as she wished to be understood. Still, it is wise not be too comfortable with this apparently obvious narrative ordering. Strict chronology was not a major concern of Eldreth's, and though, when pressed, she could usually tell me her age during the events recounted, most often my attempts to put things in temporal order would evoke her label for the first sixteen years of her life: "Oh, yes, that was before I left home" or "That was before I ever got married." More importantly, although Eldreth tends to portray these years as a joyful and carefree time, her accounts of them are far from simple rhetorically. Her pressing desire to establish a sense of herself as an inherently good person as attested to by authoritative witnesses from her earliest years bespeaks an unexpected anxiety about challenges to her moral standing. Her narrative focus on the years prior to her marriage also serves crucially to define her as more than the wife and mother most current acquaintances know her as. Furthermore, I became increasingly aware that she was

28

telling two kinds of stories that I found difficult to bring into focus together, one of growing up in an established agricultural community, the other of incessant family disruption as her father sought industrial wage labor. On the one hand, attempting to reconcile these disparate images required me to challenge my own vision of "rural Appalachia" in the early twentieth century. On the other, I realized that in constructing her version of her past, Eldreth likewise grapples with romanticized visions of a preindustrial Appalachia, partly rejecting but partly accepting versions of mountain history made by other actors for other purposes. Ultimately, her concern to establish herself as a good and valuable person both in terms set by local discourses and in my eyes is reflected in the themes she emphasizes. This concern also, however, conflicts with and suppresses an incipient critique of the actors and forces that placed her family in a precarious economic position.

A Focus on Childhood

The stories from Eldreth's childhood provide a glimpse of life in the mountain south in the 1910s and 20s as experienced by a young, but by no means sheltered, person. Work and making a living, relationships with family and neighbors, religion, the supernatural, play and joking, and the place of music in people's lives figure prominently in these earliest accounts as they will throughout her life. It is hardly surprising that an older person should enjoy reminiscing about her childhood, but it is all the more valuable, consequently, to interrogate this obviousness, asking what purpose these accounts fulfill for her.

Admittedly, the alacrity with which Eldreth spoke about her childhood in our conversations was partially a result of my collusion. Since I initially conceived of Eldreth as an interesting person to study because she was a bearer of old, "traditional" songs, I constantly asked her when and from whom she had learned the pieces she sang. I, unconsciously (and, as it turned out, erroneously), conceptualized Eldreth's childhood years as the period in which she must have acquired the bulk of her song repertoire or at least that portion in which I, as a folklorist, was supposed to be interested. I questioned her a number of times about childhood memories and her influences during what I assumed was the most important originary period for her repertoire, and I probably expressed particular interest whenever she indicated that she had learned a song from her grandmother or another relative older than herself. Thus in talking frequently about her early experiences and taking me on trips to visit places she had lived as a child, Eldreth was in part responding to guidance and privileging on my part.

Still, Eldreth's interest in talking about her childhood was not simply an artifact of interviewer pressure. Nor am I the only interviewer to note an emphasis on the subject's early years in an older woman's life account. These stories provide Eldreth with two crucial and connected rhetorical moves. They enable her,

relying primarily on the remembered testimony of her parents, to define character traits she claims as inherent, portraying herself as an exceptionally and
uniquely good child, cooperative, obedient, and strongly oriented to the needs of
others. As a result, they lay strong claim to an identity that preceded and to some
extent transcends the identity as wife and mother most salient to her family and
community.

As in accounts throughout her life, Eldreth relies as much as possible on the
evaluation of her behavior and character by situationally authoritative speakers
and tends to use the behavior of other characters, in these instances often her
siblings, as foils to highlight her exemplary nature (see Sawin 1992).

BE: Usually when Momma'd go visiting sick people, usually she'd take me with her. I
       was the only one that ever got scared; I was the only one that got to see. It was
       nerve wracking. I'd go along, she'd lead my hand.
PS: Why would she take you rather than the other ones?
BE: Well, I think I was always pretty well behaved. Clyde and Maud was rough, she
       couldn't take them anywhere.
            Lots of times when she'd go off she'd tell me to watch after Clyde and Maude—
       and they was older than I was—and if they got into anything to tell her. They'd get
       plumb mad because I'd tell her, but Momma would tell me to watch them. I
       thought I had to, which I guess I did. I'd sit in my little chair with feet up on the
       rungs. When she came in she'd ask me, and they'd get a whipping.
            And she said she used to tie me in a chair, I must have been awful little, cause
       I know I couldn't walk. She'd put me in a chair and tie me in with Dad's shirt and
       go hoe corn for half a day and she'd come back and I'd be asleep in the chair. With
       the others she couldn't do that, she'd have to take a quilt and put them in the field
       right where she could watch them. I remember Uncle Payton a-telling her one time
       when he come in. Said, "I'd never leave this young'un alone like this. Someone
       could come and take her," but Momma could leave me alone.
                                        ⸺
       [Dad] made his banjo heads out of groundhog hides. It almost turned me against
       meat. I had to hold the groundhog while [my father] skinned it. He could ask some
       of the rest of the children. "No" or "I don't want to, Poppa." Well, anything my
       dad'd say do or my momma either, I'd do.
                                        ⸺
       And Momma told me the last time that she was up in my house, she said that I she
       said, "Honey, you're different from ary young'un I raised." So, I asked her, I said,
       "Momma, in what way?" She said, "I don't know, but, Honey, you're different."

It is worth noting that, in these stories, Eldreth's investment in a discourse
that endows her with an essential and unchanging nature is significantly at odds
with my effort to analyze her ongoing self-enactment. As we shall see in subsequent chapters, however, she is at other times quite willing to depict herself as

changing and developing in response to social interaction. This is only one of the rhetorical options she employs. The claim to an inherent nature is useful to her in several respects, however. First, it allows her to depict herself as unique, quite different from her naughty older sisters or, by extension, from any other apparently insignificant woman who lived in the same circumstances. Hearing these stories over and over again, I got a strong feeling that Eldreth had felt perpetually unvalued and taken for granted throughout much of her life, that she often struggled for attention, and that she had to make the strongest and most unambiguous claim for her worth when she got a chance. Only later did it occur to me that she may have felt insecure in current audiences' evaluation of her as well. Having been singled out as a singer and storyteller for unexplained and possibly arbitrary reasons, she had good cause to want to justify the exceptional attention she was receiving. Second, these foundational stories establish an interpretive frame, encouraging listeners to recognize accounts of later deeds as further manifestations of her exemplary, generous, and moral nature.

The third purpose of Eldreth's emphasis on her childhood is implicit but powerfully contestive. In insisting that her character was established in childhood, either though inherent traits or (as we shall see in further stories) through the example of family members she admired, Eldreth effectively rejects the definition of herself as simply "Mrs. Eldreth," Ed Eldreth's wife, a woman formed primarily by her contact with her husband. Indeed, it is highly significant that she describes this period not as her "childhood," but as the time "before I left home" or "before I ever got married." Recall, similarly, that Eldreth only delimits the years of her marriage as a perceptual unit in negative terms: "The happiest days of my life was before I ever got married and since I've been a widow." In attempting to construct a chronology of her life, I realized that Eldreth had told me more stories about her sixteen years "at home" and the years since her husband's death than about the nearly five decades of her marriage and that many of the stories from the period when she was married focus on interactions with neighbors, sisters, her mother, and some of her children and surprisingly few on interactions with her husband. Oral historian Rosemary Joyce observed a similar gap in the talk of an Ohio woman with whom she worked—"most of her married life remained vague and even obscure after many interviews" (1983:24)—a lacuna she could not get the woman to fill, despite her persistence. Joyce argues that Sarah Penfield's reluctance to talk about her married life "could have been caused by the aging factor, by an unconscious sublimation of a difficult life stage, by a conscious direction toward happier, less traumatic times, or, more probably, by all three" (1983:24–25). I would suggest, rather, that Eldreth (and perhaps Penfield as well) privileges the years before she married in order to excise her husband from the story or at least diminish his perceived influence on her identity. She was required for many years to make her husband the center of her life: she worked for him, waited upon him, and tailored much of her behavior to suit his standards and desires as master of the household. The *story* of her life is her own, however, and she elects not to make that man the center of her story, indeed, to relegate him to the margins.[1] To insist that she is still the person she had become "before she ever got married" is to deny the destructive power of her husband's neglect. Carolyn Heilbrun, analyzing literary accounts of women's lives, notes that biographers of women have had to "reinvent the lives their subjects led" because "the choices and pain of the women who did not make a man the center of their lives seemed unique, because there were no models of the lives they wanted to live, no exemplars, no stories" (1988:31). Eldreth, who tells her life in fragments, leaving listeners to assemble the whole, subtly but effectively decenters her husband without having to confront the generic expectations of biography head on.

ONE CHILDHOOD OR TWO?

But even if childhood stories are comparatively easy for Eldreth to tell, they are not equally easy for listeners to make sense of. Indeed, she seems to be telling two distinct stories of two very different childhoods. On the one hand, she describes growing up in a close-knit rural community—"We lived real close to Grandma Milam"—and on the other, she relates that her parents had constantly to uproot the family as her father sought wage labor—"We moved thirty-three times in the sixteen year before I left home." For Eldreth all the disparate episodes are evidently parts of a single tale, but I long had trouble keeping what seemed like two incompatible images in focus at the same time. In order to hold onto one, I had to let the other one fade or squint to push it out of my field of vision. Was her childhood a rural idyll or an experience of disruption and exploitation? What do we need to learn in order to be comfortable, as Eldreth manifestly is, with the coexistence of these two apparently contradictory versions of her early life?

The first prominent strand in Eldreth's growing-up stories depicts a life of hard but rewarding work, self-sufficiency, and interdependence among neighbors in a stable, multigenerational community. This was the version that I was initially most attuned to hear because it corresponded with my preconception of her participation in a "traditional Appalachian culture."

> Dad raised his turkeys. We did; we all did. And our chickens. And we had our beef; we raised our beef and our hogs. Momma done a lot of canning. We made our corn crops and we cleared our new grounds. We had a little farm of our own. And we done all that work. Well, I guess we had to to survive.
>
> —
>
> Back years ago, if they had sickness in families, why, Momma would cook stuff and take, and Dad and us young'uns'd all get out and we'd get their wood and take it in, put it on their porch, and do their feeding and everything, what had to be done, till they got back able to do their work.

I learnt the songs that [. . .] I heard [Grandma Milam] sing when I was about, I guess eight or nine, somewhere along there. And we lived real close. Momma, sometime she'd send me down there, and she'd say, "Now, you go down there and back." And she[Grandma]'d be a-baking biscuits or something. And I'd say, "Grandma, I've just got to have a biscuit and blackberry jelly before I leave." [Laughs.] I'd always get me a biscuit and blackberry jelly. She could make the best blackberry jelly I believe I ever ate in my life and the best biscuits. [. . .] She was a real good cook. And then I used to go with her to the Methodist church. She always led me.

Growing up in this context Eldreth learns the core values of hard work, honesty, and neighborliness, both by example and participation and through the explicit inculcation of maxims she still repeats.

And he'd put two of us little young'uns in a row of corn, you know, when he'd be a-hoeing, in front of us. Two of us little young'uns, we wasn't either one as big as Drew [her grandson, then seven years old] and we had to pull weeds through them rows.

And one time Grandma Milam's churning and I told her, I said, "Let me churn, Grandma." And she said, "Well." And I went to set down. She said, "No, don't set down. You're supposed to stand up to churn." She said, "Lazy peoples sets down to churn."

My daddy used to say, "If you tell anybody the truth, they can believe you," and you'd know. But he'd say that you could lock against a rogue, but you couldn't lock against a liar. So, it works like that a lot, you know it? So, that's two things I'm real strict about is truth and honest. And if we stick to that, I think we'll be able to make it, don't you?

Intertwined with the story of a stable community reproducing a moral and well-socialized member is another—darker and more desperate, although not entirely devoid of good memories or humor. For Eldreth did not simply grow up on a little farm her parents owned. Rather, the family was repeatedly dislocated as her father moved them around from land they owned to rented land to places where he could temporarily get wage labor. As my insistent questions reveal, I had a hard time connecting this strand with the other stories I had heard or otherwise making sense of the whole.

PS: Did you grow up | did you stay in Ashe County most of your life?
BE: Well, we moved to Pennsylvania; we lived up there for a while. And, uh, we lived in Damascus, Virginia, for a good while and done farming. And then we lived in

Glade Springs, Virginia. I believe the best I remember Momma said in the years that I was at home we moved, we moved thirty-three times in sixteen year, I mean the years that, now, that I from the time that Dad and Mom was married. And she said she kept 'em counting and it was thirty-three times.

PS: Were you usually moving to a different farm or did your father do different jobs?

BE: Yeah, he done different jobs. And back years ago when we first moved to Pennsylvania, well, you know, they's so many people told us, "Oh, it's just like heaven in Pennsylvania." And all the jobs you could find and everything. That was years and years ago. And went up there and he couldn't find a job nowhere, only grubbing.

PS: What's . . .?

BE: That's getting out and using the mattock and doing ditching and all things like that. We didn't stay there too long because he didn't like that kind of work. But now when we lived in Glade Springs, Virginia, we farmed. And when we lived in Damascus, Virginia, he worked at a dye plant. It was the stinkingest place I've ever been in my life. I stayed sick the whole time. I couldn't even stand for Momma to put butter in the bread pan, set it on the stove, I was so sick. Well, we had to move from Damascus because I couldn't stand it. It was terrible. And now I couldn't even go anywhere and I My son-in-law told me one time, he said I I said, "I smell a dye plant." And he said, "A dye plant? It's four miles to a dye plant from here." And I said [laughing], "I don't care. I smell it." I never forgot that smell. It was just a terrible odor.

PS: Amazing. But people were willing to work there?

BE: Oh, yeah. My daddy worked there. I don't think it bothered him. It didn't bother none of the rest of 'em. I was the only one that I couldn't stand the smell of that, used to get so deathly sick. But now when we lived in Creston, North Carolina (that's where I's born), he done a lot of farming there.

PS: Did he own a farm or did you kind of rent land or . . . ?

BE: Well, when we lived in Creston we lived on a neighbor's farm and did farming there. But, now, when we lived over on Buffalo, next to West Jefferson, he had his own farm. He had a farm and he had I we al— I I always called it the little white house on the mountain. It's a pretty little house, but we done a lot of farming there. And, so, we raised our hogs. We had our hogs. We had our beef. We raised our own beef. We had our chickens.

———

PS: How many brothers and sisters did you have by that point when you were living up there [Damascus, Virginia]?

BE: Let's see, uh, Louise was the baby one. Let's see, there was Clyde, Maud, myself, Joe, Rose, Grace, and Louise. Yeah, because when we went to get on the train the conductor's a-helping each one get on? And he was excited to death. He said, "The mother of seven children." [Both laugh.] I guess that's the most that ever rode that train one family. And it took us a long time to get there, you know. We'd have to stop and stay overnight. We didn't go straight through.

PS: Is that for getting to Glade Springs or //for . . . when you were going to Pennsylvania?//

BE: //That's to Pennsylvania.// That was a-going to Pennsylvania, I mean, when we had to ride the train. I know Grandma Milam, she had | she come over there and stayed three or four days with us before we left? And she baked and she boiled a whole ham. And made the suitcase full of biscuits, homemade biscuits, and then she sliced the ham and fixed it in the way that we had plenty of food to go on; we didn't have to stop any place, I mean, you know, to eat out.

———

PS: How did your Momma manage if you were moving so often, like if you | you had to be some place to get the crop in that you planted there? Did he just kinda move in between seasons?

BE: Yeah, he'd always get his crop gathered in and then most of the time he'd just barely get it in in the fall and then he'd sell out, and here we'd move.

PS: Mostly did you buy pieces of land and go live there //or rent?//

BE: //No, we'd just// | When we'd go other places we just rented. But now when we lived over on Buffalo, next to West Jefferson (that's in Ashe County) we owned our own home and our farming land, too, that we had. So we done a lot of farming. We didn't make our living just with whiskey, bootlegging, because, I'll tell you, we done a lot of work, everything that was coming and going and working for neighbors and working out jobs. Course, now, I never did no public work, but I made up for it when we was at home.

———

BE: But I always liked to drag out extract and pulp wood, after I got it down to the level, you know, where I could use our team? Me and Clyde had a team apiece, a team of horses. And we had to saw this extract. [. . .] Chestnut, they took it and they made extract out of it, like, now, flavoring and things like that?

PS: When you cut that timber, was that on land that your family owned or your father owned?

BE: Yeah, we'd cut extract and pull it out. And then we lived on a doctor's place after we left | after we sold out ours where we lived, we lived on a doctor's place for a long time. And they got out "curly timber," they called it, and hauled it and make lumber out of it? And then we done a lot of farming on Dr. Graham's place.

———

We moved so much, 'n here and yonder, so many times my daddy just. . . . He moved so much that Grandpa Milam told us one time, said, "Your Daddy moves so much that the chickens has got till they lay down and cross their legs to be tied."

For years I made some sense of these two conflicting strands by imagining that Eldreth's family returned periodically to their own farm, perhaps holding onto an agricultural rhythm by making a crop in the summer and working elsewhere in the winter, but I was wrong. Only much later, in response to pointed questions I finally asked while putting finishing touches on this book, did Eldreth actually explain that her parents had purchased the farm she fondly calls "the little white house on the mountain" when she was four or five years old and sold it only a few years later in preparation for the ill-fated move to Pennsylvania to join some neighbors who had fared well there. After that, they periodically rented land in the same neighborhood in which they previously lived but owned their own place again only well after Eldreth and her older sisters had married and left home. Without intending either to mislead or misunderstand, Eldreth and I inadvertently colluded, it seems, on an image of residential stability that gave that little white house much greater longevity and prominence than it had really held in the Killens's lives. It is worth remembering, too, that had Romey Killens hit the Pennsylvania job market at a slightly better time, the family might well have joined the stream of permanent out-migrants, and Eldreth's Ashe County childhood might have been the beginning of a very different story.

TWO INTERPRETATIONS

It is certainly possible—as a first approximation—to read Eldreth's accounts of the variety of activities in which her family engaged during her childhood as a single, straightforward account with no particular moral valence. At times she seems to juxtapose accounts of wage work and agricultural labor matter-of-factly, in keeping with historians' recent confirmation that the pattern of combining basically subsistence agriculture with various cash-earning strategies—occasional wage labor, selling timber, collecting herbs, and moonshining—was already quite common in Appalachia in the nineteenth century and extended into the early years of the twentieth (Reeves and Kenkel 1988:199). Still, Eldreth was born in 1913, the year before the Norfolk and Western Railroad extended a line into Ashe County from Abingdon, Virginia (Fletcher 1963:210, 236). Her growing up thus coincided with a period of economic change in that specific locality occasioned by intense local resource extraction and increased access for local people to commodities from and travel to other parts of the country. Eldreth's parents led a life quite different from the settled security of her Milam grandparents, who owned a substantial tract of good bottom land. When Eldreth was a young child, she recalls that they lived close to Creston and her father worked for "a Knox man" who was very wealthy, though she remembers nothing of his specific business. Likewise, she says, her parents "worked out" the cost of the little farm they briefly owned and apparently could not raise sufficient cash to own land again for at least a decade after the move to Pennsylvania failed to fulfill their hopes. Supplementing subsistence farming with various means of raising cash may have been a well-established economic strategy, but uprooting a growing family twice a year every year and traveling to distant locales without good assurance of finding tolerable work was not. Grandpa Milam may have made a joke about the chickens so used to moving that they "lay down and cross their legs to be tied" when a person approaches them, but he was pointing out a difference between his life and his son-in-law's. And was he merely laughing, or was this a matter so serious that it could be broached only in a joking manner?

Certainly, whenever Eldreth describes her father working in the dye plant or finding the job "grubbing" in Pennsylvania or the family cutting trees for "extract" and timber, she manages to slip a reference to the farming they did into the account as well. She seems to be nervous about leaving listeners with the image of her father as a landless wage slave or her family as lacking the means to raise their own food, that is, about letting listeners define the family as other than self-sufficient agriculturalists. Interestingly, also, she seems not to recognize a pattern or a logical strategy in her parents' decisions. Even if my image of periodic return to their own farm was inaccurate, it seems likely that her father must at times have made a crop on rented land during the summer and then moved the family to a place where he could get other employment during the winter. I broached that idea to Eldreth but could not get her to confirm it. Evidently she experienced the moves as much less strategic and more chaotic.

It is also worth noting, especially for the contrast it will establish with developments later in her life, that Eldreth as a child recognizes differences of wealth within the mountain community but not differences in class interests. She does not perceive those who have money and property as taking advantage of those who do not. Indeed, social intercourse is frequent, comfortable, and supportive. Those with more seem to operate with a sort of *noblesse oblige* toward their less well-to-do neighbors. Eldreth's Milam grandparents live nearby and are actively involved both in making their own living and in modeling hard and virtuous work to their grandchildren. At various points when she is a little older, Eldreth lives with her grandparents and with an aunt and uncle and works for them, receiving room and board in return. The Knox man's wealth explains his position as her father's employer but occasions no further comment. A wealthy cousin owns an early phonograph, and Eldreth describes learning certain prized old songs and "how to speak proper" from her, without any touch of jealousy or reproach. Dr. Graham, from whom they rented the last family home in which Eldreth lived with her parents, visited them familiarly, told Eldreth stories, and even, she once mentioned, lent her his fancy saddle horse to ride when the girls would race horses in the lane after church on Sundays. Elsewhere the family might suffer from the indifference of strangers, but at home in the mountains those who had more took care of those who had less.

Eldreth's handling of the fragmentary accounts of her childhood thus suggests two contrasting but not entirely incompatible interpretations. On the one hand, the two strands of her report are probably not as contradictory in her mind as they initially seemed to me. On the other, I believe that her need to foreground an image of her family's agricultural self-sufficiency makes her complicit in downplaying ways in which her family actually was exploited by capitalist intensification during the early decades of the twentieth century. I now certainly recognize that I was confused by adherence to a romanticized view of the Appalachian past, promulgated, at the time I began working with Eldreth, both by folklorists and by social historians influential in the Appalachian studies movement of the 1980s. Her complex version of rural life is actually consistent with historians' current understanding of the region's economic development, the longtime mixture of land uses, land ownership patterns, and classes that characterize what John Alexander Williams calls Appalachia's distinctive "farm and forest economy" (2002:124ff). On the other hand, Eldreth has her own reasons for investing in a romanticized vision of the past (congruent with my original image) that links morality with agricultural self-sufficiency. Her need to give that rhetorical spin to her accounts deflects her from articulating a critique (for which she certainly has evidence) of the ways her family was exploited in precarious economic circumstances.

My difficulty in reconciling the two strands of Eldreth's childhood story was certainly in part the result of a preconceived image of what life in the mountains in those days was supposed to have been like. From shortly after the turn of the century, folklorists—both scholarly, like Cecil Sharp (1932), and applied, like settlement school workers (Whisnant 1983)—regarded "Appalachia" as a source of traditional cultural practices as yet untainted (or only recently displaced) by mass-market products. The people's characteristic individualism and egalitarianism had likewise been traced by sympathetic observers, beginning with John C. Campbell, to descent from frontier settlers who survived by means of each family's own labor and the resources it controlled (Campbell 1921, chap. 6).[2] Folklorist collector/popularizers, like the musical Lomaxes and Seegers, further promoted a consistent image of Appalachian resourcefulness and traditional artistry precisely to counter powerful negative images of depraved and shiftless hillbillies (J. A. Williams 2002:304). Cultural critics like David Whisnant (1983) and Henry Shapiro (1978) had begun to expose this view of a pure folk culture in the mountains as romanticized and in fact calculated to serve the interests not of local people but of new capitalist enterprises that were transforming the region. In this analysis, an area marginalized after the Civil War had suddenly been rediscovered in the 1890s as a source both of material resources (coal and timber) and workers for the industrialization of other parts of the United States and of pure Anglo-Saxon cultural and genetic stock to dilute the effects of immigration from eastern and southern Europe (Whisnant 1983). Still, in exposing the cultural and economic exploitation of the region during the late nineteenth and twentieth centuries, these accounts tended to bolster an image of the region as a rough utopia of self-sufficient yeoman farmers up until the arrival of the extractive industries (Caudill 1971; Eller 1982; Gaventa 1980). Only after the turn of the century, in this account, was that economy destroyed, and "Appalachia" came into being as a periphery to be exploited for the benefit of "America." Although Appalachian historians were already aware of disparities in wealth and the influential dealings of local elites, I encountered the egalitarian yeoman farmer image as almost an article of faith among those committed to a positive interpretation of mountain folk and their cultural activities when I set out to understand Eldreth's stories in the late 1980s.

Specifically, the most influential historical account of the region in which Eldreth lived documented that in the first two decades of the twentieth century, the mountain counties of western North Carolina were drawn into the timber boom that was already consuming adjacent parts of Kentucky, Virginia, and Tennessee. Companies and their wealthy owners bought up huge tracts of land, much of which was denuded without care for local needs or sustainability (Eller 1982:99–112). The federal government acquired additional acreage, balancing conservation, water control, and multiple use but managing the land primarily as a timber reserve (1982:112–121). Workers were both pushed and pulled off their farms by, respectively, changing land ownership patterns and the opportunities for employment in logging and the related industries of milling, tanning, and furniture making (1982:121). Ronald Eller's study of the industrialization of the Appalachian South lead him to conclude that farms and the collaborative family work discipline of subsistence agriculture deteriorated during these years so that when the timber companies shifted operations to the Pacific Northwest after World War I, people were forced to search for other industrial work (1982:123). In Ashe County specifically, the railroad that was built in 1914 was aimed to get as close as possible to an extant "timber resources depot" at West Jefferson and resulted in the establishment of hundreds of sawmills to process timber to be shipped out (Fletcher 1963:264). I thus imagined that during her childhood Eldreth's family would be experiencing only the very first wave of transformation from a purely self-sufficient agricultural livelihood based on widespread, equal, stable land ownership. As critical historians of the region now agree, however, this image has proved to have been a temporary foil necessary to Appalachian studies activists' campaign to highlight the real depredations of the extractive industries, but it has had to be modified in light of another decade and a half of careful scholarship (J. A. Williams 2002:362).

Since I first started listening to Eldreth's stories, the "new Appalachian historiography" has radically revised understandings of the region's history (for example, Billings and Blee 2000; Billings, Pudup, and Waller 1995; Dunaway 1996; Salstrom 1994; J. A. Williams 2002) in ways that shift our perspective on her self-narration. These authors challenge or at least complicate both the earlier claim of Appalachian "exceptionalism" (that Appalachia prior to the late nineteenth century was a purely egalitarian folk society in contrast to other regions of the country) and the idea that Appalachia was suddenly transformed at the end of the nineteenth century into an "internal colony" (Eller 1982) (that is, that, as happened in European and North American overseas colonies in Asia, Africa, and South America, a society of self-sufficient farmers living in harmony with their environment were rapidly transformed into a workforce exploited and commodified, like their land and resources, solely for the benefit of outside capitalist enterprises allied with nationalist forces). It is now clear that Appalachia was involved in the global capitalist economy from the earliest stages of European settlement. Indeed, the goal of the initial contact with the Cherokee was to obtain deer hides and slaves for national and international trade (Dunaway 1996:32ff). Starting in the eighteenth century, the region was developed not as a precapitalist paradise of small family farms but (in the terms of Immanuel Wallerstein's world-systems theory [1974]) as a "semi-periphery," with several definitive characteristics. Small-scale extractive industries like salt making, tanning, milling, and production of iron ore proliferated (Dunaway 1996, chap. 5; J. A. Williams 2002:127–129). Both industrial and agricultural products were produced in quantities exceeding local needs and were transported for trade out of the region, by whatever means were available, well before the construction of railroads (Dunaway 1996, chap. 6). Wage labor, slavery, indentured labor, and various forms of land renting and sharecropping were much more common than envisioned in the earlier idealized model of an egalitarian society of yeoman farmers in the southern mountains (Billings and Blee 2000, chap. 3; Dunaway 1996, chap. 4; Inscoe 1989; J. A. Williams 2002, chap. 2). Large tracts of land were acquired very early by absentee speculators and the "settler elite," who bought and sold the land as a commodity. Poorer settlers and later arrivals consequently found it very difficult to acquire land for farming (Billings and Blee 2000, chap. 2; Dunaway 1996, chap. 3; J. A. Williams 2002:35, 109–118). Furthermore, the image of egalitarian smallholders, however rhetorically attractive for defending the industriousness of mountain whites, made it easy to forget "how much of the wealth and the infrastructure that made possible the industrialization of Appalachia was extracted from the coerced or underpaid labor of African Americans" (J. A. Williams 2002:221).

Sociologist Wilma Dunaway paints the bleakest picture of the economic background to the fortunes of families like Eldreth's, arguing that by 1860 shifts in the global economy had fully peripheralized the region such that its infrastructure and industry were geared completely to extracting resources and producing profit for outsiders rather than providing for the needs of local people for either materials or jobs (1996:320). By this same date, "nearly two-thirds of Southern Appalachia's agricultural households were semiproletarianized into coerced labor arrangements or into unstable wage employment. Such work lives left them impoverished and seasonally unemployed for three to five months per year." These workers could neither gain access to enough land to support their families completely nor, since they did produce some of their own food, command sufficient wages to support themselves completely without farming (1996:90). John Alexander Williams offers a more hopeful image of the chances of the landless, arguing that "the extent of land ownership [in the nineteenth century] is still a matter of debate," that only "the most pessimistic view argues that between one-third and one-half of Appalachian households owned no land and had no hope of inheriting or buying it" (2002:109), and that squatters frequently obtained effective use of plots within the large holdings of absentee land-lords (2002:109–112). Still, as he summarizes the current consensus in his recent sweeping synthetic history of the region, "Social historians have pretty much demolished the old belief that mountain society before industrialization was a manifestation of the Jeffersonian smallholder ideal" (2002:136).

Clearly, then, the kind of mixed strategy practiced by Eldreth's parents (com-bining industrial wage work, resource extraction, home production for sale, and subsistence farming) was not a new development for their generation. It would have been expected, according to a long-established pattern, that someone like Eldreth's father, who had moved to Ashe County from neighboring Surrey County as a young man with very little money, would not have been able to pur-chase enough land to support his family solely by farming. The family's econom-ic hardships and their need for frequent and disruptive moves may well have been exacerbated by the recent arrival of large-scale corporate extractive indus-tries. The intergenerational economic difference in Eldreth's family, however, would probably not have been seen as the result of new outside forces blocking a young man from achieving something that was assumed to be his due. Comfortable land owners and marginal wage laborers and renters had coexisted in the same communities for generations. Paul Salstrom further suggests that "the industrialization era [in the early twentieth century] may well have intensi-fied both the practice and the attitude of voluntary reciprocity within 'their own family groups'" (1994:xvii), so the new development in Eldreth's self-account might, ironically, have been the evidence of cooperation within the extended family rather than her father's participation in wage labor. From this revised per-spective, then, one might argue that Eldreth's relatively matter-of-fact juxtaposi-tion of the agrarian and wage-earner images simply reflects the actual, function-al coexistence or even interdependence of what I had erroneously conceptualized as two contradictory social and economic systems. When wage work looked more promising than farming, they moved to a place where her dad had hope of being hired; when they took the train to Pennsylvania, Grandma Milam resourcefully made them a suitcase full of ham biscuits. The two ways of making a living sup-ported each other. Eldreth's family would not necessarily have experienced their life in terms of the imposition of a new, capitalist/industrial work rhythm that disrupted the continuity of family or the natural cycles of a life organized by agri-cultural production.

Still, what are we to make of Eldreth's own imperfect comfort with bringing the two strands of her story together and with her inclination to privilege the agricultural side of her family's economic strategy? Eldreth herself, it seems to me, clings to an image of the interdependent community of self-sufficient farmers as the cradle of the moral person and promotes listeners' perception that such a community is where she is really from. She always claims the mountains as "home," even though she also spent parts of both her formative and adult years in communities of industrial workers.

It is also significant that Eldreth tends to construct the stories about farming, raising their own food, and interacting with her parents and grandparents (though also those about cutting timber for sale) as what Pauline Greenhill has called "generalization narratives," that is, accounts rendered in a continuous historical tense that describe what people used to do rather than events that occurred on a specific occasion (1994:34).[3] The accounts of her father's wage work, in contrast, are usually much more specific reports, limited to what happened on one occasion. Generalization narratives have the rhetorical effect of depicting the activity as a typical and repeated event, the kind of occurrence that transpired so regularly that participants have lost count of and have amalgamated individual instances. Little Bessie, this kind of account suggests, was always over at Grandma Milam's, always picking up songs, always helping out her father or mother. At the same time, details like the biscuit and blackberry jelly or a child's disgust at skinning a groundhog give the accounts an evocative specificity that grounds them in particular times. Such reports give an impression of stability and continuity.

Indeed, Eldreth arguably invokes the "chronotope"—a characteristic organization of space and time—that Bakhtin calls the "idyll of agricultural labor." In stories so structured, "life and its events are inseparable from this concrete, spatial corner of the world where the fathers and grandfathers lived and where one's children and their children will live" (1981:225). For Eldreth, this solid "corner of the world" was Ashe County, where her maternal grandfather had always lived "as far back as I can remember. . . . And I never heard neither Daddy or Momma say anything about him being anywhere else. So I reckon that's where he was from." In telling these stories Eldreth asserts the claim about human character that this chronotopic deployment of time and space sets up, namely, that she is who she is because of her ancestors and their rootedness in a place and its ethic. In this atmosphere Eldreth depicts herself absorbing and being formed by explicitly articulated, timeless rules for living. She repeats her elders' maxims to this day in ostensibly verbatim quotations, always attributed to the original speaker, as befits an authoritative word (Vološinov 1973:120). She thus claims both for her ancestors and for herself a moral value based upon hard work and absolute truthfulness, attributes crucial to her discursive self-construction. Her claim to revere truth grounds the validity of everything she says about herself and others.[4]

To put it another way, Eldreth herself is deeply invested in the idea that her childhood was part of "the good old days." Eldreth is scarcely unique in this kind of attribution. Raymond Williams notes with critical humor the perpetual location in authors' childhoods of successive, receding true "Old Englands," noble and agrarian, but he equally warns against dismissing such images as mere nostalgia (1973:12). And there does seem to be something specific to the region about the precise qualities with which Eldreth endows those childhood years. As Jeff Todd Titon noted about a Virginia congregation he studied, "Without necessarily having been a time of churchgoing, the mountain past became sacred in a far deeper sense, a golden age" (1988:138). Eldreth holds onto a markedly similar vision of "life in the mountains in the old days, when people had to depend on each other, when people helped their neighbors, [when] church on Sundays was the center of the community" (Titon 1988:140). Where does this image of a specific kind of community (rural, isolated, agrarian) as the encapsulation of the moral past come from for Eldreth and what is its significance?

One source is doubtless the Baptist church, with its emphasis on each generation falling farther away from the ideal set in the past (Bruce 1974). Both the hymns and the Bible discussion at the small church that Eldreth attends are full of references to "that old time religion" that is "good enough for me" and the need to return to the moral clarity and rectitude of past generations. In her specific case, I also suspect that she has internalized and applied to her own childhood an image of an idyllic rural past articulated in popular urban song compositions. As we shall see in the final chapter on singing, a substantial portion of Eldreth's repertoire consists of nineteenth-century Tin Pan Alley tearjerkers and early country music favorites that express a nostalgia for a perfect, but disappearing, rural life, a life that the writers had never experienced and that indeed never existed in that idealized form. "In a quiet country village stood a maple on the hill, where I sat with my Geneva long ago" begins a favorite song that Eldreth, ironically, learned from her father's brother, who traveled widely in the United States in search of work before returning to North Carolina.

The idea that the preindustrial rural community of a few generations back was a model of neighborly egalitarianism, the Jeffersonian ideal of an America built by solid, landed farmers, has different valences and purposes for Eldreth than for popular song writers in the 1880s or 1930s catering to the nostalgia of the uprooted or for anti-immigrant factions in the early twentieth century touting the southern mountains as a wellspring of pure Anglo-Saxon stock or for early collectors trying to record and promote authentic folk music (Whisnant 1983) or, for that matter, for Appalachian studies activists in the 1970s and 1980s seeking an image to inspire regional pride and a blameworthy enemy in the coal and timber companies. Eldreth, however, cannot help but be discursively implicated in and reinforced by the many other voices that have promulgated versions of this image. As Sheldon Pollock argues, there is no originary moment for a local culture. The sense of a localized culture as distinct (and in this case valuable) is inevitably generated through interaction with some translocal or outside entity, often one that wishes to subsume or marginalize it (2000).

I believe that there are two reasons this version of the past is so true and so discursively powerful for Eldreth. It enables her to make a strong claim to a personal rectitude inherently challenged by her father's mixed methods of earning a living and (as we will explore in greater detail in the next chapter) by her ongoing poverty. As a version of an irretrievable past, however, it also does not commit her to any actual critique of the causes of destructive social change. Eldreth is impelled to associate herself as strongly as possible with an unambiguously moral, indeed revered, origin because the other obviously storyworthy fact about her childhood is that making bootleg whiskey was one of the economic strategies to which her father resorted and in which she as a child was involved. In discussing the matter, she seems to respond most strongly to local images of bootlegging not only as illegal but also as a lazy person's way to make a living and to her own beliefs about the immorality and danger of drinking. The vehemence of her condemnation and her desire to discuss it with interviewers may also, however, reflect her awareness of outside stereotypes of lazy, lawless hillbillies making moonshine, a consistent condemnation of mountaineers and rationale for outside intervention, from the days of post–Civil War missionaries to President Lyndon Johnson's War on Poverty (J. A. Williams 2002:201, 305).

It appears that Eldreth originally hoped to keep this facet of her family history a secret from performance audiences but got used to addressing the issue after her granddaughter Jean, more inclined to confront and play with stereotypes, began bringing it up on stage.

> Dad worked hard. Jean's the first one that ever told that, you know, about him doing | about bootlegging. I tried to get her not to tell that. [. . .]
>
> Somehow or other I just felt like from just a little young'un that it was wrong after Dad told me to | he set this big tub of corn out aside of a big old stump and gave me a little hammer and I had to set and beat that, just till I could pick up just handsful of it and put it in another tub. And that's what he made corn whiskey out of. And I'd sit there all day long and beat that stuff, mash we called it. And I never knew nor never thought about it a-being wrong till one day he told me if I saw anybody coming to | to run. And from that day forward I knew it was wrong. He didn't tell me it was wrong, but I was small, but I knew when he said to run. Keep from getting caught, you know. [. . .]
>
> I despise it, I really do. One day I's a-setting talking to Momma and I said, "Momma," I said, "I've often wondered how many purple drapes was hung over caskets from the liquor that was made in our families and sold." And she said, "What do you mean by saying something like that?" I said, "I've studied a lot about it." And she said, "Well, why?" I said, "Well," I said, "Liquor gets a lot of people killed in wrecks" and everything, which there wasn't many cars then. Everybody used horses, horseback riders.

Eldreth perceives that then and now people think of making moonshine as a lazy way to make a living and as something that, even as a child, she knew was illegal. She cannot quite assimilate this activity into her picture of the moral, neighborly community from which she claims to spring. She treats it as an anomaly, an exception to the family's usual behavior: "So we done a lot of farming. We didn't make our living just with whiskey, bootlegging, because, I'll tell you, we done a lot of work." And she emphatically sums up accounts of her father's other labors for the family—"Dad worked hard"—before launching into a description of the whiskey making. She also finds a clever narrative means of defending her father while simultaneously using him as a foil. She depicts herself as a moral person, mourning those killed because of her father's whiskey, but does so in a reported incident, within which her mother can challenge the implied criticism of her dad. And then she can allow an older and more pragmatic self to excuse him, suggesting that it was not as bad to make whiskey in the past, since people get killed from drinking by getting into car wrecks, although in those days people mostly traveled horseback instead.

Similarly, Eldreth delights in the family musical talent that she has inherited but seems to feel that she must constantly defend her father because he played for parties where people drank and even drank a little himself:

> My granddaddy Killens was a musicianer. He made his living a-playing music. And then my daddy, he played music too. I've told the children, I'd give anything if they could just a heard my daddy before he got down play the fiddle and the banjo. It just seems like he could just about make it talk; it's so plain, you know. And he'd have us a-singing. But he never did | I never did hear him sing unless he's a-drinking a little. If he got to drinking a little then he'd get to | oh, he'd just sing up a storm. He enjoyed singing and playing this music. But he'd always | I can remember when he'd set on the porch and read the Bible till twelve o'clock of a night before he'd even go to bed. He didn't have time, I don't reckon, to read it of a day. 'Cause we worked hard. I'm telling you.

Anxiety over maintaining her respectability never entirely leaves Eldreth. Her resulting tendency to make the rural idyll version of her childhood central and to treat activities that do not fit into that image, including her father's waged labor, as an aberration keeps her from articulating the kind of political critique that her experience might easily have inspired. That semiproletarianization was not new in Appalachia during Eldreth's childhood does not change the fact that she and her family were exploited and forced into desperate economic improvisation because of their incorporation into a global capitalist system that benefited others at their expense. She has experienced the travails of constant moving and watched her parents overuse land they farmed until there was nothing more to be extracted from it. She has seen hillsides denuded of their forest cover and smelt the sickening environmental pollution created by a chemical plant located in the midst of people's homes. Strikingly, for someone who identifies so strongly with her music, the first song she remembers making up describes her incorporation into industrial work rhythms defined by clock time.

> I remember when Dad worked at Creston and that's the way I learnt the time of day, how to tell when six o'clock quitting time come. I'd go backwards and forwards across in front of the fireplace and I'd ask Momma what time Dad'd be in. And she'd say, "Six o'clock." And I'd march backwards and forwards from, well, before

six, and clap my hands in front of and behind me and sing, "It's six o'clock, quitting time," a-looking for Dad to come home.

And, as Raymond Williams argues for the English case, claims that a golden age of cooperative agrarian life has just passed away, though not to be taken absolutely literally, do mark periods of exceptional change in rural economies, that is, specific local advances in the capitalist transition (1973:36, 291).

Significantly, however, Eldreth's investment in the self-justifying discourse of respectability makes it much more difficult for her to criticize the systematic exploitation and degradation of her family or the environmental and social destruction that extractive industries wrought upon the mountain South during her childhood. In one sense this is true of any nostalgic vision of a golden age just a few years past. These images inchoately recognize a shift from the valuing of personal connection toward commercialism, but they mystify analysis and shield those who hold them from any commitment to create a more humane future, since such values are posited as incompatible with "progress" (R. Williams 1973). Eldreth's felt need to make claims in this idiom for her family's moral standing further hamper her awareness of the critique that Williams would say is inherent in her attraction to the image. To the extent that she depicts her family as self-sufficient farmers, it is harder to paint them simultaneously as abused wage slaves. To the extent that she valorizes hard work, it is harder to criticize economic exploitation. Indeed, one might argue, following Joan Scott (1991), that Eldreth's "experience" is so (inevitably) determined by internalized discourses that what she in fact experienced was valuable work against steep odds rather than excessive work for too little return. She tells a number of stories about dangers to which children and families were exposed "years ago," but all the dangers she construes as such are natural rather than hazards created by human negligence and greed. During the 1918 flu epidemic her father sprayed their house with sheep dip (a disinfectant) in an effort to block the contagion. When an uncle was bitten by a rattlesnake, his wife kept him alive by cutting both his leg and a freshly killed chicken open with a razor and using the chicken carcass to draw out the poison. When she was a tiny child playing out in a pile of sawdust, a snake wrapped itself around her legs so tight she couldn't move, and her mother whipped it off with a "willow hickory." In each case individual courage and cleverness averts a bad outcome.

Conversely, the threat to Eldreth's health posed by the dye plant and the threat to all of their lives from the precarious economic position they were put into by false expectations of well-paying work in Pennsylvania are presented not as dangers heroically overcome (still less as evidence of structural exploitation) but as experiences of individual misfortune. And Eldreth's desire for individual attention and praise for herself and her family further blocks any incipient critique. These incidents exist in what Bakhtin calls the chronotope of "novelistic time":

In this everyday maelstrom of personal life, time is deprived of its unity and whole-
ness—it is chopped up into separate segments, each encompassing a single episode
from everyday life. The separate episodes . . . are rounded-off and complete, but at
the same time are isolated and self-sufficient. The everyday world is scattered, frag-
mented, deprived of essential connections. (1981:128)

These are personal stories rather than examples in a larger scenario with wider
political import. The tragedy of her parents' moving themselves and seven children to Pennsylvania in expectation of a good job and her father instead being
reduced to the most backbreaking of menial labor assumes less salience in
Eldreth's narration than the train conductor's admiring exclamation over "the
mother of seven children." Her experience of being sickened by the smell of the
dye plant becomes a story not of a greedy company carelessly poisoning the environment in which its workers must live but of Eldreth's individuality and sensitivity. And her parents' willingness to move away from Damascus (ostensibly)
because the dye plant made their daughter sick reveals parental concern but does
not identify the plant or the company running it as an enemy to be actively van-
quished. If she does not understand what her family went through as exploitation, she cannot draw on that experience to criticize exploitative structures. In
Eldreth's mind the only remedy for poverty is taking personal responsibility for
hard work, not agitation for structural change. Her childhood stories demonstrate how an effective lack of critical social consciousness can be produced by
the necessity to invest oneself in advantageous positions in discourses concerning personal worth.

CONCLUSIONS

Eldreth tells two kinds of stories about the years before she got married that sit
uneasily with one another. The fact that she does, relatively unselfconsciously,
present these stories together as aspects of her childhood experience coincides
with the revised historical portrait of Appalachian economic development.
Capitalist extraction, renting of land, supplemental wage labor that did not pay
enough to enable workers to give up subsistence farming, and a precarious livelihood for the landless were not new in the region during Eldreth's childhood and
were not unexpected. Her combination of accounts of travel and industrial labor
with stories suggesting that she was always and essentially a member of a small,
deep-rooted community also probably reflects the attitude of her parents. Those
other strategies may well have been supplemental and secondary means of making it possible to continue to live (most of the time) in a rural mountain community that claimed their loyalty although it could not offer them a decent living (see Roseman 2002). Nevertheless, the glitches and hesitations in Eldreth's
accounts where the two discourses come together and the insistence upon adding

a mention of farming to any account of industrial work tell a different tale. Eldreth's need to lay claim to an inherent moral rectitude and her investment in a romanticized view of agrarian life blocks her ability even to experience as such and certainly to criticize the kind of structural exploitation a historical, political analysis would conclude her family went through during her childhood, which coincided with the final incorporation of the region as a capitalist periphery. Her desire to hold onto the image of her childhood as a simpler and better time, when people lived by the values of neighborliness and hard work and when she had these values instilled into her, is partly a defensive reaction against the labels of shiftlessness and degeneracy so often applied by outside observers. It is also, however, a means of resisting the definition of herself wholly in terms of her subsequent role as a wife. This was the childhood that formed her essential character, as reliable witnesses attest. And these were, she repeatedly insists, "the happiest days of [her] life" before her marriage to Ed Eldreth solidified her poverty and set her up to be abused and exploited because of her gender as well as her class. Eldreth's stories of childhood, then, serve as the first of several examples in which her need to defend herself against certain undesirable personal implications makes her complicit with the overall hegemonic control of her exploited region.

3

"If you had to work as hard as I did, it would kill you"
Work, Narrative, and Self-Definition

During my initial stint of fieldwork I began most days by speaking with Eldreth on the telephone. As part of my greeting I regularly asked, "What have you been up to?" She just as regularly responded with a remark like "Oh, not much, I went out to the garden and picked beans and strung them and canned twenty quarts of beans this morning." I was consistently taken aback by her response—both by what she had accomplished before I had done more than eat breakfast and because I intuitively expected her to stop after the "not much" and shift to another topic rather than giving me a literal answer—but I somehow never broke myself of the habit. Thus I formed a cumulative impression that Eldreth was determined to make me aware and appreciative of how diligently she works. Eventually I recognized that there was another twist to these interactions. I had unwittingly played a locally appropriate speech role, initiating a kind of conversational exchange that meant different things to Eldreth and to me. As Anita Puckett observed in the southern mountain community she studied, "One type of stylized conversational opening is 'What are ya doin?' Residents often respond with detailed narratives of recent tasks or activities that are engaging and occasionally humorous" (2000:131).[1] In other words, Eldreth and I were both following conventional means of initiating conversation, but we had different notions of what the convention entailed. I expected her to take advantage of the "What's up? Not much" pair to defer having her activities become the focal "first topic" of our conversation, but she did not necessarily see that as the more polite option (Schegloff and Sacks 1973). Still, my impression stands. Although it was a miscommunication that drew my attention to the deep and complex involvement

49

of work in Eldreth's identity, many less confused conversations confirmed my conviction that I had accidentally glimpsed something profoundly true and significant. In our interviews when I asked her to fill me in about her life, she returned again and again to the topic of work, telling stories that highlight the many kinds of work she had done and asserting by means direct and indirect just how hard she had worked throughout her life. I thus came gradually to the conviction that in order to show Eldreth that I had understood and to respond to her purposes it was crucial to acknowledge my appreciation of her labor and to accord it prominence in this account.

Work is absolutely central to Eldreth's sense of self in two respects. First, over the course of her life Eldreth has created her identity and her relationships with other people not only, perhaps not even primarily, through talk but also through her labor, her specific deeds, accomplishments, and investments of energy. Her most definitive social relations entailed working *with* and *for* other people. Her labor and its products made life possible for herself and her family. Second, being hardworking is a cardinal virtue in Eldreth's system of values, a crucial but not unambiguous determiner of a person's moral worth. In steering our conversations repeatedly to discussion of her work, Eldreth, I believe, was thus offering two kinds of guidance for my project.

First, she was warning me not to neglect the bodily, practical dimension of her self-creation, not to mistake the songs and stories in which I had initially expressed interest for the whole of herself. Indeed, she implicated me in the intertwined bodily creation of selves and relationships with gifts of jars of homemade jams, soups, and sauerkraut that I gratefully consumed. At the same time, of course, she recognized in practical terms that I could not go back in time to witness or participate in her self-fashioning through labor, so the one means she had to make me appreciate this dimension of herself was precisely to tell me stories *about* it. Eldreth's response to me thus describes the limits and warns against the excesses of a language-focused analysis that, as Marx argued in *The German Ideology*, depicts consciousness in idealist rather than practical terms (1998). At the same time, however, her response suggests the potential of verbal communication, if understood in its richness as social interaction, to bridge the gaps between consciousnesses. Marx also recognizes that talk—as interaction and communication—is itself a form of practical consciousness (1998:49); and Bakhtin builds upon this Marxian perspective in advocating analysis, not of words but of socially situated and relationally motivated utterances (1986). I thus honor Eldreth's desire to foreground her identity as a worker and her identity as created through work both by conveying her accounts of her labors and by engaging in a dialogical analysis of her talk as an engaged, practical, social form of self-construction at many levels.

To understand Eldreth's stories as utterances entails recognizing that they are rejoinders in multiple ongoing conversations. That is, they are dialogic in the sense discussed in the introduction, having been formed in anticipation of the

Bessie Killens (Eldreth) as a toddler (lower left) with her older sisters Clyde and Maud, her mother Flora Milam Killens, and her younder brother Joe, ca. 1915.

Bessie Eldreth with her sister Clyde Eller (center), one of Clyde's sons, a cousin, and a cow Clyde "kept as a pet." This photograph was taken in the early 1930s, after sisters Bessie and Clyde, inseparable though competitive as girls, had both married and started their own families.

Bessie Eldreth with her sons Bob and Denver and a nephew, taken about 1956. After Eldreth started performing in public, some of her sisters threatened to send this picture to the newspaper in order to humble her, evidently because her simple cotton dress and sturdy shoes and the boys' bare feet reveal the family's relative poverty.

Bessie Eldreth in the 1970s, around the time folklorists started inviting her to sing publicly.

Bessie and Ed Eldreth in the late 1960s.

Eldreth with grandchildren Drew and Stacey Eldreth, summer 1988, visiting a cabin in which one of her aunts lived when she was a child.

receptive understanding of multiple listeners, not all immediately or palpably present. In telling me these stories, Eldreth not only shapes her remarks to her image of me but also responds to internalized discourses, which reproduce the voices of past interlocutors, and anticipates the responses of distant future readers, those to whom she speaks through me. In depicting her hard work, Eldreth thus not only communicates brute facts about her experience but also positions herself relative to multiple, even conflicting, discourses regarding the moral valence of labor and laborers. According to subtle local gradations in value, working hard defines one as a moral and worthy person, while working too hard or at inappropriate kinds of labor can be shameful evidence of social degradation. In one sense Eldreth proudly depicts herself as hardworking and self-sacrificing, while at other levels she must struggle against potential negative implications of those very labels. Seen as utterances implicated in multiple discourses, Eldreth's stories about her work reveal the ideological component of her self-construction and the complexity of identifying herself as "a hard worker."

A WOMAN'S WORK

When I put together all the stories Eldreth has told me about the work she has done, I am amazed by her knowledge, determination, versatility, and resourcefulness, as well as by the amount of sheer physical, intellectual, and emotional energy she has expended to surmount the challenges she encountered. Eldreth knows how to do—and for many years actually did, starting nearly from scratch—practically every task necessary to sustain human life at the material level. She has raised her family's staple foods from field grains to garden vegetables; tended farm animals and extracted their products, including milking cows and churning butter, collecting eggs, dressing chickens, and processing pork; collected wild foods like berries; preserved hundreds of cans of vegetables, soups, pickles, and jams to feed her family "from one year to the next"; and used these stores to cook three meals a day for a dozen or more people. Eldreth has cut timber with saw or axe, both for sale and for her own use, and has repaired and improved several of the rickety houses in which she lived. For years she scrubbed clothes on a washboard, having made many of the clothes and the lye soap with which she washed them. She has sewn quilts by hand as well as saved feathers from her chickens to make into pillows. She has worked not only for her own family but for neighbors and relatives both in the house and in the fields.

Eldreth does not talk about bearing her eleven children as a form of productive labor, though well she might. Like all women, however, once she was married and had borne a child, she was expected to assist her neighbors and sisters with the births of their babies, and she does describe this as a significant form of women's work. She became a favorite birth helper, one of those most often summoned; and although the family would also send word to the doctor and Eldreth sometimes ended up assisting him, just as often she would have to deliver the child herself before he arrived. Once her children were grown, she babysat for nieces, nephews, and grandchildren.

Although Eldreth was not wholly isolated from commercial products, in many arenas of work she accomplished the whole process from the first steps, at least during the Depression and into the 1940s. Cooking a cake of corn bread began for her not just with mixing the batter from scratch and putting it into the oven but with growing the corn and taking it to the mill to be ground into meal, raising and slaughtering a pig and rendering the lard, and cutting down and chopping the wood for the cookstove. And if we recall that she did all of this while bearing a child approximately every other year and dealing with at least two in diapers constantly for twenty-five years, the amount that she had to do seems utterly overwhelming.

The few subsistence activities that Eldreth avoided doing are notable in that they define individual preferences and economic pragmatism rather than cultural patterns. Eldreth admits, for example, that she personally could never bear to kill a chicken and always had to get someone else to do that task. Tools had to be bought. So did men's clothes like overalls, as well as the shoes that she and her children consequently frequently went without. Notably, she did not engage in the spinning and weaving so often depicted and promoted during this period as a typical Appalachian occupation (Becker 1998). She learned and devised means of providing adequately for her family with minimal cash expenditure, making pragmatic choices about when to use her own labor to accumulate and process materials instead of paying the much higher price of items manufactured by others. Her considerable self-sufficiency, then, was a necessity born of poverty, not the result of adherence to something we might identify as "Appalachian culture." Although, as we have seen, she remembers her childhood fondly and portrays it as a happy time, when she gets started on the topic of labor she eschews nostalgia and shows no patience for those who romanticize the past through which she lived: "A lot of people talk about they'd like to see the good old days back years ago when everything was so cheap. Whew! They better be satisfied with what they've got."

In doing so much subsistence labor Eldreth was not unlike many of her neighbors or, indeed, other working-class people in rural America in the first half of the twentieth century. Buying, among food staples, only sugar, salt, coffee, and wheat flour and trading eggs and butter at the local store for occasional luxuries are common reports from the 1930s and 1940s. And Eldreth was likewise scarcely unique (in her community or other rural U.S. communities in which I have worked)[2] in continuing many of the thrifty habits of growing and processing much of her own food, even in the 1980s when trips to the Winn Dixie supermarket for twenty-five pound bags of self-rising flour and cans of Crisco had long replaced taking grain to be ground at the local mill or rendering her own lard. Eldreth also happened to get married on the eve of the 1930s

Depression, so her memories and stories reflect the fact that she took on the responsibilities of a family just when times were hardest for everyone. It is worth noting, however, that the difficulty and urgency of Eldreth's labor and her sense of herself as a laborer were influenced by her having always been among the poorest people in her community. Eldreth's stories reveal in passing that there were people in her community substantially wealthier than her family, for instance, the "Knox man" for whom her father worked, the doctor who owned one of the only cars, and the rich cousin who had an early Edison cylinder player when Eldreth was a child. This was the class who owned properties, both houses and land, that they rented to people like Eldreth (and her parents before her) or who hired her to do fieldwork or housework. In talking about her work, Eldreth thus positions herself relative to and anticipates the attitudes of both those who enjoy contemporary conveniences and those who "years ago" did not have to work as hard as she did.

Stories about Work

The conventional wisdom about women's (as contrasted with men's) personal narratives and the constructions of self realized therein is that men are more likely to discuss individual attainments and challenges overcome, while women are more likely to emphasize cooperation and relationships (Johnstone 1990; Tannen 1990).[3] Eldreth contravenes these expectations with many stories in which she is the central if not absolutely solo actor, responding to a human need with her labor. Or rather we might say that she talks about both work and relationship and thus about how work establishes her relationships with significant social others.[4] Similarly, although Eldreth employs certain regionally distinctive ways of speaking as narrative resources, I see no reason to label her narrative technique a specifically "Appalachian" style. Rather, Eldreth's ways of telling stories respond to her specific experiences, those of a historical subject defined by gender, class, and the particular time period in which she lived. Her favored topics and techniques also respond to her particular rhetorical goals as she anticipates the attitudes of listeners both past and present.[5]

The everyday, repetitive women's work that must have taken up the bulk of Eldreth's time—the cooking and cleaning whose products were daily consumed and daily renewed by her efforts—tends not to make it into her stories except as the kind of glancing references from which I constructed the general account of her labor, above.[6] The instances of work that she does spontaneously narrate tend to be those that involve a striking image upon which to dwell, those in which she herself feels that she went beyond usual expectations (often meaning beyond the bounds of what women would ordinarily have done), or those in which someone else comments approvingly on her labors, as exemplified by the following story sequence.

Pigpen and Porch

BE: I went to the mountain once. I bought me a pig. (Now this sounds so silly.) I bought me a little pig. And I sold my shoes, off my feet, and paid for the pig [laughs].

PS: Where, where? At a fair or at a . . . ?

BE: No, they's some people that had some little pigs to sell. And I sold my shoes that I had on my feet and went barefooted for two dollars and bought the pig for two dollars. //That's what my pig cost me.//

PS: //You just, like,// gave | traded these shoes to //these folks for . . . ?//

BE: //Yeah,// yeah, I traded my shoes, bought the pig. And, uh, it was. . . . Then I brought it home and I went to the mountains and took the axe and cut down some trees just the size, you know, just big enough to make the foundation of a hog pen, pigpen. And I drug 'em in, and then I sawed 'em the length that I wanted my hog pen built. And I built me a pigpen and put my pig in it.

PS: Wow.

BE: And floored it, I put the logs, you know, on the ground. And then I floored it and nailed the plank across the logs and built the sides up. Made me a real pretty pigpen, put my pig in it.

[Sighs.] Went over at Momma's once then, and she said, "I have needed me a kitchen porch built." And I said, "Momma, I could build you a kitchen porch." And she said, "Could you?" And I said, "Yeah, I know I could." So I went right to work. I got me the hand saw. I dug out little places, four corners, you know, and put cinder blocks in under 'em. I put the | fixed the plank, you know, from agin the house to | laid 'em on the cinder blocks. And then crossed 'em. And then I nailed the | sawed the plank and nailed the plank on the kitchen porch and made her a purty little kitchen porch. She told me after that, she said, "Prettiest little porch I ever had was the one you built for me."

Now I used to | I could do anything just about. I sheeted the whole upper side of our house with | and sawed the planks with a hand saw. And then covered it with tar paper? And I bought the | I picked beans for some people that lived closest ('Course, now, I had to go over towards other side of West Jefferson to pick the beans) but the people that I got the | bought the lumber of was, uh, Aster Lewis that had a sawmill. And then I picked beans and got Lyle Osborne to haul it for me. And I covered my upper side of my house.

PS: Wow!

BE: And they's some people that lived out there on the hill from us and that man told me one time, he said, "I've sat out there on top and watched you cover that house," he said, "You work just like a man."

To whom had Eldreth told stories like these before me? Puckett's observations about the frequency with which people exchange "detailed narratives of recent tasks" suggests that Eldreth may have shared versions of such stories with neighbors who were engaged in similar labors and with family members on whose behalf she worked. It also seems likely, however, that Eldreth has adapted her narrative style to explain what she did to people who did not experience such work themselves. The detailed explanation of her construction of the pigpen is a probable example, a kind of recitation that a contemporary with similar skills would not need to hear but that makes a strong impression on a person who has never considered the details of such a task. As we will discuss in later chapters, in certain other respects and in discussing other topics Eldreth does not adapt her stories to the likely understanding of present listeners, mentioning people and places as if they should be as automatically familiar to me or to a festival audience as to her. And I never got the sense that she thought consciously about elaborating stories to educate new audiences in the way that storyteller Ed Bell, studied by Bauman, expressly articulated that he did (1986). Still, labor stories in the form in which I encountered them are well suited to communicate with later listeners, people who did not share or benefit directly from the work—grandchildren, public audiences, me, and other ethnographers. That is, the stories function to substitute for the work itself in interactively constructing Eldreth's identity as a worker.

NEGOTIATING THE VALUE OF WORK

Eldreth is clearly proud of all the work she has done. She seems in many instances to have a good sense of what kinds of work will impress those to whom she is talking, including tasks listeners might not expect a woman in a "traditional" cultural context to perform. An excerpt from a conversation Eldreth had with me and two other ethnographers, Dorothy Holland and Cecelia Conway, shows both how she shapes her current narration to anticipate our understanding and need for information and how she feeds off the admiration her account elicits.[7]

Cutting Timber with Clyde

BE: But before I left home, we'd get out pulpwood, chair timber, extract. [. . .] The extract's out of chestnut, pulpwood's out of poplar. You know, they make paper out of pulpwood. [. . .] Me and my oldest sister had a team of horses apiece, you know. We hauled extract down to the road on a wagon, we had a wagon apiece. And we hauled the extract down to the road till a man could take it on this big truck into West Jefferson.

DH: What did you have to do to get it?

BE: [Sigh.] Cut down the trees with a crosscut saw. Have you ever saw a crosscut saw?

DH: Yeah.

BE: Cut down the trees, trim 'em up. And then take rock hammer and wedges and bust
       'em up into stick length, not stick length, but now like the cord had to be four foot
       high and eight foot long. And we had to cut that extract and haul it into town.

DH: You and your sister did that by yourselves?

BE: We'd pull it out with the | Some of the places'd be too bad, you know, to take hors-
       es in? We'd put a strip of hickory bark around our waist and nail it [a chain] to the
       end of the logs? Nose | You know when I say "nose the logs"?

DH: Yeah.

BE: And nail it to them and pull 'em out //down to the . . . .//

CC: //Good heavens, the two of you?//

DH: //My God!//

BE: Done it a many of a time.

In other instances, however, Eldreth seems less than confident in talking
about her labors. She hedges her claims in odd ways, makes apparently unnecessary preemptive defensive remarks, or piles up more examples than seem necessary to convince her audience of the worth of her efforts. In the pigpen story, for
example, she begins by ostensibly framing the whole account as a sort of joke:
"Now this sounds so silly," as if afraid of the judgment listeners will make if they
contemplate seriously the poverty and desperation that led her to trade what was
probably her only pair of shoes for a pig that would eventually feed her family.
Conversely, whenever she happens to describe herself as *not* working, she immediately corrects that self-characterization in a classic, revelatory false start
(Polanyi 1978): "I know one time I's setting there and, uh, well, I wasn't a-setting there, I's a-getting supper."[8] This behavior suggests less a failure to read her
current audience accurately than an involvement in multiple simultaneous discursive interactions. Eldreth *is* talking partly to her partner in the present conversation, sensing and reacting to the listener's evident reactions to her. But she
is also responding to those historical local discourses relative to which she has
over the years developed her sense of self and her self-presentation as a moral
actor. And since, these days, her immediate audience usually consists of me or a
group of Elderhostel participants or schoolteachers or others she identifies as
"rich people," she also sometimes anticipates the negative attitudes about "poor
people" that she attributes to wealthy outsiders (even though it seems unlikely *to
me* that her present listeners actually hold such views).

Eldreth, I eventually realized, is trapped in a discursive catch-22, whereby working hard is the fundamental means of establishing one's moral and social worth, yet
having to work that hard (for any of a number of reasons) labels one as aberrant,
unworthy, or shameful. In order to appreciate the discrepancies between my actual (positive, sympathetic) reaction to her accounts and the kind of reaction she
seemed in many cases to anticipate, I had (as discussed in the previous chapter) to
revise my image of regional economic and social arrangements. Imagining the
region as having been, up until the arrival of extractive industries in the 1890s, a

strenuously egalitarian society of self-sufficient yeoman farmers, I could not at first understand how her individual labors could be construed in any but praiseworthy terms. Understanding, rather, that surplus production for profit, waged and coerced labor, and significant economic inequality were established in the region by the very first European settlers and continued to develop throughout the antebellum period (Billings and Blee 2000; Billings, Pudup, and Waller 1995; Dunaway 1996; Inscoe 1989; Salstrom 1994; J. A. Williams 2002) casts her experience in a different light and provides grounds for appreciating the apparent defensiveness of her self-characterization.

Working from the revised historical picture, Wilma Dunaway crucially asserts that the moral ranking of people according to their social position and kind of work was already long ensconced in this region by the first decades of the twentieth century (that is, by the time Eldreth was born). "Respectability" was defined by the 3 or 4 percent of the Appalachian elite who owned large tracts of land, were highly educated, and did not engage in any type of manual labor. Smaller land owners, shopkeepers, governmental officials, clergy, and even wage earners like teachers and engineers could also be considered honorable so long as they were committed to education and self-betterment. Mere wage workers and sharecroppers, however, had no claim on social capital, and those who could not escape from poverty were blamed for their own impoverishment. "Hardworking people" (and by definition successful) were respectable and deserving; the "shiftless poor" were not (1996:258–259). Allen Batteau documented the extension of these attitudes into recent decades and their corrosive effect, noting that people labeled "just renters" were "thought of as transient [and] unreliable" and "lacked full status in the community" (1983:148) and that clients of various sorts were made to go through humiliating "rituals of dependence," whose "common outcome is the orchestration and manipulation of feelings of shame and inferiority" (1983:146). Shirley Brice Heath observed the internalization of this ideology among mountain folk who had moved to the Carolina Piedmont to work in the textile mills. "Men and women blame themselves and each other for not working hard enough when there is not enough money . . . For them, work equals money; if one works hard enough, there should be enough money, and if there is not enough money, someone is not working hard enough" (1983:41). Those who hold to an egalitarian ethos and a strong Protestant work ethic, yet are faced with mystified structural inequalities, are caught in a no-win situation, rhetorically as well as economically.

Depicting oneself as hardworking is thus crucial to moral standing but can be treacherous for those who lack land or property. If you have to work so hard just to survive, that means you are poor and your respectability is automatically suspect. Given the cruel logic according to which wealth is taken as after-the-fact evidence of praiseworthy self-exertion, admitting that you engage in manual labor and nevertheless continue to be poor undermines the very claim to being a respectable hard worker. In this system, Eldreth, who lived in rented houses until she was nearly sixty and who frequently hired herself out to neighbors for wages, must have felt herself to be in a precarious moral position. She was long ago discursively positioned such that everything she says about her labor must defend her against a local allegation of dishonor and unworthiness. Many of the remarks and stories I have recorded from her make sense as a response more to this historical, social, and moral context, rather than to actual immediate listeners. The often-heard or feared voice of local social criticism sounds more loudly in her ears than my recent questions.

Eldreth's investment in the image of herself as moral and praiseworthy because she is an exceptionally hard worker proves partially problematic for her in two more specific respects as well. One conflicted issue involves what forms of labor are deemed appropriate for each gender. Given her husband's combination of disinclination and disability, Eldreth had to take on a lot of what he would ordinarily have been expected to do if she was to keep herself and her children from starving, and that put her in a rhetorical position that, while defensible, clearly required explicit negotiation. The strictness of the division between male and female roles and the sanctions for breach are themselves a matter of some debate. John Alexander Williams characterizes the nineteenth-century mountain family as emphatically patriarchal, yet also notes that "particularly in the absence of sons, fathers sometimes trained their daughters to do men's work" (2002:123). Puckett, in her study of discourse in a Kentucky community, argues categorically that "when someone violates basic 'rights' activity patterns, such as when a woman 'works like a man,' then 'it's not right' and sanction, at least as gossip, is likely to follow" (2000:58). Kathleen Stewart, in contrast, sees gender roles in the West Virginia community she studied as themselves discursively negotiated.

> Ask about gender differences and there will be loud and universal claims that men work in the mines and women keep the house, that men bring in the money and women get up and fix the breakfast, etc. But because such claims are made with such certainty they, like any other *braggin* talk, will also elicit an immediate counter claim that begins with the words "still yet." "Still yet" there is nothing more ridiculous than a woman who will not split wood or haul coal or shoot off the head of a thief in the night just because she is a woman. Nothing is so ridiculous as a man so "babified" he cannot cook himself a meal if he has to. (1990:46–47)

Eldreth's behavior suggests, similarly, that the rules of the speech/labor economy were situationally flexible, at least up to a point. There seem to be two dimensions that influence how far Eldreth could go without incurring gossip and scorn for doing "man's work," her age and marital status and the perceived regularity or permanence of the role. She grew up in a family in which all but two of the children (including the three eldest) were girls, so the boundaries of who did what may have been more permeable; and, indeed, the willingness of Eldreth and some of her sisters to work in the fields and woods was probably encouraged as crucial to the family economy. As described previously, Eldreth relates chopping down trees with her sister as a teenager without the slightest hesitation. Once she is a married woman, however, limitations become firmer and violations riskier. Eldreth, I would argue, has become expert in making a virtue of necessity, as the story about putting siding on her house demonstrates, but it does take some effort. We cannot know what her neighbor truly meant by "You work just like a man." In Eldreth's telling, however, it comes off as a straightforward compliment and confirmation of her own pride. It is worth noting, however, that she reinforces this interpretation both by first adducing her mother as a character witness who praises her labor without reference to its gendered nature and by telling other stories in which she herself praises her mother and grandmother in the same terms.

Stewart argues that in the perpetually back-talking, wisecracking community she studied, "gender 'ways' are so conventionalized and so dramatically performed that they tend to be clearly externalized as discourses rather than internalized as identities" (1990:46). Eldreth, however, participates in a much more reticent "Appalachian" discourse community and has a more precarious social position because of her economic standing. Interestingly, I discovered just how strongly she had internalized the gendered labor divisions from her long suppressed reaction to something I did. My former husband, in a gesture both feminist and practical, taught me to change the oil in my own car, and I proudly sent Eldreth a snapshot documenting my new accomplishment. A decade later, after I had visited her with a new partner of whom she approves because he "treats [me] right," Eldreth finally revealed that she had been horrified by the photo, having taken it as evidence that my husband was forcing me to do kinds of work I "had no business doing."

Still, in her own case at least, any individual task could be given a positive spin. Eldreth drew a firm line, however, between working *like* a man on a single occasion and taking on the kind of regular, extradomestic, wage-paying job that was evidently seen as a male prerogative and responsibility. Although she describes having done housework, work in the fields, and even timber cutting for other families for pay, she is adamant in insisting that she never held a "public job." And although she understands that times have changed and she is by no means critical of her daughters, daughters-in-law, and granddaughters for having taken a variety of regular wage jobs, it is a point of pride that she herself never did. She even recounts having turned down an offer of a job in an insurance office, preferring to go on cleaning houses to get the cash she needed. She might, as a practical matter, have eschewed a job with set hours because it would have (or would have been seen as having) taken her away from her family and her woman's household duties for too long. I also suspect, however, that in Eldreth's mind, committing herself to a job would have identified her as the family's main breadwinner; and that would have been tantamount to an open admission that things were not going as they should in her marriage. That, in turn, would evidently have brought suspicion and shame on the wife more than the husband, or so she feared. Ed's unwillingness to work very hard to support his family was probably an open secret, widely known but rarely discussed explicitly. Apparently, however, as long as Eldreth could maintain the fiction that she was not really providing most of the family's support, she could likewise hold onto her respectability.

A second problem for Eldreth arises from the fact that the work that confers moral standing is defined in contrast to leisure and to easy ways of making a living. This means that, to the extent that she is involved in such activities, Eldreth must defend herself against the implication that they are immoral. We catch hints of this anxiety especially in passing remarks. I remember only one instance in which Eldreth described accepting charity, and she framed even that as a form of effort on her part: "One of these days if we get a break, I'd like to show you just how far we walked. I'd walk from Three Top to West Jefferson to get a change of clothes for the young'uns, I mean, give to 'em. I didn't buy 'em, give to 'em." And recall her immediate self-correction when she happened to describe herself as "setting there," rather than engaged in housework, in establishing the scene for narrative action. Most crucially for Eldreth, the music that she loves and that is so much a part of her special identity tends to be regarded as a leisure activity and is thus susceptible to criticism in this moral economy of work. In the previous chapter we observed Eldreth's determination to portray her father as a hardworking and thus worthy man even though he played fiddle and banjo and even made bootleg whiskey. In the chapter on singing we will similarly note her tendency to characterize her music as either a productive accompaniment to work or a socially useful contribution in its own right.

Internalized local rules for moral conduct are not the only submerged discourses influencing Eldreth's self-characterization as a worker. In speaking to current extra-local listeners—ethnographers and members of public audiences—Eldreth necessarily anticipates a response based on past experience and at times projects onto those with whom she is interacting attitudes they may not actually hold. Eldreth certainly has reason to be suspicious of outsiders who express an interest in mountain people and mountain culture. She complains particularly about antique dealers, who once unabashedly went door to door offering to buy items out of people's homes, hoping to get bargains from owners ignorant of their possessions' worth on a wider market. The iron bed on which I sleep when I visit was a cherished gift to Eldreth from her mother, and she never tires of describing its value and how often she has refused offers for it from dealers.

Interestingly, however, Eldreth tends to identify the people who form most of her performance audiences not so much by their extra-local residence (although they come from all over the United States and even from other countries) as by wealth. When the topic of her performances at the Smithsonian's Festival of American Folklife (where we got to know each other) comes up, she regularly repeats the observation, "We met some rich people in Washington, didn't we, Patisha, but they was nice." As the slightly defensive tone of this remark suggests, she anticipates "rich people's" possible disdain and, reciprocally, is prepared to disdain those who would not respect her. The most significant aspect of the label, however, is its implication that she perceives the distinction between herself and the people who come to Elderhostel programs or whom she meets when traveling to perform in terms of class rather than culture. These are "rich people" precisely and definitively because they have not had to do the kind of hard, subsistence labor that has made Eldreth who she is. In this respect she pragmatically situates herself at odds with one of the ways in which a folkloristic perspective tends to position her, as an exemplar of old-time Appalachian culture. From the moment of the region's "rediscovery" by other Americans in the late nineteenth century, the self-styled mainstream conceived of Appalachians as "our contemporary ancestors" (Shapiro 1978; Whisnant 1983). The second wave of interest in Appalachia as a repository of "valuable folk culture" (in the 1960s and 1970s) was connected with a conception of "the folk" as conservative people who prefer and intentionally perpetuate older ways of doing things (Glassie 1968). Once I became cognizant of Eldreth's use of the "rich person" label for her audiences, however, I realized that I had never heard her use the terms "Appalachian," "hillbilly," or even "mountain folk" to characterize herself or her family.[9] Similarly, the sight of an old washboard on sale at an auction provoked a negative outburst:

> And some of 'em said, "Oh, there's an old-timey washboard." And I said, "I wouldn't have that thing in my house," I said, "They ain't no way that something like that would go in my house." I said, "I worked too hard washing on them things a-washing for everybody in the neighborhood," I said, "to help support my young'uns." And I said, "I hate 'em."

While appreciating the attention she receives when she performs, Eldreth thus emphatically, if implicitly, rejects those who would treat "country" living as merely a style or a nostalgic memory and insists upon the substance and value of what she has accomplished. Eldreth is proud of her ability to make things from scratch and does prefer some homemade products to their "modern" alternatives (for example, her own corn bread and pinto beans to the fast-food hamburgers and pizza her sons occasionally bring home). That she sees the washboard as a symbol not of simpler times but of backbreaking labor should serve as a potent reminder, however, that what she wants to be admired for is her energy and resourcefulness. She is not charmingly old-fashioned (as Fabian puts it, an "other" ostensibly separated from us by time [1983]) or culturally distinctive. She insists upon being recognized as poor and hardworking and upon being respected as such.

I eventually realized, also, that Eldreth saw me as a person who really did not have to work very hard (months of "fieldwork," not unreasonably, appeared to her simply as an extended period in which I had no job and nothing else to do but hang around in Boone and come out to talk with her day after day). I did not grasp how I must have looked to her, however, until I volunteered to help some neighbors set out cabbage seedlings and arrived at her house at day's end exhausted and wearing muddy jeans, instead of freshly showered and wearing the skirt and blouse I had thought respectfully appropriate for visiting her. The delight with which she fed me supper after my labors that day made me aware of how my usual preparations for what was to me the work of interviewing her marked me as a nonworker in her eyes. Eldreth is so dedicated to being welcoming, so willing to embrace any individual on a friendly basis that she did not draw a line between us on those grounds. Over and over again, however, she would sum up a conversation with the remark that has become the title for this chapter: "If you had to work as hard as I did, it would kill you." Indeed, everything that she has said to me must be considered in light of the fact that, in the wider project as in our individual conversations, one of my principal purposes, in Eldreth's eyes, is to serve as the foil by contrast with which she can depict herself as meritoriously hardworking.

Interestingly, since she has gotten to know and trust me better, Eldreth will at times blatantly apply the painful label "poor" to herself. When I proposed bringing my parents to meet her, for example, she responded, "Come up and show them how poor folks live." She was partly teasing me, and the phrase serves also as a conventional politeness, a disclaimer of one's ability to provide fully adequate hospitality. My inclination, however, had always been to avoid the subject, to act as if there were no economic discrepancy between us. Eldreth, in contrast, refuses to let me deny that difference but simultaneously demands that I disavow the very label she has applied to herself (to the extent that it has pejorative connotations), asserting positively that our friendship transcends, though it cannot erase, class differences.

In interacting with the people who come to hear her sing and tell stories, Eldreth now negotiates between her longstanding impression of outsiders and her present, positive experiences. That it is noteworthy to her for rich people to be "nice" not only suggests the kind of contempt she anticipated or at least dreaded but also subtly yet brilliantly turns the moral tables, since her remark implies that people like herself are usually kind and generous, while one should expect rich folks not to be. And while the new kinds of people with whom she has had an opportunity to talk in recent years do not entirely liberate Eldreth from dealing with the older discourses that she has internalized, they do offer new opportunities for her to negotiate a positive interpretation of her identity as a hard worker. These audiences contribute to Eldreth's self-construction in two distinguishable ways, corresponding to the particular possibilities of two novel kinds of conversational interaction—the public performance and the ethnographic interview.

The kinds of performances in which Eldreth is invited to participate usually involve some framing by a folklorist or musicologist, whose purpose is to situate her music in its cultural context. This means that Eldreth herself and her life experience frequently become as much an object of interest as her singing. As often occurs in a festival setting, everyday life is transformed into a performance and becomes susceptible to unusual attention (Bauman, Sawin, and Carpenter 1992). Eldreth, prompted by her presenter, simply mentions that she raised eleven children or that she regularly cooks dinner for thirty or forty people on Sundays, and she receives applause. It must be sweet for Eldreth to receive overt admiration from precisely the class of people who did not have to work as hard as she did and whom she would once have expected to look down on her. A particularly poignant and delightful moment transpired in the summer 1988 Elderhostel taught by Mary Greene. After discussion of the thirty or forty people who regularly stop by Eldreth's house on Sundays after church and have a bite of dinner, a woman in the audience asked Eldreth if she had a dishwasher. She first replied, "No," and then suddenly switched to "Yes," holding up her two hands. The laughter and applause that she evoked rewarded as remarkable both her present verbal cleverness and also the thousands upon thousands of dishes she has washed and dinners she has cooked.

While public audiences praise and validate everyday activities long taken for granted, interviews offer opportunities for frank discussion of topics that Eldreth seems not to have felt comfortable broaching previously with family and neighbors. In interviews she finds herself in the uncommon yet not unwelcome situation of being the object of undivided attention and of being involved in the kind of extended, thoughtful conversation that may be conducive to the sharing of secrets. She also, not incidentally, has often found herself talking with women who hold explicitly feminist views. While neither I nor the other interviewers in the handful of additional taped conversations to which I have access articulated a feminist philosophy explicitly, we evidently managed to communicate our beliefs in subtle ways. For example, in the conversation with Holland, Conway, and me, cited above, Eldreth reveals that she is hesitant to share anecdotes that are critical of her husband. Our well-deployed silence, however, communicates and eventually persuades her that she does not have to bite her tongue in this company.

Dish Pan

And then I did it [cut timber for sale] after I left home. Some things a body shouldn't even talk about, . . . [hesitates, but we remain completely silent, emphatically refusing to reinforce her self-censorship, even with an "um hmm."] but, you know, me and two or three of my boys, no, me and one of the boys and one | the oldest girl. After I got married we got us out a big load of extract. Well, back then it'd a-brought about $30. And we got out a big load. And my husband didn't help get it out. And, uh, after we got it out, got it busted, and got us a man to haul it, he said that he's | he'd take it to town. He didn't want me to go, and so I didn't go, and he took it to town. And do you know what I got out of that big load of extract? I got a tin dishpan. He kept the rest of it [laughs]. That's the truth.

Similarly, in a conversation with me about her participation in a religious camp meeting held near the town of Todd during the 1950s, Eldreth inserted a brief but telling record of a conversation with a friend.

But he [the pastor who led the religious meeting] called me a little slave, he said, | I asked Miss Ruth Greer one time, and I said, "Why does he call me a little slave?" And little darling. And she said, | I said, "He don't know whether I ever worked hard or not." And she said, "News gets around."

Those who cared about Eldreth could tell that she was "slaving," working too hard and not receiving proper appreciation and reward. And they tried to tell her so, but not so directly as to cause embarrassment. At the time, she called up that sympathetic naming only in order to deny it—"He don't know whether I ever worked hard or not"—and thus to deflect the potentially shaming connotations she has internalized. In the context of a conversation with me years later, however, she could transform the earlier interaction, telling the story to adduce contemporary witnesses to her self-sacrifice and her husband's neglect (see also Sawin 2002). A colleague who read this work in manuscript faulted my inattention to the Christlike pattern he saw in Eldreth's life of redemptive self-sacrifice.[10] I cannot, of course, disprove that Eldreth at some level gained comfort and strength from taking Christ as her model. It is striking, however, that she herself never makes that connection in discourse. The church she attends stresses God as the source of rules and Jesus as both savior and friend more than Jesus' life as pattern for one's own conduct. It is worth noting, furthermore, that the idea of Christ as a model may be less accessible to women than men. Consider Begoña Aretxaga's observation that the explicit Christ imagery accorded male Irish Republican Army hunger striker Bobby Sands was never applied to female IRA prisoners who protested in self-sacrificing ways (1997). Indeed, as we shall see in the next chapter, even when Eldreth praises her own and other women's risking bodily harm to save their children, she tends to characterize such self-sacrifice as just what a mother would (naturally) do. Limitations on available imagery and terminology do influence a speaker's discursive self-presentation.

In all of her stories about work, Eldreth was responding at some level to an implicit, hostile question: If you were indeed such a hard and worthy worker, why are you still poor? The benefit to her of the conversations upon which this book is based is that they allowed her, in ways previous conversational contexts discouraged, to respond to that challenge more or less directly. At times she simply slipped in a remark in passing, referring, for example, to those who were relatively secure financially during the Depression and who maintained their position by exploiting people like her: "The ones that could give you fifty cents for all day long working, they thought they had it made." At other times she wrested control of the conversation to make a point I was not expecting:

PS: What kind of work did Ed do, different stuff or . . . ?
BE: Well, for a long time he didn't do anything much. That was a whole lot of my problem, that I had to work so hard, I'll be honest with you. That's where I had to do a lot of hard work. He'd | It didn't seem | he didn't | He didn't seem to let it bother him whether he really worked or whether he didn't. He didn't work for his family like he should have. I wouldn't want [gestures toward the tape recorder], you know what I mean, but it was true, he. . . . After we'd been married I guess, probably, maybe fifteen year he done some sawmill work and he got his hand cut almost off his | in the edger saw, when he was sawmilling. And then that knocked him out of work from | for several year and he couldn't do nothing, only what he could do with his left hand. And then he got that emphysema, and it finished him up.

By imputing blame to others who took advantage of her and to the husband who failed to do his share even when he could, Eldreth is able to defend herself against the implication by which she seems to be haunted, that her poverty was her own fault and thus a sign of moral failing.

According to Eldreth's own accounts, her husband was not the only person whose actions contributed to keeping her in poverty. And her analyses, as we have seen, do not take account of wider forces, like exploitative labor policies of industries in a capitalist periphery or the speculation that led to the Great Depression. Her husband, however, is the one from whom Eldreth expected better treatment, the one who entered into the labor partnership that constituted a marriage in that historical context but did not keep his half of the bargain, either emotionally or financially. It is notable that she also describes doing all kinds of very hard work with her father and siblings before she "left home" to marry and that it seems likely that her work load decreased gradually after her children grew up and she became part of a much larger informal productive unit in which employed adult children provided for some of her needs while she babysat or cooked for them. Nevertheless, during our first interview she identified a demarcated period—from her marriage to her husband's death—as the time during which she had to work *too hard*. In Eldreth's terms there can hardly be a more damning criticism than "he didn't work for his family like he should have," and many of her accounts effectively set her up in contrast to her husband, precisely as the person who did work for her family, not only as she should have, but actually above and beyond standard expectations. Eldreth's conflicted feelings about her marriage and her role as partner are intimately intertwined with her sense of herself as an overtaxed and underappreciated worker. Her self-defense as a hard worker who could not escape from poverty constitutes an implicit criticism of the gender system that trapped her in an exploitative relationship from which she could not escape. Economic marginalization and gender exploitation are inextricably connected in her experience.

CONCLUSIONS

As I worked on this manuscript and realized how central I thought Eldreth's own work should be in the account of her self-construction, I called her to check out that impression. Her initial response was, "I can hardly believe I ever worked that hard," although after a moment's musing she proceeded again to tell me stories of specific instances of extreme and exemplary labor, continuing until our conversation was deflected onto another theme. Like pain and other bodily experience, the memory of hard labor does not linger in the flesh (Scarry 1985) unless it caused injury and disability. Telling the stories again, however, is a means of making the work of years past a continuing component of the subject's ongoing identity, that is, of the self reflected back to Eldreth by those who know her story and see her as the person she narrates.

Focusing attention on the details of one's labor is a common and conventional local mode of verbal interaction, an available form for describing and enacting one's social worth. It is something of a stereotype, especially for the generation that experienced the Great Depression as did Eldreth, for an elder to criticize his or her younger listener with some variation of the "if you had to work as hard as I did" theme. That Eldreth is thus scarcely unique in her emphasis on labor and its products does not, however, change the fact that work is a crucial component of both her self-concept and her sense of her own worth. Her stories describe labors that her listeners could not have witnessed, directly imprinting the image of her as a hard worker. They simultaneously enable her to negotiate with a contradictory and unfair social system that blames and further punishes the poor, while depriving them of full credit for the hard work they do. In her conversations with me Eldreth also seemed aware of the necessity of characterizing her labors so as to make an impression on those—prominently including me and those who might read what I would write about her—who must stretch their imaginations to envision the sheer physical effort and the desperate resourcefulness that was her daily lot for many years.

> 'Cause we worked hard. I'm telling you. I said to somebody just a while back, "It would kill the young people today," I said, "they'd be people, more people than ever had been a-committing suicide if they had to work like the people used to work." They'd starve to death because they didn't know how to start. Wouldn't they? It's true.

It is not clear to me to what extent Eldreth may appreciate the work that went into this book as a form of labor in any sense comparable to her own. On the one hand, she has often generously expressed her willingness to "help you in any way I can with your work." And in recent years, on the too frequent occasions when I have postponed a visit because of being busy at the university, she resignedly accepts my excuse with what I take as a cherished compliment, "I know you work hard." On the other hand, the months and years of transcription, analysis, and writing are necessarily invisible to her. Still, I offer my labor as a response to hers, the "responsive understanding" (Bakhtin 1986) that provides evidence that I have tried my best to listen and comprehend.

4

"I said, 'Don't you do it'"

Tracing Development as an Empowered Speaker

through Reported Speech in Narrative

It is not until [a mountain woman] has seen her own boys grown to men that she loses entirely the bashfulness of her girlhood and the innate beauty and dignity of her nature shines forth in helpfulness and counsel.

—Emma Bell Miles

Several observers have noted the personality alteration that a widow seems to undergo after an appropriate period of mourning—the quiet, unassuming, unopinionated, deferential lady becomes aggressively opinionated and, perhaps, even raucous.

—Patricia Duane Beaver

Bessie Eldreth's stories are full of reported speech. Indeed, in many instances the reported conversation and the relationship between actors therein depicted or the relation between words and actions is very much the point of the narration. Changing patterns over the course of Eldreth's life in the kinds of conversational interaction described—especially differences in the kinds of speaking attributed to men and women—suggest how she eventually, although only late in life, became able to contest her husband's dominance and mistreatment. At the same time, stories so constructed serve two crucial functions for Eldreth in her present interactions. They allow her to promulgate positive evaluations of her accomplishments in a socially acceptable form, and they model for current listeners the ways of responding to her words and deeds that she would encourage them to emulate.

68

LEARNING TO SPEAK AS A WOMAN

Classic analyses from the two ends of the past century make remarkably similar claims about the lives of working-class mountain women. Only in old age does a woman come into her own, exert some influence, and enjoy evident respect. This change is reflected, or one might better say enacted and reproduced, in a marked alteration in her conduct as a speaker. Eldreth now exhibits more of the helpfulness noted by Miles (1905:37) than the raucousness observed by Beaver (1986:104), but her self-accounts suggest that she has indeed changed. That she, like women of her grandmother's generation, did not emerge as an empowered speaker until late in life provides strong evidence of the conservatism of the community with which she interacted and whose expectations she had internalized. That she did so emerge suggests the possibilities for self-transformation possible even in apparently conservative and circumscribed communities.

What does it entail for a woman to become an empowered speaker? One facet—explored in earlier chapters—is primarily semantic: she invests in particular discourses or discursive positions through which she portrays or enacts herself as valuable. Thus Eldreth claims worth for herself both as a hard and responsible worker and as a person whose inherent good nature was fostered by a neighborly and honest community. Another facet is primarily pragmatic: she learns to speak effectively—to be heard, to have her wishes acted upon, when necessary to defend herself or criticize others' failure to treat her respectfully, and to occupy authoritative speaking roles convincingly (Cameron 1985:145). For Eldreth, to an even greater extent than for most women, inserting herself into positive discursive positions has been a complicated, uneven, and constantly revisited process. Prevailing discourses on gender and class put her in double binds. She has been exposed to relatively few sources of alternative, progressive discourses, and her prior self-positioning sets her up to be suspicious of or resistant to them. In the pragmatic arena, however, Eldreth's shift towards empowered ways of speaking is more obvious and unidirectional. Over the course of sixty years she has transformed herself from a silent girl forced to do things she profoundly wished not to do into a quietly determined woman who stands up for herself and others. How did this happen? And how could I possibly know about the process?

To answer the second, methodological question first, we can track Eldreth's development as a speaker because she has left a record of sorts in her stories. Commonsense notions conceive of the informal, personal, true narratives that we all employ in conversation as accounts of what happened or what was done on a particular occasion. Close empirical study of personal narrative has long revealed, however, that such stories are often equally or primarily accounts of what was said. If the story concerns the teller's interaction with other people, a crucial part of what transpired will probably have been a conversation. Important acts include speech acts (Austin 1962). Furthermore, in informal oral narration just as in novels, short stories, and journalistic accounts, reporting what somebody said can be an efficient and effective way to suggest a character's qualities or state of mind, to move the action along or, alternately, to provide evaluation of that action (Labov and Waletzky 1967), to make the story more vivid, or to increase listener involvement (Tannen 1995). Eldreth's stories are so full of reported conversation, in fact, that her rare action-focused stories stand out and make a listener wonder who failed to speak or what was left unsaid.

This does not mean that we can treat Eldreth's stories as exact records of what all parties said on past occasions. "Reported speech" is better understood as constructed dialogue (Tannen 1989). Even in true first-person accounts, conversation ostensibly quoted is inevitably a strategic fiction, shaped semantically and pragmatically by the narrator for the purposes of the enclosing narrative. As narrators recreating a past interaction in which we were involved, we need not have an intention to deceive or manipulate; but we nevertheless tend unconsciously to employ words that we represent as verbatim quotation in order actually to summarize longer, messier interactions, to attribute a single uttered opinion to a group (whose members presumably did not actually speak in unison), to verbalize unspoken thoughts, and in other ways to serve the story's larger purposes (Tannen 1989, 1995). I obviously lack any means of verifying in Eldreth's stories the existence or extent of isomorphism between the words a person actually spoke on a given occasion in the distant past and the words Eldreth reports herself or someone else having said. Still, Puckett observed that older speakers in the mountain community she studied "are extremely capable of reproducing speech very close to the way it was spoken to them" (2000:114). It likewise seems reasonable that a woman who prides herself on her memory (for song words, among other things) and who makes limited use of literacy skills might retain and convey more reliable impressions of significant conversations. Minimally, the consistency with which Eldreth represents certain groups of people talking in particular ways, independent of the subject under discussion, leads me to posit that she endows speakers in her stories with re-creations of characteristic kinds of speech interaction that constituted her relationships with relatives, neighbors, and friends. Still, what we can study is Eldreth's representation of her own and others' ways of speaking, even if that pragmatic representation is far less consciously rhetorical than, say, her explicit claims for the value of her work and upbringing.

To return to the substantive question, if Eldreth herself changed dramatically as a speaker over the course of her adult life, how did this happen? If we think of the self as a dialogic construction, constituted and reconstituted in communicative interactions with other people, what makes it possible for a speaker to take on new speaking roles and in that way to enact herself differently? Presumably, one must be offered alternative models or opportunities for conducting oneself as a speaker: the people with whom one interacts have to change, or new people with different notions have to become part of one's speech community. Another possibility is that one becomes sufficiently aware of discrepancies between individuals' behavior and an accepted norm to feel justified in pushing them to change. Not all the influences on Eldreth came from her immediate speech community or even from human sources.[1] However, the stories Eldreth tells about definitive interactions in her life before her public performances began—quite apart from the interactions with supernatural agents that we will consider in the next chapter—reveal how significantly her self-constitution through speaking changed from the time of her marriage to the last part of her husband's life, forty-five years later. They also provide clues as to why she was able to change. Men in the community provided authoritative validations of her work and contributions, even though her husband did not join them. Women shifted gradually from reticence, competitiveness, and miscommunication to explicit support, attentive listening, and effective interpretation of each others' silences. And as Eldreth and her cohort aged, younger generations emerged who were at least partially immune to the constraints internalized by older generations. Eldreth became a different kind of self-constituting speaker in the course of her interactions with this slowly changing speech community.

One story in particular depicts the tremendous change in Eldreth's conduct as a speaker, starkly juxtaposing the teenager's powerless, self-enforced silence with the grandmother's forceful and effective speech. After I had spent about a month with her in Boone, Eldreth stunned me during a late-night conversation by revealing that she had been very unhappy in her marriage and that her husband had neglected both her and their children. She shared the following poignant tale a little more than a week later in the course of the conversation with folklorist Cecelia Conway, anthropologist Dorothy Holland, and me. The story itself depicts Eldreth's transformation as a speaker before she had much exposure to people outside her local community. Ironically and inevitably, however, these earlier changes are evident to me only because she represents them in personal narratives that she told much later. The contexts within which she told those stories—conversations with me and with other sympathetic feminist scholars, who encouraged her to elaborate when she mentioned difficulties with her husband—exemplify the opportunities for further transformation that interaction with new types of audiences subsequently provided. Eldreth, I gradually realized, had in recent years begun to talk about some of these experiences with some of her children, as the story within this story reveals. With her family, however, she was still often guarded and hesitant, anticipating—rightly or wrongly—her children's negative responses to her complaints or at least an unwillingness to hear their father criticized. This story in fact represents one of the few openings in which someone else's pressing need evidently allowed her to feel justified in bringing her experiences up as a counterexample. In conversation with me and especially with these other concerned and forthcoming feminists, in contrast, she needed no excuse simply to explore her past exploitation and suffering as a means toward more accurately understanding her life experience.

My momma wanted me to marry him

BE: But my problem, a whole lot of my problem . . . I think I told | I might a told you
       [Conway] or I might a told *you* [Sawin]. If I didn't, I | I'm a-saying it now.

      But my Momma wanted me to marry him, so that he could | so I could | you
       know my | the first one that ever married out of the family married his brother
       [Eldreth's sister Maud married Ed Eldreth's brother]. And she [Eldreth's mother]
       insisted so many times and so much on me a-marrying his brother, so that, uh (I
       said this to you last night, didn't I?)
DH: Yeah, you were telling me.
BE: So that, uh, me and my sister could be together.
CC: Umm [sympathetic understanding].
BE: And my aunt, Carrie Burkett, was against it. She begged her not to do it.
DH, CC: [Sympathetic murmurs.]
BE: And that's what I said last night. I told Carl and Libby [son and daughter-in-law,
       parents of granddaughter Paula]; they was talking about this boy; he's a real smart
       boy, hardworking. He's a nice, real nice Christian boy, as good as you'll ever find.
       Paula's nineteen and he's twenty-three. Paula says she don't love him. And Carl
       and Libby said something about, uh, . . . they'd like | just like for her to marry him.

      I said, "Don't do it . . . to her." I said, "Don't you do it." I said, "Never . . . try to
       get a young'un to take somebody that they don't love."

      [Quieter voice.] The day I married, I lay down in an open field aside of a stump
       and I cried till I thought I was gonna die.
CC: //Oh.//
DH: //Oh, God.//
BE: //I didn't want// to get married. I didn't | I didn't | I didn't care that much for him
       to start with.

The frame story represents a tragic low point in Eldreth's life, the moment
when she exercises least control over a decision that determines her future and
happiness. It is the only story Eldreth tells about getting married, which makes it
all the more notable that neither of the principals has a speaking role. The decision for Ed and Bessie to marry is represented as having been reached in an
obliquely referenced discussion between Eldreth's mother and aunt. Ed Eldreth
does not appear at all. Bessie Eldreth is reduced, heartbreakingly, to wordless crying that she feels she must prevent others from witnessing. And even all these
years later, even when speaking to a trio of sympathetic women, Eldreth does not
appear fully confident of her right to talk about it. At first she is defensive, "I'm
a-saying it now," and then she holds back on describing the crucial scene, only
introducing it after she has talked about her disagreement with Carl and Libby
and has thus effectively forced her own hand, needing the story of her earlier distress to explain her outburst to them. In that inserted scene, however, she shows
how far she has come. Eldreth is now the older woman whose analysis should be

respected and the voice of bitter experience. It is not easy for her to take on this role, even with the son and daughter-in-law who chose to live next door to her. The abruptness of her passionate order suggests that she held herself back until she could no longer stand the direction their conversation was taking. Ultimately, however, Eldreth not only assumes the advocacy role that her aunt took on her behalf, arguing that a woman should not be made to marry for reasons other than love, but she also prevails where Aunt Carrie failed. Where her aunt "begged her [mother] not to do it," Eldreth dares to give a direct order to the parents, "Don't you do it."

GENDERED INTERACTIONS AND TRANSFORMATIONS IN SPEAKING

How did Eldreth achieve the self-transformation as speaker that the marriage story depicts? I reproduce an extended series of her narratives that sketches the trajectory of these years, provide examples of the kinds of speaking interactions in which Eldreth remembers herself being involved over the course of her lifetime, and suggest how shifting interaction patterns enable her gradually to become a partially different kind of speaking subject. These stories are among the most dramatic and memorable that Eldreth tells, depicting defining moments in her life and emphasizing her courage, selflessness, skill, and compassion. I arrange the stories chronologically to highlight change over time, and for each I will indicate Eldreth's approximate age at the time the events took place. In addition to Eldreth's own development as a speaker, three patterns stand out: men and women take markedly different speaking roles; friends interact differently with Eldreth than do family members (that is, supposed intimates), although members of younger generations act more like friends; and the way women interact with each other changes significantly over time.

Stealing Ed from Clyde
(Eldreth is between thirteen and sixteen; the events described precede and lead up to her marriage. She had alluded to these events in a humorous vein in an earlier, untaped conversation. I asked her to talk about them again when we had the tape recorder running, expecting a funny story. Although I did not anticipate it, this inquiry provided Eldreth with an opening to talk critically about her husband and her marriage with me for the first time. Maud and Clyde were Eldreth's two older sisters.)

BE: Well, have you got anything in mind? Anything you want to ask me?
PS: Tell me . . . you were telling me about how you met Ed and stealing him from Clyde
        . . . [both laugh]. Tell me that again.
BE: I will. Uh. My sister | one of my sisters [Maud] married a Eldreth and my other sis-
        ter [Clyde] got to going with his brother. And, uh, so he'd come to see her.

And back when I was, oh, I'd say maybe thirteen, fourteen, me and Clyde'd go to church; or go anywhere that we went together, you know. And we'd be a-walking along; and she'd go looking back, you know, and I'd just | I's just a-playing, you know, hard to get. [Both laugh.]

PS: I can see it.

BE: I's just playing hard to get. So I'd be a-walking along, I'd just ignore 'em, you know, when anybody'd come up to me, and . . . she'd say, "Now that's my boyfriend; I'm going to get him." They'd come right up and take hold of my arm; we'd walk off together. Oh, that would just burn her up. I did that so many times.

And then, uh [sigh], she got to going with this . . . Eldreth boy. And, uh, I think she | I think she liked him pretty good. So one day I decided, "Well, I'll take him from her, too. I'll get him. Which I shouldn't have. And, uh, when I heard him a-fixing to leave, I slipped upstairs out on the balcony and sat down with a book. And when, uh, he got out the lane (he's a-walking) he got out the lane a little ways and I whistled and he looked back. And then I dropped my head, and he knew where I was at. So then that week I got a letter from him.

PS: Um hmm.

BE: And I went to writing to him, and he went to coming to see me, and he quit her and went to coming . . . [phrase dissolves in laughter]

PS: [Responsive laugh.]

BE: So I married him [sigh].

Baby Cases

(Eldreth describes a series of events that probably began before she was twenty, that is, shortly after her own eldest children were born, and continued for fifteen or twenty years. Mary Greene told me that Eldreth had been a midwife, and I asked Eldreth about that in our very first interview. She responded with a long series of stories that are notable in terms of both the reported speech and the lack of speech on the part of significant actors. After the sequence reproduced below, Eldreth's stories became more abbreviated until they consisted of little more than a name. I am not sure how long she might have gone on, because I interrupted her with a question that turned the conversation in a new direction.)

And, uh, let's see now, I deli— | I delivered | I've delivered the babies, by myself. I know one time | now I delivered the baby, Marie Rash's on Three Top. Now her sister was there with me, but she left, she wouldn't stay, she just . . . took outside. And I stayed right with her till that baby was borned. And when Dr. Robison got there he said he didn't | couldn't understand why they sent after him, that they had as good a doctor there as they could've had.

And then . . . I was with | I assisted him in different other cases. I was with Mabel Rash when . . . her baby was born, well, I was there by myself when, when she gave birth to one and it was born dead. And, uh, I took that baby out of the bed. And it | I | I ain't never hardly forgot that. And that was | that was rougher than anybody ever knowed because it being stillborn, you know. And, uh, I | I ain't never forgot, you know, the feel of it and everything.

But then I was with another lady when, uh, when her baby was born, but I was with Dr. Robison then, I assisted him, you know. He'd | I'd go with him places . . . in the neighborhood. And he told me one time, he said that he'd rather have me for a nurse, assistant nurse, than any nurse that ever stood by him.

And, this lady, her baby was . . . stillborn. And, uh, he went to reach the baby, you know, to, uh, this other lady that was with me, and she said, "Lord, I can't do that." And, I just reach out my hands, took it, and I said, "Somebody has to." I'll never forget how that doctor looked at me, how much he appreciated that. And, they had a little old wood cookstove—it was real cold weather—and we went in there and I sat down and I put that baby on my lap. I fixed it up real purty and dressed it, put clothes on it. And then she did help me lay the baby out.

And, uh, then I was with Lorna Belle Brewer, another lady over there, and, uh, I helped deliver her baby. And Dr. Robison come, and he said, "I don't see why you send after me," he said, "when you've got a doctor right here to take care of . . . of the babies and the mother."

The Mean Horse

(Eldreth must have been in her early twenties, since her third child, a son Clyde, named after her sister Clyde, was about two years old.[2] This is another of the stories Eldreth told me in the same conversation as the story of stealing Ed from her sister, as part of her gradual revelation of her negative feelings toward her husband.)

I know one time I's setting there and, uh, well, I wasn't a-setting there, I's a-getting supper. And my husband come in and he said, "I guess that horse has killed s—" | they had, May Rash's had a *mean* fighting horse. And he said, "I guess that that horse has killed some of them young'uns." And I started out, and he said, "You ain't a-going out. It'll | that horse'll kill you." Said that it had got out the gate. Somebody'd left the gate open and it'd come out right down amongst, in that bottom, right amongst | I guess there's eight or ten children playing. [Sighs.]

And I took out and I met that horse in the road and just screamed and throwed up my arms up over my head? and scared it. And it took around me; it didn't try to h— | paw me or anything. And took on down through the bottom, and I went up through that bottom just a-flying.

Well, all the children had made it safe and got to the house but Clyde. And he was | he's about two. Toddling along. And I run up through there just as hard as I could go and grabbed that young'un on my hip, and, young'uns, now I'm a-telling you the truth—this looks unreasonable and I'm | I've never known how I done it—but I come over a garden fence that had about eight planks . . . on a fence. I got over that fence with that young'un in under my arm—I used my other hand, you know, to climb.

And as I fell on my knees in the garden | as I looked up that horse was a-standing on its hind feet on the other side of the garden fence. It's after me. It's a-trying | well, it'd killed me if it'd a got to me.

"But I did save the little young'un"

(This must have happened a few years later than the "Mean Horse" story, since Eldreth's eldest children are old enough to understand the danger their cousin is in, to go for help, and to describe what has happened. In order to appreciate the risk Eldreth takes, it is important to realize that she and her neighbors believed that a woman should stay in bed and do no work for ten days after giving birth and that exposure to water was especially dangerous. In response to my questions about this story she told another about a neighbor who had tried to please her miserly husband by doing the family's wash too soon: "And her baby was little. And it set up dropsy on her, misting the water and standing over the steam of the | where the clothes | where she's a-washing, set up dropsy on her and killed her.")

BE: And there's something else, yeah, I told you about my sister's young'un getting in the creek, didn't I, about drowning?

PS: I kind of think so, but I'm not sure. Tell | do tell me.

BE: Yeah, uh, me and Maud lived close together and she'd go work, you know, one day and I'd stay at home and then she'd stay at home and I'd go work. Took it turn about. Our husbands was both lazy. [Laughs.] And we took it turn about, you know, a-working.

And she left . . . and I's a-having to stay at home then 'cause my baby, Grace, was just seventeen days old and I wasn't able to go to work then, and I's keeping her little two-year-old. And it was in October. And, uh, my oldest two, Lorena and Clyde, and her oldest two was carrying some water from the creek bank for me to wash out some diapers. And I hadn't been out and it's a cold frosty morning, up in October. And, uh, the children come in the house, they's just screaming, and said Jean had fell in the creek and she's two year old.

And I, I really didn't know which way to go, but anyway I just went the way the children come and I didn't know whether she had washed on down or what. When I got out to the creek, why I seen her in the water and she's just . . . she's a-laying so far down under the water and she wasn't a-going on down and she wasn't a-coming up. And she's two year old. She had both arms stretched over her head and her eyes just as wide open as could be. She was about gone. And I jumped in that water up to my waist. And my baby was just seventeen days old. And I drug that young'un out. And I turned her with her head down? and carried her with her feet up next to me, to my face, to the house. I had to carry her about as | I'd say about a hundred yards or maybe a little further. And, uh, I worked with her till | and when I, when I set her down she fell over just like she's dead as a hammer. And I just kept working with her and that water's running out her nose and mouth.

PS: What did you | working with her like pushing on her?

BE: No, I's just, uh, working and a . . . trying to keep her moving and keep life in her, till, uh, till that water run out of her nose and mouth. And she began to show a little sign of | that she | of life. And I kept on till I got her brought to. And, uh, then I got some clothes and I dressed her real good all over and I put her in the bed and covered her up. And by that time—I had forgot, you know, that I was wet. And I was, I was soaking wet from right along there [indicates waist height] plumb down. And, uh, it was real chilly, so I knew then that I'd better do something . . . for myself. And I run and I change my clothes and pulled 'em off and put on dry clothes and got towels and dried myself off and dried that baby.

And, uh, and, uh, when, as the saying is, the news got around, people's a-saying it'd kill me, you know. That me a-going in that water like that and the baby so young that I didn't stand a chance. And I know Johnny Rash come down there and he said, "I wouldn't be in your shoes for your socks." And I said, "Well, I'll just put it like this," I said, "just to have went in the water like that for nothing, I wouldn't risk it either, but," I said, "I'd rather have died than for that young'un to a-drownded and it so close to my back door." And, uh, I said, "If it had been a little colored young'un I would have got it out just the same way; I wouldn't have let it a-drownded."

And about two o'clock the next morning my sister come, I heard her knocking on the door. And I answered the door and she wanted to know if I was all right and I told her, yeah, I was just fine. And she said she wanted to come see about me.

And, uh, I don't know how many people said it'd kill me, you know. And Ed Zank | Liz Eldreth, she's | I went up there a day or two after that and she's a-crying and she said, uh, "Bess," she said, "the Lord was with you," she said, "that's why that you | that it didn't make you sick." And she walked that floor and cried just as hard as she could cry. And a-telling me, a-saying that the Lord won't let it hurt you. "The Lord won't let it hurt you." And, you know, it didn't, it | I didn't even take a cold. And | but I did save the little young'un.

Joe Cox's Funeral

(Eldreth was in her fifties in this story from the 1960s. She insists that this was not the very first time that she had done special singing outside the regular church service, but the event certainly seems to mark a significant transition in the social recognition she receives for her singing.)

Well, you know, I sung at Joe Cox's funeral, that used to live down at Todd? He was always the one, you know, that'd ring the church bells. And me and him was always most of the time the first ones there. And he passed away. And they got to hunting for the song "Will you miss me when I'm gone?" And they couldn't nobody find it. Nobody didn't have it. And none of 'em didn't know it. And, uh, Verna Lee

Green's girl, she said, "I bet Mrs. Eldreth'd know that song." And I just looked at 'em, kindly, you know, give my head a shake, you know, "Just don't say nothing." But I didn't say that, I just looked at 'em and shook my head. They went on in there. And she must've told Arnette Reagan that, that I knew that song, 'cause we went on in our Sunday school class and Arnette said, "Now, Bess, I want to know. Do you know the song, 'Will you miss me when I'm gone?'" And I just shrugged my shoulders and looked at her. And she said, "You do, don't you?" And I said, "Yeah, I know the song." And Mary June Risk, she was my Sunday school teacher, and she said, "Now, Mrs. Eldreth," she said, "this is a request and," she says, "it can never be filled." And I said, "Well, I can't *today*." I said, "I just don't see how I can, Mary June. 'Cause," I said, "I have to go to the hospital and get Ed out." I said, "He's coming home today." She said, "I will make arrangements," she said, "I'll go get Mr. Eldreth or I'll send somebody," she said, "so you can sing that song."

Well, I rushed home from South Fork. And I went in there and sat down and got me a pen and a paper and set down and wrote the words plumb through that song at the dining room table. And then I turned around and went back, back to the church. And by that time, you see, when I stayed for services and everything and the funeral then at two o'clock, it rushed me. So I come on home and fixed . . . and wrote the words down and remembered every bit of the song. And Arnette said, "Now, Mrs. Eldreth, if you get nervous," she said, "I'm going to get Preacher Byrd to sit up there behind you, and if you get nervous I'll just tell . . . I'll just have him set you down." I said [very calm voice], "I think I can do it," just like that, you know? And I got up there and sang that song, "Will you miss me when I'm gone?" And when I started out, the undertakers took hold of me when I started out the church door? And they told me, said, "Lady," said, "I have never heard that song sung so beautifully." I thanked 'em and went on out.

But, now, I didn't . . . you know, that's kindly of a sad song anyway. And they said that Mrs. Cox, his mother, was the one [with a] *special* request to find the song. You see, he played that song all the time. He had a guitar and he played that song and sang that song all the time. Said that everywhere you'd see him setting around, he's a-playing that song on the guitar. And it was special requested that I sang it. So, I did, I sang it. After I got up there and started singing, I didn't . . . it seemed like it didn't bother me a bit in the world then.

"I'd like to have a house built right up there"
(By the early 1970s, when Eldreth was in her late fifties, she had saved enough money from her own work to afford a plot of land and materials to build a house. Her daughter and son-in-law drove her around to look at potential properties.)

PS: Why did you move over to this house? Did you live in | over by Todd before this?
BE: Uh, we lived down at Todd when the house burnt up. You see, I got washed out once and burnt out twice. And, uh, we moved, uh, up on [Highway] 194 in a real old

house. And, uh, it was a-leaking pretty bad, needed fix | needed some roof on it. And one day I come through there and I said, "I'm going to get out and I'm gonna see if I can find me some land and I'm going to have me a house built." [Sigh.]

So Virginia and Don told me, she said, "Well, Mom, where would you want to look for some land at?" I said, "Just anywhere." Well, we come out through here and we went a-way up yonder on that hill, and it was just almost straight up and down. Well, I didn't talk in favor for that 'cause I never did even say a word when we went up there. I didn't like it. So, Virginia said, "Don, we might as well turn around and go back." Says, "Now Mom's not a-gonna | won't buy this, because she's not interested in this." Says, "She's not talking."

PS: [Laughs.]

BE: So I come on back by and I started to pass down through here, and I said, "I'd like to have a house built right up there." And Don says, "Well, let's see if we can find the owner of the land." So we went on out yonder and Raymond Jones owned the land | Roland Jones | owned the land. And we asked him, and he said, "Yeah," it was for sale. Just got an acre and, uh, he's gonna sell it.

"I built it to live in"
(Even after her sons began building her house, one more obstacle stood in Eldreth's way before she could move in and feel secure.)

When I built my house where we live now, they's a man, George Mars (he got killed in a car wreck) he came down there right after we just moved in, didn't have the house plumb finished. And he told me he'd give me $50,000 for the house.

That was when my husband was living, he said, "Take that money," said, "grab it," said, "and I'll stick it right here in my overall pocket."

And I told him right in front of that man, I said, "I'm going to tell you something." I said, "When I bought this land and had this house built," I said, "I built it to live in." I said, "I've never had nothing but an old shack, and most of the time we were renting this place that the houses leaked." And I said, "I've got one now that I can say it's mine and I'm keeping it."

And I've still got it. It's in a right pretty place, isn't it?

"If you want you a biscuit, you pick it up"
(Eldreth is in her sixties and has moved herself and her ailing husband into the new house that her sons finished for her in 1972. Not surprisingly, this especially direct story and the previous one are among those Eldreth shared during the conversation with Conway, Holland, and me in Chapel Hill. As comments in the middle of the narration indicate, Conway's supportive questioning had encouraged Eldreth to share stories with her that she had not previously felt comfortable sharing with me.)

CC: Tell Dottie that story about telling your husband what he can do [laughs], finding your voice.

BE: One Sunday evening, one of my boys called me and said they's in a wreck and wanted me to come get 'em. Well, they was both together when they wrecked the car, and I was real nervous, I thought, you know, I didn't know how I'd find 'em. I asked if they was hurt and they said no, that they didn't get hurt, but they had to have a way home.

So, I had my biscuits made and, when they called, so I left my biscuits setting on the stove. And when I come back the first thing that my husband said to me [petulant voice], "Your biscuits are a-setting there right where you left 'em." I never opened my mouth, never said a word. I went on in there and put the biscuits in the stove and baked 'em and put my supper on the table. (I don't know whether I've told her [Sawin] about this or not.) And I put my supper on the table. And my grandson and his wife was there. And, uh, they's setting there at the table.

Well, I got me a spoonful of green beans and one biscuit and started to the living room. And he was | he said, "You get back here and reach me a biscuit."

Young'uns, so help me, I | I poured his coffee and set it like this [just above his place at the table], set him a plate here [just in front of him], and set the biscuits here [right next to his place]. I started back to | and I looked at the table. My goodness, all he has to do is pick 'em up. And I think I just, I don't know how I felt. But I said, "I'm" (by that time I was crying), I said, "but I'm going to tell you something, now." I said, "If you want you a biscuit, you pick it up there." I said, "You've sat on your [intentionally not speaking the word] (Right in front of them people, black, only I said that, "black") till you've got calluses bigger than my hands.

CC: [Laughs.]

BE: (to PS) Did I ever tell you what I said?

PS: You didn't tell me that!

BE: And I walked on in the other room just a-bawling. He ate supper and went out on the porch. And Danny [her grandson] (she's met Danny) | I've never saw a man tickled in my life as good as Danny was tickled. And he said, "Mamaw, I wasn't a-laughing 'cause that you was so upset in the way Papaw done you." But said, "What tickled me so good was what you said to him." And said, "I had never, as long as I had even stayed with you'uns, I had never heard you raise your voice to Papaw till this time."

And I don't know what hit me; I just turned loose.

And Carolyn, Danny's wife, she jumped up and she *would not* let me wash the dishes. She cleaned my kitchen, just made it shine all over. Clean as a pin. Says, "You're not a-touching a dish." She said, "You're just exhausted."

The speaker who changes most dramatically over the course of this sequence of stories is Eldreth herself. The sixty-year-old who clearly states which land she wants to buy and who directly challenges her husband's unreasonable demands is a far cry from the sixteen-year-old who steals her sister's boyfriend as a joke and then has no voice to protest when she is pushed into marrying him. For much of her life Eldreth seems to have been willing to "accept the authority of her husband as a natural fact of life," even though Ed signally failed to confirm the requisite "deep sense of the complementary nature of [a husband's and a wife's] roles and of the obligations of a good man toward his family and their needs" (Beaver 1986:98). Through most of her adult life Eldreth must have seen herself as competent and responsible and her husband as lacking those qualities, yet she nevertheless largely internalized the ideology that knowledge drawn from a woman's experience cannot justify a direct challenge to a man's knowledge and dominance (see Belenky et al. 1986:29). What effected the change this sequence of stories reveals? If as an older woman she is accorded rights to certain speech roles or behaviors that a young woman is not, how are these new roles made available to the changing speaker and what are the steps in what must be a cumulative process? Ways of talking are presumably not the sole or sufficient cause of Eldreth's transformation. The financial independence and ownership of her own home that years of labor had conferred, as well as a belief in her own capacities generated by having successfully provided much of her family's support and raised eleven children, must have played important roles. And, as we shall see in the next chapter, encounters with supportive supernatural forces emboldened Eldreth to confront her husband in rare, though influential, instances. Still, as Beaver argues generally about women of Eldreth's generation in the region, "finally, old women are privately and publicly acknowledged for their expertise. Recognition of expertise breeds self-confidence" (1986:104). What we see in the stories are Eldreth's gradually accumulating models, reasons, and justification for speaking her mind. Most crucial, I would argue, is her increasing assurance that her contributions are being recognized, her expertise appreciated, and her preferences heard.

Men's Talk: Praise vs. Exploitation

One clear pattern in these stories is the simplicity and directness with which most of the men speak. Men express themselves in straightforward, pithy, and thus eminently quotable declarative sentences. They do not hedge or hesitate. Their role seems to be to assess or characterize others' deeds—in these instances, Eldreth's actions—and they apparently feel no qualms about making authoritative evaluations. The men can be extremely critical, as when Johnny Rash declares Eldreth a fool for jumping into the creek to save her niece, "I wouldn't be in your shoes for your socks." But they can equally offer positive evaluations, as in Dr. Robison's litany, culminating with "I don't see why you send after me when you've got a doctor right here to take care of the babies and the mother," or the undertaker's compliment, "I have never heard that song sung so beautifully."[3]

The explicit positive assessments serve Eldreth well at two levels. Initially, it must have been gratifying to receive praise or to have the self-appointed authoritative evaluators of the community put a positive stamp on her accomplishments. Further, however, these concise appraisals are easily recyclable in narrative. Although in rare and dramatic instances—like the "Mean Horse" story—Eldreth concludes a narrative by offering a positive evaluation in her own voice as narrator, she evidently prefers to construct stories in which she does not have to make any claims for the value of her own actions because she can quote one of these remarks to provide the necessary evaluation. Self-praise is more strictly proscribed in this speech community than in most. Mountain people's intolerance of anything resembling bragging and the tendency to disclaim one's own abilities have been commented upon by ethnographers from John C. Campbell (1921, chap.6) to Elmora Messer Matthews (1966:xxix, 28, 54, 75) to Patricia Beaver (1986:162). The person who violates the prohibition on self-praise risks being censured as "proud," with gossip to that effect serving as a powerful deterrent. Among Eldreth's friends and family, people are noticeably careful to avoid calling too much attention to their own skills or accomplishments. In the speech of older people, especially, every statement of intended action seems to be followed by an "or at least I'm going to try to . . . " or an "Of course, I don't know if I'll do any good at it." Even her grandchildren, however, refrained from listing their accomplishments in school or sports for their elders in the way middle-class children I know are encouraged to do. And in Eldreth's church, any deed like preaching or solo singing that might draw attention to the skill of the person doing it is prefaced by heartfelt disclaimers of performance—usually along the lines of "Now, I don't claim to be a singer, but you all just pray for me while I try to do [hymn title]"—that are employed so regularly as to serve as reliable markers of intended performance (see Bauman 1977:16, 1993a:20). These readily repeatable compliments thus enable Eldreth to draw attention to the merit of her deeds without, usually, evoking censure.[4] To the extent that effective self-praise might still provoke social sanctions, this is a rather transparent subterfuge, but Eldreth is comfortable with it; and her family and friends seem to be tolerant of her desire thus to (re)circulate positive evaluations of what she has done (Sawin 1992).

Fascinatingly, Ed Eldreth appears to be the exception to the rule, the man who fails to talk as other men talk, as well as the man who fails to do what other men do (or at least should do). Although we cannot know for sure to what extent this reflects his actual practice and to what extent it is the result of Eldreth's prerogative as narrator, Ed is most often notable for his silence and inaction. In important respects Eldreth seems to be editing him out of her life, giving him minimal mention (as noted earlier), and furthermore either refusing to perpetuate what he said or, when she does bring him into a story, portraying him as ineffectual at best. She tells no stories that focus on the criticisms that he probably frequently leveled at her, thus (as Elaine Lawless argues about the lacunae in the life stories she tried to collect from battered women [2001:64]) protecting herself from reliving those moments by refusing to report them. In the story about

Eldreth's "stealing" him from her sister, Ed is more object than agent. We hear that Bessie "got a letter from him," but its content does not merit description. The decision for Ed and Bessie to marry, as noted above, seems to have been made primarily by Florence Killens; she is the only actor who is said to desire the marriage. We cannot even tell if Ed actually proposed to Bessie or if his intention was just assumed. In any case, he is not represented as the originator of the request.

In the "Mean Horse" story Eldreth makes striking rhetorical use of her husband's failure to speak in order to depict his deficiencies without naming them overtly. Ed does initially have a speaking role. He is the bearer of news—"And he said, 'I guess that that horse has killed some of them young'uns'"—and even of warning—"And I started out, and he said, 'You ain't a-going out. That horse'll kill you.'" Far from suggesting honest concern, however, his decision to describe the situation as a *fait accompli* rather than to try to affect the outcome and his feeble attempt to stop his wife from getting involved only paint him as a coward. Once Eldreth ignores his disingenuous attempt to stop her, risks her own neck, and pulls off the miraculous rescue—"This looks unreasonable and I've never known how I done it, but I come over a garden fence that had about eight planks on a fence. I got over that fence with that young'un in under my arm"—her husband does not even commend her. Does he not care even that much about their children, or does he refuse to praise her since to do so would be to admit his own cowardice by comparison? Whatever the explanation, he looks bad. Eldreth's action is so dramatic and her courage so self-evident that the story works without the kind of modestly distanced evaluation that quotation of other people's compliments provides (Sawin 1992). This story is noticeable, however, as one of very few that Eldreth constructs without such an evaluation.

Ed's deficiencies appear egregious and evident, but it is important to note that in many respects his verbal behavior, although different from that of the other men in Eldreth's stories, may actually have been within regional bounds for a husband interacting with his wife. Puckett argues that in the mountain community she studied—and I have observed in Eldreth's everyday interactions—people know their place in networks of interdependence and understand their (highly gendered) rights and responsibilities relative to others. A person within his or her rights need only express a need, and the other person will know to volunteer (2000:68ff). I have often observed Eldreth and her family follow similar patterns in their everyday interactions. Thus in simply stating that the horse had gotten loose and was threatening the children, Ed's speech might have been construed as appropriately indicating a need whose fulfillment Eldreth would understand as a mother's duty, not a father's. Likewise, when requests are appropriate, markers of politeness like "please" are generally unnecessary and even excessive (2000:89). Similarly, perhaps, praise or thanks would not be called for in situations where responsibilities, prominently here a mother's duty to safeguard her children, are clear. The positive evaluations Eldreth receives from people like the doctor or the undertaker, then, simply index the distance in their relationship and indicate that she has done more than would strictly be expected of her. By extensively describing the horse's malevolence and her own extreme efforts, however, Eldreth strongly suggests that this was an extraordinary situation requiring an out-of-the-ordinary response. Ed should have helped or, failing that, should at least have praised her. Still, Eldreth does not voice this criticism overtly, instead leaving it to those who have heard her tell so many stories that conclude with a quoted compliment to deduce both Ed's failures and her invitation to listeners to condemn them. And I believe that even in thus leading listeners toward criticizing her husband's conduct, she probably felt that she was taking more of a risk than may be obvious to feminist readers.

One might similarly see Ed's order to his wife in the biscuit story as an example of regionally appropriate or at least tolerable behavior of a husband to his wife. Puckett notes that although adult men would never dare to tell each other what to do in this direct way, a "'doin for' imperative" is appropriate from an older person to a child or from a man to a woman, and "willing compliance" can index love or at least a relationship running as both parties believe it should (2000:169–175; see also Beaver 1986:93, 152). Indeed, the story indicates that Eldreth has complied without overt complaint for many years. Earlier in the conversation during which she shared this story, Eldreth started to criticize another instance of her husband's ordering her around and making her wait on him. As with other negative remarks that she hazarded (as discussed in chapter 3), however, she almost self-censored and continued only when listeners' silence assured her of permission and sympathy.

> When we were first married, [Ed] was twenty-one years old. We didn't have a bathroom in the house to have running water you know. Young'uns, this is terrible. I shouldn't say this, should I? [No response.] He'd sit in the living room and wait for me to bring him a wash pan of water to wash in and a towel.

In the biscuit story—which she may well have dared to share precisely because of our earlier supportive response—Eldreth still goes to great length to show how unusual the situation was. Two of their sons had been in an automobile accident, even if they claimed they had not been hurt. Her duty to go get them was more pressing than her duty to feed her husband his supper at the usual time. There is even, deeply buried, the radical suggestion that Ed could have gone beyond a man's usual noninvolvement in cooking (see Beaver 1986:100) and taken care of himself at least to the extent of putting an already prepared pan of biscuits into the stove. Eldreth piles up all of these justifications on top of the obvious mean-spiritedness of Ed's demand—"You get back here and reach me a biscuit"—and the evidence that it was a pure exercise of power, since the biscuits were already within easy reach: "My goodness, all he has to do is pick 'em up." For years she had bridled under Ed's authority because he had so little sense of his family's needs, but she had felt constrained not to speak. Now she is proud and daring enough to quote not only her defiant rejection of her husband's unreasonable demand—"'I'm going to tell you something, now.' I said, 'If you want you a biscuit, you pick it up there'"—but also her scathing condemnation of his laziness—"You've sat on your [black bottom] till you've got calluses bigger than my hands"—even though she leaves some of the words implied. Puckett notes that while some women gladly comply with their husband's explicit requests as a way of showing love, others do so under duress, for fear of reprisals and even physical abuse (2000:192). Ed's behavior, here as in the "Mean Horse" story, lies technically within area norms, but Eldreth frames the interaction and shapes his words to make it clear that he is being petulant, petty, and abusive. Thus both her willingness to defy him and her decision to tell a story that justifies her response are acts of significant daring.

What enabled Eldreth finally to find her voice, speak back to her husband, and draw the line between acceptable requesting behavior and gratuitous, cruel abuse? What empowers her, in recent years, even to label marriage an inherently unfair institution and to declare that she did not want to marry again because "I never want another [man] to wait on"? One answer is suggested by the discrepancies between Ed's talk and other men's talk that she represents in her stories. Men can and do treat women with gratitude and respect, but not, in Eldreth's experience, when they have the right to control a woman's labor that marriage confers. Intimacy creates exploitation, not appreciation. Another source of strength and resolve appears to have been a significant change over time in the ways that Eldreth and other women interacted verbally with each other.

Women's Talk: From Competition to Support

Stories from when Eldreth was young almost exclusively depict women failing to communicate or miscommunicating, either willfully or inadvertently. During their teen years Eldreth and her sister Clyde slept in the same bed and worked cooperatively to cut and drag out timber, enjoying the common preference for outdoor work that differentiated them from their sister Maud, who worked in the house. Even in situations where they might have had a choice of companions, they preferred each other's company: "Me and Clyde'd go to church; or go anywhere that we went together, you know." Courting, however, sets up conflict and competition between them. The girls' implied early sympathy and synchrony give way to "communications" between them that are actually designed to mislead or to use each other as mere means to communicate to someone other than the ostensible addressee. In the first part of the "Stealing Ed" story, Clyde employs her sister as a foil, saying, "Now that's my boyfriend; I'm going to get him," ostensibly to her sister, but evidently hoping that the young man in whom she is interested will overhear and respond positively. Eldreth says nothing to either her sister or the young men walking home from church, but she knows perfectly well that this constitutes a form of "playing hard to get" that the boys will find more attractive than Clyde's direct expression of interest: "They'd come right up and take hold of my arm." In ostentatiously "walk[ing] off together" with the boy her sister wanted, Eldreth not only flaunts her own attractiveness and communicative success but also responds to Clyde's statement of a wish precisely by blocking its fulfillment. And she clearly enjoys twitting and frustrating her sister: "Oh, that would just burn her up. I did that so many times." In pursuit of male attention, the sisters short-circuit communication between themselves, speaking, in formal terms, to each other but really to a potential suitor, communicating most effectively by pointedly refusing to speak.

Eldreth likewise tells a whole series of stories about the practical jokes she and Clyde played on each other, jokes I will consider in more detail in the chapter devoted to that topic. Practical joking turns precisely on the management of information so as to produce false impressions (Bauman 1986); but while joking can be artful and humorous to some, the girls' examples, because unelaborated, constitute recriminations thinly disguised. Notably, also, the sisters' jokes are occasioned by events having to do with courtship and their emerging sexuality. The girls neither confide in each other about the welter of new emotions they are feeling nor try to make sense of their experiences by comparing notes. Instead they appear to respond to their confusion and shame by taking out their anxieties and aggressions on each other, on the person to whom they are supposedly closest. The final joke in the series is Eldreth's decision to "steal" Ed from her sister just to see if she can. Although she succeeds, the last laugh is on her, since she is induced to marry a man whom she does not love and who will turn out to be far from an ideal husband. Her further inability to protest her mother's plans may simply reflect her acceptance of an elder person's right to make decisions and to tell a younger person what to do. Later in the discussion about her marriage, Eldreth reminded us, however, that "Momma loved me as good or . . . I'd say better'n ary young'un she had." It thus seems equally possible that in grasping for the security of a role she already knew, the compliant child, Eldreth missed an emerging opportunity to express her own preference that her mother would actually have been willing to consider.

Supportive and forthright conversations among women only gradually appear in Eldreth's life, however. Once married, she and Ed move to the "Three Top" community where her sister Maud is already living, and she begins to make friends with the other young women. As the stories about the baby cases and about her niece's near drowning reveal, these women depend tremendously on each other. They could neither bring their children into the world nor assure their care while they worked to support them without each others' help. And yet the kinds of talk in which Eldreth depicts them engaging continue in many instances to be oblique and mystifying. In the birth stories the reportable conversations occur between Eldreth, Dr. Robison, and, sometimes, another helper whose words, like Ed's, mark her as an inept foil for Eldreth's competence: "Lord, I can't do that." The mothers neither speak nor are spoken to. Obviously this would make a different kind of story and deflect attention from the positive evaluations of Eldreth's contributions. I discovered, however, that whenever I tried to get Eldreth to talk about midwifery, her only response was to tell these baby case stories. At first I simply thought that she was uncomfortable talking to me about birthing because I was not then married. I gradually realized, however, that actually working with the other woman's body, coordinating with and assisting in the birth process, was not something that the women themselves had talked about at the time. Neither mothers nor helpers received explicit verbal training. A woman learned by giving birth herself and then, suitably initiated, by going along as a birth helper and learning that role from experience as well: "I just got to going, you know, where that there's places where that they | the babies'd be borned and I'd, I'd wind up a-helping, and be right there." When I tried to check my theory with Eldreth, she not only confirmed my perception but seemed by her abrupt answers to want to cut off even that discussion of the topic:

PS: Did people talk and advise? That's what I was thinking about because all the friends with X's wife [whose baby shower Eldreth and I had recently attended] and all my friends who are married and have had kids. There's so much more talk these days to explain to women what they can do and how they can help. Did people talk among themselves and—

BE: No.

PS: like tell a new mother—

BE: No, they didn't.

PS: —what to expect? Huh?

BE: Everything seemed like it was kept so quiet.

Giving birth and helping with a birth were arguably treated like the many kinds of labor (men's and women's) that one appropriately learns by watching, doing, and seeking specific correction rather than through explicit verbalized instruction (Puckett 2000:152–153; Briggs 1986). Yet Eldreth's comment that "it was kept so quiet" also hints at a silence enforced by shame that surrounded women's bodies and their functioning.

Maud's minimal and not even directly quoted line in the drowning story— "She wanted to know if I was all right"—similarly suggests these young women's inability to articulate their feelings and concerns to each other. Was Maud furious with her sister for not protecting her daughter better or grateful that she put herself at risk to save the child, or was she struggling with a mixture of anger and gratitude? We will never know, and it is not clear if Eldreth knew or felt she ought to know. Certainly it is not germane to the story she has to tell. Much of the foundational feminist work in the ethnography of speaking depicted women collaborating to generate meaning and thus to support each other in making sense of their lives and the social forces that constrained them (for example, Kalčik 1975; Johnstone 1990; Hall and Langellier 1988; Tannen 1990). It has been easy to forget that these characterizations were generated mostly on the basis of the speech behavior of white middle-class women involved in or born since the advent of the women's movement (Sawin 1999; Coates 1999). The kind of introspective sharing of personal experience that seemed natural to young women of my generation was not in fact something that Eldreth and her sisters and friends engaged in until much later in their lives, as we discovered when Holland and Conway questioned her about her dissatisfaction with her marriage:

DH: Was your sister's life like that, too, I mean the | did she feel like you did, do you think?
BE: [Pause.] I think so.
DH: Could you talk about it to her? Or did you have anybody to talk to?
BE: Yeah, uh, yeah, we discussed some things between us, but [pause], just for the past few year [pause] that I ever discussed this with anybody, and it . . .
CC: //Oh.//
DH: //Oh, wow.//
BE: //And it seems like// that I've carried this //all these years.//
DH: //Burdens.//
CC: //Whew.// So you all didn't even talk about it when you were young, living there, going through it?
BE: Unh uh, no.

In the story of her niece's near drowning Eldreth does, however, start to experience support from other women and to have modeled for her a woman's forceful insistence upon the validity of her own interpretation. Having taken what everyone believes is a serious risk by jumping into the cold river just a few days after her own baby's birth, Eldreth finds herself not thanked or praised for her altruism but chastised for not taking care of herself. Her neighbor Johnny Rash becomes the mouthpiece for the general gossip, coming over to tell her callously, "I wouldn't be in your shoes for your socks." Her sister-in-law, Liz Eldreth, however, steps in to defend her, insisting that God transcends human logic and will abrogate physical laws to reward those who sacrifice themselves for others: "And she walked that floor and cried just as hard as she could cry. And a-telling me, a-saying that the Lord won't let it hurt you. 'The Lord won't let it hurt you.'" Given some support, Eldreth not only defends her actions—"'Well, I'll just put it like this,' I said, 'just to have went in the water like that for nothing, I wouldn't risk it either, but,' I said, 'I'd rather have died than for that young'un to a-drownded and it so close to my back door'"—but elaborates a broader personal ethic—"I said, 'If it had been a little colored young'un I would have got it out just the same way; I wouldn't have let it a-drownded.'" In Puckett's terms, Eldreth certainly had "rights" to do what she did because of her "place," both her responsibility over particular territory and her role as a woman to take care of children (2000:56ff); but it is nevertheless notable that she defends herself out loud and represents herself, perhaps for the first time in her life, contradicting a man's assessment. Readers may flinch at the way Eldreth unselfconsciously alludes to the assumption that a "colored" child's life is worth less than a white child's. And she does not deny the validity of the distinction per se, although it is hard to imagine her going through that kind of explicit metacritical process then or now. Nevertheless, she employs the prejudice precisely to insist that she will not conform to it and to further index her Christian duty to serve "the least of these," in her society's definition. Ultimately, Eldreth is able to build her narrative self-justification on her sister-in-law's supportive analysis: "And, you know, it didn't, it | I didn't even take a cold. And | but I did save the little young'un."

In the drowning story Eldreth faces down unflattering community opinion, but it is not until decades later that she feels able to challenge her husband's exploitation and mistreatment of her. Two further significant changes in her interactions with women transpire in the intervening years, as exemplified by the story of her singing at Joe Cox's funeral and the story of looking for the land upon which to build her own house. The funeral story clearly depicts a turning point in Eldreth's life. The women's speech behavior in it is remarkable in two respects. Eldreth is characteristically and appropriately modest, remaining silent and not volunteering that she indeed knows the song they are looking for, one of many Carter Family numbers she had committed to memory when they were popular twenty or more years earlier. The women in her church know perfectly well how to interpret her reticence, however, and how to break through it:

> Arnette said, "Now, Bess, I want to know. Do you know the song, 'Will you miss me when I'm gone?'" And I just shrugged my shoulders and looked at her. And she said, "You do, don't you?" And I said, "Yeah, I know the song."

Furthermore, they understand the system of expectations and responsibilities that puts Eldreth's duty to take care of her husband above all other claims. They dare, however, not only to negotiate in pragmatic terms, finding another driver to bring Ed Eldreth home from the hospital (as someone had to do each month when the Medicare payments would no longer cover hospital nursing for his emphysema), but even to challenge the primacy of Eldreth's duty to her husband. "'Now, Mrs. Eldreth,' she said, 'this is a request and,' she says, 'it can never be filled [unless you sing the song].'" The other women, then, construct Eldreth not simply as a wife but as a specialist, a person who possesses unique skill and knowledge and thus has a responsibility to share these more widely in the community. The semantic dimension of their discourse was doubtless significant in Eldreth's subsequent self-conception. Equally important, however, is the (for this speech community) highly unusual pragmatic speech act of not only working within dominant community discourses but actually moving out to a discursive met-alevel where the claims of alternative discourses could be juxtaposed.

The story about searching for land to buy reveals a further means whereby the habits of reticence and self-silencing that Eldreth has internalized can be overcome. Her daughter Virginia has learned to read her mother's silences:

> Well, I didn't talk in favor for that 'cause I never did even say a word when we went up there. I didn't like it. So, Virginia said, "Don, we might as well turn around and go back." Says, "Now Mom's not a-gonna | won't buy this, because she's not interested in this." Says, "She's not talking."

By acting as interpreter, Virginia makes her mother's wishes part of the effective discussion and thus makes them available to men like her husband who are perfectly willing to be of service in fulfilling those wishes, if they know what they are. How many thousands of times, I wonder, had Eldreth expressed either her desire to do something or her disapproval of something her husband did or said through a silence that he conveniently ignored? Silence is an effective weapon only if one's opponent is willing to acknowledge its meaning (Herzfeld 1991). Either pushing another woman to speak what is in her mind or correctly interpreting a crucial silence for her becomes a means whereby women, through communicative cooperation, begin to challenge men's control.

Beaver argues that an older woman's increasing power is bolstered by the support and appreciation that she receives from grown sons (1986:104). The willingness of Eldreth's sons to collaborate to build her house, though not the subject of one of her stories, demonstrates how sensitively and generously they responded to her needs. Not surprisingly, perhaps, considering her sons' primary model of male speech behavior, the one story Eldreth tells that describes a specific incident of support is another report of silence and indirection. Once he got a job, her eldest son, Fred, would leave money on the floor of his room, pile his dirty work clothes on top of it, and then come out and tell his mother to go pick up his clothes to wash them. I have not been able to get Eldreth to explain if this subterfuge was necessary to prevent Ed from taking the money, or if Fred felt it would shame his father to have it known that he was contributing to the family's upkeep, or if he was embarrassed to take the donor role relative to his mother. The invisible infusion of funds helped Eldreth take care of the other children, and she appreciated her son's kindness tremendously, but it did not give her an opening for taking a different role with her husband.

The biscuit story further suggests that grandchildren can play discursive roles that children cannot. An adult who has intimate access but is not a regular part of the household can disrupt established dyadic communication patterns between spouses. Eldreth must have put up with her husband's niggling meanness for forty years, never challenging him in front of her children, feeling that even, or especially, for them she must maintain a veneer of propriety. Even though her children must have recognized that their father was being unreasonable and hateful, as long as she said nothing, none of them apparently took the initiative to support her or tell him he was in the wrong. She finally reaches her limit in front of Danny, her eldest daughter's eldest son. He in one sense continues to play the standard male role of the evaluator: "I had never, as long as I had even stayed with you'uns, I had never heard you raise your voice to Papaw till this time." The effect of Danny's statement is not, however, to judge Eldreth but rather to confirm that what Ed said was wrong (he refers to it as "the way Papaw done you"), to highlight the significance of what she has done, and to prevent her from later disavowing the gigantic step he just witnessed. His young wife, however, responds to Eldreth's outburst in an ambiguous way. Her insistence on giving her grandmother-in-law a needed break might also be interpreted as a confirmation that Eldreth had been mistreated and overworked in the past. Her words, however, although sympathetic, constitute an embarrassed attempt to reinstate the conspiracy of silence, given that she characterizes the outburst as an aberration caused simply by exhaustion rather than a long overdue speaking of truth to power. Where Danny recognizes the significance of what has transpired, Carolyn tries precisely to explain it away in a fashion reminiscent of Eldreth's behavior at the same age. Thus, changing responses from men as well as women of younger generations assist Eldreth's ongoing self-reconstruction, even though the women may not themselves feel the right to new roles.

Fascinatingly, other older women may serve as catalysts precisely because they themselves are going through similar transformations. The most trenchant and direct critiques of the gender system to which they all conformed can thus come from surprising sources. Not long before her death, although years after Ed's, Eldreth's mother broached the subject of Eldreth's unsatisfactory marriage with her:

> I'll tell you what she told me . . . a few year ago; it's not been all that long, but anyway she told me, she said, "I want to tell you something." [Sigh.] She said, "I wish that you had a told me and I had a known some of the things that you went through with him."

The immediate reaction that Eldreth reports depicts her as still the more conservative speaker: "I said, 'Momma, after I'd done married him,' I said, 'it's too late then.' That's what I told her. She said, 'Honey, you could a come back home.' But it wouldn't a been the same. Would it?" At the time of the reported conversation, evidently, Eldreth could neither give up the opportunity to portray herself as moral by categorically condemning divorce nor, perhaps, let her mother off the hook by joining her in a futile game of "what if?" Still, in telling the story Eldreth brings the account of her life full circle, revealing that even the person who made her marry Ed realized, in the fullness of time, that it had been a mistake. And she also, in the particular context of a conversation with feminists, opens herself to an overt discussion of the rules and why they had been so hard to challenge.

CC: But it was so hard back then to do that . . . kind of thing.
DH: Yeah, //to leave.//
BE: //Well,// you hardly ever in the world heard of a separation then.
DH: Um hmm.
BE: You got a bad name if you | if people separated. Didn't they?

Eldreth has not been entirely changed as a speaker, nor should we expect her or anyone to abandon the speech habits of a lifetime. A few years after hearing these stories, however, I was able to witness in real time (rather than to hear a much later story about) a process in which Eldreth struggled both to act as an authoritative evaluator for herself and to dare to reveal that that is what she had done. She started spending time with a widower who had once been the pastor of her church and who was now apparently quite wealthy. In phone conversations (I was living in Indiana at the time) she said she liked and respected this man; and she described having fun with him, recounting one story in which they went to pick beans together and got to laughing so hard that a neighbor stopped to tease them about it. It seemed that her definition of marriage as servitude rather than companionship, encapsulated in the oft-repeated phrase, "I never want another one to wait on," was about to be challenged. I was initially delighted at the prospect that, after all those years of marriage to a man who did not appreciate her, she might have found someone to treat her well. I was thus initially saddened when Eldreth reported that this man had repeatedly asked her to marry him but that she had turned him down. I was especially distressed because the only reason she gave at the time was that one of her daughters had been against it on grounds that it would keep their family from being reunited in heaven. Had Eldreth allowed someone else to be the authoritative interpreter of the situation, giving up a chance at happiness in order not to contest a conservative discourse that another woman applied to her life?

It was not until a few years later, when I again visited her in person, that Eldreth offered further explanation. Her suitor, she now revealed, had offered to marry her and share his beautiful home and sizeable bank account, but on the condition that Eldreth give up the singing performances and related opportunities to travel that she so enjoyed and instead stay home to take care of him. It thus became apparent that her own interpretation had been accurate, that even an apparently ideal man of her generation would understand marriage as implying her responsibility to serve him, and that she had in fact acted according to her own maxim. I suspect that her daughter's interpretation became a convenient subterfuge, a way of explaining her decision without overtly challenging beliefs her listeners might hold. I also wonder, however, if the different explanation was occasioned by changes in what she knew of me, specifically the fact that I was getting divorced at the time of the later conversations and thus could be assumed to share some of her bitter experience and evaluation. And when, another decade later, the family gathered to celebrate Eldreth's ninetieth birthday, her eldest daughter, Lorene, easily drew her mother into sharing critical reminiscences of Ed with a granddaughter and me while we prepared food for the party. As in the narrated instances, who Eldreth effectively *is* changes with the interactional opportunities offered by talking with different people.

SITUATING LISTENERS, GENERATING SUBJECTIVITY

In the kinds of stories considered in this chapter, Eldreth relies upon reported speech for a variety of purposes—to depict the characters of those involved, economically convey the action, mobilize praise for her deeds—that direct attention to something other than the speech itself. As both Dell Hymes and Greg Urban have argued, however, the point of a story full of reported speech may be to exemplify proper and improper speech roles or proper and improper relationships of speech to action, as much as to describe and comment upon the more obvious extradiscursive elements of the story (Hymes 1981; Urban 1984). This, indeed, is one of the respects in which the act of telling a story about oneself functions as a means of identity creation. Eldreth situates her listeners—be they friends, grandchildren, interviewers, or a festival audience—as witnesses not only to her (depicted) actions but also to former interlocutors' verbal responses to what she has done and sometimes to her responses to those responses. Thus, I would argue, she not only invites present listeners to make their own evaluation of a deed she describes but also illustrates for them the kinds of evaluations that she approves or rejects. In effect, Eldreth models for audiences how they should (and should not) respond to her, assigning preferred speech roles not (only) by taking the reciprocal role (Davies and Harré 1990), but by modeling a recommended future positioning. Listeners are encouraged to adopt an attitude not (or not only) on the merits of an argument or philosophical belief but rather on whether or not they want to be associated with the kind of person who takes on a particular speech role or says particular kinds of things in the story.

The stories that conclude with a reported compliment thus not only recapitulate a positive evaluation in a safe way. They also train those who hear the story that it is appropriate and praiseworthy to offer an explicit positive comment on an action that they admire or from which they benefit or, better still, to compliment the person performing the action. Eldreth often chooses as her authoritative commentators people she herself reveres, like Dr. Robison. Their stature contributes to the efficacy of their remarks, while at the same time listeners are given to understand that people who make a practice of offering this kind of positive evaluation are themselves good and admirable. Indeed, Eldreth also models other respectful and appreciative speech behaviors. In a group of stories about women for whom she cleaned house, she not only reports their appreciative evaluations of her work but approvingly describes one who always addressed her as "Mrs. Eldreth," while she called her employer by her first name.[5] Conversely, of course, those who treat her meanly or fail to praise her when they should are condemned by their own unworthy speech. Her husband in particular is cumulatively depicted as completely unreasonable, controlling, selfish, and greedy. "Your biscuits are a-setting there right where you left 'em" portrays Ed Eldreth as lazy (unwilling even to put a pan of prepared biscuits into the oven to bake) and petulantly selfish (more concerned with his supper than with the well-being of sons who had been in a car crash). "You get back here and reach me a biscuit" shows his desire to control his wife beyond, and indeed counter to, any reasonable need he might have. "Take that money, grab it, and I'll stick it right here in my overall pocket" reveals his lack of appreciation of his wife's labors and his utter disregard for her needs (money in his pocket, to fritter away as he wishes, is more important than the house Eldreth has toiled and saved for; the profits of her labor should belong to him). No one hearing such stories could possibly want to emulate Ed by responding ungratefully or without admiration to Eldreth's accounts of her trials and labors.

Furthermore, Eldreth also shows present audiences how crucial the presence of earlier listeners was in allowing her to enact her self-transformation and thus make it a social reality. In the biscuit story, Eldreth can offer no explanation for why she spoke up that time after having bitten her tongue at similar slights for so many years: "And I don't know what hit me; I just turned loose." Evidently, her entire family of children had participated in the conspiracy of silence over Ed's abusive treatment of his wife. However, the insertion of new actors into the exploitative relationship transforms the impacted dynamic. Through the witnessed outburst (and others like it), Eldreth's mistreatment by her husband finally became a potential topic of discussion for the whole family rather than an undeniable presence so uncomfortable that no one would mention it. Toward the end of Ed Eldreth's life and especially after his death, the children at last started to question their mother about their father's behavior toward her. As Eldreth depicts it, interestingly, they are now insistent enough to refuse to accept the reluctance to volunteer information that she herself has cultivated all these years. By asking, they give her permission to speak and to continue her self-transformation.

BE: (to PS) Well, now, you've met Fred, haven't you?

PS: Uh huh.

BE: Lives over at Creston. He came over there [to Eldreth's house] one day. He got to questioning me about some things. And I looked | I just looked at him. And Carl [the son who lives next door to Eldreth and spends time with her daily] was a-setting there, and Carl looked at me so quick. I never said nothing. And he said, "Mom, I want to ask you something," he said, "Is there something that you're not telling me?" I said, "Well [sigh], you asked me, didn't you?" "Yeah, I'd like to know." So I told him . . . a few things, that'd been twenty | oh my goodness, that'd been . . . , oh, it's been fifty year ago. I'd kept that | and never told | said anything."

New extracontextual listeners—especially ethnographers or journalists who produce records of what she has told them—also provide new opportunities and produce new kinds of resources that Eldreth can use to break old silences, vindicate herself, and set the record straight. Her husband was not the only person against whom she harbored a grudge. The gender double standard was not the only means by which she was exploited. She has gradually allowed it to emerge that she often felt taken advantage of economically by her relatively well-to-do neighbors as well. After telling me the same set of "baby case" stories for years, during a visit to one of Cecelia Conway's classes at Appalachian State University in 1994 Eldreth amazed me by adding another episode. This one described how Dr. Robison, arriving, as he often did, after she had successfully delivered the baby, praised her efforts but nevertheless collected his fee and did not offer to share it with her! In a story about a brother-in-law for whom she worked during the Depression, a newspaper article enables her to get the man to admit his former lack of generosity.

A Dollar Check

But I went to see my brother-in-law a while back, he was in the hospital.

And he had got one of the *Democrats*, you know [an article about her in the local newspaper, the *Watauga Democrat*]. And he said, "Bess," he said, "they was a lot of truth in that paper."

I said, "Yeah, there was." I said, "It's all the truth."

He said, "But you never had to work that hard, did you?"

I said, "Now you wait a minute." (Him laying right there in the hospital and right in front of his two girls. I said, "I've clumb that mountain for you a many of a day," I said, "Work ten hours and when I'd come out you'd give me a little old dollar check."

And his young'uns looked so funny at him.

He said, "That's right, ain't it?" He said, "That's the truth, ain't it?"

I said, "Sure it's the truth."

See, he didn't want to own up, you know, that I had done work like that. And I just pointed out to him, I said, "I've worked for you a many of a day," I said, "back on the tops of that mountain," I said, "in that rattlesnake country, for five cents a hour," and I said, "When I come off | I'd put in ten hours and I'd come off and you'd give me | write me a check, for a dollar."

As in the biscuit story, the presence of the man's daughters as new witnesses appears to be essential. It is shocking for her to challenge him "right in front of his two girls," yet they provide pressure because she knows he does not want them to see him persist in a lie. But the newspaper article, which includes the report of her labors over the years that she had shared with the journalist, is the crucial catalyst. It seems unlikely that she would have brought up the topic spontaneously or asked her brother-in-law to acknowledge all these years later that he had paid her minimally for her tremendously hard work. The newspaper, however, circulates her self-account and brings it into the public domain, including into the awareness of those who already know her. She still has to defend her claim, but the publication of the account broaches a subject that would otherwise never have come up. I also now realize that, in telling me this story, Eldreth must in part have been modeling the specific role that I, as someone who intended to write about her, could play. Indeed, when I brought her a copy of my dissertation she took the two big black volumes down to the offices of the *Watauga Democrat* and arranged an interview. In it, as the resulting article reports, she told the interviewer, "This girl wrote a book about me. In fact, she wrote two books." I now realize that I should hardly have been surprised by what she wanted to do with the dissertation. Like every conversation in which Eldreth is involved, my interactions with her and any records I produce of them become potential resources that she can use in her ongoing self-shaping. May this account likewise serve her well.

CONCLUSIONS

Granting the premise of this analysis—that reported speech in personal narrative represents characteristic types of speech interaction—Eldreth's stories are still inevitably imperfect and haphazard documents. Many crucial interactions surely never made it into stories; many that did, I never heard. Eldreth clearly deploys reported speech selectively to paint favorable portraits of herself by evaluation or contrast. Furthermore, these stories do not answer all the questions we would like to ask about her discursive self-construction. As the conversations surrounding some of these tellings suggest, Eldreth will, when gently encouraged, go a little farther in analyzing her own motivations or revealing discrepancies between her beliefs at a given moment and what she felt safe saying at the time. For the most part, however, these stories are the well-formed product of Eldreth's reflections, the self-accounts she shares when asked, and we must make of them what we can. What they reveal, if only in possibly distorted glimpses, are the concrete interactions, the ways of speaking or not speaking, through which Eldreth's formative relationships were realized. Eldreth's changing self is a pragmatic dialogic accomplishment. In the abstract, the self is thus revealed as a product not merely of the semantics of discourse or of disembodied social rules but of specific speech acts—moments of acquiescing or challenging, confiding and comparing—and of the changing opportunities for them offered by one's likewise changing partners in talk and life. In the specific, these stories show how women within Eldreth's speech community have been heavily complicit in subjugating other women to men's control and how challenges to the worst abusers and to the gender system emerged as a result of women's gradual and partial, yet collective and mutual, transformation. The stories also, crucially, model for present audiences the ways in which they should and should not respond to Eldreth's labors or her reports thereof. Those who praise her will themselves be praised as generous and wise; those who take advantage and fail to appreciate her will be revealed as greedy and cruel. Thus Eldreth effectively creates herself in the minds of those who have been schooled in how to respond to her, not only as hardworking, moral, generous, and resourceful, but also as deserving of appreciation. And every story, every interaction becomes potential grist for further stories, further interactions, in Eldreth's ongoing self-shaping.

5

"He never did say anything about my dreams that would worry me after that"
Negotiating Gender and Power in Ghost Stories

We have seen that the ghost imports a charged strangeness into the place or sphere it is haunting, thus unsettling the propriety and property lines that delimit a zone of activity or knowledge. I have also emphasized that the ghost is primarily a symptom of what is missing. It gives notice not only to itself but also to what it represents. What it represents is usually a loss, sometimes of life, sometimes of a path not taken. From a certain vantage point the ghost also simultaneously represents a future possibility, a hope. Finally, I have suggested that the ghost is alive, so to speak. We are in relation to it and it has designs on us such that we must reckon with it graciously, attempting to offer it a hospitable memory out of a concern for justice.

—Avery Gordon

Bessie Eldreth tells ghost stories. More specifically, she tells stories about being haunted, of being visited—without warning or permission—by spiritual presences whose message or import she must struggle to interpret. In contrast to her ordinary stories of personal experience, which she only occasionally has an opportunity to insert into conversation (except with an endlessly receptive listener like me), these are stories people ask to hear. They are self-evidently interesting, eminently tellable. Her grandchildren begged her to terrify and delight them with these tales. She has been invited to perform them for public storytelling events along with other people who are happy to be identified as "storytellers." While these tales may thus appear innocuous and merely entertaining, they recount experiences that Eldreth found deeply troubling at the time. Not only is the moment of contact unsettling and frightening in itself. The ghost's manifestation also propels Eldreth into difficult conversations and negotiations with the people around her. Unspeakable stories come back to life as those whom she presses for an explanation tell about past events that would otherwise have been left hidden. Men and women jockey for control, parlaying their own attempts at courage and their partner's fear into influence in their present relationship. These stories and those who tell and hear them are haunted by the injustice and inequality that constitute this society's dirty secrets, by the gender double standard, by men's sanctioned ability to control women, and by the wealthy's capacity to exploit the poor. The relationships between messenger and message and between message and interpretation exhibit an ambiguity and slippage equally appropriate to the uncanny and to the conception of subjectivity as negotiated in struggle with hegemonic forces. They tell us about the parts of Eldreth's life that she could not speak about directly, that flicker around the edge of her consciousness, and that she is as likely to repress as to acknowledge. Precisely because these ghost stories are eminently "presentable," however, they have served (in a way her more direct narratives of personal experience could not) as means of articulating coded protests against mistreatment to which she was subject because of her gender and her economic situation.

I too am troubled by these ghosts and struggle with how to make sense of Eldreth's stories about them. Appropriately, I have difficulty finding a comfortable space within which to elaborate my analysis. I obviously eschew the classic anthropological stance that strictly distinguished the scholar's "modern" rationality from the subject's "primitive" belief in magic. Neither, however, can I wholeheartedly embrace the current folkloristic remedy, which insists that the only respectful approach is to accept ghost stories at face value and argues that tracing a connection between uncanny events and social forces inevitably and inexcusably "explains away" our subjects' experience of the supernatural (Hinson 2000:327ff; Hufford 1982, 1983). Avery Gordon suggests a way to escape from this dichotomous way of thinking, arguing that "to write stories concerning exclusions and invisibilities is to write ghost stories. To write ghost stories implies that ghosts are real, that is to say, that they produce material effects" (1997:17). Everyone, Gordon reminds us, every society and individual, is haunted by injustices and violations, by all that structures of power seek to deny or keep at the margins to whisper about and scare people with. Whether we understand them in terms that are psychological (return of the repressed) or sociological (subjugated knowledges) or literal (supernatural agents), the ghosts lurk to remind us of what we forget at our peril. It helps to remember that Eldreth herself anticipates that her audience may have difficulty believing these accounts. "Now young'uns," she frequently remarks, "this may sound like ghost stories, but they's absolutely true."[1] To argue, as I do, that both the stories and the experiences they relate are in some senses "about" gender inequalities and the negotiation of power does not, in my mind, preclude or contradict Eldreth's conviction that she has experienced contact with spiritual forces. I do not understand these stories in quite the same way that Eldreth does, but I feel impelled to grapple with them and with the difference between our understandings. I must, in Gordon's terms, "reckon with [them] graciously, . . . *out of a concern for justice*" (1997:64), out of a concern to make apparent the coded protests against injustice deeply buried in Eldreth's narration.

In Eldreth's practice, the convenient and apparently self-evident label "ghost stories" has an ironic effect in making the private and hidden public and publicizable. Because listeners recognize the genre as entertaining, exotic, and inherently significant quite apart from the identity of the narrator, Eldreth has been invited to tell these stories both by her grandchildren and by audiences interested in "storytelling" or in "Appalachian culture." Neither audience would similarly request the recitation of her personal narratives of ordinary experience, in part because such stories are not obviously performable, in part because the everyday events of an individual woman's life would not as readily be seen as interesting or significant. I vividly recall one of Eldreth's grandsons coming through the kitchen when we were taping an interview, pausing long enough to gather that she was telling one of her nonsupernatural stories, and remarking dismissively, "Mamaw, we've heard it." And I admit that I sometimes tire of hearing the same stories over again. In listening to tapes of her song performances, however, I was surprised to discover that in public she shares only a select few everyday stories, usually at the prompting of the presenters. The out-of-the-ordinary-ness of these ghost stories (which for nonlocals marks the distinctness of Appalachian culture as nonmodern) thus makes them the most welcome, public means for Eldreth to talk about her life experience. Given how prominent gender conflict is in these accounts, the ghost stories thus serve as a surprising vehicle through which Eldreth has been able to explore in covert form an issue that both she and many listeners would find too controversial if it were the evident topic.

Eldreth tells three distinguishable kinds of stories about encounters with the supernatural. We might call them moral exempla, ghost stories proper, and premonitions. Eldreth does not herself differentiate the first and second groups, speaking of both as "ghost stories." It is notable, however, that the stories she heard from her parents or grandparents involve unambiguous reward or punishment for unambiguously good or bad deeds. The stories about hauntings that Eldreth herself experienced or that she helped her mother, sister, or aunt make sense of, in contrast, involve confusion and negotiation over what happened, how to interpret it, who deserves blame or praise, and how to react. The "warnings" Eldreth has received are likewise ambiguous in that the meaning of the premonition and the very validity of her interpreting an experience as a premonition only gradually emerge. Because the ghost is a sign, stories of the supernatural necessarily have a double temporal grounding. The unexpected appearance in the present refers to something other than itself, an event in the past or the future. The accounts of the two events, the story of the sign and the story of the signified, can be told in either order. The relationship between the temporal ordering of sign and signified and the ordering of the episodes in the story is likewise distinct and characteristic for each of the three types.

Because Eldreth has frequently been invited to tell her ghost stories, I have been able to draw texts from two earlier sources in addition to my own interviews. On March 19, 1980, Eldreth told ghost stories for one of "Four Evenings of Blue Ridge Tale Telling," organized and videotaped by Professor Thomas McGowan at Appalachian State University. McGowan generously offered me a copy of the tape. On April 28, 1981, Katie Spitzer and Judy Cornett audiotaped an interview with Eldreth in which they requested that she tell ghost stories. Spitzer was a student at ASU in a folklore course taught by Professor William Lightfoot and wrote her class paper on two of the ghost stories. She apparently asked Cornett, who was conducting oral histories in the area and had interviewed Eldreth previously, to arrange the introduction. Spitzer filed the tape, with permission for others to use it, in the Appalachian Collection at ASU. I am grateful to the scholars who provided me these resources. Eldreth, I consequently know, produces her ghost stories in similar but not identical ways in different tellings. The availability of multiple versions allows me to choose the best-crafted versions and to comment upon occasional significant variations.[2]

EXEMPLA

Eldreth, as noted above, applies the single label "ghost story" to accounts of her own experiences with the supernatural, relatives' experiences in which she was peripherally involved, and others' experiences that they told her about after the fact, as well as to what we might call "traditional" ghost stories, that is, ones in which the characters are not identified as local or known. It consequently took me a while to notice that there are marked differences in structure and mood between tales that were probably presented to her as long past events and tales of her own experiences or those she was told as recent personal experiences whose meaning was still debatable.

This first group, then, consists of tales that Eldreth in effect retells, having heard them as stories (rather than having experienced the event and constructed the story), probably when she was a child. These stories also tend to revolve around relationships with neighbors rather than the more fraught family and romantic relationships that dominate the later, more personal ghost stories. They present the haunting as a distant *fait accompli*, and the ghosts in them tend to manifest themselves in relatively conventional forms. These stories are distinctive in the clarity of the moral they convey and the simplicity and directness of their narrative structure. The tales begin with the event that will prompt the haunt-ing and then proceed to the supernatural manifestation, so there is relatively lit-tle suspense. The fact that the event occurred and was resolved some time ago means there is little need or even room for negotiation over what the event might mean. Still, they model—for us as listeners as for Eldreth when she first heard them—the idea that the hauntings are meaningful, that it is their purpose both to impart hidden knowledge and (as Gordon argues [1997:64]) to correct an injustice. Interestingly, even though these stories seem to have quite distinct messages, Eldreth often suggests their linkage in her mind by telling them one after the other.

Pointing Hand

BE: Here's another little | little ghost story. I call it a ghost story.

     This girl was a-staying with, um, a lady, and *her* daughter had, uh, . . . stole some money this woman had. She just broke in the . . . her safe—whatever she had—and she stole it, her own daughter. And packed it on the innocent girl that was . . . a-working, a-staying with 'em. And they said that girl cried all the time, 'cause that she was 'cused of it, she didn't get it. Well, uh, . . . finally she killed herself, //'cause//

KS: //The innocent one?//

BE: The innocent one, uh huh, she killed herself, 'cause it | they kept | 'cause that woman kept blaming it on her. And 'bout nine o'clock *every night* they was a hand on the wall. That hand would | a finger would point . . . at a certain place.

     And they was so . . . disturbed about it that they wanted to know what was a-going on. Well, they tore the . . . the ce— | so much of the ceiling out, you know. And there's where that | her own girl had hid the money. And she had stole it her-self and hid that money.

     Well, after that girl died, it was her | it was *her* finger, it was her hand, that pointed that money till | till that woman found it. And after they . . . tore the ceil-ing out and got the money out the finger never pointed no more; the hand wasn't there on the wall no more.

     And the girl . . . told her momma that she was the one got it, she couldn't live with it no longer without telling that she was the one who put the money there. And the innocent one . . . *killed* herself over it. And then they found it in the ceil-ing where that | where | the guilty one had put it there. And it her own daugh-ter. Now I just can't . . . see things like that a-going on.

Aunt Polly Reynolds

PS: What's the story about, um, there was a | oh, I know the one, but it was some-body's, um, a woman that it was either you or your momma took care of and then . . . the | finding the money in her—?

BE: Polly Reynolds.

PS: —in her clothes, yeah.

BE: Yeah . . . uh, she | it was | that was a lady used to live up on, uh, | over on Three Top, up, called it, up Ben Bolden. And, uh, one day Grandma decided she'd go see her. And she said when she went in, she said Aunt Polly—we always called her Aunt Polly—said, when she went in said, Aunt Polly said, "Miz Milam, I have been laying here just a-praying that you would come."

And Grandma said, "Well, Aunt Polly, would you like to go home and stay with . . . with me?" And she said, "Yeah, I would, I'd give anything in the world to go stay with you." And she said, "Well, I'll go home and I'll send Lindsey after you with the . . . horse and wagon. And bring you down here."

And she went home and told Grandpa and he went and got her. And took her to their house. And she was real sick 'n she didn't live too long.

And when she passed away Grandma had all of her | she had . . . some awful pretty . . . things, you know, and, uh, said 'bout as pretty a bedspread as she ever laid her eyes on. And Grandma folded them up and | and buried 'em with her, put 'em in the casket with her. And, uh, she had some | her clothes, now, that she had, Grandpa took *them* and dug a hole at the lower side of the garden and put 'em in and buried 'em.

And, uh, the next night they saw a light down there. They said they just kept | said every night for—well, I don't know just how many nights—but they saw a light down there where Grandpa buried the clothes. So he told Grandma | so he told Grandma, said, uh—no, *she* said, "Lindsey, go down there and | and dig them clothes up." Said, uh, "I c— | every night since you buried them clothes there they've been a light down there."

And he went and dug 'em up. And they went through 'em, through the clothes. And, uh, in the hem of her . . . petticoat, why, they found three hundred dollars where she had it sewed in her | in the hem, you know, of her slip. And, uh, they got that out and, uh, buried the clothes back. And said they | from that day till | till this they's never no light seen there any more.

PS: Wow.

BE: After they got the . . . the money out.

The old stories that Eldreth has incorporated into her own repertoire are probably not the only ones she heard as a child. But it is not hard to see why these particular tales are ones that would appeal to Eldreth and that she would want to perpetuate. "Aunt Polly Reynolds" depicts her beloved maternal grandparents as generous, selfless, and unconcerned with material things and shows them being richly rewarded for their kindness to a neighbor in need. This story is almost a parable in depicting the unexpected rewards that will be given to those who, in proper Christian fashion, show kindness to the poor and weak in their community. In another version Eldreth even reports that her grandfather slaughtered a yearling cow (an unconscious approximation of the "fatted calf"?)

so Aunt Polly could have a last meal of beef that she craved. The "Pointing Hand" story is equally clear in condemning theft and deception but also has an edge of class criticism. I imagine that Eldreth, who supported her family cleaning houses and hoeing fields for her neighbors, must have come to identify with the hired girl who is victimized but also triumphantly vindicated. The poor working person has no social standing, no ground upon which to combat the unfair accusation, and is driven to despair and suicide. As a ghost, however, she returns with power not only to prove her innocence but also to impel the true thief to confess and presumably save her own soul. Ultimately, she is revealed as more moral than her rich employer. In both instances the ghost rights a wrong, in the one case simply insuring that generous people are suitably rewarded, in the other actually vindicating the falsely accused and punishing the exploiter.

From an early age, then, Eldreth was given to understand that supernatural forces could come into ordinary lives, that the dead could return to complete unfinished business, that as ghosts they might wield more power than they had when alive, and that ghosts might seek to right injustice. Although another story describes a man frightened to death by a supernatural encounter without explaining what he did to deserve that fate, these childhood stories that Eldreth retells predominantly depict supernatural intervention as a force for social good, a means of making things as they ought to be. The ghosts Eldreth was thus alerted to recognize seem to have been primarily what Gillian Bennett calls "benevolent manifestations," which "are not only caused by events in the mundane world, but are also purposefully *directed* towards them" (1987:52). In these formative stories the meaning of the ghostly sign is obvious to listeners, and the characters in the story, likewise, seem to find the spectral hand and the sourceless light easy to interpret or resolve. In both instances the people who see the sign understand fairly quickly that they need to explore the physical location to which the ghost calls their attention, and they immediately receive an unambiguous explanation. Consequently, although atypically for Eldreth's stories, reported conversation, if included at all, portrays agreement rather than argument or negotiation. "Pointing Hand" involves no speech (a probable indication that this was a traditional tale, not an account of the experience of an acquaintance). "Aunt Polly Reynolds" employs speech either to make a request that is immediately complied with ("And [Grandma] said, 'Well, I'll go home and I'll send Lindsey after you with the horse and wagon. And bring you down here.' And she went home and told Grandpa and he went and got her") or to show that people are already in accord ("Aunt Polly said, 'Miz Milam, I have been laying here just a-praying that you would come.' And Grandma said, 'Well, Aunt Polly, would you like to go home and stay with me?' And she said, 'Yeah, I would.'") The disfluency Eldreth displays when describing the conversation over how to respond to the light ("So he told Grandma, said, uh—no, *she* said, 'Lindsey, go down there and dig them clothes up'") only reveals uncertainty about who told whom, since they had both already arrived at the same conclusion.

Gender seems not to be a major issue in these stories. The acts that are rewarded or punished—generosity and theft—would be regarded in the same light for either men or women. And the one couple portrayed, Eldreth's grandparents, is striking for being so thoroughly congruent in their wishes and plans and so supportive of each other. The problematic issue of class difference is not far beneath the surface, however. Eldreth's relatively well-to-do grandparents are arguably commended for making appropriate use of their surplus, sharing the wealth with a neighbor in need, while the employer's daughter is punished for being greedy herself, for playing upon the stereotype of the poor as desperate enough to steal, and for taking advantage of someone whose social subordination robs her of any recourse.

Ghost Stories

Once she is a little older, Eldreth begins to experience supernatural encounters herself, as, at about the same age, do other women she knows. These ghosts, however, seem quite different from the purposeful and potentially benevolent actors about whom she had been told. These manifestations are disturbing and potentially frightening. There is no unanimity among those affected about the significance of a ghostly appearance or how to respond to it. These supernatural actors resemble the traditional evil ghosts of British and American lore who haunt the sites of their lives or deaths and whom Bennett identifies by their lack of evident purpose: "Evil occurrences are meaningless and intrusive disturbances of the natural order; they have causes but not functions" (1987:52). Although these stories all concern either Eldreth's own experiences or events she heard about from her female relatives very soon after their occurrence, they likewise follow the narrative structure of a conventional suspenseful ghost story, beginning with the haunting and then going back in time to discover its source. Because of the need for those who experienced the haunting to seek explanations, these accounts are almost always constructed with a story within the story in which someone describes what happened previously in that house. These stories are also full of contentious reported conversation, as husbands and wives negotiate over how to respond to the crisis.

Four stories—three of Eldreth's own experience and one from one of her sisters—will serve as examples to establish a pattern regarding the import and impact of supernatural experiences in these young women's lives. The particular stories that I include in full span a transitional period, from the time when Eldreth is old enough to be left to take care of younger siblings through the early years of her marriage. Pay attention as you read them to the signs that indicate the presence of the ghost, the explanations offered for the haunting and who supplies them, Eldreth's own changing feelings, and the conversations as those affected work out how to respond.

Doctor Graham House

PS: You were telling | you told me about that | the one . . . house, the haunted house, but | and then there's another one where the babies were . . . crying.

BE: That was over on Buffalo, when my little brother was small. Yeah, now that was, uh, that was the Doctor Graham house.

Momma had went somewhere and she hadn't got back. And it's | it's real dark. And she'd left the baby with us to take care of. And we's setting on the steps and we heard this baby a-crying. It wasn't | it wasn't the little baby of Momma's; it | we just heard the baby a-crying, you know.

We got up and run in the house. It went just like it's a-coming to the door. We run in there to the bedroom and it was sound asleep, which it wasn't big enough to even a stoo—; it wasn't even sitting alone; it's a real tiny baby. I don't know why we 'ud a thought it was *it*. And we run back outside and sit down on the steps and we heard . . . heard | went like babies crying again and we . . . run in there and got the baby up and set on the porch with it.

And, uh, then some time after that, Doctor Graham, he come over there. And he always liked me. I was just a young'un, but he was . . . he was seventy-five. And I's in there making up the bed. And he said, uh, he asked me if I wasn't afraid in there. And I told him, "No." And he said, uh, "Well, Mary Black . . . Mary Black's twins—she had twins and they both died in there in that room."

And, uh, so I didn't . . . I didn't think anything about it at the time. But, anyway, he | he said that house is haunted. "This house is haunted." Now he was | he was serious about . . . haunt tales. And, uh, so then I asked him after that, got talking about it, and he said that, uh, they'd heard babies cry there ever since Mary Black's twins died in that room in there.

But | but my momma told me after that that—now she lived close when her and Dad was . . . well, you know, years ago, us children wasn't nothing like grown. Well, I don't even remember . . . that, but she said that, uh, that they said that Mary Black killed both of the babies, that she was unmarried? and that she killed both the babies when they were born in that | at that house. And, now, Doctor Graham, he didn't tell me that she killed 'em, but he said, "Mary Black's twins both died in that room in there."

So, now, I don't know. Momma told me that . . . that she killed 'em.

Bob Barr House

Now, this is the Bob Barr house at Creston. I stayed with my Aunt Edna Milam down there. And Uncle Carter carried the mail. And they had a little baby. And, uh, they had, uh, this was a great old big old-timey house.

And I slept off in the bedroom and they slept kinda like the living room, but they slept over in another room. And I kept hearing things in there. And I kept telling Aunt Edna, I did, I told her that I was afraid. And, uh, you'd just hear groans and moans and things just like that somebody's a-turning over . . . noise or something.

So I told Edna I was going to go home, that I couldn't | I was afraid to sleep in there. And she pulled my bed up to the door—left the door open and pulled my bed up to the door—and said, "Now, if you hear anything," says, "you jump out and run to me and call." And, uh, so she got my bed up to the door. Well, I heard that same noise and I jumped out and run to | to her and Uncle Carter?

And, uh, he carried | he—sometimes he carried the mail and he did, well, he carried the mail all the time, but sometimes he'd come in so late, you know, way in the night. And, uh, we could light a | a lantern, now a *lantern*, in that . . . bedroom, where I slept, and you couldn't to save your life make that lantern burn. It'd go out. And you'd carry it on the porch, it'd go out. Get down in the yard, and as long as you was up on that little knoll, going off of there, that lantern would go out. And when we'd get off of that little knoll, light that lantern, we'd carry it for a mile and it wouldn't go out.

Well, me and Edna used to run and | and hide behind the side of the little big gate where Carter'd come in—we didn't want him to know we was scared to death. And, uh, after he'd go up, then, we'd slip along behind the car and while he parked the car we'd run | run in the front door. And, uh, he finally found out how scared we was, 'cause we got to leaving and going to a neighbor's house, to Bill Osborne's over across at Creston, staying there till—sometimes it'd be twelve o'clock before he | before he'd come in.

And, uh, and they said it was | said that Bob Barr died in that room. Now, I don't know what happened, but . . . but he was a real old man; he died in that room.

First Married

Let me check my list what I'm gonna tell you first.

Now this story that I'm going to tell you tonight happened in 1930 in November. Me and my husband had just got married and we moved to a | a two-story house and, uh, no one had ever told us this house was haunted.

So one evening I's sitting there and I's a-piecing on some little quilts. And, uh, while I's a-sitting there I heard just like a clothesline upstairs—I'd never been up the stairs—but it went just like the clothesline was real tight, you know, and someone hitting on this clothesline.

And, uh, when my husband came in I said, uh, "Go upstairs and get me that clothesline." He said, "What clothesline?" I said, "There's one up there, because I heard it." So I insisted and he went on up there and he said, "There's not a clothesline up them stairs nowhere." And I said, "Well, I heard that clothesline."

Well, he went on out to chopping some wood. And, uh, then, uh, I had fastened the door good when he went out and when he went on out, why, the door slammed and it | I had it fastened real good. And the door slammed real hard. And I jumped up and ran in there in the kitchen to . . . close the door—I thought it had blowed open—and it was just like I left it. So I just went back and sit down in the living room, started back at my | piecing my quilt. And this door slammed again. And I ran in there again and it was still like I left it.

Well, I began to sort of wonder then about that door, so—we had a pretty big flat rock in the house—and, uh, I propped the door open wide and went back, and when I sat down here come that door slam again. And I went back and it was just like I propped it open. Well, it did that the second time.

Well, the second time I decided they must be something wrong and, uh, I ran back through and I | I went outside. I just had on a short-sleeved dress, and it was a-snowing; it was cold. And he said, "What are you out here without a | without a coat on for? It's cold out here." I said, "I'm going to stand here till you cut the wood." And [laughs] I didn't tell him that I'd got scared. So he cut the wood and I took me a load in and he took in a load. We went on in the house and set down.

Well, the very next morning my Grandad Milam come up and wanted him to help butcher hogs. Well, he went on down there to butcher hogs and, uh, I kept hearing these sounds and I | I got a little afraid. And, uh, I just kept going on with my work because it was too cold to a walked about three mile in the snow and the wind a-blowing like it was. And when he came in I told him about again | about sorta being afraid, but I didn't want him to know that I had really *got* afraid.

So, uh, that night we went to bed and, uh, about two o'clock in the morning, I have never heard such a pitiful . . . moans and groans and crying and taking on. And, uh, I just laid there and listened to it. And I never said a word to him. But, really, I enjoyed it, hit sounded just like a lovers' quarrel. They would cry—this man and woman both [who were going by?] or whatever. They would cry and then they would, uh, like that they was a . . . in an argument again.

And, uh, the next morning when we got up my husband said, "Let's go down to | let's go up to Pap's and stay tonight." And I said, "It's too cold." We didn't have a vehicle then. I said, "It's too cold and I'm not going anywhere." And, uh, he said, "Well, let's go down to your Grandpa Milam's and stay tonight." And I said, "I told you, I'm not going *nowhere*." He said, "Well, you can stay here if you want to, but I'm not staying." He said [laughs], he said, "Did you hear that here last night?" [Audience laughter.] And, uh, I said, "Yes, I heard it, but I was enjoying it." [Audience laughter.] "And, uh, it | it really thrilled me." So he said, uh, "Was you awake?" I said, "Yes, I laid and listened to it." And, uh, I said, "Did you hear it?" And he said, "Yes, I heard it." And I said, "Well, why didn't you . . . say something?" He said, "I was too scared." [Audience laughter.] He said, "I wasn't gonna say nothing 'cause . . . it'd a scared me to death if you'd | I'd a knew you was asleep."

So, uh, when he | I saw how bad he was scared then I grabbed my coat and we went to Grandpa's. And it was down at Creston—we lived at Longhope then—so we went to Creston. And, uh, when we went in my grandpa said, uh | Ed got talking about us a-getting scared. And, uh, Grandpa laughed real big and he said, uh,

"You got scared out, didn't you?" And, uh, I didn't want to own that I was a little scared, too, at the time, and then after I saw he was scared, I was scared. So the faster I | we went down that road, I was a-looking back because I didn't know what was gonna be behind me, 'cause I *had* really got scared then.

Got on down there and, uh, Grandpa got to teasing us about being scared. Uh, I said, uh, "Grandma," I said, "this sound[ed] just like Maimie—that was my aunt— and, uh, B.J." I said, uh, "It had their voices," and I said, "they cried and they quarrelled and they took on," and I said, "something awful." And, uh, Grandma said, "Well, now, I'm not going to tell you this to scare you out, but," she said, uh, "we had to move from that house on that account." She said, "Maimie would a went stone crazy if she'd a had to a stayed there. She said she couldn't stand it."

And, uh, so after they told us about the | about the house *was* haunted, then, uh, the next morning we come back to the house, but we went on, we didn't | I don't remember whether we even stopped or not. We went on to *his* Daddy's and we got a wagon and a team of horses and we moved out.

And [laughs] so we didn't | we didn't go back to visit that house anymore, but later one of my neighbors and friends, he asked me if, uh, I wasn't afraid in that house. And I said, "No, I wasn't afraid." Well, he said, "this house is haunted." And, uh, he said they was, uh, an old lady that was found out there in the ditch lying at the back of this house. And said nobody knowed whether she had just died there or whether she had been murdered. And said nobody never found out. But, you know, we never did go back to visit the haunted house anymore. We was too scared [laughs].

Bad Girls

Well, I'm going to tell you one about, uh, when my sister moved to Virginia, her and her husband, that was when they first got married. And they moved in a big old house and, uh, no one didn't tell *them* it was haunted.

And, uh, my sister was setting there and she was | she had her nephew with her, and her husband had went down to a | a house to get some chickens to bring up and some of their stuff. And, uh, they heard some noises in the house and went like they's a-going around the house. And, uh, she got afraid, so her and this | her nephew left with her and they went to, uh, down to where, uh, they'd went after chickens. So they slipped along behind her husband and this | and this boy's father to keep them from knowing that they'd got skeered. And they'd caught the chickens; and they [sister and nephew] hid behind the chicken house till they got the chickens and then they walked along . . . out of . . . kindly out of sight till they got back home.

And, uh, it was a big old dark hall and they couldn't keep a light a-burning. And they lit the lantern and it would go out. So they lit the lantern and started off the bank and it went out. Well, then, after they got off the hill, why, the lantern would burn.

And when they got back they hadn't been to bed but a little while till they heard these | these babies a-screaming. And it'd sound just like that they'd start at, uh, one end of the house [gesture with right hand to indicate one side] and they just scream, and cry, and go plumb around the house [circular hand motion with right hand]. It was a real big house.

And, uh, my sister tried to get her husband to leave the house that night and he was afraid, too, but, anyway, they didn't leave that night. And the next day they went to this | to their landlord, the one that owned the home, and asked him if they was anything to be heard there that | told them about the babies crying so much around the house.

And, uh, this lady said, [elbow propped on chair arm; leans head on fingertips] "Well, now, it's not a thing in the world to hurt you all, but if you see it's the imps it could scare you to death."

And, uh, they went back and, uh, that night it started again, the same babies a-screaming. And, uh, she give, uh, her husband right smart of money to leave the house, so they left that night.

And, uh, that woman said | when they went back again she said, "Well, I'll just tell you," she said, uh, "they was some bad women that lived in this house. And, uh, they had some little babies and they drownded them in the well." And, uh, they had been using the water out of the well, and she hadn't told them. And, uh, after they'd | after they left, why, they got someone to clean the well out [raises hand away from body, hand closed], and they found about three or four skeletons of little babies in the well where these bad girls had drownded the babies. And that's what happened.

Now that | they say that was really true that these bad girls had drownded the babies and they had been drinking the water off of the [nods] off of the bones in the bottom of the well. That was in Virginia. [Smiles and gets answering laughter from audience, then drops right hand back into lap and tips head back with a sharp exhalation, whoosh, as if to comment on story—that's an intense one—then a little chuckle as if to comment on her own tendency to tell such stories.]

It cannot be a coincidence that Eldreth's experiences with supernatural agents begin at about the time that she becomes marriageable and end with the end of her marriage. Her first awareness of a ghost (in a slightly earlier episode in a series of stories about Doctor Graham's house, to be considered in the next chapter) occurs when she is trying to find a place in the attic to hide love letters. The last incident of which she has told me (and which we will consider later in this chapter) happens just after her husband's death. Whether one posits that sexual maturity or sharing one's life with a man heightens a woman's sensitivity to the supernatural or, in a more sociological vein, that the ghosts are in some sense attracted by or a manifestation of the tensions in the relationship, it does appear that Eldreth is visited by ghosts during precisely the same years when she has to negotiate her status as a sexual being and her power relative to men. Eldreth's experiences with these ghosts differ in interesting ways from those of the one other group for which the gender implications of narratives of supernatural contact have been extensively considered: middle-class British women of about the same age as Eldreth studied by Bennett (1985, 1987). The British women almost never expressed belief in traditional malevolent ghosts, but the extent of their belief in the benevolent intervention of the "good dead" in the activities of the living was surprisingly high. A substantial proportion of believers talked about deceased husbands, mothers, or other beloved relatives who remained present in the house or came to the teller in a time of crisis (1987:50; 1985:94). Bennett correlates this tendency with these women's devotion to and satisfaction in lives of service to their husbands and families, noting that such experiences "give the highest sanction to traditional female values and are thus the strongest justification for the lives the women have led and the duties which they have given their lives to performing" (1987:212; see also 1985:96). Eldreth has arguably had less exposure than those middle-class, urban women to rationalizing "traditions of disbelief" (Bennett 1987; Hufford 1982). Indeed, other people whom she respects shared and modeled her beliefs. Still, particularly given her awareness of counterexamples—like the "Aunt Polly Reynolds" story—that closely resemble the British women's stories, it appears that Eldreth's experience of what she and others interpret as conventional, purposeless, evil haunting is connected with her troubled and contentious marriage, her dissatisfaction with the role she was forced to adopt. Ghosts, Gordon reminds us, are "symptom[s] of what is missing" (1997:63), and so much was missing in Eldreth's life: her husband's respect and love, adequate material provision, emotional and financial security. These are certainly ghosts with which we must reckon out of a concern for justice.

Gender figures especially prominently in these accounts. Two unusual features immediately jump out at me from these and Eldreth's other ghost stories. First, women are frequently to blame for the haunting, and their crimes involve violating women's specific roles as wives and mothers. Second, women are very reluctant to let men know when they are frightened by the ghosts. Several additional features also merit our attention: the relationship between those who experience the haunting and those who can explain it; the relationship between the situation of those who caused the haunting and the situation of those who experience it; and the specific qualities of the sign whereby the ghost manifests its presence.

These stories can be confusing. I admit that they tend to blur together in my mind. The wealth of circumstantial detail combined with the consistent structure tends to make the incidents seem interchangeable; it is not easy to remember which death created which kind of haunting for which people with which response. Indeed Eldreth's obsession with names and specifics of action that mean nothing to her listeners suggests that, in contrast to polished storytellers who self-consciously adapt their rendition to the understandings and interests of an audience (Bauman 1986, chap. 5), she is still using these stories to work through issues primarily of concern to herself. Additionally, I believe the stories can feel confusing or conflicted because Eldreth is often talking at cross-purposes, in some respects condemning women in the most conventional patriarchal terms, in others standing up for women's rights to have a say in decisions within marriage and even subtly criticizing men's abuse of their power. Indeed, this is one of the places where the "non-unitary" nature of women's subjectivity (Hollway 1984) is evident not only in contrasts between the different genres that Eldreth employs but within a single genre and even a single story. In responding to contradictory demands, confronting the injustices she and other women experience, yet grasping at opportunities to bolster her social standing, Eldreth cannot enact herself as a consistent individual.

Multiple discourses are intertwined in these stories. I will tease out three in particular: one having to do with the cause of the haunting, one to do with fear management and the appropriate response to a haunting, and one to do with the social implications of the haunted house.

Cause

Hauntings, in Eldreth's stories as very commonly in the British and American ghost-story tradition, are caused by deaths, sometimes just mysterious or lonely deaths, but often murders. The implication is that the dead cannot rest and must return to call attention to the unusual circumstances of their deaths or to expose the murderer.[3] Eldreth's repertoire includes murders blamed on men and women in approximately equal numbers. Given the actual preponderance of male murderers and the prevailing sense among Eldreth's neighbors specifically (as well as in American culture generally) that men are wilder than women and more prone to violence,[4] the disproportionate incidence of women as murderers exaggerates and calls attention to the possibility of women's misbehavior. When men murder in Eldreth's ghost stories, it seems to come out of nowhere; no explanation is asked for or offered beyond simple "meanness." When women murder, in contrast, their crime is clearly an extension of a prior abrogation of their proper role as submissive wives and devoted mothers. Mary Black, who murders her twins, is unmarried. The women who drown their babies in the well are "bad women," that is, presumably, prostitutes. In a later story, a "woman who was going with her uncle" (note, not "a man who was going with his niece") is identified as the protagonist, accused of arranging for the uncle to murder her husband and suspected of subsequently murdering her uncle/lover/accomplice as well.

It is not part of the convention of the ghost story to inquire into the motives of the murderer. Still, it is worth noting that neither Eldreth nor her sister is represented as asking those who report the originating events about the motivations or background of the women who murdered their babies and husband. Nor does Eldreth as narrator evince the least sympathy for these women's probable desperation or entertain the idea that they might have been driven to do what they did by unbending social conventions or by violent, exploitative, irresponsible men who should share the blame for these tragedies. What made the "bad girls" turn to prostitution? Had they been deserted by their families or perhaps raped and dishonored so that no one would marry them? How many other babies were they feeding when they despaired of caring for more and drowned the latest arrivals? Where was the father of Mary Black's twins? Was he willing to help take care of her and them? What would have happened to her and them if they had lived? Was the woman who convinced her lover to kill her husband evil, or might she have been abused, terrified, and out of options? Eldreth certainly knew from experience both how difficult life could be with an unkind and uncaring husband and how much more terrifying it seemed, in the face of social condemnation, for a woman to try to make it on her own. Additionally, the model of the murdered girl ballads that she learned from her grandmother would have informed her that a living child would constitute a strong paternity claim that could expose an unmarried mother to grave danger from her erstwhile lover. Given the availability of pat answers from those who offer explanatory stories, however, she neither asks further questions nor compares these instances with those described in other genres or with her own experience.

These female characters supply the only models in Eldreth's imaginative universe of women who do the things that she was prevented from doing by the pressures of convention—with incalculably destructive effects in her own life. These are women who choose their partners, who act to end bad marriages, who control their sexuality and fertility. Images of unruly women like these, when tolerated as part of ludic enactments, have served through the centuries to keep the idea of female autonomy, equality, and self-determination alive (Davis 1975:142–151). In Eldreth's stories the women are ghosts as surely as their murdered babies. These ghosts speak to Eldreth not only of their own tragedies but also, as Gordon suggests, of losses and paths not taken in her own life (1997:63), of the tragedy of being trapped in a loveless marriage and the possibility, however perilous, of a woman refusing a husband's control. It is probably unreasonable to suppose that Eldreth would overtly sympathize or identify with baby murderers, but her use of these characters suggests how established discourses make women complicit in their own disempowerment. Eldreth takes up a position within this discourse in implicit contrast to the bad women. She is the good woman who *has* taken care of her babies (and grandbabies), no matter how little support she got from her husband, and who *has* honored her marriage vows, even though she was not happy. By supporting the status quo and joining in the unquestioning condemnation of these other women, she can clearly and immediately get credit for the way she has lived her life.

The precariousness of Eldreth's own economic and moral standing probably made it especially risky for her to explore controversial issues. She could not afford, as I can, to "reckon graciously" with these ghosts, to listen when they speak of other options, to risk being seen as like them, and condemned like them, if she reveals any sympathy. Rather she is, in Bourdieu's terms, an "agent who 'regularizes' [her] situation . . . win[ning] the group over to [her] side by ostentatiously honoring the values the group honors" (1977:22). I hesitate to call Eldreth's approach "resistance" of any sort, but there is a significant parallel between her self-positioning in this discourse and the "everyday forms of resistance" that, as James C. Scott argues, allow the powerless to "defend [their] interests as best [they] can" without venturing open rebellion (1985:29). Such techniques may succeed in defending the practitioners against the most onerous demands of the system without exposing them to the dangers of direct repressive response from those in power. However, women who do not explicitly analyze and challenge the gender system (like peasants who do not explicitly analyze and challenge the class system) buy certain practical gains at the cost of leaving the hegemonic order intact or possibly even strengthening it by their appearance of assent (1985:32–33). Eldreth acquires the immediate tactical advantage of positioning herself (and thus potentially being perceived) as virtuous but in so doing actually strengthens the gender order that condemns women who seek to control their own sexuality, fertility, or life choices, the very system that made other options unthinkable for her. What we witness here is the effective, self-stabilizing functioning of a gender hegemony (R. Williams 1977:110) and its articulation with the discursive construction of the self.

It is commonly assumed that evil and frightening ghosts are random and purposeless. Their appearance is not ordinarily thought to be related to the activities of those whom they haunt. Those who experience ghosts are simply victims who happen to end up in the place to which the ghost is tied. Eldreth's anxiety about her family's standing, however, seems to impel her to anticipate and defend herself against negative assumptions—namely that the haunting was brought on by immoral behavior—that her present listeners seem unlikely to make. In another version of the story at the Doctor Graham house, Eldreth actually establishes the idea of a linkage herself—"And, uh, my Momma and Poppa used to drink a lot. My Momma's oldest sister had went to look for them. And left us there with the baby"—and is then able to offer only a feeble excuse— "You know, things like that happens." In a story that occurs much later in her life, however, Eldreth again informs us that on a particular day she heard ghostly footsteps in her kitchen at precisely those moments when she allowed herself to read her daughter's romance magazine, but she then vigorously defends herself against the implication that she was doing anything wrong or avoiding her woman's responsibilities, insisting "I never did make it a practice reading *True Stories*" and "I'd got all my washing and I'd scrubbed the floors and had everything done up." In terms of both cause and trigger, then, Eldreth positions herself discursively as a virtuous, responsible, and compliant woman, and in so doing reinforces the gender double standard and the condemnation of women who refuse to be controlled by a social system hostile to them. At the same time, however, by continuing to tell these stories, she does repeatedly juxtapose herself and these tragic, audacious women in listeners' minds, keeping open the possibility that someone will listen differently to these ghosts. Eldreth can go only as far as to say to these female ghosts, these other mistreated, marginalized women, "I see you are not there" (Gordon 1997:16). She dares not tell their stories from their point of view, give them a voice, or acknowledge that they were dealt with unjustly, since she is herself so hard-pressed to retain her own respectability. She, at least, however, lets them linger as shadows, absences that hint at a presence, silences that adumbrate the challenging that could be spoken, the accusations that could be leveled, and the alternatives for women that could be articulated.

Fear

Significantly, the people who experience ghosts in these stories are girls of an age to be interested in boyfriends and marriage or young couples attempting to set up new collaborative households. In contrast to Grandma and Grandpa Milam's long-standing, harmonious relationship, which brought them a benevolent haunting, these unsettled new or potential relationships are vulnerable to malevolent influences, to flitting, half-seen images of all that they want not to be. The senseless, frightening invasion of the house by the ghost may mirror the sense that one's body and sphere of action have been invaded by an alien force. Lonely deaths and marriages that never got started, spouse murder and infanticide quite appropriately haunt the promising new marriage and test the partners. It makes good sense that those who are haunted would be afraid of all that they wish to repress, deny, and banish from the realm of possibility.

I cannot tell you in a single word whether Eldreth is or is not, was or was not, afraid of the ghosts whose manifestations she encountered. She says different things at different times about different experiences, and her feelings often change in the course of the events she narrates. Nevertheless, it is extremely striking that, while other actors are universally and automatically frightened by the ghosts, Eldreth in at least some instances portrays herself as initially unconcerned and even pleased. Of the ghost voices she and her husband heard in their first house, she remarks: "I have never heard such a pitiful . . . moans and groans and crying and taking on. And, uh, I just laid there and listened to it. And I never said a word to him. But, really, I enjoyed it, hit sounded just like a lovers' quarrel." She rarely persists in this attitude, even when she achieves it, and in another version of the "First Married" story she actually laughs at herself for feeling that way: "As Momma used to say, maybe I didn't have sense enough to *get* skeered." Still, she calls attention repeatedly to what may be either unusual courage or some sense of kinship or lack of difference that keeps her from finding the ghosts alien and frightening. In thus acknowledging the ghosts, Eldreth at least partially domesticates them. A ghost dragged into the light is much less frightening than one relegated to the shadows. Certainly after years of a disappointing

marriage, and perhaps even as it was beginning, Eldreth seems to know that looking straight at the worst that can happen diminishes its power to hurt you,
although she shares this revelation only in the veiled generic form of a ghost
story. I even wonder if Eldreth herself partly recognizes that these "supernatural"
forces are simply not that foreign. They are manifestations of the lives and relationships of other people—people not so different from herself—and if they continue to manifest themselves and to try to influence the lives of the living, that
is not incomprehensible or so different from supposedly normal practices, like
telling stories of one's own experiences to teach and warn members of younger
generations. Men, who have the power to counter force with force directly, see
these manifestations as foreign and threatening. Women, who are used to paying
attention to relationships, waiting for opportunities, and finding indirect ways to
get things done, may feel that these spirits are kindred spirits, that their indirect
and misunderstood ways of operating are an extension of the way women must
work in a world where they have little overt power.

Whatever Eldreth's "real" feelings when she encountered those ghosts, however, it is clear that the acknowledgement of fear or the representation of fear-
fulness is something that women, including Eldreth, must carefully manage.
Men, because they are presumed to be brave and because they have the controlling power in the relationship with their wives, tend to be direct in admitting
their fear. Women, however, are quite willing to admit their fear to each other
but are reluctant to admit it to men. When Eldreth stayed with her Aunt Edna
and Uncle Carter in the Bob Barr house, she unabashedly reports: "I kept hearing things in there. And I kept telling Aunt Edna, I did, I told her that I was
afraid." Her aunt comes up with a sympathetic solution: "So I told Edna I was
going to go home, that I was afraid to sleep in there. And she pulled my bed up
to the door . . . and said, 'Now, if you hear anything,' says, 'you jump out and run
to me and call.'" At the same time, however, Edna models the imperative to
withhold knowledge of her fear from her husband: "Well, me and Edna used to
run and hide behind the side of the little big gate where Carter'd come in—we
didn't want him to know we was scared to death. And, uh, after he'd go up, then,
we'd slip along behind the car and while he parked the car we'd run in the front
door." Similarly, when Eldreth's sister and her nephew were too afraid to stay
alone in the house in Virginia, "they slipped along behind her husband and this
boy's father to keep them from knowing that they'd got skeered."

Following those models, when Eldreth repeatedly heard a tightly fastened door
"slam open" in the house she and her husband rented just after they got married,
she ran out into a snowstorm in a short-sleeved dress but made excuses about her
behavior to her husband: "And he said, 'What are you out here without a coat on
for? It's cold out here.' I said, 'I'm going to stand here till you cut the wood.' And
I didn't tell him that I'd got scared." Eldreth's sister's experience in the "Bad Girls"
story reveals that a woman's admission of fear gives her husband a means to control her or extract concessions. Having "tried to get her husband to leave the

house [one] night" and had him refuse even though he was afraid, too, the sister must eventually "give her husband right smart of money to leave the house." Thus, in this discourse men and women hold the same position relative to the supernatural, but different positions relative to each other. Men have little to lose by admitting fear; women risk handing their husbands a tool with which to con-solidate their control. Eldreth's treatment of the subject does not explicitly criti-cize this power imbalance, but she does repeatedly impress upon listeners that fear of the supernatural not only operates on individuals but also influences relation-ships *between* the men and women who have these experiences.

Furthermore, even in a society where gender roles and expectations are very structured and set, there is some possibility at this early stage for marriage part-ners to negotiate the modes of interaction and the balance of power that will pre-vail between them. The characteristic extended dialogues in these stories show the new couples establishing patterns for reacting to the crises that will affect their families. Although, as discussed in the previous chapter, Eldreth evidently lost and only much later regained any right to promote her own opinions and contest her husband's, in these stories she depicts herself holding her own, assert-ing a lack of fear, which she may or may not really feel, to be sure that her hus-band perceives her as the stronger one in this interaction. (This is most evident in another version of the "First Married" story.)

> Next evening he said, "Let's go down to your grandpa's and stay all night tonight."
>
> I said, "I'm not going down there." I said, "It's too cold." You see, we'd a had to walked and it's about three mile.
>
> And, uh, he said, "Well, you can sta—" I he said, "Let's go up to Pap's and stay then tonight."
>
> And I said, "No, I'm a-staying right here."
>
> He said, "Well, you can stay if you want to." But he said, "I'm a-leaving; I ain't a-going to stay." He said, "Didn't you hear that last night?"
>
> And, uh, I said, "Yeah, I heard it, but I liked to hear it." I enjoyed it.

Thus even in these stories of frightening hauntings, supernatural presences that are welcomed open up a space within which the conventions of gendered power become negotiable, anticipating the friendly and supportive spirits who later visit Eldreth with empowering premonitions.

A related and highly distinctive feature of the hauntings is the uniqueness and specificity of the signs through which the spirits manifest their presence. Sometimes there is a logical and poetic connection between the sound and the ostensible cause, as when they hear baby steps or baby cries in the houses where babies were killed. Other times the association seems arbitrary, as when they hear a lovers' quarrel in the house where an old woman died. In contrast, however, to the highly conventional signs like the ghostly light that reveals the treasure in the "Aunt Polly Reynolds" story (Baughman 1966, motif E371.10*), Eldreth hears not just the sound of ghosts quarrelling (1966, motif E402.1.1.8*) but the voices of her Aunt Maimie and Uncle B.J. She likewise experiences not just a ghost opening doors and windows repeatedly (1966, motif E338.1c) but the sound of a specific door slamming, even though she has propped it open with a rock. In a later story the ghost of a drowned man makes itself known with what Eldreth describes as "the sound of a car door falling in the creek." In the version of the "First Married" story given in full above she gives an even more precise and concrete characterization of the sound, "I heard just like a clothesline upstairs—I'd never been up the stairs—but it went just like the clothesline was real tight, you know, and someone hitting on this clothesline." And in another version she adds yet another detail: "But it went just exactly like somebody hitting a clothesline with a knife, you know, how they rattle? where it's . . . drawed tight?" Sound is a fascinating medium for the ghosts to employ because a listener automatically forms a very specific image of the source without having to (or in these instances being able to) secure visual corroboration. The clarity of the sound image gives Eldreth the confidence to persist in her interpretation—despite contradictory evidence—with her husband: "And, uh, when my husband came in I said, uh, 'Go upstairs and get me that clothesline.' He said, 'What clothesline?' I said, 'There's one up there, because I heard it.' So I insisted and he went on up there and he said, 'There's not a clothesline up them stairs nowhere.' And I said, 'Well, I heard that clothesline.'" This bolstering of faith in her own perceptions and analysis likewise anticipates the supernatural support she receives in later premonition encounters.

Haunted Houses

A third discourse in which Eldreth positions other characters more obviously than herself inquires who is to blame for any injuries that the residents of a haunted house suffer. One kind of answer is supplied by the "cause" discourse, and it is emphasized by being situated as the last word in many of the tales. About the "Bob Barr House," "they said that Bob Barr died in that room. Now, I don't know what happened, but he was a real old man; he died in that room." And about the house where she and Ed lived when they were "First Married," a neighbor "said they was an old lady that was found out there in the ditch lying at the back of this house. And said nobody knowed whether she had just died there or whether she had been murdered. And said nobody never found out." In these instances, then, no one is obviously to blame, and the sources of the inconclusive information are left correspondingly vague. At the "Doctor Graham House," however, Eldreth hears from two authoritative sources: "Doctor Graham, he didn't tell me that she killed 'em, but he said, 'Mary Black's twins both died in that room in there.' So, now, I don't know. Momma told me that she killed 'em." And at the house where the "Bad Girls" had lived, the owner is likewise the source of the information that "these bad girls had drownded the babies." Blame is firmly fixed, both by Eldreth's mother, whom we can easily imagine being motivated to instruct her daughter about the terrible things that can happen to a unmarried woman who gets pregnant, and by the landlords, who have good reason to deflect responsibility from themselves.

Another kind of answer is supplied by the opening lines of several stories: "And [my sister and her husband] moved in a big old house and, uh, no one did-n't tell *them* it was haunted"; "Me and my husband had just got married and we moved to a two-story house and, uh, no one had ever told us this house was haunted." People who can anticipate what the new resident will experience but withhold that information are also, in Eldreth's construction, culpable. The almost identical phraseology emphasizes that this is how she is inclined to begin a ghost story if left to her own devices and not prompted by a question that steals some of the introductory material. The pause marked by an "uh" calls attention to the linkage between the two clauses and to the evaluation implied. Eldreth does not seem inclined to blame Doctor Graham, who (she often remarks) was "sweet on" her and who volunteers the information, perhaps to tease her, in the least frightening form. Nor is she evidently critical of her grandparents, even though "Grandpa laughed real big and he said, 'You got scared out, didn't you?'" and her Grandma eventually admits, "'Well, now, I'm not going to tell you this to scare you out, but,' she said, uh, 'we had to move from that house on that account.' She said, 'Maimie would a went stone crazy if she'd a had to a stayed there. She said she couldn't stand it.'" Eldreth paints a similarly respectful por-trait of Jack Holman, another neighbor and landlord, who answers her directly when she tells him what she has experienced in his house:

> And then I asked him, I told him what I'd been a-hearing.
> And he said, "Well, I told you that I'd tell you the truth." He said, "This house is haunted." He said, "We started hearing things in the house and outside and 'round the house right after I found Dad dead."

Eldreth expresses outrage, however, at the landlady who not only failed to warn her sister that prostitutes had lived in the house and were suspected of drowning their babies in the well but also lied about it, answering initial queries with a fic-tion about "imps."

> When they went back again she said, "Well, I'll just tell you," she said, uh, "they was some bad women that lived in this house. And, uh, they had some little babies and they drownded them in the well." And, uh, they had been using the water out of the well, and she hadn't told them. And, uh, after they left, why, they got some-one to clean the well out, and they found about three or four skeletons of little babies in the well where these bad girls had drownded the babies. And that's what happened.

> Now that | they say that was really true that these bad girls had drownded the
> babies and they had been drinking the water off of the | off of the bones in the bot-
> tom of the well.

It is significant that (with one exception to be discussed in the next section)
all of the hauntings that Eldreth experiences in a house occur in a *rented* house.
We spoke earlier of the vulnerability and suspect respectability of those identified by the community as "just renters" (Batteau 1983:148). Typically, in southern mountain speechways, the "old home place" continues to be known by the
owner's name, regardless of who actually lives there (Allen 1990:162). Eldreth
reveals her tenuous claim to these homes by labeling many of the houses and stories about the events that transpired there with the owner's name: "Now, this is
the Bob Barr house at Creston." The owners know the houses are haunted, but
they withhold that information to their own advantage. They cannot be sure
that renters will experience the hauntings or find them intolerable if they do, but
they prefer not to risk the reluctance to rent the house that might be inspired by
the news that other people have encountered a ghost there. Renters' lack of full
rights is reinforced, however, by the owner's assumed privilege of judging what
the renter will find adequate and acceptable (Batteau 1983:148). In this respect
the ghosts materialize the potential for a landlord to turn the necessary provision
of shelter into a grossly lopsided and exploitative interaction by supplying an
unsafe or unwholesome place to live. Eldreth does not lay blame on landlords
who are neighbors and who care about her and treat her with respect, thus banishing the specter of exploitation. She does castigate the nameless landlord
(interestingly, a woman) who dishonestly tries to pretend there is no problem
and exposes her tenants not only to the risk of being frightened but to the loath-
some experience of drinking water steeped in murdered babies' bones. Class divisions exist and pose a danger, but their effects, in Eldreth's experience, can be
mitigated by neighborly concern and respect.

By pointing a finger of blame at the owners but then shifting her gaze, Eldreth
also hints that there is another responsible party, though she dare not speak his
name, and that the ostensible class issue camouflages a gender issue. Throughout
her marriage, Eldreth, as she now says, "ain't never lived in nothing but a shack
from here to yonder." She lived and raised her family in substandard housing—
including two houses that burned down and one swept away by a flood—because
her husband was unwilling or unable to work hard enough to provide better. The
first and only house she has ever owned was one that she saved the money for
out of her own labor and that her sons built for her when she was almost sixty
years old. Until she built her own snug house and carved her initials on the
doorstep, Eldreth existed among those marginal "people who [because they] do
not own the land they live on are automatically excluded from" what Barbara
Allen calls "the genealogical landscape" (1990:162). Eldreth thus positions herself as a victim, not of the ghosts, but of her husband's laziness and irresponsibil-

ity. He had the responsibility for providing a home for his family; he was the one who exposed that family to threat—ghostly and substantial—by failing to provide their own home and land and keeping them instead in rented places that were still "possessed" in two senses by potentially threatening others. The cruelest and most evasive ghost in these houses is her husband's neglect, a ghost that retains its power because for so many years Eldreth cannot name it aloud, though she can use her popular ghost stories to hint obliquely at its presence.

Premonitions

Eldreth, even as a young woman, is not always frightened by the ostensibly purposeless and hostile supernatural visitors that other people automatically find terrifying. As she matures, she continues to encounter such "ghosts," but she also periodically receives supernatural "warnings" which, though troubling, are ultimately beneficial and thus presumably beneficent. The possibility of such premonitions is also something Eldreth learned about as a child:

> And I knew one family that—well, Momma said that they was six children and a father and mother and they all got that flu.
>
> Well, said that [sighs] this woman told some of 'em, said, "I had the saddest dream a week or two ago that, uh, I's in the prettiest green field and all the | the little green grasses withered and died."
>
> And, uh, 'bout | 'bout a week or two weeks later they every one took that flu and all six of her children died with it.
>
> And they said she | Momma said she never did go back to the table to eat, said she'd just get her a little saucer or something and set down in the corner somewhere, wouldn't go about a table 'cause | on account of the children all dying.

These visitations may take several forms: a feeling, a presence, a dream. In contrast to the ghosts, whom others also perceive and know about, these warnings come to Eldreth alone. Lacking corroboration, she must defend not only the significance of these uncanny experiences but also the very validity of her own perceptions and her decision to interpret them as "warnings." Eldreth's stories about her premonitions have a typical and consistent structure that, logically, reverses the ordering of episodes in the ghost stories. The warning arrives first. Eldreth recognizes that it is a sign of something, but she is not provided with foreknowledge of what that will be, and she responds, if at all, on the basis of instinct rather than informed preparation. This generates suspense until, in the fullness of time, it becomes apparent to what calamity the premonition was referring, and Eldreth is vindicated for interpreting it as a warning. In only one instance of the three she has related to me is Eldreth empowered to protect her family and then only at the cost of suffering a lesser injury herself. Because her husband is the primary doubter, however, these supernatural manifestations create rare opportunities for Eldreth to speak back to him and to insist upon the validity of her own perceptions and interpretations. These are the apparitions who, in Eldreth's experience, "also simultaneously represent a future possibility, a hope" (Gordon 1997:63), an alternative life in which Eldreth can dare to contest her husband's control.

In one story, probably from the 1960s, Eldreth invites her husband, "Ed, go to church with me," even though he usually refuses. The invitation is an appropriate act for a believer, since it opens the possibility that she could serve as an instrument for God to touch his recalcitrant heart. When Ed retorts, "I ain't a-going to church tonight," Eldreth finds herself gripped by an inexplicable "feeling" and surprises herself and him by exclaiming, "I hope and pray to God, something shakes you out before I get back." When she gets home from church Ed reluctantly admits that they had an earth tremor (which affected the house but not the church) and Eldreth gets to exult that what she involuntarily prayed for actually came to pass.

In a story from the early 1970s, shortly after she has moved the family to her own new house, Eldreth senses a figure that appears to be her daughter-in-law come into her bedroom during the night, approach the bed, and pinch her. In the morning Eldreth, again without knowing precisely why, becomes upset at the idea of her son going down the mountain to his job in North Wilkesboro and convinces him to stay home. Later that day, she and her daughter-in-law go out to do errands, taking the car he would have driven, and the brakes fail. Fortunately, since they were on their way to the hospital to pay a bill, they crash in a place where they can receive immediate help, whereas the son would probably have been killed had the brakes given out on the tortuous grade down off the Blue Ridge escarpment between Boone and Wilkesboro. When the women arrive home, however, their husbands express more concern about the damage to the car and the uncompleted chores than about their wives' injuries, although they eventually apologize.

Eldreth's most poetic story, concerning the great flood in 1940 that wreaked so much destruction in the mountains, is also the earliest incident and the one in which she most conclusively and satisfyingly proves herself right. In this particular telling, her handling of my interruption also demonstrates how much she regards this story as a polished piece, not, as I initially imagined, as just a conversation about the facts of a historical event.

The Flood

And during the flood we went through all that mess. That's the 1940 flood. Everything we had washed out. My husband's sister, everything she had washed away. Aw, they was chickens, calves, and hogs, and . . . everything else that washed out in that flood. And then they's over on | next to Jefferson, over on Beaver

Creek that . . . two or three or four that drownded. And I I they's one child, and man and a woman. It was I it was rough.

PS: How did people keep from going hungry if everything had gotten . . .

BE: Well . . .

PS: washed away?

BE: Well, I reckon they, as the saying is, I reckon they survived.

I had the prettiest garden that time that I ever had in my life. And the prettiest peas; they was I they was every bit of waist high and hanging just as *full* as they could hang of peas. And had an awful pretty sweet potato patch . . . in the garden, prettiest you ever saw, and it was I it was in August, and the flood. And hit I hit just, well, the water was . . . from bank to bank, just as muddy as it could be. And when that house . . . bursted loose it was just I hit just spread out on that water.

I'd canned over 500 cans that summer. I just worked like everything filling cans, you know? I had ninety-some cans of strawberries and strawberry preserves, wild ones that I had picked back on the mountain and carried 'em off and canned 'em and everything. And when it . . . everything just . . . seemed like it went smooth and easy.

And three weeks before that, I told . . . Ed, I said, uh, "I had the awfullest dream last night." And he said, "You're always dreaming something." And I said, "Well, I I I never dreamed a dream in my life that worried me but what something didn't happen." And I said, "I dreamed that me and you was going up and down the creek bank through here picking up naked chickens." And I said, "They didn't even have a feather on 'em."

And, uh, about three weeks later . . . it started raining. And it was rain, rain, rain, raining. The water kept getting up and it'd softened the mountains, you know, and everything, till it come them slides out.

And, uh, after the water went down . . . we had a hundred and sixty-eight head of chickens. And we had one hen and some little biddies was all we had left. And a rooster. And that rooster, hit had got up on a stake up on the bank a little bit— the water was surrounded around the stake—and it stayed up on that stake and crowed . . . just as hard as it could crow. But it never I it didn't wash it off of the stake. It was I hit'd got up above the water, you know, on the bank. Oh, if it had been down any further, why, the water was higher than this house, . . . muddy water and logs a-rolling and everything else.

And after the water went down I went down through there; me and Ed was walking along the creek bank. And I don't know how many chickens I picked up, just took 'em by the feet and held 'em up. And I said, "Ed," I said, "you hooted at me," I said, "three weeks ago when I told you I dreamed of walking up and down the creek bank picking up naked chickens." And, young'uns, they was just exactly like they'd been picked; they didn't have a feather on 'em. And I just held 'em up and showed him. I said, "Right here is what I told you three weeks ago." He never did say anything about my . . . dreams that would worry me after that.

Eldreth's accounts of the premonitions are revolutionary in decisively depicting her as a knower and her intuitive perceptions, however inchoate, as a valid form of knowledge (Harding 1987:3; Belenky et al. 1986:18–19). As Catharine MacKinnon has argued, to be *objectified*, to be the *object* of knowledge and action (never the subject) is what defines women as a class in patriarchal culture, while men are defined as those who know and act upon women (1982:536–541). Eldreth's husband wants to deny her the status of knower/subject in these extraordinary cases, as in everyday life, but in these few instances she fights back and wins. She may not know *what* the premonitions mean, but she knows that they are meaningful. When her husband challenges her claim, he is proved wrong. The supernatural becomes a powerful ally, enabling Eldreth to stand her ground.

As with "women's intuitions" more generally, however, the source and nature of Eldreth's special knowledge expose her to accusations of irrationality. In the flood story, her husband initially dismisses her belief that the worrisome dream could be a premonition: "You're always dreaming something." And in the earthquake story, he responds to the coincidence of the tremor with her prayer for something to "shake him out" by accusing her of being "crazy" rather than admitting the possibility that she possesses foreknowledge or extraordinary capacities. Eldreth, however, is consequently empowered and vindicated in direct correlation to her husband's being subordinated and proved wrong. Ed never gives his wife the satisfaction of apologizing for his doubt or actually conceding that she was right, but he must at least shut up and keep his criticism and doubts to himself: "He never did say anything about my dreams that would worry me after that." His attempt to discredit her as "crazy" serves only to reveal his fear and resentment of a woman he cannot, in this respect, control. In the pinch story, Eldreth's son, who, in marked contrast to his father, accepts the validity of his mother's foreknowledge or at least honors her concern enough to act upon her recommendation, is consequently saved from death.

Eldreth's sensitivity to "warnings" is not an unmitigated benefit. The supernatural visitations can be frightening. The knowledge she receives is only partial. It allows her to save Carl from the car wreck but not to protect herself and Libby. Nor does it enable her to keep the products of so much of her labor from going to waste in the flood. As in the ghost stories, then, the supernatural intervention seems to have more to do with the imbalances in intimate human relationships than with the material world or other aspects of people's lives. Like the vision of the children's deaths experienced by her mother's friend, the premonitions do not confer the kind of usable foresight (for instance, explicit warning that a flood was coming) that might drastically alter Eldreth's life or establish her conclusively as the possessor of extraordinary knowledge. They do, however, provide sufficiently specific images (the desire for a "shake-out," the vision of naked chickens on the creek bank, the conviction that Carl should not go to work that day) to give her the satisfaction of being proved right in the end. Like her lack of fear of ghosts, her premonitions embolden Eldreth to stand up for herself and to extract a modicum of respect from her husband. In this respect, also, Eldreth's application of the experience exceeds the model she learned as a child.

In the ghost stories, neighbors or relatives often step in to provide information and guide the interpretation. Eldreth uses reported speech in those narratives not only to depict the affected couple's negotiations but also to portray wider conversations about how to interpret the haunting or to allow the owner or previous resident of the house to offer an explanation of prior events. That is, she demonstrates that knowledge and authority are shared and negotiable among friends and family members, and she often depicts someone outside the marital dyad as the source of authoritative knowledge. In the premonition stories, Eldreth departs radically from that practice and presents herself in unambiguous terms as the authoritative speaker. She quotes her own retort to her husband, often more than once, and concludes the narrative briskly with an authorial evaluation confirming and insisting upon the rectitude of her stance. In the earthquake story, "I said, 'I *told* you,' that's the way I spoke it, I said, 'I *told* you I hope and pray to God something shook you out before I got back.' [. . .] And it did." In the flood story, "And I said, 'Ed,' I said, 'you hooted at me,' I said, 'three weeks ago when I told you I dreamed of walking up and down the creek bank picking up naked chickens.' And, young'uns, they was just exactly like they'd been picked; they didn't have a feather on 'em."

It is also important to note that Eldreth does not draw a firm line between spiritual supporters conceived as ghostlike and personal intervention by God. It is not clear, for instance, what exactly inspired her to blurt out the remark to Ed about something shaking him out. She has no doubts, however, about who caused the subsequent earthquake. She concluded one telling of that story by remarking:

> They've never been but one perfect person on this earth and it was God. [. . .] But I'm gonna tell you something, if I'm not serious . . . I'd better not pray . . . for something to happen, 'cause it will. [. . .] Now I have prayed prayers that would absolutely shock me when I *knew* they was answered. Now that's the dying truth.

I was never able to get Eldreth to discuss her conception of the relationship between God and ghosts or supernatural actors. In her experience, however, God himself may be one of the sources or even the ultimate source of the intuitive support that occasionally enabled her to portray herself as an authoritative knower and renegotiate the balance of power with her husband. Her practice thus appears to resemble instances of ritual spirit possession (those that have been analyzed as enabling women to express discontent and manipulate men without fully taking responsibility for nonapproved behavior or directly criticizing the system [for example, Lewis 1971:116]) more closely than the kind of explicit attack on societal gender norms voiced by nineteenth-century American spiritualist mediums (who lectured while in trance about marriage based on economic necessity rather than on love as the root of women's oppression [Braude 1989:117–118]). Still, while Eldreth could argue that she acts involuntarily—as the spirit moves her— in the premonition stories, she far exceeds her own practice in the ghost stories, portraying herself as—rather than in contrast to—a woman who takes responsibility for interpreting her own experience. These are apparitions with whom Eldreth can reckon graciously—since their origin is unknown and possibly heavenly—and they empower her to expose and confront her husband's lack of appreciation. Indeed, it long struck me as strange that Eldreth could simultaneously maintain beliefs as divergent as those implied respectively by the ghost and premonition stories. In part this seems to be explained by the separability of distinct discourses or conversations and the self-positioning they offer. When talking about the causes of hauntings, Eldreth can situate herself in opposition to unconventional women, while when talking about premonitions, she can portray herself as unconventional without sensing a contradiction. It may also reflect cognitive processes, according to which beliefs acquired from an explicit verbal source are readily isolated from beliefs acquired through direct experience (Strauss 1992). Eldreth's most recent uncanny experience, however, forces her to breach the boundaries between these discourses and ways of thinking.

A FINAL REVENANT

Once Eldreth moves into the house that she owns and paid for with her own hard-won earnings, she appears to be safe from threatening ghosts, although she continues to experience empowering premonitions. The most recent ghost experience that she narrates, however, occurred in her new house shortly after her husband's death. This latest story is distinctive in being the only one in which not only the process of interpreting the uncanny event according to given models but even the process of deciding which models to employ is played out in the course of narration.

Light in the Bedroom
(Eldreth had just finished telling the story about "Aunt Polly Reynolds.")

> You know, I've thought about that, about | when my husband died, he | they was | about that light, you know, that would flash up in my bedroom so much. Did I ever tell you about it?

PS: I think so.

BE: And, uh, it was | for a long time it would kindly | it'd dashed me, you know. But I got till I, when I'd turn the light off I'd close my eyes real tight. But now, honestly, that light would go down in under the cover with me. It did. That light'd | when I'd turn that cover down and after the light was turned off, that light'd go down under that cover as pretty as I ever saw a light in my life.

And, uh, I had a quilt on my bed that I thought might be the cause of it, that I that was on *his* bed when I before he died. And I rolled that quilt up and sent it to the dump. Because I felt like that maybe that's the reason.

But I still saw the light. It didn't make I it didn't change a thing. But the light . . . for a long time, well, for two or three year or longer . . . probably than that, that light would flash up.

But I've not seen it now in a good while.

I told this I I was talking to somebody about this where I'd went to sing one time, and these people said, "Well, you know, maybe," said, "maybe it was the Good Lord watching over you." I said, "Well, I've thought of that, 'cause," I said, "it was I it was as bright a light as I ever saw." And, I said, "I I a few times I've thought, well, it might be my husband."

And I thought I and then I said, "But he wasn't that protective over me when he's living." [Laughs.] I had them all laughing, those people, I said that.

In the formation of narratives from experience, contradictions may be exposed when the narrator is forced to choose among available models both for understanding and reacting to events and for constructing a narrative about them. In Eldreth's case, the opportunity to perform her stories and the incorporation of metastories about storytelling into the texts themselves also prove to be important resources in completing a small but significant shift in self-presentation.

The light that "flashes up" in her bedroom and even follows her under the covers frightens Eldreth. As she says, "It'd dashed me." She needs to find an interpretation. The possibility that the light might be a premonition is summarily ruled out by the lack of a subsequent remarkable event. However, given that this house has no previous owners or residents to ask for advice or information, she is not going to be provided a ready-made explanation as in the ghost stories. Rather Eldreth must choose an explanatory model to account for the phenomenon and, as in the premonition stories, arrive at and maintain an analysis entirely on her own authority. Three kinds of models suggest themselves. First Eldreth considers and rules out ordinary causes. In another rendition she begins the story by describing that process explicitly:

Well, shortly after my husband passed away, I went in the bedroom to get ready to go to bed. And they was the prettiest light; it was something like . . . that big [uses both hands to indicate a circle the size of a softball]. Hit was so bright that it hurt your eyes. And it was just I just going all over my bed. And I looked at the windows. I thought, "Well, could that be a flashlight, someone's flashing a light in at the window?" Well, no, it wasn't; it was too bright for that. And then, uh, I had curtains, you know. I keep curtains over my windows good.

The next obvious possibility is to equate this light with the light in the story of her grandparents' caring for Aunt Polly Reynolds. This comparison provides both an explanation and a model for action, since it connects the ghostly light to the possessions of the recently deceased person. Such a possibility would make sense, since the quilt on Eldreth's bed is one her husband slept under before he died. And although Eldreth does not articulate the further comparison, it is potentially complimentary to imply that the light could be intended to reveal something Ed had hidden to reward her for nursing him during his long, agonizing battle with emphysema, just as her grandparents selflessly nursed their neighbor. The very structure of the story implies a mismatch, however, since this story must begin with the unexplained light rather than with a report of what she did for her husband. Eldreth nevertheless acts on that potential connection and throws the quilt away: "And I rolled that quilt up and sent it to the dump. Because I felt like that maybe that's the reason." Her grandparents responded to the light they saw by bringing back into the house apparently worthless clothes that had belonged to a destitute woman, and they were rewarded. Eldreth, in contrast, far from receiving a reward, has to sacrifice something valuable, a quilt she had probably made with her own hands. Her willingness to make such a drastic move suggests how threatening she finds the light and how much she is willing to give up in order to get rid of it. But the technique proposed by her grandparents' model does not work: "But I still saw the light. It didn't change a thing."

This leaves Eldreth with a model that she mobilizes only implicitly. If the light is not a natural phenomenon or a premonition or a clue to a reward or just a bit of spirit tied to the deceased's possessions, then it must be a hostile ghost. Since hauntings, as she understands them, are always caused by deaths in the haunted location and since Eldreth's house is quite new and has never belonged to anyone else, she is sure that her husband is the only person who has died there. It thus seems clear that this revenant is her husband. This conclusion has a number of unpalatable corollaries, however. First, comparison with the causes of haunting in Eldreth's other stories might imply that this ghost's appearance results from evil behavior by a woman who stepped outside her proper role. Such a conclusion hardly seems fair, given how dutifully Eldreth nursed her husband through years of disability and illness, but the bad feelings she harbored toward him may not have let her conscience rest easy. Second, her husband's return in the form of the light (which even shares her bed) suggests that she will never be rid of him, that he will always be there to observe and control her. Furthermore, as a ghost, Ed finds a peculiarly effective means of striking at his wife. Her sensitivity to supernatural contact provided her with one of the few means she ever had to challenge her husband's domination, and he did not like that. Once he is dead, he enters that supernatural realm and can contact her as a ghost. The supernatural channel had supplied Eldreth with knowledge and power to fight her husband; he takes over that channel and uses it to punish and frighten her.

Furthermore, as both Ed and Bessie Eldreth knew from the model of earlier stories and from their own common experience in the house they lived in early in their marriage, the only way to escape from this kind of senseless, malevolent haunting is to abandon the house to which the ghost is tied. Given their history together, Eldreth's new house—the one she paid for herself without his help—must have been a daily reproach to her husband, a concrete reminder of his failure to fulfill his responsibilities. Eldreth is proud of that house and happier and more secure there than she ever was in any of the homes he provided. Driving her out would be a logical and terrible revenge, one that Eldreth is determined to resist. Eldreth does not dare to state this conclusion overtly, but the behavior that she reports as a continuation of the story allows her to give some strong hints of what she is thinking.

In various versions of the story, Eldreth describes herself as responding in two ways to the light once her quilt ploy fails to banish it. First, she simply resigns herself to its continued presence—"But the light . . . for a long time, well, for two or three year or longer . . . probably than that, that light would flash up"—and tries to find ways to keep it from bothering her—"And I got till I wouldn't . . . I would *not* turn the light off, my bedroom light, till I got ready to crawl in the bed and then I'd close my eyes real tight to get in the bed." This simple decision is more significant than it may appear. Ed Eldreth is dead and should, at last, be out of his wife's life. But as a ghost, he refuses to disappear and leave her alone. Even more frightening in this form because less predictable, he haunts her. Clinging to patriarchal power, he lingers vindictively, half-absent, half-present, refusing to allow Eldreth the closure his full absence would confer, refusing to let her get on with a new life from which he is absent (Gordon 1997:64). In determining to find a way to ignore the light and not to be frightened, Eldreth harkens back to the spunky, curious girl she was when she first married Ed and to the actual lack of fear she felt when encountering some of her first ghost experiences. She also demonstrates that she has internalized the lesson that she articulates in the discourse about fear of the supernatural, namely, that men can control women if women admit fear. Perhaps most importantly, she determines to pit her will against Ed in a way she rarely dared to when he was alive. This encounter with the revenant light represents her first exercise in practicing the freedoms of widowhood. Earlier ghost experiences became part of the negotiation between members of a couple as they passed through the liminal stage occasioned by their entering into a marriage. Here we see Eldreth again negotiating power with her husband as she passes through the liminal stage involved in reconstituting her identity as she moves back out of the marriage because of Ed's death.

Eldreth's second technique for responding to the light specifically involves talk and storytelling: she goes on discussing the experience as an unexplained phenomenon, which invites other people to offer interpretations. In so doing, she follows the same procedure as for her other ghost experiences and acts in an appropriately unassuming fashion, even though in this instance she has no expectation that anyone else can actually tell her more than she already knows. If friends or family members offered suggestions, these are not preserved in her current narratives, but eventually an audience member at an Elderhostel performance gives Eldreth just the opening she wants (as she describes in another version of the story):

> And I told them about this at Camp Broadstone and one of the guys asked me, said, "Well, did you ever think about it that, uh, about it could be . . . the Good Lord, watching over you?" I said, "I did think one time that, uh, hit might be that it was my husband, that light keep coming back. And I said, "But I don't believe that now because he wasn't that protective over me when he was living."

In the guise of a sassy and sarcastic quip appropriate to the mood of her singing performances, Eldreth finally gets to say what she really means. Her husband "wasn't that protective over [her] when he was living." He did not take care of her as he should have. He did not fulfill his responsibilities. A good, loving, responsible husband might conceivably come back in the form of a beneficent light to watch over his grieving widow, but not Ed. Although she has no direct model for it in her experience or tradition, Eldreth here refers implicitly to the concept of the caring, protective dead that Bennett's informants found so persuasive (1985). Eldreth, it appears, can imagine the good dead, but not her husband among them. Her immediate rejection of the idea that the light represented the "Good Lord" watching over her seems out of character for a woman with such a strong faith in a personal and loving God and a conviction that the divine and the ghostly may not be all that separate.[5] Her unwillingness even to entertain this well-meant and comforting suggestion is, however, in character with her general tendency to turn conversational openings to her own predetermined purposes. It also lends strong support to the notion that she had been waiting for someone to utter a remark that would allow her to advance her own hypothesis in response without introducing the idea unprefaced. She cannot directly exorcise the frightening ghost light, but by asserting her own interpretation of it and implicitly criticizing her husband out loud in public, she can defeat Ed's intention and thus quench the light in a different dimension.

Significantly, this metastory about the conversation at the Elderhostel performance with emphasis on the audience's responding laughter has become an essential part of the story about the light. Including this episode enables Eldreth to voice her critical statement quite overtly while pretending that she is simply quoting a cute, funny remark that she happened to make on one occasion. The audience's laughter—that reported in the story and that evoked by each new telling of the story—is an important component that accomplishes two rhetorical goals simultaneously. In one sense it helps to mask Eldreth's critical intent; if people laughed at the original comment and still laugh when she reports it, it cannot have been too threatening. Note, however, that Eldreth very carefully cultivates this response by framing the statement as a mere throwaway line. Here Eldreth employs a strategy—common in the efforts of women and other oppressed groups to give covert expression to ideas that the dominant group would not tolerate if overtly expressed—that Radner and Lanser label "trivialization." She employs "a form, mode, or genre that the dominant culture considers to be unimportant, innocuous, or irrelevant" and hence inherently unthreatening (1993:19).

Eldreth also cannily exploits the difference between her former and present audiences. The cultural tourism in which festival and Elderhostel audiences engage offers her (like many performers transforming their material to appeal to tourists) an opportunity to include different messages than she would for local listeners (E. Cohen 1988). Mountain neighbors and grandchildren took the possibility of haunting seriously and could honestly be frightened, if simultaneously entertained, by the stories. The conventionally well-educated, nonlocal people who make up her current public audiences may enjoy the chill of a well-told ghost story, but they are also prone to laugh off that feeling in order to confirm their disbelief. Although Eldreth would absolutely reject their lack of belief, she encourages that laughter and turns it to her purposes. In telling "Light in the Bedroom," she manages to mobilize her audiences to laugh not only at her witty remark—"He wasn't that protective over me when he was living"—but also at her husband, about whom the remark is made. The comment is funny in being unexpected. If the husband of an evidently virtuous woman shows up as a ghost, it should be to protect and watch over her.[6] Eldreth's audiences may not believe that she sees ghosts, and they probably know little of her married life; but if they laugh at her story, then a whole roomful of intelligent adults has effectively confirmed that Ed Eldreth did not fulfill his marital responsibilities. Audience response is crucial to the dynamic of this story; the laughter provides the only closure possible. Eldreth cannot actually get rid of the light; she has exhausted the techniques she knows about for banishing it to no avail and has resolved herself to wait until it goes away. She cannot entirely keep the light from frightening her, and she cannot even openly articulate what she thinks is happening. She can, however, beat her husband at the game she perceives him to be playing. He is trying to get revenge on her and to scare her out of her precious house. She can strengthen her own resolve and prevent the light from having too severe an effect on her if she can get other people, through their confirming laughter, to agree with her that Ed was in the wrong in the past and that she is a good person, while he was not.

CONCLUSIONS

Ghosts are inherently ambiguous, and therein lies their power. Neither fully present nor fully absent, they keep us from forgetting things we ought to remember and things it would be better to forget. They may represent the alternative that we can recuperate in order to challenge a hegemony—or the stubborn

vestiges of a hegemony—that we seek to banish. They are strange and challenging and frightening. Over the course of her life, Eldreth has developed narrative
means of making sense and use of her ghosts in order to bolster her precarious
social position. Ghosts that speak of women's exploitation and cry out for justice
are so threatening that she can just barely give them a hearing, although she does
not banish them entirely. Those that offer the power of knowledge to a person
who will take the smaller risk of admitting her sensitivity she welcomes more
openly.

The experiences of "Light in the Bedroom" present Eldreth with an unprece-
dented narrative task. She is convinced that the repeated appearance of the light
constitutes a haunting, not a premonition, but there is no one else who has
greater knowledge of what has happened in her own house than she does and
consequently no one to turn to for an explanation. If the event is to be made
meaningful, Eldreth herself must make that meaning. This is what happened
with her premonition experiences, but in those cases Eldreth had an ally. She
dared to take interpretation into her own hands—and even to defy her husband
when he tried to deny that the experiences were meaningful—because she felt
she had a strong, benevolent supernatural force behind her. In the premonition
stories Eldreth acts on the basis of her own impressions, conclusions, and interpretations, thus treating this intuitive, women's understanding as a valid form of
knowledge. But because she is buoyed along by benevolent supernatural support,
she is not required fully to acknowledge that that is what she is doing.

The experience of the light in her bedroom requires Eldreth to take that last
risky step. Here the supernatural apparition reverts to its old, frightening, senseless form. The light must be a manifestation of her husband's not-necessarily-
friendly ghost, rather than a benevolent supernatural force sent to warn, protect,
and aid her. Yet unlike in her other ghost experiences, in this case she has more
extensive knowledge of relevant prior events than anyone else. The onus for
interpreting the experience falls on her, and she must acknowledge that interpretation as her own. The ghost stories and the premonition stories have been
constructed in terms of opposed ideologies: "women must be tightly controlled
within patriarchal gender roles or evil will result" versus "women have valid
knowledge and the right both to act upon it and to defend it against male
doubts." Thus, her ghost stories condemn unruly women and elevate Eldreth herself in contrast as obedient and self-sacrificing, while in her premonition stories—where supernatural forces support rather than threaten her—she justifies
and celebrates her own rare acts of defying her husband and proving him wrong.
The ghost stories concede, even declare, that it is wrong for women to think,
choose, and act on their own initiative, whereas the premonition stories insist
upon the validity of women's independent reasoning from their own experiences.
Eldreth has evidently been able to keep these ideas separate in her mind by
restricting them to different discourses in differently structured story types. With
"Light in the Bedroom" the two narrative structures collide and with them the

dominant discourses and inherent ideologies of each type. Eldreth is trying to tell a story of her own ghost experience, but she finds herself constrained to use something more like the premonition story structure. The resulting process of reexamining generic expectations and renegotiating the fit between content and form appears to precipitate in Eldreth's mind a similar reexamination of the ideological underpinnings of the two story types. This process is neither fully conscious nor articulated in explicit ideological statements. The narrative produced, however, provides evidence of the kind of growth resulting from perceptions of discourse conflict that the model of nonunitary, discursively constituted subjectivity predicts (Hollway 1984; Weedon 1997).

Eldreth's marriage to an irresponsible and unkind husband exposed her in an extreme degree to the abuses inherent in a cultural system that expects women to submit to men simply because of the gender difference. A patriarchal society positions women so that their hegemonic formation and their life experience are likely to be odds: the rewards promised to women for compliance with the system are rarely as great as those that perceptive women recognize are being withheld and accorded to men. It is fully to be expected that a woman for whom the contrast was especially stark should feel motivated to invest both in conventional definitions of good and bad behavior for women and in vehicles for fighting back against specific gender-based abuses and that she would consequently need to develop a discursive and structural system for compartmentalizing opposing ideas. The example of Eldreth's supernatural repertoire also demonstrates, however, that a system developed to deny contradiction and to contain its power also sets up the conditions for comparing new, unclassified experiences against the range of models and structures through which particular kinds of experiences have been expressed. "Light in the Bedroom," the culmination of Eldreth's ghost-story repertoire, reveals in detail how the opportunity to compare and choose between alternatives in a structural and discursive system can result in a new expressive form and an accompanying movement in gendered self-definition. Ghosts, to the extent that they offer unsettling alternatives to the status quo, represent a hope for change, a hope for a different future.

Still, it is important to remember that Eldreth continues to tell all of these stories and that the transformation I identify in "Light in the Bedroom" is only a part of her ongoing narrative self-construction. The conservative (and, from my point of view, deeply counterproductive) representation of herself as virtuous in the ghost stories continues to be as valuable and appealing to her as the direct representation of herself as empowered in the premonition stories. Few listeners, hearing a handful of stories in a performance, are probably even aware of the change over the course of her lifetime that I have traced. Furthermore, the framing of these accounts within the genre of entertaining "ghost stories"—a label encouraged by folklorists but proposed and happily accepted by Eldreth—serves further to trivialize or distract from their potentially controversial subject matter. These stories are as much about male-female relations and the shaping of gendered identity as they are about ghosts and premonitions. During her husband's life-time, they served as thoroughly camouflaged ways of exploring not only her supernatural experiences but also the intolerable stresses of her life as a woman and the unfairness of having to obey and serve a man far less hardworking and moral than she was. That even years after his death she still feels comfortable addressing these issues only in an oblique and deniable form exemplifies the recursive nature of self-construction and the consequent near impossibility of complete self-transformation. Ghosts are frightening; it is not easy to tell allies from enemies. As a feminist reader, I regret that Eldreth does not recognize the maltreated women as her ghostly sisters or banish her husband in more-than-symbolic terms; but I acknowledge the courage she has exercised in dealing with what are, after all, *her* ghosts.

6

"I'm a bad one to go pulling jokes on people"
Practical Joking as a Problematic Vehicle for
Oppositional Self-Definition

To those with whom I have shared Eldreth's stories, she often comes across as a tragic figure, unappreciated, trapped in a loveless marriage, struggling for subsistence and respect. Despite or perhaps even because of the hardships she has faced, however, she is also an inveterate practical joker and gleefully self-identifies as a person who loves to "go pulling jokes on people." In order to portray her accurately, as I believe she would have herself seen, it is thus crucial to include an account of these pranks.[1] Still, her joking puts me as ethnographer in a bind. Eldreth herself clearly regards the practical jokes as (mostly) harmless fun and likes to perform and to talk about them (even some that in her view went too far) as evidence of the irrepressible and joyous side of her character. I, in contrast, dislike practical joking and have great difficulty finding anything amusing in causing another person discomfort or distress, even in supposed fun. The jokes that Eldreth has pulled since I have known her, I have to admit, are relatively harmless—starting to slide past someone sitting in the church pew and then startling the person by plopping herself down on a lap or pretending to drop a full glass or a plate of food just before the person to whom she is handing it gets a grip on it. The jokes she describes from the past, however, often involve what strikes me as real cruelty, not only to other adults, but even to children, and several stories describe her use of a disparaging blackface disguise. Still, I recorded these stories during my early fieldwork, when I felt that I had to repress any negative reaction to the things Eldreth told me and so never told her that I was dismayed at her actions and implied attitudes. This means both that I allowed her to position me (though I realized it with horror only much later) as a listener who apparently agreed with opinions I in fact reject and that I never gave her a chance to respond. It is, however, at least clear to me (from her response to reactions I failed to suppress) that she probably sees my distaste for practical joking as a middle-class affectation, a lack of a sense of humor coupled with a failure to grasp the emotional and physical toughness of people whose lives included so much hard work. Ultimately, I would argue, an analysis of Eldreth's practical joking must be conflicted. I believe that joking to some extent momentarily allowed her to slip free from the requirement to be a constantly self-monitoring perfect daughter, mother, wife, or good Christian lady. To an even greater extent than in her ghost stories, however, in search of her rhetorical goals Eldreth grasps at whatever tactical resources are available and is thus complicit in victimizing—actually or symbolically—those few persons who were in an even weaker social position than she was.

I as newcomer was not immune from Eldreth's joking, but even the funniest story I can tell—one in which I was the accidental prankster but still did not get the last laugh—reveals the tension between Eldreth and me over the matter. One afternoon when I stopped by her house, Eldreth was not feeling well. Quite uncharacteristically, she was sitting still in the living room rather than bustling around, cleaning house or cooking. She even acquiesced in my offer to make her a cup of tea. The jar of tea mix was sitting where I always found it, next to the coffee pot on the kitchen counter, but I had to search the cupboards for the sugar canister. When I brought Eldreth the cup, she took one sip and burst out laughing. I had brought her tea "sweetened" with a heaping teaspoonful of salt! She seemed equally delighted by my demonstration of incompetence in the kitchen, my having played a joke on her, even inadvertently, and my discomfort at both, which meant that I had simultaneously played a joke on myself. My horrified apology just amused her more and gave her the chance to tease me, pointing out that I was indeed "sorry" in the local sense of being inept.

THE PROBLEMATICS OF PRACTICAL JOKING

Practical jokes are "enactments of playful deceit in which one party . . . intentionally manipulates features of a situation in such a way as to induce another person . . . to have a false or misleading sense of what is going on and so to behave in a way that brings about discomfiture . . . in the victim" (Bauman 1986:36). The successful joke depends upon the creation of a "fabrication," "a nefarious design . . . leading—when realized—to a falsification of some part of the world" (Goffman 1974:83). Practical joking necessarily walks a fine line between cleverness and cruelty, acceptability and bad taste, stretching the bonds of friendship and breaking them. Richard Tallman distinguishes "benevolent" from "malevolent" pranks on the basis of intention but notes that in either case misunderstanding will lead to the opposite effect from that intended (1974:264).

And Richard Bauman and Erving Goffman situate all practical jokes as part of the larger category of "routines of victimization," emphasizing that even those that may be considered "benign," in that the victim is not seriously injured, use the victim's distress as the source of humor (Bauman 1986:36; Goffman 1974:87). Even at its best, practical joking involves a "release from suppressed tensions" (Tallman 1974:260) and may contain an element of hostility, all the more distressing because the victim is under pressure to show she is a good sport by not getting mad and by acknowledging the cleverness of the prank (Bauman 1986). Ideally, a benevolent joke will actually strengthen or at least not damage the friendship between those who survive it (and this seems to have been the case in the stories Eldreth tells), but the most reportable accounts, in Eldreth's case as in Bauman's study of masterful practical jokers (1986), seem to be the ones that really did go beyond the bounds of taste or even safety.

Additionally, joking is a prime area for inversion and deception, for pretending to be other than you are or hiding who you really are or both. Thus, to an even greater extent than the ghost stories, Eldreth's jokes allow her to enact facets of her self that she does not find it easy, appropriate, or perhaps even possible to explore overtly. On the one hand, the joking frame facilitates protective denial—"That's not really me; I was just joking"—and thus permits the joker temporarily to inhabit proscribed roles. On the other hand, however, joking tends to reveal assumptions about self and other so apparently obvious as not to require explicit mention. In playing "the other," the actor demonstrates by contrast who she most deeply feels she is. These two opposed tendencies can operate simultaneously, making the interpretation of joking complicated and indeterminate. Still, this kind of playing around is a crucial component of the constitution of subjectivity because it incorporates aspects of the self that contradict or hide behind the predominant, socially acceptable face. Furthermore, as with many other facets of her experience, I know about Eldreth's practical joking mostly through her own accounts. Eldreth stopped engaging in the kinds of joking to which I most strenuously object—blackface impersonations and activities so dangerous that, as she herself says, "we had to cut that out"—decades before I met her. She still talks about those events, however, so I am left to interpret both the jokes themselves and the import of her stories about them in her dialogue with me.

Practical joking has been a part of Eldreth's experience throughout her life. Her participation displays significant parallels with her ghost experiences and serves like them as a barometer of the degree of pressure she was under. She was introduced to the practice as a child through others' activities or accounts thereof, and joking at this stage appears, if not exactly harmless, not to have had lasting negative effects on the victims. The stories she still tells of this period, however, depict only two categories of acceptable victims—family members and black neighbors. Eldreth begins to participate intentionally in joking as a young marriageable woman. Her early jokes are, in fact, connected to the ghost experiences that start during the same period of her life. The jokes she plays as a teenager and as a young married woman, however, are almost out of control and have potentially dangerous outcomes or long-lasting deleterious consequences. She learns to throttle back her jokes to avoid such negative impact, but those she perpetrates as an adult nevertheless reflect serious strains in her assigned female role and in the social fabric. Many of them entail a momentary refusal or reversal of expectations laid on her as a woman, specifically her role as a nurturer. The more elaborate, planned jokes often involve Eldreth disguising herself in blackface, simultaneously engaging in a denigrating portrayal of a black person and using the power of a figure whom she knows the joke victims will distrust or fear to further her agenda. Pretending, teasing, and inverting roles can be a lot of fun and a source of salutary laughter in Eldreth's life, but joking is not only a joking matter.

CHILDHOOD

Although there are many contexts in which traditional practical jokes are perpetrated on successive generations (of college students, campers, workplace novices, and the like), the jokes that tend to be judged most skillful are unique and context dependent, falsifying some aspect of the immediate and specific world in which victim and perpetrator operate. What Eldreth learned from the models to which she was exposed as a child was not specific repeatable jokes, but the skill of devising a joke appropriate to the situation at hand.

The stories Eldreth tells about jokes she observed or heard about as a child are highly variable in terms of situation, means, and both the identities of and the relations between trickster and dupe. One involved the men who worked at a local sawmill and took their meals with a neighbor of the Killens family. On one notable occasion as she poured coffee for her boarders, this elderly woman inadvertently grabbed the cup in which she had deposited her false teeth. The man sitting next to her noticed, but elected not to stop her, and passed the cup with the teeth in the bottom of it to one of his fellows to drink. Another involved Eldreth's brother, Joe, who, one day when they were out working in the woods, managed to "get Dad in a bees' nest." Since his laughter gave him away as the perpetrator, he paid for the joke by receiving a whipping from his father. A third involved her grandmother Milam, who kept bees and, while removing the honey one time, found some of the "bee bread" that was prized for eating unless, as in this instance, it was spoiled by having "young bees" in it. Grandma Milam nevertheless gave that bee bread to two young "colored girls," playmates of Eldreth's mother, who did not know any better.

All three of these childhood joke accounts entail cleverness on the part of the trickster, an ability to recognize and immediately act upon an opportunity for playing a joke that is presented to them. Eldreth presents all three as motivated more by the desire to pull off a good joke than by any established enmity toward the victim. She even treats the story of Joe causing their father (whom she adored) to receive multiple bee stings as a funny joke. And although Joe got spanked, the incident evidently caused no permanent rupture between father and son. Still, it is hard not to bring different interpretations to joking between adult male coworkers, children challenging the power of an adult, and, conversely, a white adult preying upon the relative ignorance of a black child. Indeed, Eldreth seems to sense that the racial issue is delicate. She made a point of disclaiming any enmity: "Momma played with these two little colored girls a lot. Grandma Milam and their mother was good friends." And she went on to tell another "funny story" about "the night the cat got into the molasses barrel," ending with a report that her grandmother had given the spoiled molasses to another "colored woman" they called Aunt Liza Weddington to feed to her hogs. Nevertheless, her grandmother's story did arguably model for Eldreth the idea that it could be funny to victimize not only one's peers (like the workmates in the false teeth story) or those more powerful (like Joe's father) but also children and people more vulnerable than oneself. I find myself put in the same emotional place by the story about the "colored girls" as by Eldreth's account of jumping into the creek to save her niece. She reveals that some blacks and whites had reasonably neighborly relations in Ashe Country. In the very same breath, however, she both demonstrates that her grandparents probably assumed that their black neighbors were inferior and tries to defend them against that charge. And it is difficult to know to what extent her defensive portrayal of Grandma Milam might reflect a desire to distance herself from the attitudes her grandmother presumably held and to what extent it simply anticipates an objection Eldreth expected me to feel—although, like Eldreth herself when she disapproves of something, I did not voice it at the time.

On a happier note, I also observed that in telling these stories Eldreth tends to mix accounts of what one can clearly label intentional practical jokes with reports of other incidents that just turned out to be funny. Some of these incidents, like my mistake with the cup of tea, could be construed as instances of people inadvertently playing a joke on themselves.

> Let me tell you this 'un. This is sorta bad, in a sense.
>
> My Dad and Uncle Bill Milam was a-going to | was a-moving with a yoke of cattle and on a sled. See, we didn't have trucks and things back then. And, you know, when you get cattle together they just seesaw. One'll seesaw this way and the other'll seesaw *this* a-way. And they pull against one another so bad, that they're in the road.
>
> And Dad—I guess I got a whole lot of my old foolishness from Dad; I know I did—he said | he told Uncle Bill, he said, "I'll tell you," he said, "we ain't going to get where we're moving to. Hit's going to be dark," he said, "I want to get them cattle a move on. And he walked out in the [laughs] woods a little ways and got some chestnut burrs. [. . .] And the silly thing, he, uh, he put these chestnut burrs under them oxen's tails.

And they run away! They | when they got to where them | where they got the cattle stopped, they didn't have one *piece* of furniture on the sled. They had to go . . . [laughs]. And the way that them cattle got stopped—now, young'uns, this is the truth—they way they got stopped, they run, you know, they run off that mountain, they run | a tree caught under the yoke and divided them on each side.

And they | instead of getting there before dark, they had to pick up furniture [listeners laugh] and put in on the sled. So it was | it was late, sure enough, when they got to where that they's going. He thought that he'd get a move on. Well, he did. He got a move on.

Similarly, once when the family lived in Virginia, Eldreth and Joe were sent to the store to try to sell some eggs. When the owner told them he would not pay cash but would trade for merchandise, Eldreth thought of a treat she liked and responded, "I'll take mine out in prunes." Only subsequently, when Joe teased her, did she realize that her instant response could be interpreted as an embarrassing request for a laxative. And other accounts, like the story of the cat in the molasses, simply take amusement in peoples' discomfiture even though it was not caused by anyone's intentional action.

In all these instances, the people inconvenienced appear to have appreciated the humor in their own situation. When she narrates these stories, Eldreth and her listeners laugh *with* as much as *at* those who suffered. And note that even though Romey Killens presumably did not intend to play a joke, least of all on himself, Eldreth mentions his decision to put the burrs under the tails of the oxen as a model for her own practical joking: "I guess I got a whole lot of my old foolishness from Dad; I know I did." Overall, my sense is that the funny stories from her childhood, intentional practical-joke stories included, contribute to Eldreth's effort to portray her childhood as largely a joyful time. People did not have easy lives, but they punctuated their labors with laughter. They could see the funny side to some of their travails, laughed at themselves when they had made their own problems, and kept an eye open for an opportunity to make something to laugh at. Practical jokes, as she initially learned about them, seem largely motivated by a desire for humor, although no one was in the least hesitant to take advantage of an opportunity for humor generated at someone's expense.

MARRIAGEABLE GIRLS

As we have seen in the previous two chapters, a lot of things changed in Eldreth's life once she began to be considered marriageable by herself and others. Practical joking, too, takes on a new valence during this period of her life and is significantly connected to both the changes in forms of talk among women and the initiation of her ghost experiences. Grandma Milam's bee-bread story, among other effects, had evidently suggested to her granddaughters that practical joking was an acceptable activity for women as well as men. As teenagers, however, Eldreth and her sister Clyde turn the jokes on each other in cruel and potentially dangerous ways.

Well, me and Clyde always took it turn about a-building fires, you know. Well, I built 'em most of the time, 'cause she didn't like to get up and it be real cold weather, you know? And she'd stay in the bed till last and I'd just get up to not argue with her.

So [. . .] one evening, late, I went upstairs and clumb up on a chair to hide some love letters I'd got, you know, stick 'em up the garret, we called it. And while I was standing up there in that chair, a steel trap—now hit *wasn't* no steel trap—but a steel | the sound of a steel trap fell out of that garret at my feet. And I looked and there wasn't nary'un there. I looked all around and there wasn't a sign of a steel trap there. But it was just like, you know, one fall down at you. But hit | it wasn't, it was the sound and all.

Well, I run downstairs just a-flying. Momma said, "Well, what was you a-doing up in the garret?" And I didn't tell her. I said, "I's just standing up in a chair." But I didn't tell her I's hiding my love letters.

And the next morning, Clyde had to get up and build the fire; I aggravated her that morning, said she had to get up and build the fire. And they was about thirteen steps . . . from the top of that step, you know, down to the bottom. And she knowed I told Momma about [. . .] the steel trap falling. And, I was a nervous wreck, I's scared so bad. And the next morning 'cause she had to build the fire she slipped and hunted up a steel trap . . . and throwed it back in under my bed.

And, young'un, I jumped out of that bed and I never hit step one. I jumped to the bottom. I *jumped* to the bottom. It could a killed me. But I didn't take time to run down the steps. I jumped to the bottom of that | of them steps. And I's a-crying like everything.

And Momma said, "What've you'uns been into?" And Clyde said, uh, "Momma, I just throwed a steel trap in under her bed." And Momma said, "Well, you ought to've knowed better than to throwed a steel trap in under her bed," said, "after she heard that steel trap fall from that garret."

And, uh, so we kindly got over that. And we had the habit of moving the beds, you know. We'd now, like this, we didn't | we just had lamp light. Well, we'd go to bed after dark, you know, but we wouldn't, uh, didn't have lights to turn on. So one night one would move the bed over here. Next night we'd have it somewhere else, in some other corner. So I run and give a leap to beat her to bed and I hit in the corner; they wasn't no bed there. Hit right on my knees. Boys, it hurt. And I was going to beat her to bed, you know; we'd scare one another when we'd go to bed.

Well, I thought, "I'll get that back on you." So the next day I didn't move the bed; I left the bed a-setting. But I had a big old . . . fur, you know, come way down my back and fastened, it looked like a . . . mouth here where it snapped in front. I went upstairs and I made the bed and I turned the cover down. And I put that in the bed, just plum down in the bed and up on the | and its head up on the pillow. And then I covered it back up. Clyde she went just a-flying to get into bed and right in on that she went. She throwed the covers down. Aaah! I'm a tell you the truth, I thought she was going to jump the banisters. She come downstairs like a *wild* cat; she's a-*screaming* . . . at the top of her *voice*. She just about had a *night*mare.

And Mom said, "What are you young'uns a-doing?" And, boys, I's afraid to tell, that time, I's just | stood there and watched Clyde. And that young'un | we never went to bed till about two or three o'clock the next morning. And she stood there afraid to *move*. And, you wouldn't believe it, she blistered her legs a-standing— behind, you know?—a-standing so close to the fire. And she blistered her legs. And she was afraid to *move* from that *fire*. I mean, away from the | she was just scared to death. And I scared her like that 'cause that she scared me with the steel trap.

We used to scare one another, just about scare one another to death, when we | when we's—tell ghost stories; all get in a big bunch and tell ghost stories. And I'd try my best to get in the middle. We had a lot of fun, though.

In the two previous chapters we have noted that both Eldreth's sensitivity to ghosts and her pattern of competitive miscommunication with other women emerged at the point in her life when she began to be perceived as a sexual being, a person whose identity is significantly determined by her gender. In this story those two matters—ghosts and miscommunication—coincide. These events transpired in the Doctor Graham house, where Mary Black killed her twins. Eldreth sometimes tells this story of reciprocal joking with Clyde as a stand-alone incident, but sometimes (as in this rendition) she includes it as one of several episodes of encounters with ghostly manifestations in that house. Even though her parents will shortly encourage her to get married, Eldreth (as suggested in the discussion of the young women's miscommunication in chapter 4) does not seem to have been provided with any productive way of handling her emerging sexuality, her new social identity, and the attention she is receiving from men. She understandably wants some privacy but also seems ashamed. She looks for a place to hide her love letters, the evidence of her new sexual identity, and although she cannot conceal her fright from her mother, she refuses to explain what she was doing up in the garret. The distinctive sound of a steel trap falling, although there is no trap to be found, strikes Eldreth as convincing evidence of a haunting. Later in her life, as we have seen, her perceptions of specific recognizable sounds will prove a resource in negotiations with her husband regarding the ghosts. In this early instance, however, the sound terrifies her and reinforces her sense of the shamefulness of her romantic and sexual interests.

As in the other stories of Eldreth's interactions with her sister during this period, Clyde responds, not with sympathy, but in a competitive spirit, taking advantage of Eldreth's vulnerability to play a practical joke on her. And Eldreth responds with a joke of her own. Eldreth insists that they "had a lot of fun" playing these jokes on each other, and their tendency to reciprocate, to "get one back" on the other, is often a hallmark of a benevolent joking relationship (Smith

1990:79). Still, these young women are emotionally sensitive and high strung. (Eldreth describes herself as "a nervous wreck" after her encounter with the ghostly trap.) In contrast to earlier jokes aimed primarily at embarrassing people or making them look foolish, from this point forward one of the things Eldreth seems to find funniest is giving people a shock, frightening the victim in a way that produces a strong visceral reaction. Furthermore, as only incipient adults they seem not to have good judgment about the possible effects of their pranks. Eldreth leaps down the entire stairway and in retrospect judges, "It could a killed me." Clyde almost vaults over the banister and is so terrified that she cannot move from in front of the fireplace even though her legs are getting burnt. The presence in this story of the girls' mother is notable. She intervenes periodically to ask what is happening but is satisfied when her daughters refuse to explain. Eldreth seems to be reminding us that their mother was there as a guarantor of their safety. They could not really be seriously hurt with her watching. At the same time, Flora Killens leaves her daughters to sort out both their competitive joking and the anxieties over their emerging sexuality on their own. These are not the sort of classic initiatory practical jokes (for example, the fool's errand) with which youngsters and newcomers may be welcomed into a group (Tallman 1974:264). The presence of practical joking during this transitional period suggests, rather, that the girls are left to initiate each other into womanhood as best they can. In contrast to classic initiates, they neither feel secure in their new identities nor form a cohort bond upon which to rely for future support.

Understanding these practical jokes as an extension of the sisters' competition for male attention and related miscommunication during this part of their lives also sheds further light on Eldreth's attitude toward her marriage. We can now recognize that her successful attempt to steal Ed from Clyde was a move in this escalating spiral of practical jokes. Indeed, it turned out to be the final move, because it backfired when her mother expected her to stop playing around and actually take on her adult role by becoming a wife. The result was the tragedy of her being put into a position where she felt she had to accede to her mother's wishes and marry Ed, even though she did not love him. Was her inability to protest her mother's plan another instance of reluctance to explain the destructive consequences of a joke? Many factors induced Eldreth's resignation to staying with her husband, most importantly the seriousness she ascribed to her wedding vows, made to God as well as to her husband. I wonder, however, if she had not also internalized a sort of trickster's honor, according to which you must accept the consequences of the joke you have perpetrated, even if you end up being your own victim.

MOTHERLY (?) JOKING AND WHITE PRIVILEGE

Even if her marriage was in some sense a joke gone horribly wrong, or perhaps because she continued to be victimized by the very success of that final girlhood joke, Eldreth has persisted in playing jokes on family and neighbors throughout her adult life. For a feminist analyst, these produce a deeply conflicted reading. I believe that Eldreth has used the deniable power of joking briefly to slip free of the onerous expectations she faced as a woman and perhaps even to enact a coded critique of her position. In so doing, however, she made use of whatever resources were available to a person with minimal social capital of her own, victimizing children and mimicking African Americans in unflattering ways. As Margaret Mills argues, it is one of the strengths of folklife studies to give us "some chance of conceptualizing what 'feels real' (pain, marginalization, the intransigence of prejudice both as suffered and as thought)" (1993:185). In Eldreth's jokes we witness simultaneously her response to prejudice she suffered as a woman and the prejudice she herself "thought" about those relative to whom she could claim some social privilege.

Eldreth's adult joking interactions with family and friends fall into two categories. The kind I witnessed seem modeled on the jokes she relates from childhood in that they involve taking advantage of instantaneous natural opportunities and momentarily subverting the normal, expected flow of social interaction in familiar, domestic settings, although she often mobilizes techniques she has used repeatedly. As described earlier, at church, sliding into the place in the pew that she always occupies, she will startle a neighbor by stopping short and sitting down suddenly on the woman's lap. In her kitchen, reaching out to offer a plate of food or glass of milk, she pretends to lose her grip, inducing the recipient to react in a sudden attempt to catch the "dropped" food, although Eldreth has in fact never lost control. These pranks I have both experienced and heard her describe in generalization narratives about the kinds of things she is prone to do. But she is clearly capable of devising entirely new jokes in response to a novel situation. In the middle of a trip to town to do errands, she reports, a daughter and granddaughter came back to the car to find her eating a piece of what they thought was chocolate candy. They asked her to share, and she obligingly dosed them with Ex-Lax!

The other, more premeditated form of joking always, in her report, involves Eldreth's disguising herself or others in blackface. Significantly, she told a whole string of stories together about incidents that must have happened over a period of twenty or thirty years.

BE: We's good at scaring one another. We got a kick out of that. We used to black our
       faces, go places.
PS: Tell me about that.
BE: That was after I got married. Me and my sister'd black our faces just as black as a
       coal and put on overalls and an old hat and go up the road a-walking. And the
       neighbors'd just fly [laughs]. They didn't know us. They got to running, run from
       us. And Maud, well, the way she got I that they caught up with her is she laughed,
       and they knowed her smile, you know, when they started to run from her. But we's

all the time pulling pranks on people. Well, we just had a good time a-doing things like that, playing, and everything.

One evening I blacked Lorene's face, my oldest daughter, just black as a coal, and her first cousin. And then I hid 'em, put 'em in under the bed, hid 'em back in under the bed? And told one of Maud's boys to go in there and get me out from under the bed? Get my *shoes*. That's what I told him, I said, "Go in and bring my shoes." And then I set some chairs kindly in the way. And that young'un, he come out of there just a-screaming. Scared that boy to death. And, boys, we got the scare of our lives then. He took towards the mountain. And we didn't know how we was going to get him back. We finally told him it was them girls a-scaring him.

And Lorene's first cousin, she didn't know, you know, that we's a-doing things like that. Anyway, they walked to the door, to her sister's, and knocked at the door. And she come to the door. And both them standing there blacker'n a coal and them old hats on and overalls. And she fainted, it scared her [laughs]. We had to quit some of that. We scared people so bad they couldn't stand that. But now we was getting a lot of fun out of that.

I blacked my face as black as a coal and went to—down at Todd, I guess that's been about fifteen or sixteen year ago—put on overalls and an old hat and went to a Halloween party they's having at the schoolhouse. And Leslie Norris come down through there. I went up through that yard a-singing: "For a long time this wul [world] has stood. It gets more wicked evwy [every] day," like a colored person, you know? And he come down through there and he said, "I thought I'd come down here and unlock the door. I had to unlock the door." And he thought we's colored. And it was getting dark, too, you know. He couldn't a told. And I got tickled and I laughed. And he said, "I'm a-telling you, I knowed we hadn't invited no colored people tonight." And he said, "I come down here just a purpose to see just what colored people *was* here."

In his study of blackface minstrelsy, Eric Lott argues:

> So officially repugnant now are the attitudes responsible for blackface joking that the tendency has been simply to condemn the attitudes themselves—a suspiciously respectable move, and an easy one at that—rather than to investigate the ways in which racist entertainment was once fun, and still is to much of the Caucasian population of the United States. (1993:141)

Following Lott's example, it seems valuable to me to try to resist this kind of collapse in understanding Eldreth's joking. Our challenge, then, is to hold in mind simultaneously both the pleasure and utility Eldreth found in these masquerades and her willingness to invest in stereotyping disparagement of African Americans in order to secure those gains for herself. In so doing, we can see her use of blackface not (simply) as the expression of a preexisting racist attitude but as a crucial component of her effort to negotiate anxieties around her own social position, which is cast in terms of gender and class as well as race (see Lott 1993:6).

A preliminary question is where Eldreth got the idea of engaging in blackface disguise. None of her childhood stories mention it, although that does not necessarily mean that she never saw her parents or others "black their faces" for a costume or joke. The material for creating this disguise was readily available and free—Eldreth described it as "just pure black from the caps of a wood cookstove." But I wonder to what extent she was generating her own depiction of African American neighbors—we know there were a few from one story, probably dating to the 1930s, in which she describes helping to lay out a woman in the community who had died—and to what extent she was emulating stereotypes of other blackface performances.

I find no direct evidence in Eldreth's song repertoire of familiarity with blackface minstrel shows, an entertainment form on the wane by the 1930s. She sang for me only seven songs with any kind of African American connection. Four are spirituals, two ("My Lord, What a Morning" and "Were You There When They Crucified My Lord?") popularized by Marion Anderson, one ("No Hiding Place Down Here") sung by one of Eldreth's favorite sources, the Carter Family, and one ("Mary, Mary, What You Gonna Call That Baby?") that I suspect Eldreth and her granddaughter learned from students at Mars Hill College, who sang it during a shared performance in the late 1970s. Secular songs with African American connections are "Old Cotton Fields Back Home," popularized by Leadbelly and the Weavers, and "I'm Sitting on Top of the World," composed in 1930 by a black string band called the Mississippi Sheiks, but famously sung by Jimmie Rodgers, the Carter Family, and Bob Wills. A Civil War era song, "No More the Moon Shines on Lorena," made enough of an impression on Eldreth that she used a version of the name in the title for her eldest daughter. Bill Malone describes it as a "northern-produced tune," and it is sung from the point of view of a (clearly romanticized) slave lamenting the death of his love but claiming he was happy working on the plantation until she was sold away. It could lend itself to blackface performance, but it was also apparently widely popular in the Confederacy during the Civil War (Malone and Stricklin 2003:2) and was recorded by the Carter Family and Blue Sky Boys, from whom Eldreth learned so many songs. Even the song she put (or now puts) in the mouth of her blackface character in one of her stories, "This World Can't Stand Long" ("For a long time this world has stood. It gets more wicked every day") was written by Jim Anglin, author of a number of Eldreth's other favorite songs from the 1930s, and again probably came to her from the Carter Family's rendition. Still, Eldreth's beloved Jimmie Rodgers, among other early country music stars, "routinely 'blacked up,'" and during Eldreth's young adulthood the new and newsmaking medium of movies featured blackface performances like Al Jolson's 1927 *The Jazz Singer* (Lott 1993:5). Eldreth may well have been aware of such performances. Perhaps it is simplest to recognize that the image of the blackface entertainer has been, as Eric Lott argues, "ubiquitous, cultural common coin; it has been so central to the lives of North Americans that we are hardly aware of its extraordinary influence" (1993:4) and that (as I will argue in more detail in the chapter on Eldreth's own singing) Appalachia was not nearly as isolated from such influential common images as stereotypes of the region led me to imagine.

Even in a highly race-conscious society, it is theoretically possible to engage in what Lott calls "metaphysical" blackface, representing an evil or frightening character rather than a person of African descent (1993:28). Eldreth's earliest story, of blacking the children's faces and putting them under the bed to scare the boy sent to get the shoes, might be of this sort. Her later examples, however, clearly involve none-too-flattering pretense at being an African American person. What, then, are the specific uses of the masquerade for Eldreth? Lott describes the impersonations by blackface minstrels as both "love and theft," a combination of racial insult and racial envy (1993:18). The "insult" part is easy to see. Eldreth, at least once the disguise is discovered, clearly approximates the "triangulated, derisive structure of minstrel comedy, in which blackface comic and white spectator share jokes about an absent third party" (Lott 1993:142). The "love" part is less easy to detect in Eldreth's practice, though not entirely absent. Many of the ways in which Lott suggests that blackface reveals a partially positive attitude do not apply to Eldreth. She does not call upon the symbolic power and freedom of the savage for political protest (1993:27) or reveal admiration for an African American musical form by expropriating it (1993:18) or, obviously, become involved in a white, male, homosexual fascination with the potency of the black man (1993:57–58).

What the various practical jokes, including the blackface enactments, do provide Eldreth is an opportunity to refuse for a few moments to uphold the image of the virtuous woman, to which she usually so desperately clings. Let me turn first to the issue of directing her jokes at children (or fictional children, like myself) and then return to the symbolic import of blackface specifically. In most of her stories, as we have seen in previous chapters, Eldreth goes to considerable links to depict herself as the definitive and emblematic good mother. She is the person who found ways to support her children even though her husband failed to do his part. She not only bore them, rocked them, sang to them, and cooked for them, she also grew and preserved much of their food and even repaired the substandard houses in which they were forced to live. She embodies the essence of motherly responsibility and nurturing. Yet in these jokes we find her instead preying upon children, startling them, frightening them, and laughing at their expense. As Smith notes, "people often play a particular joke on a particular person as a way of creating poetic justice or of indirectly criticizing their behavior" (1990:78). Eldreth preys on those who depend upon her, not so much to criticize them as to resist the social expectation that they embody.

It is also notable that Eldreth plays jokes *with* her sister and *on* children and neighbors but that her husband is never involved either as co-conspirator or dupe. To the extent that these interactions were intended in good fun, Ed's absence as a fellow joke player hints again at the lack of warmth in his relationship with his wife. Ed never takes the role as playmate that I have heard neighbors of Eldreth's age who had happier marriages describe with their husbands. It appears that Eldreth may never have dared to play a joke on her husband. While joking can be a means of communicating a veiled or at least deniable criticism against those more powerful and while women who have ways and opportunities for talking candidly with each other have been observed preferentially to tell and enjoy narrative jokes that are hostile to or critical of men (Mitchell 1978, 1985), Eldreth evidently sensed that it would have been much too dangerous actually to act out any such critique on her husband. Absent the kind of joking relationship that she apparently did have with both her sisters, it was presumably too likely that Ed would interpret any joke played on him as hostile and treat it as justification for serious retaliation.

Eldreth's tendency to play jokes on children strikes me as a fairly direct example of the persecuted turned persecutor. Powerless to escape—or even very overtly to protest—her own exploitation by her husband, Eldreth, in this interpretation, launches jokes against children that pass her pain and anger on to those weaker than herself. Surely there is a note of hostility in the sisters' pitting some of their children against others, setting up a joke that scares one of their sons so severely that he runs off into the night and is afraid to come back into the house. And I can attest from my own experience that Eldreth's dropped-plate ploy, which several grandchildren told me she had pulled on them, produces a startle response and a rush of adrenalin that makes it very hard to appreciate the joke with any kind of good humor. I think it is important to acknowledge, however, that Eldreth, especially as a very young mother, had a different notion of appropriate child rearing than the nurturing of the emerging psyche in which parents of my generation have been trained and that she probably had a sense of her children as sufficiently resilient emotionally to take some rough treatment. She even implicitly frames the frightening pranks as suitable means of entertaining children by similarly treating as jokes the later instances in which children got more scared than they had bargained for by stories they had actually begged her to tell:

> They said, "Aunt Bessie, will you tell us some ghost stories?" I said, "Yeah, get on in here." And I got to telling 'em ghost stories—and now some of them boys was twelve and fourteen year old—and I'm a-telling you the truth, them boys got so scared, what I was telling, them ghost stories, that you wouldn't believe it. It was 2:30 in the morning and I couldn't get them boys to go to bed. They's | I had 'em scared, you know, they's afraid. And I laid in there and laughed till I about cried. I said, "Now, young'uns, I'm going to tell you something," I said, "You look what time it is," I said, "It's 2:30." And I said, "You've got to get in the bed." "Aunt Bessie, we're afraid. Aunt Bessie, we're scared."

Ultimately, Eldreth acknowledges that she and Maud learned from their mistakes that they were being too rough on the children, "We had to quit some of that." Yet while conceding that that some recipients experienced their jokes as hostile, she does not admit that that was their intention.

It is also interesting to reflect on the apparent permissibility of this rough joking in light of the tenacity with which people in the region insist, in nonplay situations, upon the right to make their own decisions. Individuals' right to decide their own course without even suggestions from others is inviolate (Puckett 2000:169). In interactions within Eldreth's family I often observed the strong rule against telling someone else what to do, that is, assuming the right to direct another's conduct or even to attempt to influence them to do what you think is best for them.[2] It makes a wonderful kind of inverted sense that the favored kind of joking in such circumstances would involve deception and trickery that makes people react, on the basis of false information, as they would not otherwise, that is, against their will. This situation makes it seem all the more plausible to me that Eldreth's jokes are coded protests against domestic entrapment, since joking would be the only place in which critical or directive messages could be safely conveyed.

Furthermore, there is at least some possibility that Eldreth's subversion of her domestic self may communicate messages that she believes the victims of the jokes need to understand—in other words, that they are in part an indirect manifestation of good mothering in Eldreth's terms, if not in mine. These jokes, especially when directed at children or grandchildren, may in effect toughen the recipients. They may serve as a sort of productive weaning, reminding her family that their caregiver may not always be available and that they need to learn how to take care of themselves. Like the jokes played on newcomers by their elders in the industrial workplace, Eldreth's victimization of those she loves may train them to be on the lookout for falsifications and not to be "put (up)on" by those who would take advantage of them (Willis 2001:198). In practical terms, this kind of joking may thus help train the dupes in anger management. I certainly discovered, on those occasions when Eldreth pretended to drop a plate or glass that she was handing to me, that my startle response developed into surprising anger that I had to find a way to dissipate, sometimes by leaving the house and walking around in the yard to cool off, if I were to keep myself from yelling at her. Developing the capacity to respond as a good sport to disappointment and even victimization may be a crucial life skill for children who are culturally disposed against taking orders but situated by class such that they will often have to.

Symbolically, however, it does seem that Eldreth is striking a blow for a woman's freedom, refusing, if only for a moment, to do the kinds of woman's work—child care and food provision—that she has in fact done consistently for decades. Minimally, in refusing to be dependable, she raises a protest against being taken for granted. Maximally, she may be engaging in a "subversion of domesticity" (Lanser 1993), momentarily demonstrating the "incompetence at conventionally feminine activities [through which] women may be expressing their resistance to patriarchal expectations" (Radner and Lanser 1993:20). Eldreth does not dare overtly to reject the image of herself as the supremely competent provider; she has too much of her moral worth wrapped up in that discourse. Temporary incompetence, however, conveys a coded protest against the unfairness of the responsibilities she has had to shoulder and the enforced limitation of her identity to that of a domestic drudge. Even here Eldreth runs a certain risk. The performance of "women's work" is so bound up with local definitions of ethical behavior that serious nonperformance would brand her as a bad woman and therefore a bad person. Her jokes could never be construed as real incompetence, but they might be read as refusal.

Perhaps in order to mute such risk, in these jokes Eldreth enacts a persona that is effectively a parodic inversion of her usual self. Parody, notably, destabilizes, challenges, and complicates the serious image but stops short of destroying it, since it depends upon the straightforward original for its existence (Bakhtin 1981:55). Eldreth thus challenges and momentarily frees herself from the dedication and even self-sacrifice to home and children that have been expected of her as a woman, yet in the same instant reminds us of how faithfully she has in fact fulfilled her maternal obligations. She is simultaneously the perfect mother and her antithesis.

All practical jokes depend upon setting up a false situation that is taken as true, then discrediting that fabrication. In order to be plausible, the fabrication has to correspond to a considerable degree with the victim's expectations of something that could ordinarily happen. The joker thus pretends that life is going along in a normal way and can be interpreted according to the usual frames. Only when the joke is sprung does the victim learn that that joker has been manipulating things under the surface to foster an appearance of normalcy and reality when the situation is far from normal or real. These jokes of Eldreth's are especially fascinating in that they enact a sort of double reverse. The first move is to suggest to the startled victim that Eldreth's ordinary persona was the fabrication. The reliable, giving, motherly supplier of food and person who takes care of you momentarily appears to have been a false image. For a split second the "real" Eldreth seems instead to be the person who drops food instead of feeding you, scares instead of nurtures you, and gives you unnecessary drugs (and diarrhea) instead of candy. She seems, briefly, to discredit as a fabrication precisely the image of herself that in most other situations she is most careful to build up and insist upon. A moment later she reverses the image again, revealing that the new "truth" was the fabrication and what first seemed a fabrication is indeed true.

But what of the blackface enactments specifically? How is race play connected to the anxieties over gender roles and class standing that seem to predominate in Eldreth's self-construction? At the simplest level, when Eldreth dons this disguise (in contrast to simply, say, pretending to drop a plate), she engages in a full, deceptive performance, trying to get people to perceive her as an African American person and, evidently, briefly succeeding. Playing this fictional part, like performing a song, allows her temporarily to slip out of the repressive and otherwise constant requirement to perform herself as a respectable woman. Devoting herself to intentional performance of any kind enables her to relax the vigilant attention to the performance of her usual self that her tenuous social standing otherwise demands (Sawin 2002; Butler 1990). And at some level, once her true identity is revealed, she also receives recognition for the skillfulness of her disguise. Blackface specifically, however, confers particular powers because it allows Eldreth to activate and play upon her neighbors' fear and distrust of African Americans. In Lott's terms, Eldreth displays a sort of "racial envy" by mobilizing the paradoxical influence of the hated. Instead of being ineffectual young women to whom no one need pay much attention, she and those she dresses up in blackface become powerful figures to whom people have strong conscious and unconscious reactions. One woman faints from fear when they come to her door. A neighbor is motivated to come out to confront what he believes is a threatening interloper in the community. Equally crucial, however, is the moment when Eldreth herself is recognized beneath the soot. Once the neighbor starts explaining his actions, essentially apologizing for having been suspicious of her while acknowledging the effectiveness of her disguise, he treats Eldreth as an insider, validating her identity as a valued member of the community. By enacting the role of someone she knows her neighbors will reject on racial grounds, she gets them subsequently to voice their explicit inclusion of her. She may be poor, pitied, marginally respectable, even "a little slave" (this being the community in which her pastor applied that epithet to Eldreth), but as long as she is white, she's an insider.

Eldreth's willingness to induce people to include her by drawing a race line reminds us how powerfully race and class have been intertwined in characterization of Appalachian people. The views of mountain people promulgated in the mainstream American culture have been schizophrenic but always highly racialized. Those who felt that the United States was being negatively affected by the influx of southern and eastern European immigrants in the late nineteenth century depicted mountain folks as a pool of "pure Anglo-Saxon stock." The myth was that

> Southern highlanders, who were isolated from southern black people and from the strange, foreign breeds invading northern cities, seemed to be a unique refuge for white Anglo-Saxonism. Here, in Appalachia, isolation had bred patriotism, a continuation of pioneer traditions, and a sturdy and vigorous nature. The mountaineers exuded a potential for uplift and industry, especially in light of their purer racial heritage and their minimal exposure to the degradations of slaves and the slave system. (Silber 2001:256; see also Whisnant 1983:110)

More commonly, however, middle-class observers despised mountain back-wardness and poverty and explained the supposed degeneracy and inferiority of "poor whites," "white trash," or "hillbillies" in terms of inbreeding and genetic segregation. Recall that rural poor whites were the object of study from 1880 to 1920 by the United States Eugenics Record Office. Classifying poor whites as racially distinct was crucial to others' claim of the superiority of the "white race" (Newitz and Wray 1997:2). Supposed racial difference was thus used to explain away differences based on class, that is, differential access to resources, education, or the opportunity to own property. Poor whites, in this explanation, were inherently inferior and were to blame for their own poverty. Given the extent to which Eldreth felt her moral standing was (unfairly) compromised by her continuing poverty, it is not hard to see the attraction to her of using racial division to get others to express their commonality across class lines. Like Irish immigrants in the northeast in the late nineteenth century, who pushed black workers out of certain jobs in order to create spheres of distinctive competence and lay claim to inclusion in the category "white," from which they had previously been excluded (Brodkin 1998), Eldreth differentiates herself from blacks in order to solidify her whiteness and rescue herself from the disparaged racial category "poor white," to which her class standing threatens to assign her. If the black face is a removable disguise, then the true self behind the disguise is defined as black's opposite. Eldreth's blackface enactments attempt the kind of uneasy purification that denies or represses an actual hybridity, rejecting as foreign and despised what is really part of one's own culture and society (Latour 1993). Because they depend on momentarily crossing boundaries otherwise unconsciously maintained, these jokes remind us that in everything else she does, Eldreth unconsciously enacts herself, her values, and her ways of being as white. Like the minstrel impersonations studied by Lott, blackface for Eldreth proves crucial to the solidification of an anxious, tenuously respectable white working-class identity (1993:8).

The salience of blackface in Eldreth's joking also requires us to rethink the attractive image of the mountains as distinct from the rest of the antebellum South in having few slaves and consequently being inherently less racist (another facet of the "Appalachian exceptionalism" critiqued in earlier chapters). From the earliest period of white settlement, however, "certain it is that slave labor was used in clearing the land and establishing backcountry mills, forges, and cow-pens. The value of this labor is reflected in the concern that white authorities manifested when they demanded the return of escaped or captive slaves on each occasion when Native and Euro-American differences were negotiated" (J. A. Williams 2002:47). Slaves provided much of the labor for the region's three "principal nonagricultural industries: ironmaking, saltmaking, and mountain resorts," although "unskilled immigrant labor also became important as the nineteenth century wore on" (J. A. Williams 2002:127). In the twentieth century black convicts were leased to work on mines, roads, and railroads. John

Alexander Williams holds up the ballad of "John Henry" as an emblem of "how much of the wealth and the infrastructure that made possible the industrialization of Appalachia was extracted from the coerced or underpaid labor of African Americans" (2002:221).

Certainly, the number of slaves was lower in the mountains than in the lowland South. John Inscoe, who has done the most extensive studies on slavery and racism in Appalachia and western North Carolina specifically, maintains that less than 10 percent of the western North Carolina populace consisted of slaves in the antebellum period, and 90 percent of whites owned no slaves (1989). In 1860 Ashe and Watauga counties had slave populations of less than 5 percent (Inscoe1989:64). Significantly, however, attorneys and doctors were among the slaveholders and there was a strong correlation between business diversification and slaveholding. "Watauga County's largest slaveholder was Jordan Councill, whose store was the nucleus around which the town of Boone developed" (Inscoe 1989:63–65). There is even a mountain in Ashe County whose official name for many years was "Nigger Mountain." Slaveholding, then, was an important part of the system that generated the class-stratified mountain society at the bottom of which Eldreth later found herself.

Champions of mountain culture, including John C. Campbell and Loyal Jones, have extrapolated from the relatively low percentage of slaves to insist that mountain whites harbored less race prejudice than did lowland whites because they were so little acquainted with blacks (Campbell 1921:94–95; Jones 1975:512). Inscoe, however, challenges this claim, citing observations made by Frederick Law Olmstead during a trip to the region in 1854. Evidently, most of the mountain residents with whom Olmstead discussed the topic of slavery seemed to have had "equal contempt for slaves, their masters, and the system itself," but almost none advocated abolition, except in East Tennessee, "the only section of the South with an ardent and well-developed antislavery movement" (Inscoe 2001:159). As folklorists, we tend, loyally, to champion denigrated cultures and peoples, but, as José Limón argues, being oppressed does not guarantee that people will not engage in oppressing others (1994). Rather, we need to remember critically the roots of folklorists' interest in Appalachia in the missionaries and folk-school teachers of the Reconstruction era. If we have "learned to view the white people of the southern mountains as unique among the mass of poor whites throughout the South," our attitudes are traceable in part to "racial and political myths of the Anglo-Saxonism and unqualified patriotism of Appalachia" (Silber 2001:256) through which those interested in the plight of the mountaineer encouraged contributors to "cultivate an interest in the southern white because he is white," deflecting attention and support away from earlier work to uplift blacks (2001:247). We are still surprised and hesitant to recognize the presence of racist attitudes in warm and welcoming communities of folk performers (Thomas and Enders 2000), but Eldreth's unselfconscious comfort with enacting a stereotype of a shuffling, broad-speaking, black hayseed suggests that we should not be. Indeed, as John Alexander Williams argues, both the existence of exploited slave and later conscript labor and the racism that kept blacks and whites from making common cause were essential components of the system that kept free labor cheap (2002:251) and families like the Killens and the Eldreths poor. It is also interesting to note that Eldreth herself hints that blackface play could end with the joke backfiring on the perpetrator: "I liked to never got that stuff off, especially from around my eyes. I had to go to church the next morning. I had to wear it or stay at home, one." Doubtless, she meant only that it was embarrassing to have to go to church with a dirty face and be identified as the prankster from the day before. To me, however, this image of Eldreth bespeaks the impossibility of completely erasing the black mask, the futility of the social purification she was attempting, and her ultimate complicity in the production of the race/class system by which she was herself controlled. At the same time, Eldreth and her neighbors are well aware of "mainstream America" judging them according to a racial stereotype of the "poor white," an essential component of which is holding negative attitudes toward blacks. The neighbor attempts to deny or disguise any racist intent, both when he thinks he is talking to an African American person—"I thought I'd come down here and unlock the door. I had to unlock the door"—and after he realizes he is talking to Eldreth— "I'm a-telling you, I knowed we hadn't invited no colored people tonight" (which implies that on another occasion they might have). Eldreth, in turn, reports his careful self-justification. We may not be convinced, but she makes it clear that she knows what we are probably thinking about her, challenging our assumptions as we challenge hers.

CONCLUSIONS

Joking turns the world upside down, making the false seem true and the true seem false. Even after the fabrication is discredited, we tend to retain a double image. The usual character of the perpetrator cannot but be inflected by the fictional identity she temporarily, but convincingly, adopted. In inverting her nurturer role, Eldreth mobilizes the shielding power of the joke to enable herself simultaneously to articulate and to deny a protest against being taken for granted in her fulfillment of a woman's work. Even after she resumes her usual role, the joke leaves a tiny gap, subtly destabilizing the assumption that that is the only natural way for a woman to behave. In her willingness to be cruel to children and in playing at blackface, however, Eldreth reveals a measure of desperation. She never dared, apparently, to play a joke upon (and thus level her criticism directly at) her husband. As a woman whose poverty has itself been racialized, she is willing to take advantage, actually or symbolically, of those few social actors with less social capital. In blackface impersonation, however, she mobilizes the paradoxical power of the denigrated, inducing fear and anxiety in those who perceive her as a threatening racial "Other." In an important sense, however, she cannot escape her own joke, since her own social insecurity is produced by the racialized class label "poor white." Neighbors may be induced to draw the color line with Eldreth on the white (respectable, not poor) side. Still, by engaging in rough, cruel, and racist joking and telling new audiences about it, she potentially reinforces or justifies prejudicial stereotypes of mountain whites.

It is a classic ethnographer's mistake not to recognize it when your subjects are having you on (Paredes 1977). It is not entirely clear whether, when she plays jokes on *me*, Eldreth is treating me as another of her "young'uns" or if she is subtly criticizing the ways I, as a rich person in her estimation, exploit and depend upon hard workers like herself. Probably she intends some of both. Certainly on the day when I served her salted tea, I marked a contrast between us, and I daresay she enjoyed coming off well in the comparison. She was the woman who had produced three meals a day, from scratch, often for a dozen or more people, for more than fifty years. I, despite all my education, lacked the practical competence to make a drinkable cup of tea or to realize that a quart container could not possibly store the amount of sugar used by a person who cooks in the volume Eldreth does. Furthermore, she was balanced enough to find hilarity in a joke played on herself, while I showed that I was so effetely hypersensitive as to be dismayed at what I had done. At the same time, however, I had established a commonality between us by joining her, albeit unintentionally and unwillingly, in the ranks of practical jokers, and she seemed delighted to level the distinctions between us and include me.

There are, however, significant respects in which I do not want to be included. In fact, I do not like either of the discursive positions Eldreth makes available to me: the person who finds racial stereotyping funny or, alternately, the mirthless class snob who condemns her jokes. When I finally dared to mention that readers might understand her blackface joking as derogatory, Eldreth disavowed any prejudice, telling a story I had never heard before about an African American neighbor whom she had invited to eat with her family when his wife was ill, although she did not grapple explicitly with the symbolism of the impersonation. For me, Eldreth's stereotypical portrayal of a rural black person is what Moira Smith, following Bauman, calls an "over-saturated metaphor," too laden with racist connotations to be funny (Smith 1995:134, n. 5; Bauman 1983b:92). Eldreth's practice, however, rejects that oversaturation, trying to hold onto the paradoxical power of the blackface character and the humor of incongruity. I would love to be able to argue that Eldreth, in mobilizing her neighbors' own negative stereotypes against them, subtly criticizes the racist attitudes upon which her blackface portrayal relies, but that is probably a fond stretch. Still, neither Eldreth nor her neighbors lose sight of the further racial stereotype that "mainstream America" holds of them as "poor whites." By having her neighbor insist that in coming out to challenge the apparent black interloper he had really just come down to the church to unlock the door for the Halloween party to which they might actually have invited "colored" guests, Eldreth's story warns us to be careful, in condemning her use of racial stereotype, not to apply a racial stereotype of our own.

7

"My singing is my life"

Repertoire and Performance

The very first time I spoke with Bessie Eldreth in her home, she made a point of defining herself as a singer: "My singing is my life, it is, my singing is my life." I had, of course, been introduced to her the previous summer in Washington, D.C., *as* a singer, so to some extent she may simply have been solidifying our connection by confirming the importance of the practice I had told her I wanted to study. Still, such a claim is not to be taken lightly. I rapidly recognized that the role of songs and singing in her life is indeed remarkable, both the size of a repertoire that she has kept in memory for many decades and the time and energy she has devoted to singing in various contexts. My perception of Eldreth as a singer shades everything I learned about her from the stories analyzed in earlier chapters. She was not only a poor working woman but also an artist with a talent that was valuable to herself and her community and that eventually garnered remarkable attention from people whose interest in her and the music she sings she could not have anticipated. Eldreth eagerly cooperated with me to make tape recordings of her repertoire, close to two hundred songs. I was also able to observe her singing in a variety of settings—around the house, to her grandchildren, in church, and at festivals and educational concerts—as well as to hear her accounts of other memorable performances and occasions for singing. In equating her singing and her life, Eldreth draws attention both to her repertoire of meaningful texts, amassed and carefully maintained over the years, and to her singing, her situated exercise of a special talent that garnered her rare and welcome praise.

Considering Eldreth as a singer confirms impressions of her gathered from her narrative practice and discursive self-positioning, yet also significantly complicates this study in several respects. First, her repertoire, simply as a collection of texts that she has chosen to perpetuate, consists of historically traceable artifacts.

This should theoretically enable us to observe the influx of one kind of external cultural influence, the effects of which seemed apparent in Eldreth's dual accounts of her childhood. To what extent does she preserve songs learned from "the southern mountain tradition" and to what extent prefer nationally disseminated popular compositions? The process whereby musical items passed readily into and out of the "oral tradition" during the late nineteenth and early twentieth centuries, however, introduces new indeterminacies. Second, her song repertoire (in contrast to a repertoire of personal narratives) consists almost entirely of learned (rather than personally composed) texts that she nevertheless voices. Thus, we have an opportunity to inquire into the dialogic relationship, not only between Eldreth and her audiences, but also between her "own" voice and the voices in the songs that she adopts or resists. These texts, as performed by Eldreth, are potentially heteroglossic in ways her stories avoid. Third, as a singer, Eldreth potentially performs, calling attention to her abilities and the artistry of her effort, in ways she does not when telling a story. Her practice draws us to inquire to what extent performing has been attractive and beneficial to her, especially because of her gender, and to what extent it has proved a liability. Examining these three facets in relation to each other, I argue that Eldreth resists or misunderstands folklorists' attempts to define her as "Appalachian." At the same time, she makes use of certain of our definitions and our attention to her both to reinforce her sense of the meanings and importance of her songs and to avail herself of a fulfilling opportunity to perform in ways from which she previously felt restricted because of the defensive gender and class self-construction revealed in her stories.

REPERTOIRE

For a song to become part of any singer's repertoire, it must matter to her in some way. The particular collection of songs that Eldreth has chosen to retain in memory and to voice with regularity reveals many things about her beliefs, values, and sense of self. Nevertheless, in studying a repertoire with an eye to what it means to the singer, one must acknowledge multiple degrees of indeterminacy. There are many potential reasons for a singer to include a particular song in her repertoire, not all of which may be accessible to the singer herself, let alone to those who study her singing (Abrahams in Riddle 1970; Goldstein 1971; E. K. Miller 1981:210; Stekert 1965:167). Furthermore, the words a singer voices when singing a song may correspond more or less closely to her own feelings or thoughts. The study of Eldreth's rendition of these preformed texts, to an even greater extent than study of the stories she herself has composed, calls attention to heteroglossia, that is, to the interaction, blending, and conflict among the multiple voices of the singer, the overall message of the song, and the individual characters/speakers in the narrative or lyric. One must also consider the potential sources of songs available to a particular singer in order to judge to what extent she is influenced by tendencies within the ambient repertoire and to what extent she has selectively emphasized or deemphasized particular themes or messages (Abrahams 1970:13).

About the project of recording her repertoire, Eldreth and I seemed to be in accord. We both recognized this as an intelligible and valuable concrete goal. Whenever we took trips in the car she would pass the time with singing, so I learned to turn on the tape recorder, and she responded by starting to plan what to sing for me when we were going somewhere together. On many occasions we also recorded sessions devoted entirely to singing, initially to catch whatever she felt like singing that day, later to allow her to provide songs that I had not taped previously. Eldreth is proud of her memory and her large repertoire: she often paused in our conversations to reflect upon how clearly she remembers events and songs from her childhood. She had herself made tapes of her singing for friends or family members and even for audience members at public performances who asked if she had recordings for sale. She saw our documentation of her repertoire as significant, doubtless in part because of her pride at remembering so many old songs that few other people in her experience now sing, perhaps also in part because that was the most plausible explanation to her of the interest I and other folklorists had shown in her singing. Recording her repertoire and putting the tapes in an archive[1] also proved congruent with her intentions since, as she explained, she feels a moral obligation to make her songs available to other singers.

> I like to share my songs with people. I don't feel like that | I don't like to be hoggish about nothing. You know what I mean. If somebody likes one of my songs or would like to have a tape or something where I've made one, why, I enjoy doing it for 'em. I feel like it . . . a talent that God gives us. Share it with somebody else. Make somebody else happy.

Unless she was ill or upset, Eldreth was always willing to sing for me, and as our collaboration progressed, she became quite eager to be sure that I "got" as many of her songs as possible. Our tapes document almost two hundred songs that she kept in memory.

Repertoire Sources

A repertoire[2] is an unruly entity to try to account for with satisfactory completeness. At this level of generality, attempting to encompass all Eldreth's songs at once, details of individual compositions are lost to view. However, patterns emerge to suggest the routes via which Eldreth could have been exposed to the items that she elected to learn and preserve. As it happens, the formative period in Eldreth's life as a singer coincides with the period during which "traditional

Bessie Eldreth with her children: back row, l to r, sons Denver, Bob, Roger, Carl, Fred, and Clyde; front row, Eldreth and daughters Patsy, Virginia, Betty, Grace, and Lorene. (Photograph by Wanda Eldreth.)

The home Eldreth's sons built for her in 1972 on Castle Ford Road in Watauga County. She saved the money to pay for the land and materials from her own work, without her husband's assistance. Of the housing her husband had previously provided for the family, Eldreth notes, "We ain't never lived in nothing but a shack from here to yonder."

Tabernacle Baptist Church, where Eldreth has worshipped and sung for more than twenty years.

Bessie Eldreth and her granddaughter Jean Reid performing at the 1987 Smithsonian Festival of American Folklife in Washington, D.C.

At the Festival of American Folklife Judith Cohn Britt, sign language interpreter, accompanied some of Eldreth's and Reid's performances. Eldreth was taken with the beauty of the signing and subsequently incorporated symbolic hand gestures in some of her performances, notably to accompany the line, "He stabbed her in her heart, and her heart's blood it did flow" in the ballad, "Pretty Polly."

Glenn Hinson presenting Eldreth and Reid on stage at the 1987 Festival of American Folklife.

Eldreth performing with Mary Greene at the 1987 Festival of American Folklife.

Bessie Eldreth singing at the Festival for the Eno, in Durham, North Carolina, July 3, 1988. While audience members may have expected a different appearance for a singer of "traditional ballads," as she was billed in the program, Eldreth honored the performance opportunity by having her hair styled, buying a new pair of "diamond ear bobs," and dressing in red chiffon and high heels.

Jean Reid singing at the Festival for the Eno, in Durham, North Carolina, July 3, 1988.

Jean Reid introducing her grandmother during their 1988 performance at the Festival for the Eno. Reid often described learning her songs from Eldreth and praised her grandmother's large repertoire.

Dorothy Holland (left) and Cecilia Conway (back to the camera) interviewing Eldreth at Holland's home in Chapel Hill, North Carolina, before her 1988 Festival for the Eno performance. Excerpts from this conversation, in which Sawin also participated, are analyzed in chapters 3 and 4.

Among the mementos displayed on Eldreth's living room wall is this collection of photographs of her performances and interactions with folklorists taken during Sawin's fieldwork in 1988. Pictured (from top left to bottom right): Eldreth with Dorothy Holland and Cecilia Conway in Chapel Hill; Eldreth with Patricia Sawin; Eldreth with her granddaughter Jean Reid, performing at the Festival for the Eno, Durham; Sawin with Eldreth's son Roger; Reid and Eldreth; audience members at an Elderhostel workshop on Appalachian music taught by Mary Greene at Appalachian State University; Eldreth with other Elderhostel participants; Eldreth with Dean William McCloud of the ASU School of Music after a workshop for music teachers; and Eldreth with McCloud's mother.

Eldreth in her dining room, showing off part of her collection of china and Depression glass and the furniture made for her by her sons, 1994.

Eldreth's bedroom, decorated in a style she now has time and resources to produce, 2003.

Eldreth has made biscuits and cornbread from scratch as part of her daily routine of woman's work for more than eighty years. Here, in July 2001, she makes her famous biscuits in a happier moment than that described in the "Biscuit" story.

Practiced hands.

Eldreth displays the awards she has received in recent years for her singing, including these certificates from the North Carolina Folklore Society and the Smithsonian Institution's Festival of American Folklife, among the family photographs and art works on her living room wall.

A 90th birthday celebration

A covered dish dinner will be held Sunday, Sept. 14, beginning at 1 p.m. at the Tabernacle Baptist Church fellowship hall in celebration of Bessie Eldreth turning 90. Hosts will be her children and their families. "We would like to invite all her friends and acquaintances to bring a covered dish and share this happy occasion with us. Cards are appreciated. No gifts are expected," said a spokesperson for the family.

Notice in the *Watauga Democrat* inviting people to Eldreth's ninetieth birthday party in 2003. (Announcement written by Betty Cable. Photograph by Wanda Eldreth.)

Sign in front of Tabernacle Baptist Church on the day Eldreth's ninetieth birthday party was held in the church hall.

At Eldreth's ninetieth birthday party a table displayed photographs and scrapbooks and other records of her life, including her certificate for the North Carolina Folk Heritage Award and Sawin's dissertation.

Article about Eldreth in the *Watauga Democrat* from 1990 (written by Mike Hannah, photographs by Gary Hemsoth), highlighting her involvement in the Festival of American Folklife and other public performances, framed and displayed at her ninetieth birthday party.

Eldreth and Sawin summer 1988.

Bessie Eldreth at age 89 in 2003, showing the view of her beloved mountains from her home.

Eldreth with fellow choir members listening to the Sunday school lesson, April 2004.

The altar at Tabernacle Baptist Church, decorated for Easter 2004.

Eldreth standing in the pulpit at Tabernacle Baptist Church to sing a solo, April 2004.

mountain music" became an object of concern and argument for two groups of outsiders. During the 1920s and into the 1930s "A and R men" from recording companies (so-called because of their assignment to discover new artists and repertoire) began to seek out mountain musicians and record their music for sale, starting what grew into the commercial, popular, country music industry (Malone 1985). Almost simultaneously, folklorists, settlement school workers, and festival organizers were trying to preserve and encourage forms of mountain music untainted (in their view) by popular sources or commercial embellishments (Becker 1998; Whisnant 1983). Thus, Eldreth was beginning to learn songs, some "traditional" but many relatively recent popular or religious compositions, at just the point that outside interests engaged in debate over the commodification and traditionality of a music perceived (by different interests for different reasons) as both peculiarly regional and fundamentally "American." Eldreth has in recent years gained a reputation as a "traditional Appalachian singer," but her repertoire exemplifies why this is a problematic concept. On the one hand, she actually sings only a handful of songs that are both anonymous and handed down by purely oral channels. On the other hand, her repertoire reveals how materials produced elsewhere became crucial components of the production of a sense of locality (Appadurai 1996), to the extent that it becomes essentially impossible either to determine how Eldreth learned a particular song or to determine what constitutes a "local tradition."

Roughly a quarter of Eldreth's repertoire at the time we tried to record it all consisted of hymns (56 items), some of which are sung regularly at the church she attends, a few of which she sings as church solos and in other kinds of performances, and most of which she has sung around home or in our song-collecting interviews. In practice, the line between what counts for Eldreth as a sacred and as a secular song is blurry, although there is a stylistic distinction. Among what we might call the not-overtly-religious songs, roughly three quarters (96 of 129 items) were composed by commercial songwriters between the middle of the nineteenth and the middle of the twentieth centuries.[3] Of these popular songs at least half were country music hits in the 1920s, 1930s, and 1940s—some recently composed, some recordings of nineteenth-century songs that had passed into the oral repertoire. Eldreth has also picked up a few popular songs from later decades. She claims eight songs as her "homemades," not distinguishing in this category between apparent original compositions and instances in which she slightly adapted the words to a recent popular song to reflect her own situation and feelings.

At most a sixth of Eldreth's repertoire (33 items) would be considered "traditional" by conservative measures, that is, excluding all songs with known authors and relying heavily on stylistic and documentary evidence of long periods of oral transmission. Eldreth sings only one Child ballad, "Barbara Allen" (Child 84), "of all the ballads in the Child collection . . . easily the most widely known and sung, both in the old country and in America" (Belden and Hudson 1952: vol.

2,111). She sings three American ballads traced by Laws (1957) to British broadside antecedents: "Knoxville Girl" (Laws P35), "London City"/"Butcher Boy" (P24), and the murder ballad "Pretty Polly" (P36B). She sings five others that Laws deemed native American ballads (1964): "Banks of the Ohio" (F5), "John Henry" (I1), "The Lawson Family Murder" (F35), "Neoma Wise" (F31), and "Wild Bill Jones" (E10). Four more of Eldreth's songs fit the criteria set by Belden and Hudson (editors of the 1952 *Frank C. Brown Collection of North Carolina Folklore*) for "folk lyrics": "Bonnie Blue Eyes" (FCB vol. 3 #284),[4] "Pretty Polly"/"Wagoner Boy" (FCB vol. 3 #250), "In the Pines" (FCB vol. 3 #283),[5] and "The Storms Are on the Ocean" (FCB vol. 3 #264). There are another twenty songs in her repertoire—including "East Virginia Blues," "Handsome Molly," "Little Maggie," and "Will You Miss Me When I'm Gone?"—that I have classified as presumably traditional Anglo-American songs, based on a combination of stylistic grounds and testimony from artists who made early commercial recordings that these were songs "we had known our whole lives."[6]

The group of hymns Eldreth sings shows a similar emphasis on fairly recent popular creations. The only two pre-nineteenth-century hymns she sings are "Amazing Grace" and "Rock of Ages"; the only documented nineteenth-century shape-note hymn is "Poor Wayfaring Stranger," like "Barbara Allen," far and away the most often encountered item from that tradition. Eldreth remembers four hymns learned from a great aunt or from her father that have the repetitive wording and marching rhythm that might mark them as songs used for early nineteenth-century camp meeting revivals (see Bruce 1974:95). As noted in the previous chapter, she also knows four African American spirituals, "Mary, Mary, What You Gonna Call That Baby?" "My Lord, What a Morning," "There's No Hiding Place Down Here," and "Were You There When They Crucified My Lord?" The bulk of her sacred repertoire consists of the kinds of late nineteenth- and twentieth-century gospel hymns written by Fanny Crosby, Ira D. Sankey, Ira Stanphill, Homer Rodeheaver, Albert E. Brumley, and many less prolific writers and kept available in the popular hymnals produced by Stamps-Baxter, R. E. Winsett, J. D. Vaughn, and similar southern religious-music publishing firms.

Eldreth's repertoire demonstrates perfectly the realization that people in the southern mountains had never been as isolated from American popular culture as the ballad collectors and settlement-school teachers wanted to believe (Whisnant 1983). The stock of songs circulating orally in the first two decades of the twentieth century (that is, even prior to the advent of radio broadcasts) already encompassed much more than the list of English and native ballads favored in folklorists' collections. An important segment of the repertoire consisted of sentimental parlor ballads, like "The Eastbound Train" and "Little Rosewood Casket," thirteen of which Eldreth sings. Composed by commercial songwriters in the 1850s through 1890s and circulated as sheet music, these retained their popularity in the mountains after passing out of urban fashion (N. Cohen 1970:10; Malone 1981:3, 1985:10; Wilgus 1965:200). These songs have been widely collected (or noticed and not collected) by folklorists in the southern mountains and throughout the United States. Laws lists a dozen such songs among often-collected, "ballad-like" pieces that he admits were "sung traditionally" but that he rejected from his list of traditional ballads for one of several reasons, in these instances because they are "melodramatic and sentimental, usually of professional origin" (Laws 1964:277–278). Belden and Hudson, more swayed by evidence of popularity and oral transmission, accorded some of these songs the status of ballad or folksong, including three that Eldreth sings: "Little Rosewood Casket" (composed 1870, FCB vol. 2 #273),[7] "Red River Valley" (composed 1896, FCB vol. 3 #260), and "Little Orphan Girl" (FCB vol. 2 #148, in sheet music in the 1850s, author unknown [Ellis 1978:662]). D. K. Wilgus notes that early twentieth-century singers were already regularly labeling as "old-time" songs that had been out of commercial circulation for little more than a decade (1965:198).

Early, "Edison"-type cylinder players and recordings of contemporary popular and classical music were being purchased by mountain families by the time Eldreth was born (1913),[8] and record companies began making commercial recordings of southern mountain instrumentalists and singers in 1923. Much of what these artists performed in the early years was their "traditional" music, that is, songs they already knew, mostly ones they thought of as anonymous (Malone 1985:44). Initially, the burgeoning radio and recording industries simply "offered new media for an existing tradition" (Wilgus 1965:197), as entrepreneurs discovered that they could sell mountain music (like other ethnic and regional repertoires) back to the "hitherto untapped market" of people who had listened to the same music being performed by their families and neighbors (Green 1965:208–209), as well as to a growing national audience responding with nostalgia to the "rapid social transformations of the late 1920s" (Whisnant 1983:183).

Commercial "hillbilly" artists thus made substantial amounts of new, but familiar, material available to mountain audiences, some already in oral circulation but not known to everyone, some actually recently composed. A. P. Carter actively collected old songs to add to the Carter Family repertoire and even went on song-hunting trips (Malone and McCulloh 1975:97–98; Malone 1985:67). Jimmie Rodgers drew on a stock of "maverick phrases" common to blues and hobo songs to create his famous "blue yodels" and other pieces that rapidly passed (passed "back"?) into a wider oral circulation and have often been collected as traditional pieces in the years since Rodgers recorded them (Greenway 1957:231). Songwriters, themselves well versed in the songs already in oral circulation, created new pieces on the old models, often encouraged by record producers who were eager to find songs that the audience would find congenial but that could be copyrighted for greater profits. To cite a well-documented example from Eldreth's repertoire, "Floyd Collins"—a ballad about the attempted rescue and death of a man caught in a cave while spelunking in February 1925—

achieved tremendous spread in oral tradition and was accepted as a folksong, not only by Belden and Hudson (1952, FCB vol. 2 #212), but even by the skeptical Laws (1964, G22). The song was actually composed by the Reverend Andrew Jenkins, author of over eight hundred popular and sacred songs, and was commissioned from him by producer Polk Brockman only days after the event (Green 1972:125; Malone 1985:49).[9]

I regularly asked Eldreth when and from whom she had learned her songs and what she knew of their origins, to the extent that it became something of a joke between us. She has strong associations for some songs and no particular memory about others. It is hardly reasonable to suppose that she would recall the source of every one of her songs, almost all learned between thirty and seventy years earlier, let alone that she would make the kinds of distinctions about provenance that scholars have filled in. Still, Eldreth's pattern of attribution, lack of attribution, and probable misattribution raises interesting questions, usually without providing complete answers.

The source Eldreth mentioned most often was her grandmother Milam:

> But, now, that was one of my songs that Grandma Milam taught me. You know, I used to do a whole lot like Jean has done by me. She wouldn't know that I was listening or whatever. I'd just be around and taking every word in. And I's a-learning those songs.

Eldreth associates a few songs apiece with her father, mother, a cousin, an uncle, two aunts, and her schoolteacher in Damascus, Virginia. She also attributes several songs apiece to two favorite early country music artists, the Carter Family and Jimmie Rodgers. Among twenty-four songs in her repertoire that were popularized by the Carter Family, Eldreth specifically said of "Wildwood Flower" and "Will You Miss Me When I'm Gone?" "that's one of Maybelle Carter's songs." She not only ascribes "T for Texas," "TB Blues," "Mississippi River Blues," and "Peach Picking Time in Georgia" to Rodgers but explained that she had learned to yodel by singing along with some of his records. And of "Blue Christmas," which she has sung at Christmastime performances, she notes, "That's Elvis Presley's song, but I made the third verse."

Conversely, there are only a handful of songs that Eldreth talks about learning from print or recordings per se. "There's No Depression in Heaven" (recorded by the Carter Family) Eldreth recalls learning from a music book she bought in a store. Two singular humorous songs, "Snoops the Lawyer" and "Ticklish Reuben," she knows she learned (apparently when she was only four or five years old, circa 1918) from a relatively wealthy teenaged cousin, Blanche Killens, who owned a cylinder record player earlier than other people in the neighborhood. It is, however, the memory of her cousin's singing that she emphasizes: "I just learned it by hearing her come off down the mountain singing it. She'd come down to Momma's and she'd sing that song. She'd start about the time she left her house."[10] It seems likely that Eldreth has been prompted to highlight the cylinder record source of these songs because local scholar Mary Greene has done extensive research on the influence of early recordings on mountain singing and often mentions the connection when she has Eldreth perform for Elderhostel programs. At a slightly later date but before she "left home" in 1929, Eldreth's own family owned a record player, and she reports learning two items directly from that source: a popular jilted-lover song, "Just Another Broken Heart," and a patriotic, dying-soldier song, "The Red, White, and Blue" (although I suspect the latter actually dates from World War II). "The Little Girl and the Dreadful Snake" (recorded by Bill Monroe in the 1950s) Eldreth mentioned learning from an LP she still owns. Interestingly, given her clear memory of Maybelle Carter and Jimmie Rodgers, Eldreth has never mentioned any of the other popular stars of the 1920s through the 1950s—including the Blue Sky Boys, the Stanley Brothers, the Bailes Brothers, Charlie Poole, Vernon Dalhart, Flatt and Scruggs, Grayson and Whitter, the Maddox Brothers and Rose, Gene Autry, Roy Acuff, Asher Sizemore and Little Jimmie, Molly O'Day, Bradley Kincaid, Ernest Tubb, Pop Stoneman, Porter Wagoner, the Louvin Brothers, and Patti Page—whose records or radio performances were likely the sources of many of her songs.

The sources of the hymns in Eldreth's repertoire present few mysteries, since songs of this type were widely available in hymnals as well as being performed on religious programs on radio and later television. Notable in her repertoire are several that have become bluegrass standards and were thus performed along with secular bluegrass numbers on radio and records. The handful of African American spirituals originally tantalized me as possible evidence of sharing between Eldreth and her few black neighbors, but it seems more likely, as noted in the previous chapter, that Eldreth learned these from recordings by the Carter Family and Marion Anderson. One, "Mary, Mary, What You Gonna Call That Baby?" was also regularly performed by the Mars Hill Singers, and I suspect Eldreth may have picked it up on the one occasion when she and her grand-daughter performed on the same program with them at Mars Hill.

The secular songs, however, present a variety of intriguing indeterminacies. The fact that Eldreth remembers learning a song orally from a relative of an earlier generation need not mean that the piece was particularly old or that it had been in oral circulation long (or ever) before her immediate source learned it. She fondly recalls her uncle Sidney Killens singing "Floyd Collins" to her, although since it was composed in 1925, her recollection that he held her on his lap while singing may not be accurate.[11] One of the few songs she says she learned from her mother is "Singing Waterfalls," written by Hank Williams and recorded by Molly O'Day in 1946. Clearly, childhood need not be the only time for a singer to acquire repertoire, even from family members, especially when several generations live close together through the younger generation's adulthood. Similarly, we might take the fact that Eldreth learned "Voice from the Tombs" (written in 1918 but popularized by a Blue Sky Boys recording in the 1930s) from her grandmother as evidence that the song made it into the mountains quickly or as a reminder that Eldreth worked alongside her grandmother, not only as a child, but also as a young adult, as part of extended family reciprocity that enabled everyone to get by during the lean years of the Depression. Furthermore, no one's memory is perfect. The thematic connection among lawyer songs is so strong in Eldreth's mind that she now also maintains "My first cousin learnt me that when I was right small" about not only "Snoops the Lawyer" but also "Philadelphia Lawyer," actually written by Woody Guthrie in 1937 and popularized by the Maddox Brothers and Rose in a 1949 recording.

Indeed, it is even impossible to tell precisely how Eldreth learned songs that are known to have been circulating orally in the mountains when she was a girl. They might have come to her through a chain of oral transmission, but she could equally have learned them (then or later) from record, radio, or sheet music or from a family member who had just learned them from one of the mediated sources. As Cecilia Conway notes, "good musicians tend to be musically receptive to new influences," and "the foremost community musicians [in the mountain south] were usually the first in their areas to own record-playing devices" (2001:36).[12] Several of the traditional songs that Eldreth remembers learning from Grandma Milam were also recorded quite early, for example, "Little Maggie," (recorded by Grayson and Whitter in the early 1920s), "Pretty Polly"/"Wagoner Boy" (recorded by Bradley Kincaid in the 1920s), and "Sailor on the Deep Blue Sea" (recorded by the Carter Family), so it is just as possible that her grandmother learned them from a recording as that she had had them handed down orally much earlier in her life. There are as many as twenty-five more songs in Eldreth's repertoire that may well have reached her via phonograph recordings, even though they were (theoretically) available in oral circulation in the region at the time. These include several more Carter Family numbers ("Bury Me beneath the Willow," "East Virginia Blues," and "Single Girl/Married Girl"); folk lyrics, such as "In the Pines" (recorded by Dock Walsh in 1926), "Short Life of Trouble" (recorded by Grayson and Whitter in 1928), and "Little Birdie" (recorded by Vernon Dalhart in the 1920s); and several of the nineteenth-century sentimental parlor songs ("Letter Edged in Black" [recorded by Fiddlin' John Carson and Vernon Dalhart in the 1920s], "My Mother Was a Lady" [recorded by Jimmie Rodgers in 1927], and "Just Break This News to Mother" [recorded by both Riley Puckett and Blind Andy Jenkins in 1925]). It is easy to surmise that Eldreth almost certainly got "Sweet Fern" more or less directly from the Carter Family, since the change from "Birds" in the original title to "Fern" seems to have begun with them (Cohen and Cohen 1973:45). Closer textual comparison of Eldreth's versions with recorded versions might provide evidence for other specific songs, although over the years she may have modified the wording so that her current versions diverge from her sources.

Perhaps most intriguingly, Eldreth never mentioned learning any of her murdered-girl ballads or her other native American ballads or American ballads from

British broadsides from anyone in particular. She described "Banks of the Ohio" as among those songs that "date back years ago," reported that she learned "The Knoxville Girl" "before [she] ever left home," that is, prior to 1929, and indicated that the stories reported in some of the songs were something with which people were familiar when she was a child: "And, you see, my grandparents used to talk about these murder ballads and . . . and where people . . . like boyfriends, they'd maybe want the girl to get married and she refused and they'd kill her before that they'd let her go." All of these most traditional songs in Eldreth's repertoire were recorded in the early years of the country music industry— "Banks of the Ohio" by the Callahan Brothers in the 1920s, "Pretty Polly" by B. F. Shelton in the 1920s, "Knoxville Girl" by the Blue Sky Boys in the 1930s, "London City" by Bradley Kincaid in the 1920s, "Handsome Molly" by Grayson and Whitter in 1923, and "Wild Bill Jones" by Ernest Stoneman and Bradley Kincaid—and were thus recirculated and popularized in recorded form. "Naomi Wise," or, as Eldreth calls it, "Neoma Wise," a ballad about an 1807 murder in Randolph County, North Carolina, was described by Belden and Hudson as North Carolina's principle contribution to American folk song (1952: vol. 2, 690; Laws 1964, F31) and has been collected in multiple oral variants that, Eleanor Long-Wilgus concludes, branch off from a text published in 1851 and have been influenced by eighteenth-century British broadsides also in oral circulation (2003). Eldreth, however, except for the unique variation on the murdered woman's name, sings a text almost identical to a version composed in 1925 by the "hillbilly" songwriter Carson Robison and issued on at least a dozen 78-rpm records, notably by Vernon Dalhart in the late 1920s (Long-Wilgus 2003:19–20).

Eldreth's vocal style is equally ambiguous, representing a hybrid of elements characteristic of traditional singing technique in the American South and elements typical of a more "cultivated" *(bel canto)* style. Several qualities mark her as an accomplished singer, irrespective of musical tradition. She stays on pitch without requiring instrumental accompaniment for reference. She is quite aware of the importance of breath control (even teasing people in the church choir who have to take a breath before the end of the phrase). Her light soprano voice is never breathy. She has a substantial dynamic range and is able to sing loudly without apparent effort and softly without losing clarity or focus. She has a strong sense of musical phrase and focuses attention on the shaping of the melodic line.

Eldreth employs two notable stylistic features often noted as characteristic of American vernacular singers who have not been exposed either to formal "art" music training or to the model of popular singers. First, she regularly and gracefully adds small embellishments to the tunes she is singing, including scoops and slides up to a pitch and an especially characteristic three-note slide off of a pitch. She inserts such adornments freely, as it feels right to her, not necessarily at the same point in different verses of the same song. Second, when singing a cappella she tends to conceive of the musical phrase as coterminous with the textual line, and (though maintaining the meter within phrases) often moves on to the next line without waiting out the metrical fullness of the preceding musical phrase.[13] This tendency becomes especially apparent on the rare recent occasions when folklorists have brought her together with musicians who share items from her repertoire but perform them with guitar or string-band accompaniment. In these instances Eldreth is frequently ready to start singing again while the instrumentalists are finishing out their musical phrase.[14]

In other respects, Eldreth's singing style contrasts markedly with the "traditional" style of mountain ballad singers. While her sound is not as supported and resonant as that of a formally trained singer, neither is Eldreth's singing marked by the nasality and roughness identified as characteristically Appalachian. Though not rich, her tone leaves an impression of clarity and openness, probably because she sustains notes through their full value and in particular sustains vowels, keeping them open for the maximum time allowed by the meter (in contrast to ballad singers, who tended to cut off notes at the end of lines and to close on and sing through voiceable consonants like m, n, and l). She sings with considerable vibrato (which she emphasizes further in highly emotive pieces like "He Touched Me"), possibly as a way of approximating a desired resonance which more highly trained singers achieve in other ways. Her focus on musical phrasing similarly contrasts with the tendency of some ballad singers to emphasize the enunciation of individual words rather than the shaping of a musical line.[15] This relatively cultivated quality of Eldreth's singing is further accentuated by her notable tendency to adopt a much more standard (nonlocal) vocal pronunciation when singing than she does when speaking. As she herself observes, she sings "more proper" than she speaks. Her song texts markedly lack the distinctive local pronunciations (for example, "hit" for "it" in phrase-initial position) and grammatical features (for example, "I was a-singing") that are an unselfconscious part of her everyday talk. Eldreth expressed great admiration for the wonderfully gravelly, nasal, harsh singing, dissonant harmonies, and marked mountain diction of a gospel group, the "Spiritual Heirs," that visited her church. But while speaking of their singing approvingly as "spiritual" and "old-fashioned," she also distinguished their style from her own. She loved that kind of singing but did not think of it as appropriate or even possible for herself. There is a subtle heteroglossia going on here so pervasive that it is easy to miss. Whenever she sings, I would argue, Eldreth enacts herself as a member of a national audience rather than as any kind of isolated mountaineer. The artists she loved and whose songs she incorporated into her repertoire were widely popular. If the music of the Carter Family or of Jimmie Rodgers or of cultivated "hillbillies" like Vernon Dalhart spoke to Eldreth of the South as a place of traditional values in a time of bewildering change, it spoke the same message to beleaguered working-class people all over the county (Malone 1985:42). Ironically, the repertoire that has inclined folklorists to identify Eldreth as a "traditional

Appalachian singer" can as readily be interpreted as evidence of her participation in the mainstream American culture of the day.

I suspect that Eldreth's sense of how it is most pleasing to sing—with smooth, clear intonation, expressive use of dynamics and tempo changes, and standard diction—is modeled primarily on the more cultivated style of the popular singers she heard on records, radio, and more recently television. At the same time, however, her singing of popular country pieces is also infiltrated by qualities of embellishment and rhythm that she must have learned from singers whose styles were well established before the advent of the commercialized, standardized country sound. Conversely, elements of her polished style could have been passed down orally with the nineteenth-century sentimental songs.

Given the likelihood that Eldreth acquired much of her repertoire from records or radio broadcasts by popular commercial performers, it is intriguing to speculate why she seems not to remember or at least to mention their names or indeed to talk about listening to the radio at all. One possibility is that she may simply have been more interested in the message or feel of the songs she made a point of learning from popular renditions than in the adulation of country music stars that emerged with the recording industry. As Ellen Stekert noted in one of the earliest individual repertoire studies, a singer is more likely to remember the situation in which and the person from whom she learned a particular song if she values it for those associations, less likely if she appreciates the song primarily for itself and its emotional or thematic content (1965:53). Eldreth gives evidence of such thinking with remarks like, "'Little Maggie' is just a, you know, not a sacred song, but I like it because she [Grandma Milam] sang it." One might detect a linkage between her memories and her musical practice. Because she was not merely listening to these songs but memorizing certain ones so she could sing them herself, Eldreth appears to have paid more attention to the content than to the performer or performance.

The other possibility, however, is that Eldreth is responding to a perception that folklorists tend to place greater value on songs learned orally. She is far less a conscious traditionalist than her granddaughter, Jean Reid, who expressed interest in learning only the oldest and most certifiably traditional songs in her grandmother's repertoire. Nevertheless, it seems possible that Eldreth has been influenced, consciously or not, by the several folklorists who have worked with her in the past and by my consistent interest in direct human sources. In dialogue with me, did she shape her memories to what she sensed I wanted to hear? Did she neglect to attribute songs to recording artists because she understood that folklorists are interested in unattributable songs?

It is also worth noting that Eldreth's repertoire—in terms of sources, though not of themes—more closely resembles those that men rather than women have been observed to accumulate. In Newfoundland outports, women tended to learn most of their songs from intimates prior to marriage and to continue singing that repertoire throughout their lives (Kodish 1981), while men tended to learn songs "in their adult years—when they [were] away on boats or in the woods, and around other men, strangers with new and unusual repertoires" and as a result "picked up more current song styles" (Kodish 1981:43; see also Ives 1978:374–395). Anne and Norm Cohen note that a split between domestic (older, less popular) and public (more current) folk music traditions also existed in the southern mountains in the 1920s, which explains why the two groups of collectors active in the area at the time—folklorists (who went into people's homes) and record company A and R men (who went to social gatherings)— documented such different materials (Cohen and Cohen 1977). In Eldreth's own Watauga County, the Hicks and Presnell women from Beech Mountain continued to sing a substantial number of the old English ballads along with more recent popular tunes (Burton 1978), while Doc Watson, from Deep Gap, who made his living as a musician, was able to perform only contemporary popular tunes in public until folklorist Ralph Rinzler drew him into the folk revival, which provided a new audience for old songs.

Eldreth, similarly, until late in life, sang her secular repertoire almost exclusively for herself or to entertain children in the home and thus did not feel pressure to conform to anyone's taste but her own. Because she was a crucial couple of decades younger than those other women, however, and was thus familiarized as a child and very young woman with media that brought new music into the domestic setting, Eldreth, without participating in performance outside her home, had access to the kinds of external influences formerly available only to men. Eldreth's repertoire thus demonstrates the extent to which commercial recordings, which brought music formerly reserved for social gatherings into the everyday domestic sphere, enabled a rapidly changing public repertoire to be incorporated into domestic singing practice. An interesting effect, noted in other private singers with access over a long period to new popular songs, is the production of a repertoire markedly like Eldreth's, quirky and old-fashioned, mixing songs that have been remembered by wider audiences with songs that were in vogue only briefly and have long since passed out of public consciousness (Rosenberg 1980:323).

From whatever source she may have learned her songs, Eldreth has held onto them as singers did before the advent of recording, by memorizing them and (as I will detail below) by making her own handwritten copies. Perceptually, then, she is well and accurately aware that she still sings a large number of songs that no one else around her knows.

Meanwhile, however, a number of developments transpired to transform perceptions of Eldreth's practice and repertoire, notably the folk revival, which recirculated to a new audience a mix of older and newer music then being performed by mountain musicians. The result is a curious partial convergence and partial mismatch between Eldreth's sense of the interest of her repertoire and the analysis suggested by knowledge of the history of early country music outlined above. Folklorists' interest has confirmed Eldreth's supposition that her repertoire is significant because she knows so many "old" songs. Ironically, however, her very reasonable sense that songs she learned sixty or more years ago are "real old" does not match with folklorists' tendency to apply that label rather to English or English-influenced ballads from the sixteenth to eighteenth centuries, of which she sings very few, those possibly learned from recordings. The truly rare items in Eldreth's repertoire, from a scholarly perspective, however, are short-lived topical and popular pieces that she has preserved as if in amber and that were not previously rediscovered by revivalists. Further, the very indeterminacies in identifying her sources illustrate the hybrid character of the musical repertoire to which people in the mountain South were exposed during the first half of the twentieth century and the fluidity with which certain songs moved among the categories "traditional" and older and newer "popular," both from an analytical perspective and in singers' minds.

Repertoire Meaning

Why did Eldreth include in her own personal repertoire certain songs out of the presumably much greater selection to which she was exposed over the years and from which she might have chosen? Given that for most of her life she sang secular songs almost entirely in private, she alone, without needing to consider others' preferences, chose a particular subset of songs to memorize and perpetuate. Eldreth seems attracted to songs mainly because of the story or feeling expressed by the words. I have only rarely heard her comment on the tunes or express preference for particular pieces on musical grounds. I thus posit that she has chosen songs because the words reflect some aspect of her experience or feelings. This does not mean that she necessarily means every word she sings as an expression of her own thoughts at the moment, of course. And it is possible to trace certain instances where she adopts the words of a song as her own, others where she maintains a separation or even talks back. In general, however, her preference appears to be shaped by what Raymond Williams calls a "structure of feeling," that is, a form, style, or guiding principle of cultural creation that has a discernable shape but is not formalized or explicitly defined. "We are talking," Williams explains,

> about characteristic elements of impulse, restraint, and tone; specifically affective elements of consciousness and relationships: not feeling against thought, but thought as felt and feeling as thought: practical consciousness of a present kind, in a living and interrelating continuity. (1977:132)

In a structure of feeling, one's values, ideology, and sense of self are caught up with and expressed by the formal and thematic qualities of the art works. And as

Gordon notes, it is precisely in such inchoate yet pervasive structures of feeling that hauntings—lingering elements of a constraining past—are transmitted and received (1997:18).

Lonesome Songs

Overall, Eldreth's songs tell stories that are sad, even tragic, and that envelope singer and listener in melancholy. She sings narrative songs about young women murdered by their lovers, dying children, self-sacrificing mothers, soldiers about to die in battle, men brought down by economic adversity, families torn apart by drink or divorce. Her lyric songs are almost entirely laments, for dead or faithless lovers, dead or aging parents, the impossibility of going home again, the disappearance of religious values and good old-fashioned ways. Eldreth herself often quotes approvingly her daughter-in-law Cathy's characterization, "You always sing such lonesome songs." Given the hardships Eldreth has experienced, it seems reasonable that at some level she has chosen or kept songs that could reflect pervasive feelings of regret and abandonment. Still, the mood of the songs could not be more different from Eldreth's usual warm, cheerful, positive, loving, even ebullient, demeanor. Indeed, her emotional separation from the mood of her songs is suggested by another remark that she also likes to quote, Professor Thomas McGowan's incredulous question after seeing her perform the murdered-girl ballads, "How can you sing those songs and smile?"

Eldreth has, I believe, amassed a repertoire that takes the songs she learned as a girl and young woman as a model for subsequent inclusions. These included the murdered-girl ballads and nineteenth-century tearjerkers that led Abrahams and Foss to comment on the "remarkable preponderance of songs on the themes of love and death" in the early twentieth-century Anglo-American tradition (1968:92).[16] Thus at an early age she learned a number of songs describing unhappy love—either confused relations between lovers leading to a tragic end, as in "Neoma Wise," "Little Maggie," and "Wild Bill Jones," or the despair of a deserted lover, as in "Wildwood Flower." New songs from each decade express similar themes: in the 1920s, "Treasures Untold";[17] in the 1930s, "The Last Letter" and "Philadelphia Lawyer";[18] in the 1940s, "I'm So Lonesome I Could Cry," "Live and Let Live [Don't Break My Heart]," "Lonely Mound of Clay," "Pins and Needles in My Heart," "Precious Jewel," "Singing Waterfalls," and "Tennessee Waltz." Nineteenth-century mourning songs like "Letter Edged in Black" established the model for a raft of laments for dead or elderly parents—"Silver Haired Daddy," "Mother's Not Dead, She's Only A-Sleeping," "No, Not a Word from Home Any More," "White Dove" ("I'll live my life in sorrow, Now that Momma and Daddy are dead"), and "Wait a Little Longer, Please, Jesus"—or for parents' losses, "Where is My Wandering Boy Tonight." Another early-established model came from the late nineteenth-century sentimental songs about dying or self-sacrificing children ("Blind Child's Prayer," "Eastbound Train," "Little Orphan Girl," "Put My Little Shoes Away") and dying soldiers ("Just Break This News to Mother").

To this group Eldreth has added "Drunkard's Prayer" (from the late 1940s, in which the drunken father runs over his own children and repentantly holds them in his arms as they die), as well as soldier songs from both the first and second world wars ("The Soldier's Sweetheart" from World War I; "Searching for a Soldier's Grave," "Red, White, and Blue," "The Soldier's Last Letter," and "Teardrops Falling in the Snow" from World War II). She has also expanded the category to include adult sufferers: Jimmie Rodgers in "TB Blues," the young man stuck in jail in "They're All Going Home But Me," the farmer reduced to despair, poverty, and homelessness when his wife is seduced by a city slicker in "Can I Sleep in Your Barn Tonight, Mister?" and the self-sacrificing mother in "I'm Just Here to Get My Baby out of Jail." The handful of songs from the 1950s to 1970s that Eldreth has adopted similarly either tell a murder story like the early ballads (for example, "Long Black Veil" and "Springtime in Alaska") or lament the misery of loss (for example, "Blue Christmas").

Conversely, Eldreth sings very few songs of happy love,[19] and she picked up neither any of the mine and mill songs, hobo songs, and other protests against the treatment of the working poor that made it into early recordings (T. Patterson 1975:284) nor any songs from other prominent streams in later commercial country music, like honky-tonk songs and songs considering drinking from the drinker's point of view.[20] Indeed, in terms of affect, if not strict chronology, Eldreth has constructed an "old" repertoire in another sense, selecting subsequent items to match the structure of feeling defined by the earlier pieces she learned. Among the items she spontaneously described as "a real old song" are the traditional ballads "Knoxville Girl," "Banks of the Ohio," "Little Maggie," and "Wild Bill Jones," the native American lyric "Pretty Polly"/"Wagoner Boy," and the nineteenth-century parlor songs "Eastbound Train" (1896) and "Sweet Fern" (1876), as well as the 1925 "Dream of the Miner's Child" (composed, like "Floyd Collins," by the Reverend Andrew Jenkins), Gene Autry's 1931 hit "Silver Haired Daddy," Karl and Harty's 1934 "I'm Just Here to Get My Baby out of Jail," the World War II song "Searching for a Soldier's Grave" (recorded by the Bailes Brothers and the Blue Sky Boys), Gene Sullivan and Wiley Walker's 1945 "Live and Let Live," "Singing Waterfalls" (written by Hank Williams and recorded by Molly O'Day in 1946), and Bill Monroe's 1946 "Blue Moon of Kentucky." Eldreth's repertoire is a perfect example of both the kind of cohesiveness and the retention of early pieces that can occur when "taste and esthetic patterns adopted at an early age remain relatively unchanged during a singer's life" (Goldstein 1971:64) and is consistent with a pattern observed more widely among "traditional" musicians in the southern mountains whereby "acquisition of new repertory and stylistic techniques was guided by principles of tradition and personal taste" (Conway 2001:36).

The majority of songs in Eldreth's repertoire are overtly melancholy if not outright tragic. Such sad songs are not entirely sad for Eldreth, however, because she associates them with the childhood that, as we saw in chapter 2, she remembers as the happiest time of her life. In practice, the structure of feeling that these songs evoke for Eldreth deemphasizes the misery and violence they actually describe in favor of the sense of security and assurance of being loved that pervaded the context in which she first heard the songs that form the basis of and model for her repertoire. In these texts, explicit statements about the superior morality of an earlier generation surface only occasionally, as in "Dust on the Bible" (1945). Nostalgia for an always already disappearing idealized rural past pervades the popular selections, however, from "The Maple on the Hill" (1880), in which the lovers who wooed in a "quiet, country village" will ultimately be buried beneath the tree that was their trysting spot, never suffering spatial dislocation, to "Rank Stranger" (1930s), in which the adult returning to a childhood home finds no one to recognize him.

The hymns in Eldreth's repertoire, similarly, offer assurance of a reward in heaven[21] conditioned by a rejection of the (current, degenerate) world, often expressed in terms such as "the world is not my home" or, from one of the hymns most often sung at Eldreth's church, "I find here no permanent dwelling" ("Mansions over the Hilltop"). A view of Jesus' life as the maximally valuable time in history establishes a model of looking backward for moral reference. This practice, however, promotes a conflation of an ideal or holy state, one's own childhood, and an earlier rural life in that heaven is portrayed as a place where the faithful will be reunited with loved ones ("If We Never Meet Again This Side of Heaven," "That Glad Reunion Day," "Where Parting Comes No More") and specifically as a place where the childhood family will be reconstituted ("If You Love Your Mother, Meet Her in the Skies" and "Supper Time" [in which Jesus calling the faithful home to heaven is likened to the long-dead mother calling her son home to supper]).[22]

The irony in this "sacralization" of childhood, the rural past, and the family is that it was articulated by popular-song and hymn writers well removed from the milieu in which Eldreth actually lived, notably from the poverty and domination by a shiftless husband that she suffered. Many of the songs she sings became so popular in the 1930s and 1940s because economic and geographical dislocation made people nostalgic for supposedly simpler times and made them identify with the yearning feel of the sentimental nineteenth-century tunes, recycled as "traditional," and the newly written songs based on these models. For Eldreth, these mournful songs serve to recall happy memories of the past and to reinforce the positive sense of herself as moral, resourceful, and hardworking that she associates with those memories. This reminds us further that, whereas it is easy to imagine that the orally transmitted traditional ballads were more properly Eldreth's cultural property, she experienced all of the songs as equally available, equally "her music." For those who use and cherish a hybrid repertoire, the expressive power of a piece is relevant while its provenance is not (Samuels 1999). Her adherence to this structure of feeling, however, seems to have steered her away from songs that would directly address her economic victimization.

Speaking through Songs

While the repertoire as a conglomerate list of texts suggests the structure of feeling that predominates, examination of a handful of individual songs and Eldreth's performance of them reveals a wide range of interactions between the singer and her song. When she sings, Eldreth evokes a general set of associations that may or may not be obviously related to the words or the story. Yet any voicing of a pregiven text involves heteroglossia, the coexistence in the utterance of multiple voices that may concur or may contest each other. To what extent, in various instances, is she directly voicing her own feelings and beliefs through the words of the song? If she does not agree with the message or identify with the story, what does the song mean to her when she sings it?

To begin, it is worth noting that Eldreth, because she did not sing publicly—except in church—until late in her life, experienced few of the influences that encourage performers to adopt songs that are effective aesthetic objects but not personally meaningful texts.[23] She has likewise until recently been free of the kinds of pressures that a changing audience may exert on a singer to drop outmoded topical songs or adapt to new aesthetic standards (Goldstein 1971). The one obvious recent influence on her repertoire has come from folklorists and festival audiences, who have probably encouraged Eldreth to sing the murder ballads and her songs from the early cylinder recordings more frequently than she would have otherwise. My tendency is thus to assume that if she sings a song, she means the words. Still, Eldreth's relatively cultivated diction and vocal style distinguish her singing voice from her speaking voice. Faithfulness to a memorized text, as well as the constraints of a metrical composition, would militate against Eldreth's adapting song words toward her usual way of speaking. Nevertheless, as mentioned previously, Eldreth herself notes that her singing is more "proper" than her speaking, and the consistent difference marks Eldreth the singer as not necessarily identical with Eldreth the speaker, although that distinction may itself be employed for a number of contradictory effects.

At one end of the spectrum are a number of overtly homiletic songs that Eldreth gives every evidence of singing precisely because she does agree with the message and wants to play a part in voicing it. These include "Drunkard's Prayer," "Wreck on the Highway" ("I saw whiskey and blood run together, But I didn't hear nobody pray"), "The Picture from Life's Other Side" (condemning the lack of compassion that might have prevented desperate suicides), and "Little Orphan Girl" (which denounces the rich man who insists he has "No room, no bread, for the poor"). An especially fascinating and distinctive piece is "Little Girl's Prayer," which begins, "Momma says Daddy has brought us to shame. I'm never no more to mention his name" and contains a spoken interlude condemning divorce because it hurts the children. "Satisfied Mind" ("One day it happened, I lost every dime. But I'm richer by far with a satisfied mind") similarly expresses Eldreth's own oft-mentioned conviction that she is more blessed than people who are financially better off. Eldreth has also written three religious pieces, "Someone's Last Day," "Someday I'm Going to Heaven," and "There Are Times When I Am Lonesome,"[24] that capture her feelings at particular moments—in the first instance, for example, on a morning when her youngest daughter called with the news of her mother-in-law's death. While consistent with other hymns in Eldreth's repertoire in mixing pathos and hope and in portraying heaven as home, these turn on images that Eldreth probably drew from her own experience, for instance, resorting to prayer during a time when she feels "lonesome" and "blue" or being induced to reflect upon the value of one's own life by the realization that today is "someone's last day."

There is only one set of songs for which I have been able to get Eldreth to articulate exactly why she sings them. I was struck by what seemed the unusual prevalence in her repertoire of songs about dying soldiers. Eldreth explained that remembering and singing these songs was a form of thinking and worrying about a group of people who risk their own lives for the general benefit but whom she thinks most others tend to ignore. Contextual observation also allows me to conclude that Eldreth's fascination with songs about people's suffering connects with her strong self-definition as a comforter. She tells various stories about feeling impelled to go help a suffering or grieving person. She constantly monitors her enormous family and often gets so worried about loved ones who are ill or injured that she makes herself sick. When we saw a news story on television about a complete stranger whose children had drowned, she indicated that she would call the man on the telephone if only she knew his number. When I drove her to a viewing at a funeral home in town, I had to stop the car so she could go put her arms around a sobbing girl she had never seen before. It seems possible also that Eldreth may identify with those who suffer (as Bill Ellis argues, with specific reference to the sentimental ballad that Eldreth calls "The Blind Child's Prayer"), not passively and "gratuitously," but with a "conspicuous suffering" that is an "act of protest" and a very effective means of manipulating other characters into desired psychological and emotional states (Ellis 1978:667). In performing these songs, Eldreth simultaneously evokes audience sympathy for those who are represented as suffering through no fault of their own—a group with which she would like to be identified—and elevates herself above that group by demonstrating the emotional resources to offer comfort.

Two songs in Eldreth's repertoire stand out for me because she has made substitutions for words she found unintelligible, evidently to enable her to align her voice more precisely with the song, that is, to mean exactly what she was singing. Gene Autry's "Silver Haired Daddy of Mine," in which a child expresses the desire to make up to her father for the stresses that have aged him, is unsurprisingly congruent with Eldreth's devotion to her own father. Eldreth has, however, transformed the stilted diction of the original, "I'd give all I own, if I could *but atone*," into the comfortably colloquial "if I could *put a tone*," which she explained as follows:

BE: It | now that 'un means that, uh, where his | her father had turned so gray, you know, sh— | they'd give all they owned if they could put a *tone* back, now like a differ—, now like his color of hair *used* to have, put the tone back . . . in his hair . . . like he once had.

PS: Like Miss Clairol [laughs].

BE: Yeah, like Mi— [laughs] | Now be still! Like Miss Clairol, yeah.

"My Mother Was a Lady," written by Edward Marks in 1896 and recorded by Jimmie Rodgers in 1927, is notable, first, in that songs that treat the theme of the exposed but virtuous woman were well received by popular audiences in the 1890s but were taken into the repertoires of twentieth-century oral singers far less often than the dying-child songs of that period. Eldreth has not only held onto a song few of her contemporaries thought worth singing but again modifies crucial words to identify herself with the central character. In this song a young woman "has come to this great city to find [her] brother dear," is working as a waitress, and is harassed by a customer, but stands up for herself and demands decent treatment. In the original, the woman bases her demand for respect on a respectability conferred by class, "My mother was a lady, Like yours, you will allow" (Horstman 1975:355). Eldreth, in contrast, insists that respectability derives from behavior and moral standards, irrespective of class, singing, "My mother was a lady; any[thing] odd she wouldn't allow."[25]

Further, of whom might Eldreth have been thinking when she sang that song? For all the years before she ever spoke back to her husband, did she imagine confronting Ed with his mistreatment and lack of appreciation? Did songs like this, which she could sing as often as she liked but which were not, after all, her own words, enable her to express resentment and demand justice in a safely distanced way? While the adaptation of wording in "My Mother Was a Lady" hints at Eldreth's desire to make the words her own, there are many other songs in her repertoire that it is extremely tempting to interpret as (at least in part) encoded criticisms of her life and lot, but for which I have not even that much concrete evidence. Do the betrayals in the murdered-girl ballads resonate for her as symbolic representations of the way she was mistreated by her husband? Do all the songs mourning lost and hopeless love remind her of the boy she wishes she had married instead of Ed Eldreth? When she vigorously intones the antidivorce diatribe in the middle of "Little Girl's Prayer" is she "protesting too much," trying to convince herself that she really was right to stay with her husband, although even some of her daughters now say she should have left him?

Talking Back

Eldreth's feelings about her husband are, no doubt, extraordinarily complex: a mixture of affection for a man with whom she had eleven children and anger at the ways in which he failed her; longing for a presence to which she had grown accustomed after attending to his needs for forty-seven years and relief at his absence; possibly some nagging guilt that she might have contributed more to the marriage;, and relief for him that his sufferings are over. The discourses made available to her, however, both in everyday talk and in song, supply few terms for these nuances of feeling. They tend to offer black or white, love or anger, joy or grief. They may even bring the two poles together, as in the murdered-girl ballads and "Someone's Last Day," but they do not elaborate on all the emotional territory around and between them. Certainly, when Eldreth wants to express feelings about a person who has gone from her life, there is only one rhetoric available, a discourse—consistent in the deserted-lover and mourned-parents songs—that voices only misery and longing and wipes away any faults the absent person may have had. In order to approximate her actual feelings toward her husband, then, Eldreth twists the words to songs or even sings but talks back to them, expressing one conventional feeling, countering this false claim with its equally incomplete opposite, hoping that listeners may perceive that the truth lies somewhere in the unspoken middle.

Whenever Eldreth sang "Those Wedding Bells Will Never Ring for Me," she would give me a significant look or emphasize those words in the chorus to remind me of what she'd told me:

> I said I'd never . . . as long as I lived ever get married again. [Ed]'s been dead soon be twelve year. And I've not even went with nobody, not one time. As far as having any use for a man. Now I love 'em all as I and in Christian fellowship. In Christian fellowship I love 'em all. But as far as ever getting married to one, no, I'd never do it.

Similarly, she sang "I'm Sitting on Top of the World" most of the way through in the regular form, from the male point of view, and then changed the last verse to "And now *he's* gone and I don't worry . . . ," referring pointedly to frequent insistence that her life had been much easier since her husband's death. Another time she sang "Little Birdie," which includes the line "I've a short time to be here and a long time to be gone," remarking between the lines that her husband used to sing it and that it reminded her of him and then stated directly at the end of the song, "No, really, I'll just be honest and tell you the dying truth, they been so many times that I wish he'd a went on and left me and never come back." This was a rare instance in which the metaphorical comment in the song emboldened Eldreth to speak forthrightly about her critical feelings.

Shortly after her husband's death, Eldreth "made" two songs that suggest how she works with limited expressive resources. In "Making Believe," it appears that Eldreth has adapted a forlorn, deserted-lover song of that title, written by Jimmy Work in 1954 and recorded by the Louvin Brothers, to describe her feelings after her husband died. In "Our Home Is So Lonesome Tonight," she has made smaller changes to what was probably a lament for a dead father.[26] As a result, her compositions feature lines like "He has gone and left us alone" and "I'll spend my lifetime Loving you and wishing you were here." These sentiments puzzled me, given what I had heard from Eldreth about her husband, so I asked her about the songs. Her response suggested both that her actual feelings were more complicated than her previous critical comments about her husband had indicated and that it was not at all easy for her to find words to express those feelings:

PS: I think you did sing that one to me before and it kind of surprised me . . . that you would write a song saying that you missed Ed when it seems all he ever gave you was pain and trouble.

BE: Well, it was true.

PS: That you missed him?

BE: In a way, in a way, I don't hardly know how to say it, but now, as the old saying is, it was pain and trouble, heartaches, heartbreaks. Now that is true. But I and then, I was studying today about I in there, I was in the bathroom? And I think of him 'bout every day. There's hardly ever a day that passes that I don't think of him. And of a night, I very often think of him, and, as Beulah said, I dream of him.[27] But I never have, I don't hardly know how to say it, I've just I I've never worried much about it . . . because he caused me a lot of trouble, he really did.

In her explanation, Eldreth shifts back and forth between opposite positions. She misses Ed, but he caused her heartaches and heartbreaks. Not a day goes by without her thinking of him, but she never worried much about his absence. Twice within these few lines she indicates the difficulty she is having expressing herself: "I don't hardly know how to say it." A few minutes earlier, when she sang "Making Believe" for me, she engaged in a spontaneous dialogue with herself, one voice singing, one speaking, that clarifies the source of her difficulty.

> Making believe that you are around, dear
> Making believe that you are still here
> I know it is sad, my heart is so glad, dear
> To know you're at rest, with loved ones are blessed
>
> Though I am so lonely [speaks: *No, I'm not*],
> I know not what to do, dear [laugh in her singing voice, then speaks: *Yes, I do*]
> I look out the window and think that you are here
> We had our little quarrels [speaks: *Big 'uns, too*]
> Like [laughs] everyone else, love, [laughs]
> We had our lovely days, like heaven above.
>
> Making believe that you are still with me
> The house is so empty it seems like a dream
> I know you are gone, to never return, dear
> But someday I'll go, to where my heart yearns, love.

Making believe, I'll spend my lifetime
Loving you and wishing you were here.
I dream of you; I know it's not true, dear
I know you are gone; it's so lonesome here.

Making believe I'll always love you
Making believe that you are still here.

In singing these songs for me—that is, privately and informally for a woman she knew was sympathetic to her expressions of difficulty with her husband—Eldreth actually articulates out loud both the song she has sung many times and the critical counterdiscourse that must have been running in her head, unvoiced. It would be tempting to suggest that the sung voice was imposed, conventional, not hers, and the spoken rejoinders Eldreth's real voice, but that would be an oversimplification. Recall that Eldreth calls this adapted popular song one of her "homemades," suggesting that she has internalized the conventional view and did in part experience her life in those terms. Her dialogic rendition of "Making Believe" demonstrates how she must simultaneously espouse and flatly contradict the forms of expression offered her, blend her voice with the words of a song and separate it out into a contradictory riposte, in order to approximate her actual feelings.

Eldreth's song repertoire does, then, in many respects express her thoughts, beliefs, and investments of self but not necessarily in obvious or determinate ways. The overall melancholy tone is partly inherited from the dominant themes of available repertoire, partly hints at her own sense of victimization but conversely at her determination to act as a comforter, and partly evokes a structure of feeling according to which sad, old songs recall the idealized times of Eldreth's childhood and reinforce her sense of her own moral worth. In singing a song, she may be agreeing with the message expressed or questioning it in her mind or some of both. Contextual information suggests her allegiances, but, not surprisingly, she rarely articulates her relationship to a particular discourse, instead infiltrating it or arguing against it, while letting it stand for a part of what she means. Occasional overt commentary or humorous back-talking suggests, however, that subtle heteroglossia may be present whenever she lends her voice to a song, such that she sings her own pain and anger underneath the conventional, respectable surfaces.

SINGING PRACTICE

My introduction to Eldreth occurred when she was performing at the Festival of American Folklife. Folklorist Glenn Hinson, who had sought her out to come to the festival, presented her on stage, engaging her in conversation, requesting specific songs, and offering a frame within which the audience could understand her performances as examples of the musical traditions of the Appalachian region. I particularly recall two of Hinson's anecdotes that intrigued me and led me to talk to Eldreth myself. First, he recounted that other people in Ashe and Watauga counties had urged him to seek out "the lady who sings in church." Second, he related that when he visited Eldreth, she offered to get him a cup of coffee and then sang to herself from the time she left the living room until they resumed their conversation. I was fascinated by the two aspects of Eldreth's practice as a singer thus hinted at—on the one hand, that she was a woman for whom singing was an informal, daily, personal practice; on the other, that her reputation in the local community confirmed her standing as a singer. Only in retrospect did the contradiction between the two images—a private singer with a public reputation—occur to me.

I soon learned that the two contexts—home and church—had offered Eldreth opportunities for distinct singing behaviors and kinds of interaction and had consequently had different meanings for her. At home, her singing was a solitary activity, possibly appreciated by children, sometimes even discouraged by her husband. At church, singing was shared, encouraged, and rewarded as a contribution to the spiritual uplift of the congregation. She had otherwise not sung in public or engaged in recreational singing with people outside her family until (in the 1970s) folklorists at Appalachian State University had become interested in her granddaughter Jean Reid and thence in the grandmother who taught Jean her ballads. Eldreth was probably known to those who recommended her to Hinson because her adult children had invited her to sing solos in the several churches they attended. Music was clearly a central feature of Eldreth's experience and self-definition throughout her life. To understand what she means when she says, "My singing is my life," we must consider the multiple contexts in which she has sung and the relationship in each between singing, gender, and work. Still, both the story about the public private singer and her initial framing for me by Hinson can serve as emblems of the extent to which Eldreth's singing career and her identity as a "traditional singer" are inextricable from her late, though influential, involvement with several generations of folklorists.

Singing is a daily activity for Eldreth, a regular part of her experience and her way of getting through the day and interacting with other people and also an important component of her self-definition. But what her practice of singing actually involves and what it has meant for her to "be a singer" differ according to the contexts in which she has sung: in and around the house, in church and related situations (like singing religious songs to comfort the sick), and (since the mid-1970s) in various kinds of public performances and demonstrations organized by folklorists, teachers, and musicians. She is also notably active in making written copies of her songs, both as records and as a form of rehearsal. It is equally important to remark that there are other types and contexts of singing in which we might have expected her to participate, although she actually has not—notably small-group singing (as in the gospel quartets common in local churches) or simply getting together with friends and neighbors to make music for mutual entertainment (although she recalls instances from her childhood and such jams continue to be popular for instrumentalists). The details of her history and practice in each context, and the separations between them, reveal the possibilities and limitations open to Eldreth as a woman with musical talent, revealing how engagement with music both constructs and is constructed by gender identity. Her practice also goes beyond her repertoire in suggesting how she is and is not connected to "traditional mountain music" as it has been defined and celebrated by folklorists. I was able to witness Eldreth singing in instances of all three oral contexts, as well as to observe her involvement with her songbooks. She also frequently talked about singing and memorable times when she had sung, however, so my understanding relies upon her stories about her own singing and analysis of the rhetoric of those stories, as well as upon my observations.

Home Singing

Singing around the house and yard, for one's own amusement and as an accompaniment for other activities, is not in itself unusual. Indeed, this kind of non-performative singing for oneself may be one of the most common forms of engagement with music, although more performative practices are likely to be what comes to mind when we consider the role of music in people's lives. The extent of Eldreth's involvement in this informal singing is remarkable, including the frequency with which she sings (according to her own report) and the effort she has put into retaining a circulating repertoire of almost two hundred songs. The stories she tells about her home singing also further reveal that she invested so extensively in this particular music-making practice because it was compatible with her self-definition as a woman, a moral person, and a worker.

Eldreth tells a number of what we might call "origin stories" that explain how she got started singing and how she amassed such a large repertoire. None of these is the single "true" story, of course. Each calls attention to one influence or one facet of her practice, and each can be rhetorically effective for different audiences or to highlight different aspects of Eldreth's identity. Still, conflict between certain stories suggests the dialogic tension inherent in identity construction. It is also ironic that, although family members and friends clearly recognized Eldreth's talent and large repertoire throughout her life, I suspect that she did not have a reason to formulate most of these stories until folklorists started asking her the kinds of questions that the stories implicitly answer, which got her to think consciously about these issues.

The people who now come to talk to Eldreth about her singing, including me, tend, in a humanistic scholarly vein, to ask her about human sources and influences. Eldreth herself challenges the assumption behind such questions, informing interviewers that she sees her musical ability as a divine gift. She thus explains the frequency with which she sings as the appropriate use called for by that special endowment.

> I think, just really, I think that it's a talent that God give me. I told some of 'em one time, I said, uh, "I'm 'fraid not to use my talent, that I sing. I'm 'fraid that if I was to quit, somebody else'd get it." And I want to keep mine [laughs].

Still, Eldreth likewise acknowledges human sources and models. She particularly loves to talk about her father and his musicianship, suggesting that her talent is to some extent inherited from him:

> My dad always played the banjo and the fiddle. And I told the children not too long ago, I said, "I'd give anything in the world if you children could have heard my daddy play music." Now, many of a time, I'd set and hear him play. Honest to goodness, young'uns, it just almost seemed like the music talked. It just seemed like he'd play it so plain that it was just like that it would almost say the words.

Interestingly, however, it was in the context of talking about her male forebears who were musicians that Eldreth spontaneously explained why she had never followed them in playing instrumental music, offering a surprisingly blunt analysis of the limitations she faced because of her gender:

> He [Grandfather Killens, her father's father] was a musicianer [a professional musician]. And Dad said that he set on the front porch *most of the time* and played music. And that's where Dad picked up his music from, his *playing*. I've often wished that I'd a took up playing some kind of instruments, but I *didn't have time*. I had to work too hard.

The claim that she "didn't have time" is doubtless factually accurate. There were just no moments in a day when she would have felt that she could give priority to playing instrumental music over whatever else needed doing. Yet this is also a symbolic statement. We have seen that leisure time was morally problematic for a poor family like Eldreth's. Working hard and continually was not only a practical necessity but also a way to justify herself, to prove that she was not lazy and thus that she did not deserve to be poor. In her experience, men could free themselves from the blaming discourse and make time to exercise their musical talents and to enjoy doing it. Eldreth, however, evidently could not construct herself outside that discourse, and she attributes the difference to gender. A poor man could be admired and celebrated for his musical talent even if it involved indulgence in leisure. A woman could not. Notably, once, years later when I took my parents to visit her, Eldreth told my mother that as a teenager she had briefly owned a piano and started to learn to play it but that her mother had sold it, without consulting her, at a time when the family needed money. The claim that the exigencies of women's work prevented her from playing an instrument is, however, the story she purveys much more often and, as such, is another means of critiquing her exploitation by her husband.

Singing, conversely, was a kind of music that could accompany a woman's work—housework, cooking, even fieldwork—speeding the labor along and not interfering with it or requiring breaks. Further, singing could actually serve as a productive means of accomplishing some of a woman's necessary tasks, as Eldreth went on to explain:

> I had to work too hard. You see, I raised eleven children. And I babysitted for all the grandchildren. Momma said, "That's where you got a whole lot of your singing is babysitting, rocking the cradles." But I never took up the [instrumental] music.

Singing as an accompaniment to work was, in fact, the example of singing as a social practice that Eldreth fondly describes being modeled for her as she learned songs from her grandmother Milam:

> I used to go stay with [Grandma Milam] a whole lot when she was able to work and go, you know. And, uh, she'd be a-churning . . . and she'd always be a-singing. And I loved her songs. [. . .] She'd be a-working and she'd just sing hard as she could sing.

For me to witness Eldreth singing while she worked took a specific request and her cooperation; but one morning she allowed me to leave a tape recorder running on the kitchen table while she went about her usual morning housework routine, washing dishes and putting them away, sweeping, going out into the yard to feed the chickens, and preparing food for the two grandchildren whom she was keeping that summer.[28] During about forty minutes captured on tape, Eldreth "sang" five songs: "He Touched Me," "My Mother Was a Lady," "I'm Just Here to Get My Baby out of Jail," "T for Texas," and "Little Maggie." In no instance did she actually sing through all the words to any given song. She usually sang at least the first couple of lines and, for one song, a full verse and chorus. She then played around with that song for several more minutes, although she never got to the end of the text. She often backtracked, resang portions that she had already sung, and alternated between lines sung with words and lines where she was humming or "do-do-ing" (her term). Once she was through with a given song and moved on to the next, she did not go back to a previous selection, although I have noticed that often a particular song seems to be on her mind, as she sings it repeatedly on a given day or successive days.

On the tape made that morning, Eldreth's singing is part of a complex soundscape, along with the swishing of dishwater, the scuffing of a broom, the distinctive clatters of dishes, pots, and silverware as Eldreth deposited them in the dish drainer or put them away, her footsteps as she walked around the house and the squeak and slam of the screen door, the opening and closing of drawers, cupboards, and the refrigerator door, the children's talk and shouting as they played together or came into the kitchen to ask questions or get Eldreth's attention, brief conversational interchanges with me, and the low hum of a male voice from the documentary film showing on the children's TV channel. It is interesting to note that Eldreth is constantly moving as she sings, but moving independently of the music, not to it. She does not, for example, coordinate her footsteps or the closing of a drawer to the rhythm of the music. This stream of singing is also resiliently interruptible, such that necessary interactions with the children she is taking care of do not disrupt her.[29] For example, at one point the grandchildren came into the kitchen to ask for something to eat. While singing the first long verse of "My Mother Was a Lady," Eldreth finished washing some dishes and then got out bowls, cereal, raspberries she had picked that morning, and milk. (The transcription begins as she starts the chorus.)

> [sings] My mother was a lady, any odd she wouldn't allow.
> You may have a sister—
> [speaks to children] *D'ya want these?*
> [sings] —who needs—
> [speaks to children] *Come on in here then.*
> [sings] —protection now.
> I've come to this great city to find my brother dear.
> And you'd not dare insult me, sir, if brother Jack were here.
> [speaks] *D'you want milk on 'em?*
> [backtracks to earlier portion of song]
> [sings] She turned [brief pause] hmm her tormentors, her cheeks were blushing red.
> Do-do-do [through melody of remainder of line]
> [calls out loudly] *Come here, Drew, you and Stacey.*
> [pause of several seconds while she waits for children]
> [starts a new song]
> [sings] I'm not in your town to stay, said the lady old and gray.
> [speaks] *Come here, Drew, you and Stacey.*
> [pours cereal into bowls]
> [sings] I'm just here to get my baby out of jail.
> [speaks to Stacey] *No, don't take it in there. Set it on the coffee table, real easy, don't spill it.*
> [sings] Yes, warden, [brief pause] I'm just here to get my baby out of jail.

Eldreth may be interrupted in her singing, either by someone else's intrusive words or by her own need to speak in order to accomplish whatever she is doing along with the singing, but she usually picks up the song again where she left off; and she is able to switch from song to speech and back again without loss of focus or embarrassment. While the kind of observation that taping makes possible depicts song and speech as a kind of dialogue, Eldreth actually seems to suppress awareness of any interaction between the song and either talk or environmental sounds, keeping the two tracks running, as it were, in separate parts of her consciousness. The two can happen simultaneously; thus Eldreth could rely on singing to help her get through the amount of work she needed to accomplish, because neither interfered with the other.

Notably, when Eldreth talks about composing songs, she likewise describes the inspiration coming to her while she is working:

> I made the words to that song one morning. My daughter called me and told me her mother-in-law had passed away. And she was real upset and I was crying with her. I just went into the kitchen and washing my dishes. And seemed like just as fast as one thought come to my mind, another did, and before I left the kitchen sink I had the words made to that song.

In naming her compositions "homemades" she similarly claims them as appropriate women's products, like her home-processed cans of homegrown vegetables, her jars of jam made from handpicked wild berries, and her daily pans of scratch biscuits and corn bread. Interestingly, in this song text Eldreth actually describes the emotions behind the song, but the connection with work is elided by conventional language. "Someone's Last Day" begins simply, "I was standing by my window one bright summer's day." Still, in describing her creativity, Eldreth makes it clear that writing a song does not interfere with the work she as a woman must do: she can and, it appears, usually does think of a song while getting "her" dishes washed.

The discourse Eldreth favors thus treats music making as requiring moral justification and characterizes her home singing as justifiable because it helped her to fulfill her duties, her woman's work: "I always felt happy, regardless what I was doing or how hard I was a-working. I sing with my hard work. Yeah, I did, I'd . . . work and sing. I still do most of the time." Yet there are at least a couple of other stories that she occasionally tells that reveal this conception as not entirely monologic. One of Eldreth's explanations for how she was motivated to develop such a large repertoire is connected to her father's whiskey making:

> He'd take that [sprouted corn] up in the field, in a wide, big, open field, you know, and a big old huge chestnut stump. And I'd sit there and beat that corn all day with a little old hammer. [. . .] I was about ten, nine or ten, somewhere along in there. I was just a little old young'un, but that was my job. [. . .] I'd set and sing all day long, just one little old song after another.

Notably, however, almost every time she tells that origin story she also stresses that she had originally been pushed into the admission:

> And Jean was the first one started telling that on me. Everywhere I'd go when she'd start talking, and she'll do it today, wait and see. She'll say, "Mamaw used to help

bootleg." She said, "Mamaw doesn't like to have this told." So I might as well tell it, 'cause I'm sure she will.

While Eldreth has thus come to trust the audience's sympathetic reaction and to enjoy making people laugh at the hillbilly, as she learned was possible from her granddaughter, she nevertheless hedges her bets. If her singing is to be associated with what she saw as an immoral as well as illegal activity, she wants to be sure audiences are told she is chary of revealing it.

Eldreth's insistent description of herself singing alone while she worked also tells us something else by implicit contrast, namely, that she almost never sang with other adults for fun. When I asked her directly, she did recall instances from her childhood of "bean stringings and apple peelings," where people gathered to complete a common task and sang together to speed the work. She also talked about teaching several of her grandchildren to sing while she babysat for them, and I observed her singing along with Drew and Stacey to teach them a song. From the time she was married, however, secular singing appears to have been almost entirely a solitary activity for Eldreth. It is possible that later in her life there were some parties in her communities at which people sang but that Eldreth did not attend, either because, as a mother with small children, she was too busy to indulge in such leisure activity (compare Kodish 1983:133) or because she was unwilling then, as she emphatically is now, to go to places where people might drink liquor.[30] In fact, Eldreth tells stories that suggest that any secular singing that would be heard outside the confines of her home might be morally suspect. She described an elderly neighbor who overheard her and stopped at her open door to comment. His remark, "Anybody who can sing like you sing. . . . You ought to be in church every Sunday," sounds like a compliment, but Eldreth's defensive reply, "I *was* in church every Sunday," reveals the criticism she believed was implied (see Sawin 2002). Similarly, Jean Reid indicated that her grandfather at least tolerated her grandmother's frequent singing in the house: "I don't think he ever minded it. I never heard him tell her to shut up. I guess that's something he just always got used to." Apparently, however, shortly before Ed died, when Eldreth owned a tape recorder and tried to make tapes to send to distant family members, he actively tried to obstruct his wife's home singing: "And I was in here recording some [songs] one time and he come in and he begin to rattle spoons and forks in the dish drainer to drown out the songs."[31] It appears that when Eldreth tried to use the home sphere to create a permanent and exportable performance product, her husband felt justified in frustrating her attempts. Eldreth was not operating in a cultural context like that described contemporaneously for Malta, where any woman who sang in public was automatically considered a prostitute (McLeod and Herndon 1975) or even Newfoundland, where men often sang at evening gatherings, but a woman who dared to go out to such events would be considered a neglectful mother (Kodish 1983). Still, similar, if less absolute, discourses guided people's responses to her singing and her reception of those responses.

I also suspect, however, that over the course of Eldreth's lifetime there were simply fewer occasions for group singing as the increasing availability of music on records and radio allowed people to be entertained without gathering to create music themselves. Eldreth's repertoire and her practice thus cross with each other in ironic ways. She is arguably old-fashioned in her practice, taking responsibility for learning and singing a large number of songs. In another context she might have been a central member of and valuable resource to a group that sang for sociability. Yet the recordings and broadcasts that supplied so much of her repertoire simultaneously eliminated the occasions in which Eldreth's abilities as a singer of secular songs might have garnered recognition and social support. Similarly her internalization of conservative gender standards both guided her choice of songs to include in her repertoire and stifled any inclination she might have had to take part in whatever participatory music making might still have been available.

Given her lack of opportunities for singing with others and despite her justification of singing as compatible with work, we should not lose sight of the effort Eldreth expended to make time for singing and (as we will discuss in a moment) for writing down song texts. Compared to the daily discourse she reports in her stories or, indeed, to the reportorial style of the English ballads in which emotion is implied by action, the popular songs she favors are explicitly and often dramatically emotional. Songs are always another's words, slightly buffered and deniable. Yet in her constant singing, Eldreth explores adoration and rejection, elation and despair, hope and defiance. Her determination to make these texts an ongoing part of her life experience speaks pragmatically of their value to her as a form of emotional sustenance in an otherwise arid landscape.

Songbooks

Another notable and revealing feature of Eldreth's home-singing practice, and one that helps to explain the size of her effective repertoire, is the fact that she has kept a series of handwritten songbooks. In the summer of 1988 Eldreth had at least six songbooks that she consulted, added to, and sang from. There were two large, cloth-and-leather-bound ledger books with numbered pages, two thick (200–250 page) spiral-bound notebooks, one photograph album with acetate-covered pages into which she had inserted sheets of notebook paper with songs written on them (and a few newspaper clippings, as well as photographs), and at least one slim spiral notebook in which she wrote songs prior to several anticipated performances.

The fact that someone we think of as primarily an "oral" singer would employ her literacy skills to manage her repertoire may not now be surprising. Folklorists have discussed a number of women who kept extensive written song collections (see Kodish 1983; Rosenberg 1980; Burton 1978). Still, this is another of the ways in which Eldreth contravenes the kind of image that may come to mind when she is described as a "traditional Appalachian singer." Eldreth's practice of reading and writing is distinct in both extent and purpose from the massive daily consumption, analysis, and production of text in which most academic readers of these words participate. Because she so frequently spends time writing down song texts, however, Eldreth makes unusually extensive use of literacy skills, compared both to the white, working-class Carolina Piedmont residents documented by Shirley Brice Heath, who use writing mostly for formulaic letters, memory aids like lists, brief notes to substitute for oral communication, and financial records (1983:217–219), and, I suspect, to members of her generation in her community and to many other working-class Americans. Eldreth does not subscribe to any newspapers or magazines and (except for song words) reads only her Bible and a bimonthly series of Sunday school lessons distributed at church. Still, I estimate that, during the time we were working together, Eldreth not infrequently found half an hour or an hour several times a week to go over her songbooks, copy out selections, and write down songs she had been thinking about. Sleepless nights gave her hours at a time for writing:

> [M]aybe if sometime when I wake up in the night . . . I'll think of one [song]. I raise up and put my pillows behind my head and set up in the bed and write it down while I think of it, while it's on my mind. I don't know how many I've wrote like that . . . in the night | of a night . . . when I wasn't sleeping good, I'd just set and write songs.

Eldreth herself certainly saw her writing down of songs as a frequent and relatively regular activity: "When I'm not real busy with something else I *always* get my books down."

In both the Piedmont and the mountains, ethnographers have noted that writing is identified as a form of women's work and that adult women perform the preponderance of writing tasks (Heath 1983:212–213; Puckett 1992). There is thus some delight in noting that Eldreth, although prevented from singing publicly or communally by certain expectations of women, could at least preserve her songs while doing what women are supposed to do. However, both Heath and Puckett also note that women can rarely take time from other responsibilities to write for purposes that cannot be readily justified to others as "practical" and necessary for the fulfillment of women's responsibilities, although these may be construed as including the maintenance of family ties through letter writing. Similarly, Eldreth sees her writing as a leisure-time activity: she talks about it as "messing with" her books. As such, it has to wait until she is "not real busy with something else." She may also be distracted from working on the songbooks for long periods by illness, worry, or a family crisis. From her teenage years Eldreth made a practice of writing down words to favorite songs and keeping them in "kinda like a letter box or something like that, just something that I could put 'em in, maybe a pasteboard box, where I'd hide love letters, too." None of these individual sheets survived the floods and fires that have destroyed her homes, however. Eldreth estimates that it was not until around 1970, when she was nearing sixty and her children had left home, that she actually began systematically creating books of her songs and found she was able to maintain this pattern of activity and time allotment. Ironically, the sleepless nights that enabled her to get a good start on her first songbooks were probably occasioned by the stresses of nursing her husband through the last years of his long battle with emphysema.

Various scholars have suggested that women's songbooks provide opportunities to engage in sociable interaction focused on song texts for those who do not or cannot sing where others can hear them. Kodish, for example, notes that in Newfoundland

> Women do not tend to sing publicly in times [house parties], but there is an active tradition of solo display of songs for which women are well known. We have evidence from the 18th century to the present of the women's tradition of keeping enormous scrapbooks, or ballad books, filled with clippings and handwritten song texts to which they might refer for their own pleasure, to settle arguments, to entertain, or to provide words for other singers. (1983:133)

Eldreth, however, seems to have had few people to share song texts and songbooks with, apart from her granddaughter Jean Reid and folklorists. In one instance that she reported to me, Eldreth took a book along when visiting a neighbor who had been ill and depressed and used it to get the friend singing with her. Conversely, on one occasion Eldreth and I visited Hattie Presnell, a member of the extended Hicks-Profitt family of singers and storytellers on Beech Mountain (see Burton 1978). Eldreth scoured Presnell's songbooks hoping to find texts to songs she only partially remembered. Eldreth herself, however, does not talk about other singers, except Reid, using her as a resource in this way. In the absence of communal singing events, there seems likewise to have been little impetus for others to learn Eldreth's repertoire and few contexts for pleasantly interacting with other singers to compare versions through the medium of writing or to search for rare texts in each others' books.

Eldreth's organization of her songbooks suggests that she modeled them after church hymnals. She evidently wrote down the songs in whatever order they occurred to her and allowed each text to cover as many pages as necessary, but then assigned a sequential number to each song (rather than to each page), as do hymnals of the kind she has used. On the inside covers of each book she made an index (again, using the same position within the book as in many hymnals), although her indices are in numerical rather than alphabetical order. Thus, the index is a direct reflection of the content rather than a finding aid arranged according to another systematic principal, but this arrangement works well for Eldreth to speed her locating of a given text. During our tapings when she thought of a particular song that she wanted to sing, she would often scan down the index with her finger and then say the number and title out loud while she searched for that page in the book—"Number one-eighty, 'Long Black Veil'"— just as the song leader does in church.

The most counterintuitive thing that I had to learn about Eldreth's songbooks is that, although she uses them in part as reference works, that does not imply all the same attitudes and practices for her as it might for me. At one level Eldreth does regard and employ her books as repositories of information that are proof against memory loss. She refers to the books when she feels called upon to sing a wide selection of songs, either when she makes a tape to send to a friend ("[T]he day before yesterday, I got the tape recorder and one of my songbooks and I fastened myself up in the bathroom and then I sang just as hard as I could") or when I want to record her singing. At the beginning of the summer during which we worked together, Eldreth would get out her songbooks when I got out the recorder and would flip through them for inspiration. Toward the end of the summer she searched the books in advance of our recording sessions to find songs she had not yet sung for me, often songs that she had not sung at all for some time ("London City"/"Butcher Boy" and the hymns she associated with her father and Aunt Mary Killens were among these). Not uncommonly in our recording sessions she would think of a song or I would request one that she had sung or referred to previously, but she would defer singing it, remarking, "I've got that song somewhere in one of my books." However, if she was singing unself-consciously, she often produced quite full versions of those same songs from memory. When she "sang from the book," it often seemed that the book served mostly as a convenient list of titles from which she could choose, since after the first few words she rarely needed to look at the text, as indeed is the case for many of the hymns sung in church as well. To the extent that her own songbooks are modeled on hymnals, it should not be surprising that she would similarly regard the book as the container of words and regularly make the text available for reference while she sings but that she would at the same time keep most of the words (as well as the tunes) in memory as well.

Similarly, when I asked about her motivation for making the songbooks, Eldreth explicitly stated that her purpose was song preservation:

PS: What got you started [writing songbooks], anything in particular?
BE: Well, just songs that I wanted to remember and I was afraid if I just let 'em go on and on and I wouldn't | I might maybe sometime forget 'em. And I wanted to keep 'em and let the children . . . pass 'em on to others that would like to hear 'em and | and for others that would like to sing 'em.

Note, however, that she says she was afraid that *she* might forget the songs. Although she has at times lent the books to Jean Reid and to me for us to copy out words, her goal was more to keep the song words in her own mind than to make textual records to which others could refer. She has little nostalgic attachment to her books as artifacts apart from their usefulness to her and no qualms about recopying worn books into new ones and throwing the old ones away:

PS: Of the books you've got now do you have any idea of how old is the oldest one? Like these ones it looks like you wrote in 1985. Do you have older ones?
BE: Well, I did have some older ones, but I wrote the songs out of those into these and then I done away with the others.

She protects the books to the extent of sheltering them from the rain and finding substitute paper for a grandchild who wants someplace to scribble, but several books contain amidst the song words tracings of children's hands and similar evidence that she is willing both to put other precious things in them besides songs and to use them to humor the children she takes care of if need be. Likewise, I have never heard her speak of the books themselves as accomplishments or seen her show them off (as well she might) as evidence of the size of her repertoire.

In this instance as in others, Eldreth seems not to envision the written text as an object with potential functions apart from her immediate use of it. For example, when she makes a song tape, she always slips into the case a sheet of paper on which she has written the titles of the songs in the order in which she sang them, thereby providing some of the information usually included on a record dust jacket. She does not, however, label either the cassette or the box with her name or the date. As with her analogous disinclination to label home-canned vegetables or family photographs, she presumably thinks that the listener's ability to recognize her voice or to remember receiving the tape from her makes specification of the singer's identity unnecessary. Even in packaging her voice so that it can be heard when she is not present, Eldreth does not seem to imagine information requirements occasioned by her own absence. As Amy Shuman notes, "the central feature of decontextualization (however unrealizable) is that one writes with an understanding of what it is like to read from another person's perspective" (1986:115). Eldreth maintains a kind of innocence arguably analogous to that of the adolescents Shuman studied. In her stories, and to an even greater extent with these artifactual records of her verbal performance, she certainly thinks about projecting herself positively but does not stop to consider how the receiver's situation or state of knowledge might differ from her own.

Eldreth's relaxed attitude toward her songbooks further suggests her awareness that (even though the books contain texts she does not often sing) with a little effort she could always create another one. Indeed, she is almost constantly in the process of creating another one:

PS: Do you just always have some songbook that you're writing ones in?
BE: Uh huh.
PS: Do you just keep writing them and keep writing them?
BE: Yeah, just one and then another.

Eldreth described having copied a worn book page by page into a new one, that is, working from one written text to create another. In my observation, however, she was mostly involved in using writing as part of several ongoing processes of working with her songs so as to recycle and revivify her repertoire.

The process she most often spoke about was re-remembering old songs that she had not sung in a long time and bringing them back into her repertoire.

> I have laid there [in bed at night] and seems like a song'll just come to me and I'll get to thinking about it and studying about it and then I'll . . . the next thing you know I'll be as wide awake as I can be regardless of it's one, two, three, or four o'clock in the morning and I'll lie there and say it over to myself until I get it. Till . . . and then the next day I'll go write it in my book.

Old songs, like her own compositions, just "come" to her as a passive receptor, but once they arrive, she can actively fix them in her mind by saying or singing them over silently and can then capture them on paper. She cannot always write down the full texts as soon as she starts to remember them, but she does keep some writing materials by her bedside, "just an envelope or a plain little piece of paper in my Bible," to jot down the titles. This enables her to get the songs going in her head again the next day and then to sing them and write them down. Once she has taken the time to write out the words and thereby fixed the song even more firmly in mind, she is likely to sing it aloud fairly often at least for a while.

I also observed that Eldreth frequently spent considerable time writing songs in a notebook (usually a new, slim spiral-bound book) just before a planned performance. I initially assumed that she was creating a portable reference work containing the texts of songs she might sing. Eldreth did take these new notebooks to her performances and in one instance when she was particularly nervous even carried the book on stage, but I never saw her consult them after she had created them, either prior to a performance or during one. Even more significantly, I realized that in creating these new books, she never copied a text from an extant text but rather wrote out of her head, taking dictation, as it were, from her mental singing. This, she confirmed, is her practice whenever she writes down a song:

PS: When you're writing songs down in a book, do you sing through it in your mind or . . . ?

BE: Um hmm.

PS: . . . do you sing it out loud or just . . . ?

BE: No, I just sing it to myself, like I's singing to myself . . . and write 'em.

In creating performance-specific notebooks, then, the process is more important to Eldreth than the product. Writing out the words while singing the song over in her head is a significant and often sufficient form of rehearsal. She may supplement the writing with actual singing out loud at another time prior to a performance but does not always feel the need.

The great majority of the songs Eldreth currently sings are ones she learned between fifty and eighty-five years ago. Her repertoire is not simply "stable" (see Goldstein 1971), however, but rather undergoes a constant process of renewal in which writing plays an important role. Eldreth's practice of literacy is not a motivating factor in deciding which songs will be retained and which jettisoned, but it is an enabling factor, a technical means that allows her to bring remembered songs back into her active repertoire. Throughout her life she probably periodically thought of songs she had not sung for a while and picked them up again. Her attraction to "old" songs (into which category a song she remembers that she used to know automatically fits) provides a constant motivation to recall and reactivate songs that were active in her repertoire previously. The songs Eldreth remembers in this way may be ones she truly has not thought of in years or ones that, when she checks in her songbooks, she will find she wrote down not too long ago. She may keep singing a remembered song or let it lapse again. Even if she stops singing a song spontaneously, she may find the words in one of her books, recall the tune, and sing it once or frequently at a later date. Now that she has the model in mind of acquiring a written text to go along with a remembered tune and partial text, as well as access to academics who are interested in songs, she will occasionally ask one of us to see if we can find the words to a partly remembered song for her.[32] With writing as a mediator, then, Eldreth constantly recycles her repertoire.

Eldreth's songbooks should be regarded not as inert objects but rather as one of the contexts in or media through which she produces and reproduces her songs. Writing was seen as an unexceptional activity for a woman, and she thus met little resistance in extending it slightly beyond obviously utilitarian purposes, even during her busiest years, and has been able to devote substantial energy to using it to preserve her song repertoire since her responsibilities have lessened.

Writing down a song involves Eldreth in singing it over (text and words) silently in her head. As such, writing not only (and not even primarily) produces a useful artifact. Rather, it is an intrinsically valuable and interesting activity—a form of rehearsal, a means of fixing a text in her mind prior to singing it out loud, and an enjoyable act in its own right. Appropriately, then, writing as process and practice has even more of an influence on Eldreth's constant revival of old repertoire items than do the reference texts that are its apparent end product. In another sense, however, Eldreth's songbooks had to be more important as processes than products. Because of a lack of contexts—beyond those she herself manufactured with her grandchildren—in which secular songs might be shared, Eldreth's songbooks did not provide her the opportunities for sociable interaction documented in other situations where women were otherwise discouraged from sharing their musical knowledge in public.

Singing in Church

The one public context in which Eldreth has been able to share her talents and to participate in music with her neighbors has been the church. She has been a member of the choir at whatever church she attended since childhood. As she notes, "I feel plumb out of place if I'm not | if I don't go to the choir, 'cause I've done it just about all my life. So the choir's where I always sit." She also regularly sings a solo piece in the course of the service. When singing for herself at home, Eldreth certainly sometimes monitors the quality of her voice production. Prior to her involvement with folklorists, however, church had been the place in which she was encouraged to "perform" as a singer in the terms elaborated by Bauman, that is, to strive for aesthetic excellence as she understands it, to share her efforts with an audience "for the enhancement of their experience," and to make the result "subject to evaluation for the way it is done" (1977:11). Musical contributions in church seem largely immune to the kind of gender discrimination that might have censured Eldreth's participation in instrumental music or secular singing outside the home. Singing in churches, her own and others to which she was invited, garnered Eldreth a local reputation before folklorists' attention gained her recognition in other contexts. This kind of freedom appears to stem, however, from a consensual framing of sacred singing as not exactly performance in all the usual senses.

Since shortly after she built her own house in 1972, Eldreth has been a member of the Tabernacle Baptist Church, just a quarter mile down the road. Most Sundays, between thirty-five and fifty people attend, almost all of whom live or previously lived within a couple of miles. At other times in her life Eldreth's experience of musical participation in church may have been somewhat different from what I observed. The church of which she was a member in Todd during the 1960s, and which we visited once, is a bit larger and more formal. She also talks about having attended a regular camp meeting around the same time, and Reid recalls going with her grandmother to Pentecostal services where Eldreth and others would "get happy" and sing and dance in an uninhibited expression of the Holy Spirit. Still, Eldreth herself does not differentiate her involvement as a child from participation at Tabernacle, which has been her church home for more than thirty years. Eldreth often remarks, "I love my little church." She "hates" to miss a service there; and, as I discovered when we came to Durham for her performance at the Festival for the Eno, she does not regard worship at another church as an adequate or appealing substitute.

Singing at Tabernacle Baptist, as at many small Baptist churches in the South, is remarkable for its combination of centrality to worship and its informality (see Titon 1988, chap. 5). During the years that I have known Eldreth and attended church with her, the Sunday morning service has always begun with the choir singing three or four hymns, a section specifically identified as "the song service." The choir and any members of the congregation who wish to join in also sing another couple of hymns during the course of worship. Every two to three weeks on average someone will offer a special solo or small group performance as part of the service.[33] In months that have five Sundays, the church holds an additional evening service on the fifth Sunday, the centerpiece of which is a musical performance by a visiting group whose participation is arranged through a personal connection with someone in the congregation. (During the summer of 1988, the visitors included a bluegrass gospel group led by the son of a church member and the "Spiritual Heirs," whose old-fashioned style Eldreth so admired.) The Tabernacle choir is likewise occasionally invited to neighboring churches to provide the special performance for their fifth Sunday, just as Eldreth has been invited by her children to visit and sing solos in their churches.

Although valued, the singing at Tabernacle Baptist is much less formal than the norm for the larger, urban, mainline denomination churches with which I had formerly been familiar. The singers are self-selected and largely untrained and the performances mostly unrehearsed. About fifteen of the forty-five congregation members at Tabernacle regularly sit in the choir, a row of three pews set at right angles to the congregational seating on the left side of the church (as one enters) between the front row of regular pews and the raised dais and lectern for preaching. Several women take turns providing accompaniment on an upright piano. The choir has an identity as a group, and the choir leader is elected along with other church officials like the Sunday school leader and the church secretary, but choir membership is a matter of willingness to serve rather than auditioning or selection. Choir members apparently like to sing more than the rest of the congregation (some of whom do not join in even on congregational hymns) and may be more musical. Vocal tone ranges, however, from sweet to strident, and people take harmony parts sporadically, if and when they are able. Eldreth insists that I sit with her and join in the choir's singing whenever I visit, and my presence is accommodated without complaint.

The manner of presentation for the hymns sung only by the choir is no different from those that all church members sing. The choir leader chooses the hymns in advance and announces them, rather than, as in some small mountain churches, "let[ting] the congregation choose just before singing [with] each member select[ing] his or her favorites" (Titon 1988:214). Still, hymns occasionally have to be changed on the spur of the moment if one of the pianists cannot manage the original selection, and this is not a source of significant concern. The one "choir rehearsal" I attended involved singing through several hymns (some familiar, some new) just as in a service; there was no attempt to go over difficult passages, no effort to assign or learn harmony parts, no attempt to synchronize timing or tone, indeed, no evident special approach to the music to mark this as rehearsal in conventional terms. The singers are aware of some desirable formal features of appropriate singing—Eldreth talks, as mentioned earlier, about teasing fellow choir members who have to take a breath before the end of the phrase—but there is no organized means for inculcating those practices. In sum, the provision of vocal music for the church is seen essentially as a voluntary and unpremeditated activity. Participating in the choir involves a mixture of using one's gifts to glorify God and having a good time with the people one likes to sit next to in church.

Eldreth's church welcomes special musical offerings by any member of the congregation who feels moved to provide one. Eldreth is only one of several individuals and groups within her church who periodically contribute to the service. During my visits between 1987 and 1989, for instance, I witnessed five performances by Eldreth, two by a quartet composed of two couples who usually sang in the choir, one by the elderly parents of one of those couples (who were formerly more active in the church than age and illness then allowed them to be), one by a young woman who sang and played the guitar, and a special Mother's Day performance by a man who accompanied himself on the electric bass. Eldreth teaches hymns to her grandchildren and from time to time persuades one of them to stand up at the front of the church and sing, with only a little help from her on the first line. The Sunday school teachers likewise occasionally get the children to prepare and sing a song. When I left Boone in August 1988 after attending church regularly with Eldreth for three months, she convinced me to perform a song with her one Sunday as a fitting goodbye. Singers have complete permission to occupy the raised dais and even the pulpit, otherwise used only by the preacher (and not by either the deacon who gives church announcements or the Sunday school teacher). Performers often had clearly planned their performances in advance, but they usually only told the choir director of their intention when they arrived for the Sunday service. The director never gave any indication that it was a problem to accommodate an individual who wished to offer a special performance or, conversely, to have the choir sing another hymn if no special performance was forthcoming on a given day. Eldreth may sing solos a little more often than others in her church, but she is not markedly unusual in being willing to stand up in front of the congregation and sing alone. Conversely, within the local continuum of semispecialist religious singers—from individuals who might sing a single song as a testimony in their own church on an important occasion, through groups that rehearse fairly often and perform locally half a dozen times a year, up to named groups that become semiprofessional, traveling most weekends and receiving donations to pay for instruments and matching costumes—Eldreth is situated toward the less elaborate end and is somewhat unusual and old-fashioned in singing by herself a cappella, though she is still part of a thriving musical economy.

Her regular practice of offering solos has provided Eldreth with an identity as a singer, in her own mind and for others. Her repeated offering of solos enables her to think of herself as a singer precisely because her past willingness subjects her to others' ongoing expectation that she will make a special contribution to the service. At a lull in the service the choir director (who usually sat in the front row of the choir, immediately in front of Eldreth's usual seat) would regularly lean back over the pew to enquire, "Do you have anything for us today, Mrs. Eldreth?" If she did not sing a solo for several weeks at a time, other church members would question her, urge her, even extract promises from her to sing, in part because they enjoy hearing her and in part, I suspect, because they know she likes to be asked. One evening Eldreth decided to surprise one of her daughters by going to a midweek service at the church in Todd that she had attended for years, but which she had visited only occasionally since moving to her new house sixteen years previously. The man who had been the choir director at South Fork Church when she was a member of the congregation still held the post. He immediately recognized Eldreth and insisted that we sit in the choir and that she sing several solo pieces, saying, "Oh, good, we can just sing one and then turn it over to Mrs. Eldreth." Eldreth seemed quite surprised at this invitation, although she was carrying copies of the words to several hymns in her purse; and she had to scramble through the hymnbook and the papers she had brought in order to come up with something to sing. Nevertheless, she was obviously delighted to have been remembered and asked to sing and was more than willing to fulfill the request on the spur of the moment.

In terms of message, style, and mood, solo and small group performers add noticeable variety to the musical fare at Tabernacle. The choir and congregation sing only out of the hymnal that the church owns (*Best Loved Songs and Hymns*, 1961, R. E. Winsett Music Co., Dayton, TN), the selections in which, mostly composed between the two world wars, are musically and textually homogeneous, generally upbeat and emphasizing expectations of the rewards of heaven. The vocal quartet in the church, by contrast, favored current, pop-gospel songs (like ones often playing on radio or TV when we visited their homes), while the young woman who accompanied herself on guitar presented hymns that sounded recently composed, in a folklike style, in order to appeal to young people. Eldreth expands outward from the church hymnal in several directions, toward the more solemn and the more old-fashioned as well as the more modern, the more high-performance, and even the more secular. For a church revival, Eldreth sang "The Old Crossroad" and "The Pale Horse and His Rider," notably more somber, textually and musically, than the majority of congregational hymns, emphasizing the inevitability of death and the awful fate of the unsaved, and thus situationally appropriate and well calculated to help a sinner achieve "conviction" of his own sinfulness and need for salvation as the first step toward religious conversion (see Bruce 1974:64–67).

Eldreth's favorite solo offering during the years I have known her has been "He Touched Me," composed in 1963 and evidently popularized by its frequent performance by George Beverly Shea on the televised Billy Graham Crusades.[34] The piece is an obvious dramatic vehicle for showcasing a solo voice. It has numerous sustained notes, and Eldreth renders it with a richer timbre and much more vibrato in her voice than when singing any other song, producing almost a coloratura effect. While consistent with the common theme in the Southern Baptist hymn repertoire of a personal relationship with Jesus and conviction of being saved, it is also especially appropriate thematically as an individual testimony:

> He touched me, yes, he touched me,
> And oh, the joy that floods my soul.
> Something happened and now I know,
> He touched me and he made me whole.

In a very different direction, Eldreth skillfully negotiates the blurry boundary between sacred numbers and songs expressing devotion to family also evident in the bluegrass repertoire. She surprised me but pleased the congregation, for example, with a performance in church of "Silver Haired Daddy of Mine." She explained before she began singing that she was doing the song for an older man in the congregation who had recently been ill and at the request of his daughter. The woman who had asked for the song as well as two others, one with an elderly and one with a recently deceased father, cried while Eldreth was singing and tearfully thanked her for the performance after the service. Although Eldreth was not taking a very big risk with this selection, the instance demonstrates how she can trade upon her established legitimacy to stretch listeners' expectations and how her success in pulling off a tremendously appropriate and appreciated performance then circularly reinforces her legitimacy as a provider of suitable religious experience (Herzfeld 1991).

And contributing to the religious experience of one's fellow church members is precisely the rationale and justification for musical performance. This idea applies more generally within the Christian tradition, of course, but it assumes a particular sense and salience within the egalitarian community of a small Baptist congregation like that at Tabernacle, where each member assumes a certain responsibility for the state of her neighbor's soul. These solo song performances very often are labeled as or lead into a "testimony," an explicit personal statement of some aspect of faith that may both confirm and model others' appropriate experience. Eldreth, for instance, used her singing of "Poor Wayfaring Stranger" to introduce such a profession. The song concludes, "I am just going over Jordan. I am just going over home," which led Eldreth to remark:

> I know I'm getting way up in years, but I'll tell you the truth, I'm a happy person . . . and I'm looking forward to going home. I really am. I believe it'd be a happy place . . . when we can all join together. I feel like we've got a . . . real close fellowship here. And I love everyone of 'em . . . from the bottom of my heart. I never pass this church that I don't say prayers for the little church, 'cause I love the church and I love the ones that go to it. But I look forward to going home.

The flip side of this emphasis on content and sincerity is the regularity with which performances are marked—indeed, marked *as performances*—precisely by a disclaimer of performance (Bauman 1993a). Like other special performers in these small churches, Eldreth prefaces every offering with a remark like "I know I'm not a singer, but I'm trying to make a joyful noise for the Lord" or "You all just pray for me while I try to do this song." To those who offer her compliments, Eldreth often responds, "Give God the praise. It's nothing I did. Give God the praise." These disclaimers have the effect of helping to set up an interpretive frame in which excellence of form and execution is officially discounted, even though such excellence may be both aimed at and noticed. In concert with the expectation that songs sung in church will be transparent statements of the singer's beliefs and feelings, the frame within which the singing event is present-ed thus makes strong claims for the primacy of its semantic content and affective impact. The singers' skill and the aesthetic and emotional quality of the per-formance may indeed contribute to the emotional and spiritual effect on listen-ers, but people should concentrate on the effect and not the means. Thus, to the extent that "performance," as isolated by Bauman, involves a Jakobsonian "focus on the message for its own sake" and full performance is identified by a domi-nance of interest in the form and execution of the communicative event over other aspects and effects (Jakobson 1960:356; Bauman 1977:7), Eldreth's singing in church should be identified as a modified, partial, or hedged kind of perform-ance. It is suggestive that during the service people are likely to respond to a song with "Amen," signifying agreement with the sentiment or belief expressed. Only afterwards will they compliment the singer on the formal quality of the perform-ance, "That's the prettiest song I ever heard."[35] An important corollary is that an adorable child trying to remember the words or an old man haltingly choking out a hymn he has sung for sixty years may move listeners to contemplation of God's goodness or of the promised rewards of heaven as effectively, if not more effec-tively, than an accomplished singer. Formal excellence may contribute to this emotional/religious effect, but it is valued primarily, though not exclusively, for that contribution rather than in itself. Emphasis on form may be a significant consideration, but it should not be the dominant function.

In most instances, then, whatever degree of skill a musician can muster is graciously and gratefully received as an attempt to contribute to the shared reli-gious experience of the congregation. A potential for conflict arises, however, in those instances where the singer's conduct is perceived as calling too much attention to the performance itself or to the performer and her abilities. The more accomplished the musician or the more evidence she gives of aiming for formal excellence, the more requisite the disclaimer of skill or intention to per-form. In fact, any special singing draws attention to the individual and his or her talents. It also takes time. There are no absolute time limits on the service, but people accustomed to going home (or out) for Sunday dinner after church start to get hungry and inattentive if the service goes on too long (as I discov-ered for myself on hot summer Sundays when my stomach began to growl while the service seemed to drag on interminably). Extra time spent on special singing also cuts into the time for other contributions. In a church to which Eldreth formerly belonged, she frequently prepared a group of her grandchildren to sing during the service. Some people in that congregation apparently loved it. Others, including the Sunday school teachers, apparently wanted more time spent on religious teaching, perhaps even found the children irritating in frequent doses, and complained behind Eldreth's back. I found out about this distressing incident, over which Eldreth actually left the church, only because Eldreth sang me a cryptic song that she had written about it, "Jealous in the Bible" (on the model of "Dust on the Bible"). Similarly, since singing is supposed to be an offering to God and a contribution to the religious experience of others in the congregation, it is not acceptable for performance to take the place of or priority over worship. In a small church, absences are noticed and keenly felt. The common greeting, "We missed you last Sunday," though an honest expression of friendly concern, also requires a justification in answer. Eldreth made a point of explaining to me that she would not sing elsewhere than her own church if it meant missing the service:

> They [people at her daughter's church] have asked me to come sing, but I hate to go leave my church on Sunday. But if it's any time like of a night or when I'm not in church, then I'll go along and sing for them.

Similarly, when the festival performance in Durham kept her away from home on a Sunday, she repeatedly mentioned how sorry she was to be missing the service at her church.

An interesting corollary to tension about overemphasizing performance is Eldreth's insistence that she actually gets more anxious about singing before friends in her little church than in front of a secular audience of hundreds:

> I don't m— | hit don't bother me. I mean, you know . . . now hit seems like it bothers me more . . . to stand up in my church and sing than anywhere. It's strange, isn't it? Than anywhere I can go, hit | hit bothers me more. And I | I guess it's | well, maybe it's 'cause everybody knows me out there [at the church]. And I | I don't care to[36] stand up and sing before . . . a crowd nor how— | nor how many, 'cause that it seems like that | ain't nobody that knows me.

In contrast to Reid, who, Eldreth enjoys reminding her and me, used to get sick to her stomach out of nervousness before a big public performance, Eldreth wants to make it clear that she worries more about singing for those members of her congregation, to whom she has a clear religious duty. She also approvingly quotes an alternate explanation that erases the question of performance and performance anxiety completely:

Well, now, I | I'll tell you, most of the time when *I* get up in *God's* house, if you're
noticing, I'll tremble. But, uh, I said that to a real old lady one time. I told her, I
said, "I don't know why it is when I stand up to | and sing or testify," I said, "I trem-
ble." She said, "That's the power of God." She says, "You *will* tremble under the
power of God." Well, I suppose you would, don't you? You *will* tremble. You feel like
it, don't you?

In contrast to any kind of purely recreational or purely performative singing,
then, Eldreth's singing in church counts as a Christian duty and thus as a fully
appropriate activity for a woman. It is not quite a form of work, but neither is it
a leisure indulgence. Even though Eldreth's husband did not himself attend
church, there seems never to have been any question of his preventing her from
participating in the service or singing there. As the story of the Cox boy's funeral (analyzed in chapter 4) indicates, however, Eldreth was concerned about the
propriety of singing even for an extension of church like a funeral, especially
when it might be seen as interfering with her duty to care for her husband or
when it involved her being singled out because of her special knowledge. Other
women's support, including in that case reframing her singing at the funeral as
itself a duty—a bereaved mother's request that could not otherwise be filled—
was crucial to allowing her to exercise her talents and enjoy doing so.

Church is the context for singing that matters most to Eldreth. Using a gift that
she believes she received from God to return Him praise and to share religious fellowship with her church is a fully satisfying form of performance for her. At the
same time, as we have noted, church performance is necessarily hedged so that
attention is deflected from the performer and toward the religious message and the
spiritual uplift it is meant to inculcate. Singers can receive credit for their artistic
abilities without being accused of inappropriately drawing attention to themselves
because the church is a setting in which performance is disclaimed and in which
sung messages are accepted as semantically and emotionally transparent.

Public Singing

Until she was in her sixties, home and church provided Eldreth with all the
scope for singing that she evidently imagined or wished for. She has never given
me any indication that she dreamed of performing for broader audiences or that
she was dissatisfied with or felt limited by the occasions and contexts for singing
available to her. The avidity with which she has since taken to the public performance opportunities offered by folklorists and musicians, however, suggests
how congenial she finds the chance to perform without the constraints inherent
in her previous contexts. For Eldreth, these new performance contexts represent
chances to share her large secular repertoire and to employ her talents for an
audience's enjoyment irrespective of religious affect, that is, to treat her singing

as aesthetic production. Ironically, most of the performances she is invited to give are actually framed by those who arrange them as demonstrations of various sorts rather than as pure performance. Eldreth, however, makes her own interpretations. The story of Eldreth's involvement with folklorists cannot be told in a single voice or from a single point of view. There are ways in which her purposes coincide with those of the people who have arranged her public performances and ways in which she ignores their definitions and frames things in her own terms. Similarly, in some respects Eldreth's example refutes the comfortable stories folklorists like to tell themselves about their relationships with "the folk" but in other ways confirms our hopes for the benefits of such collaboration.

To begin, as discussed earlier, Eldreth was not "discovered" by me or by any other lone folklorist scouring the mountains for traditional singers in the mode of Cecil Sharp but got involved indirectly through her granddaughter. Reid, who has an exquisite, rich voice and who contemplated trying to make a career for herself in country music, started singing publicly in talent contests in junior high school. One of her music teachers (who may also have been working on a master's degree at Appalachian State University) took a special interest in her in part because of her beautiful voice and in part because of the older songs she had learned from her grandmother. The teacher took Reid to Raleigh to sing for a convention of music teachers, who were focusing on folk music that year (about 1972 or 1973). There Reid attracted the attention of various scholars of Appalachian culture and music, notably Professor Cratis Williams, one of the earliest and most influential proponents of Appalachian studies and then a dean at ASU, who was excited to find someone of her age singing the old ballads. Over the next several years Reid made more contacts with academics interested in encouraging her singing and received increasing numbers of invitations to sing in public: for the North Carolina Folklore Society, at the Jonesboro Storytelling Festival, at the Bascom Lamar Lunsford Folk Festival, for classes at ASU, and on short notice for a group of international scholars being toured around by the United States Information Agency (USIA). She also appeared on television in 1976 for one of a series of "Bicentennial Minutes" about American traditions, although she complains about having been stereotypically posed with a dulcimer, which she does not play, and next to a mountain waterfall, which drowned out her singing. People asked Reid where she had learned her songs and expressed interest in hearing her grandmother sing. Initially, Eldreth accompanied Reid primarily as a chaperone but soon began to sing along with her. Eldreth began singing in these public venues in 1975 or 1976, shortly before her husband died, as Reid explained, "'cause I remember Papaw [her grandfather] used to get real jealous . . . about me taking her places," and went out more often after his death in 1977. In 1979 Reid went off to nursing school in Charlotte and was unavailable for performances for three years. Eldreth began to perform by herself and became the person whom event planners knew about and contacted. Once Reid started working as a nurse in Lenoir and through the 1980s, Eldreth and Reid again frequently performed together unless Reid could not get time off from work; in the 1990s, after Reid's sons were born, Eldreth again most often performed alone. Thus, Eldreth's "career" as a public performer should not be seen as an obvious matter of the most representative "tradition bearer" inevitably rising to attention. Rather the chance temporal coincidence of Reid's coming into contact with folklorists as a teenager but then being less available to perform, the U.S. bicentennial that focused attention on American traditions, a revitalization of regional festivals thereafter, and Eldreth's arriving at that period in her life when an older woman could have more flexibility and control over her time resulted in an involvement in public performance that would not have come about under other historical or personal circumstances.

Initially Eldreth was shy on stage, but she got over that fairly quickly, in part out of a determination to sing well. As she pragmatically says, "I used to get real nervous, but it hurts you [as a singer]." By the time I met her in 1987 she appeared comfortable, natural, and unselfconscious in performance. In fact, she usually looked like she was having a wonderful time, laughing and joking with the audience, responding to the presenter with funny quips, and talking quite spontaneously about herself. Audiences responded well to her warmth and unpretentiousness. I have seen people cluster around her after a performance, wanting to talk to her and hug her and get their pictures taken with her. Eldreth loves to talk about how the children crawl into her lap when she sings at schools or how the people in New York just had to get close to her after a performance: "And they's so many, one didn't turn me loose till another one'd be a-hugging me and kissing me and really crying on my shoulder." She has sung for scholars and international visitors, and she and Reid were filmed by actress Stella Stevens for a documentary on "The Southern Heroine," but she takes it all in stride. Reid articulated what she saw as the benefits of the situation for Eldreth:

> I think this has been good for my grandmother, 'cause I think it's kept her alive and kept her going. It's kept her spirits up, because my grandmother has always had a hard life and she's always had to struggle for every little bitty thing that she's had. [. . .] And I think really when she says that these last years have been the happiest in her life? I really think that's true, because she can be a center of attention now. And she's praised and she's oohed and she's aahed and she really loves it and she's never had that before. And she's never been . . . she's just never been treated that way before. And I think that's been really good for her. She has deserved something like this for a long time. She really has.

Similarly, the opportunity to travel, to perform, and to be made the center of attention exemplifies a freedom to order her own life that Eldreth did not enjoy through most of her years—one, as her decision to reject her wealthy suitor reminds us, that she was loath to give up. As she explained just before her performance at the Festival for the Eno:

But now I can | as the saying is, "I feel free." I feel like I could do what I want to | do what I want to do? And don't have to wait for somebody to say, "No, you can't do that." Now the children'll say, "Mom, go on and do what you want to do." And I'm doing what I want to do [i.e., by coming to Durham to perform].

Eldreth's style and repertoire in these public performances exhibit expectable continuities with those appropriate to the contexts in which she previously sang, but she has also evidently been influenced by the analyses and preferences of those who organized the performances and invited her to sing. Her involvement in these public events has primarily given Eldreth an opportunity to share what was previously her secular home repertoire with wider audiences. The two presenters with whom I have seen Eldreth interact, Mary Greene and Glenn Hinson, were both intent upon educating audiences about the complex history of "Appalachian music." They consequently encouraged Eldreth to include her favorite religious songs and her own compositions, especially "Someone's Last Day," as well as pieces—like "Philadelphia Lawyer," "Long Black Veil," and Jimmie Rodgers yodels—that demonstrate both the continuities between "traditional" mountain singing and modern country music and the breadth of an active oral singer's sources. Because of the "folk" or "old-fashioned" framing of these events, however, Eldreth's performances tend to emphasize the native American and British broadside–derived portions of her repertoire. "Neoma Wise," "Knoxville Girl," "Little Maggie," and the two versions of "Pretty Polly" show up in her performances with particular frequency, along with the two early recording curiosities, "Ticklish Reuben" and "Snoops the Lawyer." After years of interacting with folklorists and festival organizers, Eldreth seems to have internalized a sense of the expected repertoire and brings out the native American ballads whether she is specifically directed to do so or not. Relatively conservative scholarly standards of what counts as an authentic American folksong have thus probably given these songs greater prominence in Eldreth's repertoire than they otherwise would have had. Reid, because of her early and influential contact with folklorists, became interested in singing almost exclusively what she identifies as the oldest and most traditional items from her grandmother's repertoire, but Eldreth shows no inclination to drop songs the folklorists do not favor.

Given that Eldreth's main models and main opportunities for singing were solos in church and singing while working, both unaccompanied, she has ordinarily sung everything she knows in a solo, unaccompanied, unharmonized style. When she teachers her grandchildren songs, they all sing the melody in unison. When she began singing publicly with Reid, they sang some songs together on stage; but Cratis Williams discouraged that as a performance practice, evidently on the conservative supposition that the old ballads would have been sung as solos. As a result, Eldreth and Reid developed distinct styles and became used to paying attention only to their own internal sense of rhythm and phrasing. By 1988, Reid commented, "We're a lot more comfortable singing alone rather than together." However, when they started working with Hinson, a folklorist with a strong interest in contextualized presentation, he encouraged them to sing together again, presumably to model the pedagogical situation and the intergenerational transfer of repertoire, so they then resumed doing one or two songs together in each performance. Thus may changing paradigms of folklore scholarship influence what is presented to external audiences as "folk" material. Furthermore, as noted earlier, participation in festivals has at last afforded Eldreth opportunities for singing sociably with other local and revivalist musicians, although her resolutely singular style does not make her fit comfortably with those more accustomed to group singing.

Eldreth is not merely a passive receptor, however, but actively observes and incorporates novel influences. When performing without a presenter, she now frequently talks about where she comes from or tells one of the stories that explain why she has such a large repertoire, supplying for herself the kind of introduction that a folklorist presenter would usually elicit. Less frequent but attractive models may also be incorporated into her performances. The Festival of American Folklife provides sign language interpreters for many presentations, and Eldreth commented on how beautiful she found the signer's interpretations of their songs. She usually sits quite still while singing; and the summer after she had been in Washington, she startled presenter Mary Greene, who thought herself familiar with Eldreth's repertoire and practices, by adding gestures inspired by the signers she had seen to graphic song lines like "He stabbed her in her heart and her heart's blood it did flow."

Eldreth is usually invited to sing for folk festivals and musical demonstrations that frame the performer as an example of something. In certain respects she has come to rely upon this presentation, but in others she resists or ignores the framing, effectively insisting upon her own interpretation of what is happening. These occasions are constructed in ways that suggest to Eldreth that the aesthetic quality of her performance takes precedence. Eldreth sits on a raised stage in front of an often sizeable audience. She uses a microphone and is often paid an honorarium. The organizers have gone to considerable trouble and expense to ensure her participation. At the same time, however, the organizers themselves tend to think of the event as (secondarily) a performance that serves (primarily) as a demonstration. The World Music Institute's series on "The Roots of Country Music" billed her as an example of "the old, unaccompanied ballad style" that immediately predated commercial recording (Allen 1988); Hinson and Greene emphasize the variety of her repertoire and the interpenetration between "traditional" and "popular" song in Appalachia; the 1987 Festival of American Folklife included Eldreth and the other people from Ashe and Watauga counties to exemplify speakers of a distinctive regional dialect; William McCloud, when dean of the School of Music at ASU, included Eldreth and Reid in a workshop for secondary school music teachers to demonstrate that it is possible to be very musical without being able to read music. Those who arrange for Eldreth's participation want her to do well, but they involve her because she exemplifies a style, historical moment, or point, not because she is simply or obviously a great singer. Eldreth's purposes are congruent with those of the organizers of such events to the extent that she is proud of and glad to share songs that it is unusual to find in contemporary oral repertoires.

I increasingly realized, however, that Eldreth predominantly sees these situations in a different light than do her presenters. These times on stage provide her with opportunities to shine, to sing as well as she can sing, to perform pure and simple, and thus to satisfy a desire to do her best for an audience and to be recognized for it that neither home nor church singing quite fulfills. She focuses on performing and seems either not to grasp or simply to ignore the efforts to frame her performance as an example of "Appalachian culture."[37] When she and Reid performed at the Jonesboro Storytelling Festival in the late 1970s, they were directed to sit on hay bales on stage while they sang. Reid is quite aware and explicitly critical of attempts to stereotype her as a hillbilly. Eldreth reports the hay bale incident with apparent puzzlement—why would they want us to sit on hay bales?—but she does keep bringing it up. Similarly, when I volunteered to drive her to Durham for the Festival for the Eno, she instructed me to pick her up at the beauty shop, so her hair would be freshly coiffed; and for the performance she wore high-heeled sandals, her best red chiffon dress, and new diamond "ear bobs." Festival audiences may have expected a mountain woman in a granny dress, but for Eldreth performance is an occasion to dress up, not to dress up *as* something.

When working with a presenter on stage, Eldreth is perfectly happy to answer questions directed to her and, usually, to sing particular songs when asked; but she seems oblivious to the overall demonstration frame. She has actually come to depend upon a presenter's guidance in order to connect well with the audience. The least effective performance I have seen her give came about when Dean McCloud was prevented at the last moment from being there to introduce her performance for the music teachers' convention. The audience was actually expecting Eldreth to sing ballads and even tried to request them, but Eldreth, flustered, kept falling back on hymns. Nevertheless, she tends not to pay much attention to the presenter's argument about, for example, different types of mountain music, for which she is supplying the examples. Instead she responds to her own sense of what she feels like singing at a particular time, thereby dealing presenters some surprises. At the Festival of American Folklife, Hinson gave an extended comment on Eldreth's humorous songs picked up from early records, "Ticklish Reuben" and "Snoops the Lawyer"; but when he asked which of them she wanted to do, she responded, "What Am I Living For?" Hinson then had to accommodate her and explain to the audience what was going on: "OK, that's not a ballad, but go ahead." At an Elderhostel workshop with Greene, an audience member asked Eldreth about her own compositions. She started looking in a notebook for the words to one of her own songs, answering some other questions at the same time, and then came out with "Voice from the Tombs." Again, presenter Greene had to offer a quick reframing for the audience: "Now she did switch gears on you. That's an old hymn." In order to do her best as a singer, Eldreth evidently feels that she needs to attend (as she does when singing at home) to her own spontaneous sense of what she is ready to sing or what appeals to her at the moment. She usually accommodates presenters' requests, but her frame of performance, rather than theirs of demonstration, determines her choice of the next song when a conflict arises. I noted a similar tendency on Eldreth's part to subtly take charge of our interviews and treat them as performances, not mere song-collecting sessions. When she was in good voice and felt like singing, she would gradually squeeze out my questions about the songs, offering only a brief reply before launching into another tune. Conversely, Eldreth always expressed reluctance to have me record her if she was hoarse or otherwise felt that she was not in her best voice. Since I tended, obtusely, to insist, she usually eventually agreed to be recorded, but always with the disclaimer that the resultant tape would be suitable "just to get the words."

When observing others, Eldreth also has a strong predilection to identify a borderline or laminated (see Goffman 1974:157) activity as a performance rather than a demonstration. Cratiṣ Williams frequently gave a lecture about Appalachian speech, in which he demonstrated the aesthetic capacities of the dialect by telling "The Three Little Pigs." Since this was a demonstration, however, he usually told about only one or two pigs and then broke off, advising the audience to fill in the rest for themselves.[38] Eldreth performed on the same program once and gives her story of their interaction a different rhetorical spin:

> Yeah, I knew Cratis, and I sang . . . I's singing at Boone once and I took my Momma with me? And it just tickled her so good. He was . . . he's a-telling us the story of the three little pigs, you know. And, uh, he just told the story of two of 'em and then when he just told the two and never mentioned the other 'un, I hollered right . . . right in the whole audience. I said, "Mr. Williams, what happened to the third little pig?" [laughs]. I got the awfullest cheering [laughs]. And he said, "I'll tell you, Mrs. Eldreth," he said, "I'll tell you what happened to the third little pig the next time I tell the story" [laughs]. Oh, it tickled Momma. Momma said, "I'd a never thought you'd a said that!"

Williams was a masterful storyteller; when I saw a tape of this lecture, I, like Eldreth and the audience present along with her, was terribly disappointed when he stopped. Notably, however, in light of her own resistance to the demonstration frame, Eldreth apparently never realized (or completely forgot) that Williams had claimed to be demonstrating, and she thus interpreted his breaking off in midstory as a breach of performance conventions.

While enjoying the opportunity to perform and the rewards of attention and praise for her singing skill, in other respects Eldreth refuses to treat performance as seriously as one might expect. She explicitly tells people, "I don't claim to be a perfect singer." Even considering the local convention of modest disclaimers of ability, Eldreth appears to maintain reasonable expectations of herself. She sings well enough for church, as well as her grandmother did, and she does not need to approximate a recording star to feel confident about appearing on stage. She is similarly casual about rehearsal (in parallel with the model of church choir rehearsals). When she and Reid perform together, Reid insists on a sung practice beforehand. Eldreth is content to think about the songs she plans to sing and possibly to sing them around the house (not necessarily in full voice) and to write them down in a book as a way of going over the words. Having thus prepared, however, she may sing entirely different songs when she gets on stage. If she feels like singing a particular song, she does not worry about whether she has rehearsed it.

Eldreth similarly always agrees to a future performance conditionally, "Good Lord willing," and tells the organizers to call her back and remind her. She thinks about audience expectations to the extent that she is concerned not to offend anyone. Eldreth mentioned that she really likes "A Little Girl's Prayer," but, because it deals with the way children are hurt by divorce, she says, "They's so many places I won't sing it for fear there might be a divorced person there and hurt their feelings." She likewise talks with some distress about singing "The Fair Maiden," in which the cowboy laments, "Those redskins have murdered my poor darling wife," and later learning that there had been several Native Americans in the audience. Even for events arranged months in advance, however, she gives precedence to newly arisen obligations to family members over prior agreements to perform. She even told me about "slipping out" of a performance once when she just did not feel like singing, going home without telling anyone and evidencing no concern about the unanticipated gap she thus left in the program.

Ultimately, Eldreth insists upon her own definition of the frame in operation, turning the opportunities offered by folklorists into what she needs them to be, which may or may not be performance for its own sake. The World Music Institute concert on "The Roots of Country Music" was held in a large church in New York City, so Eldreth interpreted it as a religious activity and behaved accordingly: "I was in the church, you see, singing in the church. I felt like it was just like I was singing in my home church." "I met a lot of people up there that I really loved, just a-seeing 'em and talking to 'em and singing for 'em . . . *and testifying,* I brought a lot of tears." Interestingly, this frame "transgression" proved very successful *as* performance. Hinson reports that the audience loved what she did and loved her. In effect, her sincerity in breaking the performance and demonstration frames to follow her religious impulse actually resulted in a more effective demonstration of the kind of singing she would do at home and thus a more effective performance. Similarly, when a group of international teenagers was brought to Eldreth's house to hear her sing and, presumably, to see how mountain folks live, Eldreth baked cakes, bought drinks, insisted that the visitors sing with her, and turned the event into a party of which she was the hostess rather than a study of Appalachia for which she was an exhibit. In talking about her performances, also, Eldreth casts them in terms favorable to her sense of self. Of the school and Elderhostel performances that she especially enjoys, Eldreth remarks, "That's my pride and joy . . . is to be where young'uns is at or elderly people," strategically casting herself again as the person with power to do good for others, even though the senior citizens who attend Elderhostels are wealthy, well educated, and now often younger than Eldreth herself. Asked to reflect on all her performing, she is likely to say something like "I guess that's my life, singing and making others happy. Just something I like to do."

Eldreth has good reason to represent her performances as a form of service rather than a search for fame. The attention and publicity she has received have occasioned some jealousy and suspicion, particularly among other women her age. The story that stuck in my mind after our first conversation in Washington concerned a visit Eldreth paid to her sister Ruby after returning from her trip to New York a few months earlier. The phone rang and Ruby, looking significantly at her sister, told the caller, "It's OK. You can come over. She's not a bit proud." Eldreth's trips and awards make appealing human interest stories for the local newspapers. These media thereby effectively brag on her part, inspiring others to use the same medium to put her back in her place:

> Momma told me, said I told me about some of my sisters, said that they was going to take that—they had the picture, you know, and I didn't have it—said they was gonna take that picture and have it put in the *Skyland Post*. Said that people would see how I looked back when I was trying to take care of the family and everything and the difference it was then to today. And I said, "Momma, honey, it wouldn't have worried me one bit. I would not have cared," I said, "because everybody knows just how hard I worked and what I went through with." I said, "It would've been fine if they'd wanted to put it in the *Skyland Post*. I wouldn't have cared a bit."

When word got around that I was writing a book about Eldreth and her singing, I also heard back indirectly that another older woman in the community had complained, "I know those old songs, too." While in earlier chapters we have seen how older women could eschew competition and offer each other crucial social support, fame beyond the community can evidently revive old jealousies. Thus, Eldreth takes pains to insist that she is not seeking fame and to enlist sympathetic listeners like me as witnesses to the purity of her intentions:

> I always felt like that, uh, I guess that's silly, but I did, I always felt like that . . . I didn't want people to think that I was . . . trying, you know, trying to *show* myself. You know what I mean? I mean, like, now, I didn't want people to, oh, give me credit for all these things that I was a-doing. I just I it was some way I it was just

that I . . . I didn't want to be *bragged on,* and all that. I always felt like that, "I'm not that . . . famous and I just I I'm just *me.*" Now that's just the way I've always felt. I never did try I want somebody to think I look at me as I was . . . special or famous.

When Eldreth talks about her public performances, she never dwells on how well she did or did not sing. Rather she comes back again and again to audience response, to the things people said or did that tell her they were pleased or amused, to the laughter, teasing, compliments, and hugs. Her definition of a good performance, here as in church, is an effective performance, one that evokes the response she hopes for. Public performances enable Eldreth to receive confirmation of her abilities as a singer and entertainer in ways not available to her when singing for herself or a few grandchildren at home or even when offering a solo in church. She controls these public interactions, however, ensuring a positive result and protecting herself by enacting and interpreting them in her own terms. To the extent that she wants to be acknowledged as a skilled musical performer, she rejects framing that treats her as a mere example for someone else's argument. To the extent that she earnestly desires her music to benefit others (and that she needs to deflect criticism of herself as a fame-seeker), she frames performance as service. In effect, Eldreth mobilizes outsiders (who may think they are doing something quite different, like learning about Appalachian "folk" singing) to affirm her identity as a singer in the community terms that matter most to her.

CONCLUSIONS

Consideration of Eldreth's singing—both practice and repertoire—throws into relief the paradoxes inherent in trying to make sense of her as "an Appalachian woman." In some respects, the discourses and practices upon which she relies for self-definition are remarkably congruent with conceptions of the region as cultur-ally distinct (rather than historically and economically connected to the rest of the nation); in others, apparent congruence hides ironic divergence; in others still, she actively rejects attempts so to type her. Her repertoire of songs demon-strates the supposedly isolated region's lack of isolation, illustrating the case that antiromantic empiricists (first in folklore and subsequently in history) have been building for the past thirty years. She learned new songs over a span of six decades, and the songs that seem oldest to her often prove to be popular compo-sitions from the mid-nineteenth and mid-twentieth centuries. At the same time, however, the structure of feeling that directed her repertoire choices, her devo-tion to the melancholy longing for an ideal agrarian past that to her signals an "old" song, ironically parallels early twentieth-century folklorists' myopia in searching the mountains for old English ballads and rejecting newer works as contaminations. The very forces of commercialization that in fact provided her with many of her most precious songs simultaneously deprived her of any opportunity to use her talent for singing and for collecting a repertoire to foster sociable interactions. I seek to destabilize any lingering image of Eldreth as some sort of pristine repository of ancient tradition, even though she in part thinks of herself that way, possibly because of the attention folklorists have paid to her and her repertoire.

As a singer, Eldreth internalized those local discourses that would have made instrumental proficiency or secular performance scandalous for a religious woman and thus confined herself to vocal music and to singing most of her repertoire only for herself. Her large oral repertoire served, however, to help her get through the huge amounts of manual labor in the house and fields that were for her a woman's lot and became practical adjuncts to her constant duties to soothe and amuse children. Church provided her a context in which to perform, to thus contribute to the essential religious experience of people she cares about, and to be appreciated for her talent. Once her children were grown, opportunities to expand upon her church singing, as in performing for funerals or in neighboring churches, built her a local reputation as a singer. Had she not coincidentally established contact with folklorists, it is hard to tell if she would ever have felt herself limited or have pined for further performance opportunities. Invited to sing publicly, Eldreth enjoys herself fully. She tends, however, to resist attempts to frame her singing as an example of "Appalachian culture," preferring that it be seen simply as a good performance. She further capitalizes on her interactions with obviously educated and wealthy audiences to gently set herself up as their equal and thus contest the negative stereotyping of mountain folks. At the same time, however, she accedes to local critiques of those who seek fame and judges her performances modestly and joyfully according to how deeply she affects those who hear her sing.

8

Epilogue

In the fall of 2002, while I was deeply enmeshed in the writing of this book, I called Eldreth to wish her a happy eighty-ninth birthday. She reported that "two girls from the college" were coming out to visit her on a regular basis. One plays fiddle, the other banjo, and they sing and play and learn songs from her. They had also asked her if she knew Dr. Robison—it sounded as if they must be doing an oral history of significant actors in the area—and she had obliged them with her stories about her interactions with him. This incident and her account of it perfectly exemplify both the stability and the situational variability of Eldreth's construction of self and likewise both her willingness to serve as a tool to further others' work and her creative use of listeners, new and old, as tools in her own ongoing work of self-enactment.

In many respects, I expect, Eldreth has presented herself to these students in much the same way she did to me and, before me, to Mary Greene and Glenn Hinson and Thomas McGowan and Cratis Williams, as well as to Elderhostel and festival audiences and many other students of regional culture, formal and informal. The consistency of Eldreth's self-presentation derives from at least three factors. The repertoire of songs and stories that she has learned and composed over the years may have gradually expanded, but for the most part she draws on the same store of well-formed texts to represent what she has done and what ideas and sentiments matter most to her. She is also, however, haunted by ghosts, both the literal ones that show up in her ghost stories and the lingering manifestations of old social attitudes and former interlocutors' voices that supply the framing discourses and quoted remarks in relation to which she shapes her accounts of self. These ghosts cannot be banished; they keep her in line, keep her endlessly responding to their discursive concerns, no matter the identity and interests of her evident current interlocutor. And she has devised consistent and productive ways of forming her stories, selecting from surrounding discourses only those remarks that fit into her focus on local personal relationships and situating them to cast her well in her ethic of care and hard work.

However, Eldreth's approach is also both flexible and generative. For the students who are visiting her now, she is in important respects a different person than she was with me (or, indeed, with earlier interviewers or her neighbors and family). To the young fiddle and banjo players, she is a teacher of music and a coperformer, dimensions of identity and practice in which I could only barely participate. Her stories of Dr. Robison, in their analyses, may form part of an objective history of rural medicine in the mountain counties of North Carolina, whereas for me the same stories revealed Eldreth's accomplishment of a specific kind of woman's work and her negotiations with authoritative men for credit and sorely needed appreciation. In one respect, Eldreth thus seems perfectly happy to answer questions and supply stories and songs without needing fully to understand the motivation behind the questions and the purposes for which her accounts will be employed or how they will be framed. At the same time, however, she obviously retains control of how she presents herself, and she turns new experiences and new interlocutors into resources for her own purposes. The laughter of an Elderhostel audience supplies the final rejoinder to her abusive husband. When invited to perform at a festival, she embraces the opportunity to sing without having to justify it as a form of productive woman's work, yet conveniently ignores the "folk" framing. Ultimately, however, Eldreth maintains a kind of studious innocence, an oblivious unwillingness to project herself fully into the mindset and needs of those with whom she interacts in new settings. Eldreth has been able to define her life as meaningful within certain bounds and even to challenge some local standards so as to improve her position. She seems loath, however, to engage imaginatively with a larger society according to whose standards she might be insignificant. Whether telling stories without explaining the characters, recounting an instance of blackface joking with only the merest acknowledgment that some might find it offensive, or singing a song different than the one her presenter had introduced, she insists upon living in a social world she defines.

I, of course, encountered Eldreth with my own set of preconceptions and expectations. This study explores who she "is" as seen through the particular lens of an interest in gender identity and in the practice of speaking. My initial inclination was to make sense of Eldreth's practice in simplistically cultural terms, regarding her singing and storytelling as a manifestation of "Appalachian culture" or an "Appalachian woman's" way of presenting herself. But Eldreth resists such typical assignments and insists upon an interpretation specific in both personal and historical dimensions. The culture in which she can be said to participate emerges in her internalization of, negotiation with, and self-enactment via particular discourses and texts, not all of which are strictly local. The discourses relative to which she situates herself tell us much about the economic history of a particular locale and the moral grading of classes in a capitalist periphery. Yet she has equally internalized romanticized notions of an agrarian social paradise, drawn in part from a popular musical culture that had its own rhetorical purposes for an imagined Appalachia. Many of her forms of self-expression—including prominently her ghost stories, practical joking, mobilization of reported speech, and playful talking back to romantic songs—appear to have been developed as means of contesting the specific forms of male dominance she experienced in a loveless marriage to a shiftless man. Yet she herself and other women were just as influential as men in maintaining a discursive climate that limited and stifled her options for resistance. Her tendency to build herself up at other women's expense, her need to code and camouflage any defiance to gender norms, and her willingness to engage in racial stereotype in order to position herself securely within a community self-defined by shared white privilege derive from the insecure social and moral standing that her class position defined. Gender, labor, race, and class are inextricably intertwined components of her subjectivity.

Yet even as complex as Eldreth appears to me, I cannot pretend that my presence and my questions elicited the full range of her discursive self-construction. There are doubtless other discourses that provide a frame for Eldreth's constitution of self with other listeners that she did not have occasion to engage in with me. I note in particular that Eldreth's daily practice makes clear that her Christian faith has deeply defined her life experience. However, her religious and spiritual beliefs emerge in this account only to the extent that she expressed them in ghost stories she knew would intrigue a folklorist, hymns that fell within the purview of our plan to record her song repertoire, or the occasional religious testimony that I witnessed in church or that she slipped into a public performance. If Eldreth articulates religious experience in other ways, I was not the person to hear it. I thus remind readers in closing that there are aspects of Eldreth's subjectivity that my interaction with her did not evoke and that my work about her cannot adequately explore.

This book is the product of a protracted and delicate negotiation, conducted as a series of friendly conversations. In one respect, Eldreth is inevitably a means toward my goals, as I employ her example to explore the intricate and sometimes contradictory processes of an individual's discursive and dialogic self-construction. Equally, however, I am a means toward her goals of being perceived by a wider audience as a talented singer, a woman who did her duty, and an extraordinarily hard worker. If this ethnography serves both our purposes, if only partially and imperfectly, then it has accomplished what conversation can.

Notes

Notes to Chapter 1

1. Authors of works recognized as classic fine-grained analyses of both text and context tended actually to have acquired a record of both through some special entrée. For example, Bill Ellis relied on tapes made by students who told the ghost stories he had required them to collect but then unselfconsciously reflected on those stories—thus providing natural context—while the recorder was running (1987). Barbara Kirshenblatt-Gimblett was able to reproduce from memory a parable she observed her brother employ in conversation (1975). More recent work on context has, however, taken an approach like mine in recognizing that the text can tell you about its previous contexts. Janet Langlois, for example, traces the transmission of a contemporary legend via comments in the story about the person from whom the current teller heard the story, comments that are a crucial part of the truth claims necessary to such stories (1991).

2. I observed that Eldreth employed a similar approach in other poorly defined situations with people she did not know, notably an Elderhostel performance, where she asked, "What do you want me to sing?" and a music teachers' workshop, where she began by asking, "Is there anything special you might like to hear?" and, receiving no answer, got more specific, "Would you like to hear a hymn or some kind of ballad?"

3. Two recent examples of the effectiveness of daring to express one's opinions and press interlocutors for what one wants to know come from Matthew Gutmann, who gained some of his most important insights into the multiple "meanings of macho" from passionate outbursts evoked when he argued with his Mexican male friends (1996), and Elaine Lawless, who discovered battered women's principled resistance to telling the part of their stories in which only their batterer has agency precisely by pressing them when they appeared reluctant to tell her about the physical violence they had suffered (2001).

4. As Billie Jean Isbell notes, additionally, it is usually simply the case that our ethnographic subjects are far less interested in us than we are in them (1995).

5. Richard Bauman pointed this out to me at a juncture when I myself was frustrated with Eldreth's apparent unwillingness or inability to reflect upon the stories she had told me.

6. This may be another explanation for Eldreth's lack of interest in stories of my own novel doings, even though she professes to care very much about me.

7.   The festival is now known as the Smithsonian Folklife Festival, but I retain the name used when Eldreth performed there.

8.   Folklorist Cecelia Conway, videographer Elva Bishop, and I collaborated on a half-hour video, "Bessie Eldreth: Songs and Stories of a Blue Ridge Life," funded by the North Carolina Arts Council.

NOTES TO CHAPTER 2

1.   Barbara Kirshenblatt-Gimblett cites an article by Daniel Goleman published in the *New York Times* that suggests that this kind of gap occurs in men's as well as women's life histories and is a product of the memory process: "Memory is selective not only for certain kinds of events but also for certain periods. The middle years in particular tend to fade" (Kirshenblatt-Gimblett 1989:126; Goleman 1987:C1). Even if this is the case, however, women's narrative neglect of their husbands holds a different political significance than the reciprocal situation.

2.   Patricia Beaver points out that the egalitarianism is reinforced by Calvinist religious traditions, according to which humans are inherently sinful and there is no possibility of improving one's real worth through individual effort, so everyone should be seen as equal (1986).

3.   Greenhill notes that interviewees often supply such accounts in response to researcher questions, as was indeed the case when Eldreth told these stories in response to my attempts to understand her early history.

4.   Eldreth's repeated insistence on her own truthfulness and her backup reliance on the word of elders whom she constructs as authoritative speakers were not necessary for her immediate listener, me, since I was prepared to take anything she said as gospel. Her approach strikes me as a preventive measure designed to fend off anticipated challenges to her veracity. In the next chapter I take up the implication that these bespeak her continued involvement in discourse with prior interlocutors.

NOTES TO CHAPTER 3

1.   Puckett is careful to point out that her exacting empirical study characterizes only the specific community in eastern Kentucky that she studied (2000). However, many of her descriptions also seemed very reminiscent of speech behaviors I had observed Eldreth, her family, and neighbors engage in. I do not want to make blanket claims about "Appalachian speech ways" or to overgeneralize Puckett's specific findings. When our observations coincide, however, I have taken the liberty throughout the book of citing her comparable findings to identify ways in which Eldreth is probably employing a conventional way of talking as a resource (rather than inventing a pattern unique to herself).

2. During the 1990s I was involved in research both with dairy-farming families in the Catskills of New York state and with rural Cajun households in south Louisiana. I wondered how people managed to feed large families on modest salaries or slim profits from a family business. In both instances I learned that a primary strategy for making do with less cash was to produce food oneself from a much earlier stage, whether that meant growing a garden and freezing or canning produce, raising and butchering a pig or beef steer, drinking some of the milk from one's own cows, collecting and boiling maple sap for syrup, enlisting children to pick fruit at a pick-your-own farm for jams or desserts, or making items like ice cream for which even purchased ingredients cost significantly less than the final product.

3. The distinctions among (1) a strictly labeled narrative or story, that is, an account of something that happened on a particular occasion and that is evaluated so as to make a point (Labov and Waletzky 1967); (2) a generalization narrative concerning the kinds of things people regularly did (Greenhill 1994); and (3) what one might term merely a discussion of past practices tend to blur both in the conversational settings among familiars in which many stories are actually told (Polanyi 1985) and even more so in the semi-interview situations in which Eldreth engaged with me and other folklorists and anthropologists.

4. Given that models of "women's personal narrative" and "women's talk" were derived largely in the 1970s and 1980s and largely on the basis of middle-class European and Euro-American women's speech (for example, Coates 1996, Johnstone 1990, Kalčik 1975, Langellier and Peterson 1992, Tannen 1990; while Yocom 1985 and Baldwin 1985 offer exceptions only insofar as they treat rural working-class women) and that such models have since been criticized as overly general and essentializing, it should probably not surprise us that Eldreth has different implicit notions of both appropriate topic and effective form (see Sawin 1992, 1999).

5. In Sawin 1999 I discuss Eldreth's rejection of my tendency to respond to her stories with what I saw as supportive analogous cases. There I argue that the differences between Eldreth's narrative practice and the practices that seem so comfortable to me and other women of my cohort have more to do with working-class versus middle-class experiences, with the fact that she grew up in the 1920s and 1930s, while I grew up in the 1960s and 1970s, and with her desire to depict herself in a particular way in conversations with particular listeners, me among the most recent, than with any difference between "Appalachian" and "mainstream" narrative models.

6. Note again the difference between Eldreth's practice and earlier observations that women are more likely than men to narrate their ordinary labors (Baldwin 1985; Yocom 1985).

7. Holland teaches in the Department of Anthropology at the University of North Carolina, Chapel Hill (where I am now fortunate to be her colleague); Conway in the Department of English at Appalachian State University in Boone. When Eldreth

performed at the Festival for the Eno in Durham, North Carolina, on July 3, 1988, Conway invited us to spend the night at her home in Chapel Hill. She wanted Eldreth and me to meet Holland and fortunately suggested that we videotape our conversation. In the transcript of this conversation, CC is Conway and DH is Holland.

8. The story that begins in this way will be discussed in detail in chapter 4.

9. In her apparent obliviousness to stereotypes of the hillbilly, Eldreth contrasts with her granddaughter, Jean Reid, who frequently sang with her grandmother. Reid, a nurse, is alone among Eldreth's thirty-plus grandchildren in having wanted to learn the old ballads in her grandmother's repertoire. At the Festival of American Folklife in Washington, D.C., in 1987, Reid reports, she constantly found herself battling images of mountain folks as ignorant, uncouth, impoverished, and premodern. She recalled as typical a question (during a cooking demonstration) regarding whether they had microwaves, to which she responded in a parodically exaggerated hillbilly accent, "Yes, maaa-am!"

10. I am grateful to Terry Evens for this observation.

NOTES TO CHAPTER 4

1. As we will discuss in the next chapter, Eldreth's experiences of wordless communications—visions and physical sensations—from a supernatural or spiritual source were so convincing that they enabled her to challenge her husband's skeptical authority on at least some issues, and her role as a singer and teller of ghost stories has allowed her to interact with educated, middle-class people and with listeners who responded to her as audience to entertainer in ways that would not have been possible with family members and local friends.

2. Elmora Messer Matthews notes that in the Tennessee ridge community she studied, it was very common to name children after living family members, especially the parents' siblings and cousins, and that such naming within a family showed a "lack of sex differentiation" (1966:28).

3. Eldreth also tells a few stories in which her mother made similarly direct positive remarks, for example, as reported in the chapter on work, "Prettiest little porch I ever had was the one you built for me." Most often, however, these remarks in Eldreth's stories are made by men. An older woman's participation, in fact, bespeaks the kind of transformation in women's speech interactions over time that the remainder of this chapter discusses.

4. As we shall see in the chapter on singing, Eldreth has upon occasion had to weather accusations of being "proud" since she started being involved in public performances.

5. This kind of nonreciprocal naming between employer and employee has a double valence, of course. The employer's elaborate care to use the respectful form of address actually reinscribes inequality while—or by—attempting to deny it. But Eldreth is either unaware of or chooses not to explore this aspect of the practice.

NOTES TO CHAPTER 5

1. Will Cramer, a student in my Folk Narrative course at the University of North Carolina in the spring of 2003, collected stories of personal experience with the supernatural for his paper, "'Have your ever seen a ghost?' Reconciling Real Experience with Disbelief." Cramer observed that his sources made the explicit assertion "this is true"only in instances when the listener was not well known to the teller. Eldreth similarly seems particularly inclined to attest to the veracity of a story when performing for a public audience—see the "Bad Girls" story in this chapter—and to me, whom she thus marks as someone she expects to be skeptical.

2. In this chapter I use versions of "Pointing Hand" and "Bob Barr House" that Eldreth told to Spitzer and Cornett, versions of "First Married" and "Bad Girls" that she told for the performance organized by Thomas McGowan at ASU, and versions of "Aunt Polly Reynolds," "Doctor Graham House," "The Flood," and "Light in the Bedroom" that she told to me.

3. See Baughman 1966: motif E411.10, Persons who die violent or accidental death cannot rest in grave; E413, Murdered person cannot rest in grave; E231, Return from dead to reveal murder.

4. For example, it seems to be regarded as regrettable but not particularly remarkable, indeed almost inevitable, that young men will drink with their buddies, drive recklessly while drunk (endangering themselves and others), get into fights, and threaten each other with bodily harm. By contrast, a woman who were to do these things would excite substantial comment. During the period of my fieldwork, a young man in the community shot and killed a man with whom his wife had been "running around." This was regarded in the community as a *tragedy* for both the killer and the victim, but as a *scandal* as far as the woman's behavior and involvement were concerned. The differential response suggests how much more remarkable and condemnable it seemed for women to behave in violent or antisocial ways than for men to do the same things. (Although nationwide statistics from a much later period cannot be applied directly to the mountains sixty or more years ago, they are suggestive. According to the FBI, during 1991 only 10 percent of the documented murderers in the United States were women [Miller 1993:E1].)

5. In some tellings, Eldreth even implicitly contradicts this denial, associating the song with a protective light whose source is divine:

    > I've got a little song that I sing about the light.
    > > Did I ever sing it to you?

    PS: Unh uh.

    BE: It's | now this is the one that I sang on the broadcasting station in Winston-Salem; I told that story about the light? and then I sung this song:

    > > Oh, a glorious light is dawning
    > > That I see, that I see
    > > And it shines, and it shines
    > > Over me, over me.

It is glowing, Jesus, showing
Love to me, love to me
Ceasing ever, resting ever [sic]
That I see, that I see

And within its holy border
I can go, I can go
Ne'er again my feet shall stumble
That I know, that I know

There's a light, there's a light
That I see, that I see
And it shines, and it shines
Over me, over me.

PS: You made that song?
BE: No, that was an old song I used to sing years ago.
       A long, long time ago I used to sing that song.

6.   Significantly, Baughman's motif index (1966) only offers two alternatives: E321,
     Dead husband's friendly return and E221, Dead spouse's malevolent return to protest
     with spouse for evil ways. The idea that a dead husband would return out of spite to
     torment a wife for having been more virtuous than he was does not seem to make
     sense to Anglo-American storytellers, although one might speculate that this omis-
     sion could reflect collectors' preference for male tellers, male bias among cataloguers,
     or the reluctance of female tellers to make such a point to male collectors.

Notes to Chapter 6

1.   My dissertation (Sawin 1993) did not mention Eldreth's practical jokes, and one of
     the most memorable events of my defense was Beverly Stoeltje's insistence that I
     include this facet of Eldreth's personality in any future account.
2.   On several occasions Eldreth or one of her adult children explained to *me* how much
     they wanted to convince another member of the family to go to the doctor for an evi-
     dent health problem, all the time lamenting that they could not, of course, bring the
     matter up with the person concerned.

Notes to Chapter 7

1.   These recordings, along with those of all my interviews with Eldreth, have been archived
     in the Southern Folklife Collection at the University of North Carolina, Chapel Hill.
2.   My dissertation (Sawin 1993) includes a complete list of the songs Eldreth and I

recorded, with annotations on their authors or traditional provenance and on well-known recorded versions.

3.   For many, I have determined known authors and dates of composition; others I so identify from stylistic or anecdotal evidence.

4.   Frank C. Brown called this lyric a "purely North Carolina product," and Belden and Hudson second his analysis on the grounds that practically all versions available to them had been collected from North Carolina or adjacent areas of neighboring states (Belden and Hudson 1952: vol. 3, 334). Songs in *The Frank C. Brown Collection* will be indicated by the abbreviation "FCB," followed by the volume number (2 contains ballads, 3 contains folksongs) and the song number.

5.   It would be more accurate to say that Eldreth sings one version of this extremely variable and well-studied song cluster. See McCulloh (1970) for a full discussion. Norm Cohen (1981:491–502) summarizes McCulloh's argument.

6.   Such memories do not, of course, guarantee that a song was of great age. Nolan Porterfield recounts the instance of Jimmie Rodgers and "My Mother Was a Lady," which Eldreth sings. As far as Rodgers was aware, this was a traditional song. Under pressure from recording executive Ralph Peer to provide copyrightable material, Rodgers concluded that he had "fixed the song up" enough from the oral versions he had learned to take out a copyright. Edward B. Marks, a New York songwriter who had created the song a little over thirty years previously (1896) threatened to sue (Porterfield 1979:119).

7.   Belden and Hudson note: "This piece rather strikingly shows how a merely sentimental song may be taken up by tradition. No doubt a parlor song originally—its author and history are not known—it has become a traditional song in the South and Midwest" (1952: vol. 2, 631).

8.   Mary Greene shared this information on the basis of field research she did for an exhibit at the Appalachian Museum at Appalachian State University.

9.   For a more detailed discussion of Jenkins and the adoption of his songs into the rural oral repertoire, see Wilgus (1981).

10.   My name is Ticklish Reuben from way back in old Vermont.
       And everything seems ticklish to me.
       I was tickled by a wasp; I was tickled by a 'jacket;
       I was tickled by a yellow bumble bee.

       Snoops the lawyer, never had a dollar.
       Snoops the lawyer, charges an awful sum.
       Snoops the lawyer, never wore a collar.
       No one ever took a word of his advice.

Both songs seem to have northeastern connections. "Ticklish Reuben" was recorded, with brass accompaniment, by the singer Cal Stewart (in character as "Uncle Josh") on Victor 1637 sometime between 1902 and 1919, probably relatively early in that time range. Eldreth's version resembles Stewart's except for a couple of minor verbal changes and one omitted line, so this recording seems the most likely source, if her memory of how she learned the song is accurate. The song was also recorded by North Carolina musicians Charlie Poole and Frank Luther, who were active in the northwestern part of the state but not until the 1930s. (I am grateful to David Camp, who traced the history of this song for me on the basis of his extensive work in the Southern Folklife Collection at the University of North Carolina.) I have not been able to locate a recording or any other documentation about "Snoops the Lawyer."

11. Sidney Killens returned to North Carolina after a stint at coal mining in Kentucky or West Virginia. Archie Green explains that although Collins was not a miner, newspaper photographs of the miners who helped with the rescue effort forged a link in many people's minds (Green 1972:125). Eldreth recalls Uncle Sidney crying when he sang the song, and it appears either that he made up a story to impress his twelve-year-old niece or that she has rationalized a connection over the years, since she remembers him claiming that he and Collins were "real good buddies" from working together in the mines.

12. Conway cites a number of examples from the generation of Eldreth's parents: "Tommy Jarrell's father, Ben, bought the first record player in the Round Peak community. In Kentucky, Jean Ritchie's father was the first to own such a machine in his mountain community. . . . A photograph of the West Virginia Hammons family ancestors shows one holding a fiddle, one holding a shotgun, and the third holding an Edison player" (Conway 2001:36).

13. This tendency is not in evidence when Eldreth sings hymns in church, where she is accustomed to the piano finishing out a line before it is time to start singing again.

14. I observed such instances at the Smithsonian Festival of American Folklife, when Glenn Hinson gathered the western North Carolina participants for informal "kitchen picking" sessions, and at a party Mary Greene gave for me just before I left Boone at the end of the summer of 1988, when the "old time" musicians with whom I had made friends through Greene urged Eldreth to sing with them.

15. I am indebted to David Whisnant for sharing his reflections on Eldreth's style of vocal production.

16. Eldreth does not sing all the subtypes of songs of love and death that Abrahams and Foss enumerate, notably, no songs of lovers' separation by family, but she does sing songs of "separation of lovers by their own devices" (for which Abrahams and Foss give "Knoxville Girl" as an example) (1968:114–115) and "American [that is, sentimental] songs of death" including (among ones they list) "Little Rosewood Casket" and "Letter Edged in Black" (1968:120–121), as well as religious folksongs in which "death is seen as something to be desired as an end to the struggle, and as a way of becoming reunited with loved ones," for which they give "Wayfaring Stranger" (1968:125).

17. The chorus runs:

> I'd be so happy, with treasures untold
> If teardrops were pennies and heartaches were gold.

18. Woody Guthrie wrote this satirical song, set in Reno, Nevada, in which the lawyer tries to woo a Hollywood starlet and is killed by her cowboy husband.

19. Exceptions include a few purely upbeat songs, like the Carter Family's "Keep on the Sunny Side of Life" and Jimmie Rodgers's "Peach Picking Time in Georgia" and, interestingly, her version of "Pretty Polly"/"Wagoner Boy." Belden and Hudson describe this as "one of those folk lyrics of unhappy love" (1952:275). Eldreth, however, sings a variant (closest to FCB vol. 3, #250C) in which the boy, as usual, declares his intention to leave because the girl's parents do not approve of him, and the girl responds by deciding to run away with him.

20. In terms of favorite themes, Eldreth's repertoire is markedly similar, though not identical, to that of Almeda Riddle, although Eldreth (fifteen years younger) sings far more twentieth-century compositions and far fewer Child ballads. Roger Abrahams discovered that Granny Riddle knew, but did not care to sing, several types of songs that existed in the oral repertoire of her region, including "courting dialogs, forlorn-lover lyric songs, good-time and frolic songs, songs of mockery . . . , ballads of sexual embarrassment, and 'coon songs' . . . " (Riddle 1970:157–158). He further notes,

> But if a theme or situation conforms to her standards of interest and beauty she will learn every song she encounters which explores the subject. This is why she sings so many dying soldier, cowboy, graveyard, railroad, and parted-lover ballads, shape-note and brush-arbor songs. Her repertoire is all of a piece. (Riddle 1970:158)

Eldreth likes many of the same kinds of songs, and her repertoire is similarly "all of a piece." As the following discussion will reveal, however, her reasons for choosing particular pieces and rejecting others are more complex than the simple "standards of interest and beauty" Abrahams attributed to Riddle, though perhaps not more complex than Riddle's actual reasons.

21. A review of titles reveals the dominance of this theme:

> "I Won't Have to Worry Anymore"
> "I've Got a Home in Glory Land That Outshines the Sun"
> "Mansions over the Hilltop"
> "My Name Is Written There"
> "Victory in Jesus"
> "When I've Gone the Last Mile of the Way"
> "Where the Soul Never Dies"
> "Where We'll Never Grow Old"

22. Swensen (1988) and Jones (1988) observe, respectively, that heaven as home and meeting loved ones in heaven are among the most common themes in the religious music of

Appalachia. And Jeff Todd Titon reports that, in the independent Baptist church he studied, many members recount having been saved as the result of a promise to a dying relative who wanted to be able to see them again in heaven (1988:175–177). It is interesting to note, however, that this belief is not universal. Beverly Patterson reports that the Primitive Baptists she studied talk rather about having a "home in the church" and place great value on the nurturing of family and friendship ties on earth because "there will be no recognition of one's family members in heaven" (1988:69). I would speculate that the appealing image of a family reunion in heaven may have been introduced into southern religious discourse by the popular revivalists at the end of the nineteenth century, which would explain why it was not picked up by the most conservative sects, ones that intentionally held to the old ways at that time.

23. I am indebted to Bron Skinner for sharing his insights into changes in his reasons for adopting certain pieces as he shifted from singing for his own pleasure to performing.

24. These are texts of the three religious pieces Eldreth has composed:

> "Someone's Last Day"
> words by Bessie Eldreth, borrowed tune
> written 1980s
>
> I was standing by my window one bright summer day
> My thoughts of tomorrow seemed so far away
> And then I remembered, it was someone's last day
> They've gone up to heaven, they've gone there to stay.
>
> chorus:
> Someone, yes, someone's last day
> Some soul has drifted away
> They've gone up to heaven, I know there to stay
> For, yes, it was someone, yes, someone's last day
>
> Mother has gone and left us here below
> We're bowed down in sorrow in this world here below
> We'll meet her up yonder in heaven to stay
> For, yes, it was someone, yes, someone's last day.
>
> chorus:
> Someone, yes, someone's last day
> Some soul has drifted away
> They've gone up to heaven, I know there to stay
> For, yes, it was someone, yes, someone's last day
>
> I know I have loved ones that's gone on before
> We'll meet them up yonder on that beautiful shore
> And when we see Jesus, "Well done," he will say
> For, yes, it was someone, yes, someone's last day

chorus:
Someone, yes, someone's last day
Some soul has drifted away
They've gone up to heaven, I know there to stay
For, yes, it was someone, yes, someone's last day
Oh, yes, it was someone, yes, someone's last day

"Someday I'm Going to Heaven"
words and music by Bessie Eldreth
written circa 1985

Someday I'm going to heaven
A place I've never been
I'll live up there forever
In a world that will never end

Thank God I'll have a new body
I'll live forever more
I'll sing and shout with the angels
Over on the golden shore

So many clouds are gathering
Sometimes I can hardly see
But I got a glimpse of heaven
What a wonderful sight to see

I could hear the saints all shouting
Around God's great white throne
Thank God, I am so happy
We'll soon be going home

I can hardly wait for tomorrow
When we will all be together again
I'll get to see my mother
And take her by the hand

We will stroll through the gates of glory
We'll be singing a brand new song
Thank God, I am so happy
We'll soon be going home

"There Are Times When I Am Lonesome"
poem

There are times that I am worried
And there are times that I am blue
There are times that I am lonesome
And know not what to do

And when I look around me
And see someone in despair
Then I look up to Jesus
And I know he answers prayer

There's someone out yonder
If I could lend them a hand
To tell them about my savior
And lead them to the promised land

Tell them that we love them
Try to show them the way
Tell them about our savior
Kneel down with them and pray

I know I love my Jesus
And I know he understands
And I know he walks beside me
And he takes me by the hand

I know he will go with me
Through heaven's open door
Then we will all be together
Over on the golden shore

Don't weep for me, my children
Don't weep for me, I say
For I have gone to be with Jesus
On that great Judgment Day

I will meet you over yonder
Over in the glory land
Then we'll all be together
We will all understand
Yes, we will all be together
And then we will all understand

25. Jimmie Rodgers sings this line as, "And yours, you would allow." Given his pronunciation ("an—ee—urs"), his version could have functioned as transitional step between the original and Eldreth's wording.

26.　　 "Our Home Is So Lonesome Tonight"
　　　　words by Bessie Eldreth, borrowed tune
　　　　written 1977

　　　　One morning my husband told children goodbye
　　　　Our home is so lonesome tonight
　　　　I know he has gone and left us alone
　　　　Our home is so lonesome tonight.

　　　　Our home is so lonesome tonight
　　　　The lamp won't be burning as bright
　　　　He's gone up to heaven, that's one thing I know
　　　　Oh, it is so lonesome down here.

　　　　He told me on Sunday that he had to go
　　　　Our home is so lonesome tonight
　　　　He's gone up to heaven, I surely do know
　　　　Oh, it is so lonesome down here.

　　　　Our home is so lonesome tonight
　　　　The lamp won't be burning as bright
　　　　I know he has gone and left us alone
　　　　Oh, it is so lonesome down here.

　　　　I know I have loved ones that's gone on before
　　　　Our home is so lonesome tonight
　　　　We'll meet them up yonder on that beautiful shore
　　　　Our home is so lonesome tonight.

　　　　Our home is so lonesome tonight
　　　　The lamp won't be burning as bright
　　　　I know he has gone and left us alone
　　　　Our home is so lonesome tonight.

27. Eldreth refers to a neighbor and member of her church, also a widow, who apparently had a very loving marriage and who often talks about how much she still misses her husband.

28. At the beginning of the tape, her singing sounds self-conscious, but I believe she fairly quickly forgot that I was recording and during most of the time was not performing for the recorder. I went into the living room and wrote field notes so as not to distract her.

29. Compare Karen Baldwin's remarks on women's conversational "visiting":

> A visit can be easily engaged and just as easily interrupted for the doing of other things. . . . the artistry of visiting can be put down at any time a diaper needs changing, a quarrel needs unsnarling, or a batch of chicken needs turning in the oven. A visit can be picked up again after interruption without any loss of coherence, or it can be accomplished right along with the washing of dishes after a meal (1985:154).

30. Mary Greene—a neighbor of Eldreth's as well as a scholar—stressed that, as late as the 1970s when she started playing in a bluegrass band, she worried that she would bring scandal on her family by being seen in the kinds of seedy bars where her band was contracted to play. She soon realized that she was safe because the kind of people who would be bothered by her being in a bar would be extremely unlikely to go into those places themselves. This illustrates, however, how strongly self-segregated are the musical/social activities of religious and nonreligious people.

31. Gerald Pocius documents an interestingly comparable interaction between Newfoundlanders Vince and Monica Ledwell. "Mr. Vince" was a recognized singer in the community, although he himself admitted that his wife was the better singer and knew more songs. He would sometimes seek his wife's advice about songs, although he ignored her attempts to offer corrections (1976:112–113). Pocius became interested in collecting from "Mrs. Mon" as well but discovered that this was a delicate matter: "In another instance, Mrs. Ledwell began to sing 'That's What God Made a Mother For.' Mr. Vince soon got up and started to bring out plates for tea, rattling them near the microphone on the table. He showed little interest in the singing of his wife, and felt that it was time to shift our attention to other matters" (1976:117).

    The situation here is complicated by the challenge that the ethnographer's interest in the wife presents to the husband's status as singer. As with the Eldreths, however, it appears that the husband tolerates the wife's singing around the house and begins to object only when her home singing starts to be transformed into a kind of semipublic performance.

32. Eldreth told me that Mary Greene had found the words to "Voice from the Tombs" for her a few years before I got to know the two of them. In April of 1990 she asked me to look for the words to two songs: "The Old Crossroad," which I was able to find almost immediately in Leonard Roberts's *In the Pine* (1979), and "Sweeter than the Flowers," which I finally discovered in Dorothy Horstman's *Sing Your Heart Out, Country Boy* (1975) while doing research on the sources of her repertoire.

33. In some parts of the South such a presentation is actually called "a special" or "a special song" (see Titon 1988:214), although Eldreth and the members of her church do not use this term in a marked sense.

34. Mary Greene and others recall Shea's performances. I have not been able to confirm her recollection via written documentation.

35. Compare Charles Briggs's analysis of Holy Week rituals in Hispanic Northern New Mexico: "As the texts are performed, a tremendous amount of formal elaboration is focused on these sign vehicles. . . . however, *estuvo muy bonito*, 'it was very beautiful'

refers to the success of the performances in generating profound religious feeling; form per se is not singled out for comment" (1988:327).

36. Eldreth employs the phrase "I don't care *to* . . ." where a speaker of Standard American English would say "I don't care *if* . . ." In other words, she means that she does not object to doing whatever she is discussing, not (as I, for example, would mean if I employed that locution) that she does not like to do it or would prefer not to do it.

37. In recent years, folklorists have turned their attention to the issue of whether the people who participate in folklife festivals actually benefit from this involvement (Camp and Lloyd 1980) and, more specifically, how participants understand and frame their experience (Bauman and Sawin 1991). A study of other participants in the 1987 Festival of American Folklife, in which I was involved, suggests that the "folklife festival" frame is sufficiently unlike any other within which participants have operated that festival participants often struggle to understand "what it is that is going on here" (1991:296). Some find grappling with and arriving at a formulation of their frame to be an enlightening exercise; others experience uncomfortable confusion and distress as a result of not understanding how they fit in and what they are supposed to be doing. In Bauman, Sawin, and Carpenter 1992 we suggested that the people who were most satisfied with their activity at the festival had arrived at relatively complicated understandings of multiple frames and laminations—for example, the difference between work and a demonstration of work—and that those who failed to make these distinctions were the most likely to be confused and unhappy. Eldreth exemplifies how the opposite approach can also have positive results.

38. I am indebted to Eric Olsen, former librarian of the Appalachian Collection at Appalachian State University, for showing me a videotape of one of Williams's lectures (at Sue Bennett College, probably in the 1970s, although the tape was undated) and advising me that Williams had given essentially the same lecture on many occasions.

WORKS CITED

Abrahams, Roger D. 1970. Creativity, Individuality, and the Traditional Singer. *Studies in the Literary Imagination* 3:5–36.

Abrahams, Roger D., and George Foss. 1968. *Anglo-American Folksong Style*. Englewood Cliffs, NJ: Prentice-Hall.

Abu-Lughod, Lila. 1991. Writing against Culture. In *Recapturing Anthropology: Working in the Present*, ed. Richard G. Fox, pp. 137–162. Santa Fe, NM: School of American Research Press.

Allen, Barbara. 1990. The Genealogical Landscape and the Southern Sense of Place. In *Sense of Place: American Regional Cultures*, ed. Barbara Allen and Thomas J. Schlereth, pp. 152–163. Lexington: University Press of Kentucky.

Allen, Ray. 1988. Notes to sound cassette *Roots of Country Music: Voices of the Americas*. New York: World Music Institute.

Appadurai, Arjun. 1996. *Modernity at Large: Cultural Dimensions of Globalization*. Minneapolis: University of Minnesota Press.

Aretxaga, Begoña. 1997. *Shattering Silences: Women, Nationalism, and Political Subjectivity in Northern Ireland*. Princeton, NJ: Princeton University Press.

Austin, J. L. 1962. *How to Do Things with Words*. New York: Oxford University Press.

Bakhtin, M. M. 1981. *The Dialogic Imagination*, ed. Michael Holquist, trans. Caryl Emerson and Michael Holquist. Austin: University of Texas Press.

———. 1986. Problems of Speech Genres. In *Speech Genres and Other Late Essays*, ed. Caryl Emerson and Michael Holquist, trans. Vern W. McGee, pp. 60–102. Austin: University of Texas Press.

Baldwin, Karen. 1985. "Woof!" A Word on Women's Roles in Family Storytelling. In *Women's Folklore, Women's Culture*, ed. Rosan A. Jordan and Susan J. Kalčik, pp. 149–162. Philadelphia: University of Pennsylvania Press.

Batteau, Allen. 1980. Appalachia and the Concept of Culture: A Theory of Shared Misunderstandings. *Appalachian Journal* 7(1–2):9–31.

———. 1983. Rituals of Dependence in Appalachian Kentucky. In *Appalachia and America: Autonomy and Regional Dependence*, ed. Allen Batteau, pp. 142–167. Lexington: University Press of Kentucky.

———.1990. *The Invention of Appalachia*. Tucson: University of Arizona Press.

Baughman, Ernest W. 1966. *Type and Motif-Index of the Folktales of England and North America*. The Hague: Mouton.

Bauman, Richard. 1977. *Verbal Art as Performance*. Rowley, MA: Newbury House.

———. 1983a. The Field Study of Folklore in Context. In *Handbook of American Folklore*, ed. Richard M. Dorson, pp.362–368. Bloomington: Indiana University Press.

———. 1983b. *Let Your Words Be Few: Symbolism of Speaking and Silence among Seventeenth-Century Quakers*. Cambridge: Cambridge University Press.

———. 1986. *Story, Performance, and Event: Contextual Studies of Oral Narrative*. Cambridge: Cambridge University Press.

———. 1993a. Disclaimers of Performance. In *Responsibility and Evidence in Oral Discourse*, ed. Jane Hill and Judith T. Irvine, pp. 182–196. Cambridge: Cambridge University Press.

———. 1993b. The Nationalization and Internationalization of Folklore: The Case of Schoolcraft's "Gitshee Gauzinee." *Western Folklore* 52(2,3,4):247–269.

Bauman, Richard, and Charles L. Briggs. 1990. Poetics and Performance as Critical Perspectives on Language and Social Life. *Annual Review of Anthropology* 19:59–88.

Bauman, Richard, and Patricia Sawin. 1991. The Politics of Participation in Folklife Festivals. In *Exhibiting Culture: The Poetics and Politics of Museum Display*, ed. Ivan Karp and Steven D. Lavine, pp. 288–314. Washington, DC: Smithsonian Institution Press.

Bauman, Richard, Patricia Sawin, and Inta Gale Carpenter. 1992. *Reflections on the Folklife Festival: An Ethnography of Participant Experience*. Folklore Institute Special Publications Series #2. Bloomington: Indiana University.

Beaver, Patricia Duane. 1986. *Rural Community in the Appalachian South*. Lexington: University Press of Kentucky.

Becker, Jane S. 1998. *Selling Tradition: Appalachia and the Construction of an American Folk 1930–1940*. Chapel Hill: University of North Carolina Press.

Behar, Ruth. 1993. *Translated Woman: Crossing the Border with Esperanza's Story*. Boston: Beacon Press.

Belden, Henry M., and Arthur Palmer Hudson, eds. 1952. *The Frank C. Brown Collection of North Carolina Folklore*. Vol. 2, *Folk Ballads from North Carolina*; vol. 3, *Folk Songs from North Carolina*. Durham, NC: Duke University Press.

Belenky, Mary Field, Blythe McVicker Clinchy, Nancy Rule Goldberger, and Jill Mattuck Tarule. 1986. *Women's Ways of Knowing: The Development of Self, Voice, and Mind*. New York: Basic Books.

Ben-Amos, Dan, and Kenneth Goldstein, eds. 1975. *Folklore: Performance and Communication*. The Hague: Mouton.

Bennett, Gillian. 1985. Heavenly Protection and Family Unity: The Concept of the Revenant among Elderly Urban Women. *Folklore* 96(i):87–97.

———. 1987. *Traditions of Belief: Women and the Supernatural*. London: Penguin.

Billings, Dwight B., and Kathleen M. Blee. 2000. *The Road to Poverty: The Making of Wealth and Hardship in Appalachia*. Cambridge: Cambridge University Press.

Billings, Dwight B., Mary Beth Pudup, and Altina Waller. 1995. Taking Exception with Exceptionalism: New Approaches to the Social History of Early Appalachia. In *Appalachia in the Making: The Mountain South in the Nineteenth Century*, ed. Mary Beth

Pudup, Dwight Billings, and Altina Waller, pp. 1–24. Chapel Hill: University of North Carolina Press.

Bloom, Leslie Rebecca. 1998. *Under the Sign of Hope: Feminist Methodology and Narrative Interpretation*. Albany: State University of New York Press.

Borland, Katherine. 1991. "That's Not What I Said": Interpretive Conflict in Oral Narrative Research. In *Women's Words: The Feminist Practice of Oral History*, ed. Sherna Berger Gluck and Daphne Patai. New York: Routledge.

Bourdieu, Pierre. 1977. *Outline of a Theory of Practice*, trans. Richard Nice. Cambridge: Cambridge University Press.

Braude, Ann. 1989. *Radical Spirits: Spiritualism and Women's Rights in Nineteenth-Century America*. Boston: Beacon Press.

Brenneis, Donald L. 1993. Some Contributions of Folklore to Social Theory: Aesthetics and Politics in a Translocal World. *Western Folklore* 52(2,3,4):291–303.

Briggs, Charles L. 1986. *Learning How to Ask: A Sociolinguistic Appraisal of the Role of the Interview in Social Science Research*. Cambridge: Cambridge University Press.

———. 1988. *Competence in Performance: The Creativity of Tradition in Mexicano Verbal Art*. Philadelphia: University of Pennsylvania Press.

Brodkin, Karen. 1998. *How Jews Became White Folks and What That Says about Race in America*. New Brunswick, NJ: Rutgers University Press.

Bruce, Dickson D., Jr. 1974. *And They All Sang Hallelujah: Plain-Folk Camp-Meeting Religion, 1800–1845*. Knoxville: University of Tennessee Press.

Burton, Thomas G. 1978. *Some Ballad Folks*. Johnson City: East Tennessee State University.

Butler, Judith. 1990. *Gender Trouble: Feminism and the Subversion of Identity*. New York: Routledge.

Cameron, Deborah. 1985. *Feminism and Linguistic Theory*. London: MacMillan.

Camp, Charles, and Timothy Lloyd. 1980. Six Reasons Not to Produce a Folklife Festival. *Kentucky Folklore Record* 26:67–74.

Campbell, John C. 1921. *The Southern Highlander and His Homeland*. The Russell Sage Foundation. Repr., Lexington: University Press of Kentucky, 1969.

Caudill, Harry M. 1971. *My Land Is Dying*. New York: E. P. Dutton.

Clifford, James. 1983. On Ethnographic Authority. *Representations* 1(2):118–146.

Clifford, James, and George E. Marcus, eds. 1986. *Writing Culture: The Poetics and Politics of Ethnography*. Berkeley: University of California Press.

Coates, Jennifer. 1996. *Women Talk: Conversation between Women Friends*. Oxford, UK: Blackwell Publishers.

Cohen, Anne, and Norm Cohen. 1973. Tune Evolution as an Indicator of Traditional Musical Norms. *Journal of American Folklore* 86(339):37–47.

———. 1977. Folk and Hillbilly Music: Further Thoughts on Their Relation. *John Edwards Memorial Foundation Quarterly* 13:50–57.

Cohen, Erik. 1988. Authenticity and Commoditization in Tourism. *Annals of Tourism Research* 15:371–386.

Cohen, Norm. 1970. Tin Pan Alley's Contribution to Folk Music. *Western Folklore* 29(1):9–20.

———. 1981. *Long Steel Rail: The Railroad in American Folksong*. Urbana: University of Illinois Press.

Conway, Cecilia. 2001. Appalachian Echoes of the African Banjo. In *Appalachians and Race: The Mountain South from Slavery to Segregation*, ed. John C. Inscoe, pp. 27–39. Lexington: University Press of Kentucky.

Davies, Bronwyn. 1992. Women's Subjectivity and Feminist Stories. In *Investigating Subjectivity: Research on Lived Experience*, ed. Carolyn Ellis and Michael G. Flaherty, pp. 53–76. Newbury Park, CA: Sage Publications.

Davies, Bronwyn, and Rom Harré. 1990. Positioning: The Discursive Production of Selves. *Journal for the Theory of Social Behaviour* 20(1):43–63.

Davis, Natalie Zemon. 1975. *Society and Culture in Early Modern France*. Stanford, CA: Stanford University Press.

Derrida, Jacques. 1976. *Of Grammatology*. Baltimore: Johns Hopkins University Press.

Dunaway, Wilma A. 1996. *The First American Frontier: Transition to Capitalism in Southern Appalachia, 1700–1860*. Chapel Hill: University of North Carolina Press.

Eller, Ronald D. 1982. *Miners, Millhands, and Mountaineers: Industrialization of the Appalachian South, 1880–1930*. Knoxville: University of Tennessee Press.

Ellis, Bill. 1978. "The 'Blind' Girl" and the Rhetoric of Sentimental Heroism. *Journal of American Folklore* 91(360):657–674.

———. 1987. Why Are Verbatim Texts of Legends Necessary? In *Perspectives on Contemporary Legend*, vol. 2, ed. Gillian Bennett, Paul Smith, and J. D. A. Widdowson, pp. 31–60. Sheffield, UK: Sheffield Academic Press.

Escobar, Arturo. 1995. *Encountering Development: The Making and Unmaking of the Third World*. Princeton, NJ: Princeton University Press.

Fabian, Johannes. 1983. *Time and the Other: How Anthropology Makes Its Object*. New York: Columbia University Press.

Fine, Elizabeth C. 1999. Ventriloquizing the Voiceless: A Critical Assessment of the New Ethnography. In *The Voice of the Voiceless*, ed. Edith Slemback, pp. 13–24. St. Ingbert: Rohrig Universitatsverlag.

Fletcher, Arthur L. 1963. *Ashe County: A History*. Jefferson, NC: Ashe County Research Association.

Foucault, Michel. 1972. *The Archaeology of Knowledge*, trans. A. M. Sheridan Smith. New York: Pantheon Books.

———. 1977. *Language, Counter-Memory, Practice: Selected Essays and Interviews*, ed. Donald F. Bouchard, trans. Donald F. Bouchard. Oxford, UK: Blackwell.

Gaventa, John. 1980. *Power and Powerlessness: Quiescence and Rebellion in an Appalachian Valley*. Urbana: University of Illinois Press.

Geertz, Clifford. 1973. *The Interpretation of Cultures*. New York: Basic Books.

Glassie, Henry. 1968. *Pattern in the Material Folk Culture of the Eastern United States*. Philadelphia: University of Pennsylvania Press.

Goffman, Erving. 1974. *Frame Analysis*. New York: Harper and Row.

Goldstein, Kenneth S. 1971. On the Application of the Concepts of Active and Inactive Traditions to the Study of Repertory. *Journal of American Folklore* 84(331):62–67.

Goleman, Daniel. 1987. In Memory, People Re-create Their Lives to Suit Their Images of the Present. *New York Times*, 23 June 1987.

Gordon, Avery F. 1997. *Ghostly Matters: Haunting and the Sociological Imagination.* Minneapolis: University of Minnesota Press.

Green, Archie. 1972. *Only a Miner: Studies in Recorded Coal-Mining Songs.* Urbana: University of Illinois Press.

Greenhill, Pauline. 1994. *Ethnicity in the Mainstream: Three Studies of English Canadian Culture in Ontario.* Montreal and Kingston: McGill-Queen's University Press.

Greenway, John. 1957. Jimmie Rodgers—A Folksong Catalyst. *Journal of American Folklore* 70(277):231–234.

Gutmann, Matthew C. 1996. *The Meanings of Macho: On Being a Man in Mexico City.* Berkeley: University of California Press.

Hall, Deanna L., and Kristin M. Langellier. 1988. Storytelling Strategies in Mother-Daughter Communication. In *Women Communicating*, ed. Anita Taylor and Barbara Bate, pp. 107–126. Norwood, NJ: Ablex.

Harding, Sandra. 1987. Introduction: Is There a Feminist Method? In *Feminism and Methodology*, ed. Sandra Harding, pp. 1–14. Bloomington: Indiana University Press.

Heath, Shirley Brice. 1983. *Ways with Words: Language, Life, and Work in Communities and Classrooms.* Cambridge: Cambridge University Press.

Heilbrun, Carolyn. 1988. *Writing a Woman's Life.* New York: W. W. Norton.

Herzfeld, Michael. 1991. Silence, Submission, and Subversion: Toward a Poetics of Womanhood. In *Gender and Kinship in Modern Greece*, ed. Peter Loizos and Euthymios Papataxiarchis, pp. 80–97. Princeton, NJ: Princeton University Press.

Hill, Jane H. 1995. The Voices of Don Gabriel: Responsibility and Self in a Modern Mexicano Narrative. In *The Dialogic Emergence of Culture*, ed. Dennis Tedlock and Bruce Mannheim, pp. 97–147. Urbana: University of Illinois Press.

Hinson, Glenn. 2000. *Fire in My Bones: Transcendence and the Holy Spirit in African American Gospel.* Philadelphia: University of Pennsylvania Press.

Hollway, Wendy. 1984. Gender Difference and the Production of Subjectivity. In *Changing the Subject: Psychology, Social Regulation, and Subjectivity*, ed. Julian Henriques, Wendy Hollway, Cathy Urwin, Couze Venn, and Valerie Walkerdine, pp. 227–263. London: Methuen.

Holquist, Michael. 1983. Answering as Authoring: Mikhail Bakhtin's Trans-Linguistics. *Critical Inquiry* 10:307–319.

Horstman, Dorothy. 1975. *Sing Your Heart Out, Country Boy.* New York: E. P. Dutton.

Hufford, David J. 1982. Traditions of Disbelief. *New York Folklore Quarterly* 8:47–55.

———. 1983. The Supernatural and the Sociology of Knowledge: Explaining Academic Belief. *New York Folklore Quarterly* 9:21–31.

Hymes, Dell. 1981. *"In Vain I Tried to Tell You": Essays in Native American Ethnopoetics.* Philadelphia: University of Pennsylvania Press.

Inscoe, John C. 1989. *Mountain Masters: Slavery and the Sectional Crisis in Western North Carolina*. Knoxville: University of Tennessee Press.

———. 2001. Olmstead in Appalachia: A Connecticut Yankee Encounters Slavery and Racism in the Southern Highlands, 1854. In *Appalachians and Race: The Mountain South from Slavery to Segregation*, ed. John C. Inscoe, pp. 154–164. Lexington: University Press of Kentucky.

Isbell, Billie Jean. 1995. Women's Voices: Lima 1975. In *The Dialogic Emergence of Culture*, ed. Dennis Tedlock and Bruce Mannheim, pp. 54–74. Urbana: University of Illinois Press.

Ives, Edward D. 1978. *Joe Scott: The Woodsman-Songmaker*. Urbana: University of Illinois Press.

———. 1988. *George Magoon and the Down East Game War: History, Folklore, and the Law*. Urbana: University of Illinois Press.

Jackson, Michael. 1989. *Paths toward a Clearing: Radical Empiricism and Ethnographic Inquiry*. Bloomington: Indiana University Press.

Jakobson, Roman, 1960. Closing Statement: Linguistics and Poetics. In *Style in Language*, ed. Thomas A. Sebeok, pp. 350–377. Cambridge: Massachusetts Institute of Technology Press.

Johnstone, Barbara. 1990. *Stories, Community, and Place: Narratives from Middle America*. Bloomington: Indiana University Press.

Jones, Loyal. 1975. Appalachian Values. In *Voices from the Hills: Selected Readings of Southern Appalachia*, ed. Robert J. Higgs, pp. 507–517. New York: Unger.

———. 1988. Sense of Place in Appalachian Music: Home and Mother, Heaven as Home. In *Sense of Place in Appalachia*, ed. S. Mont Whitson, pp. 160–164. Morehead, KY: Morehead State University.

Joyce, Rosemary O. 1983. *A Woman's Place: The Life History of an Ohio Grandmother*. Columbus: Ohio State University Press.

Kalčik, Susan. 1975. " . . . Like Ann's Gynecologist or the Time I Was Almost Raped": Personal Narratives in Women's Rape Groups. In *Women and Folklore: Images and Genres*, ed. Claire R. Farrer, pp. 3–11. Austin: University of Texas Press.

Kirshenblatt-Gimblett, Barbara. 1975. A Parable in Context: A Social Interactional Analysis of Storytelling Performance. In *Folklore: Performance and Communication*, ed. Dan Ben-Amos and Kenneth Goldstein, pp. 105–130. The Hague: Mouton.

———. 1989. Authoring Lives. *Journal of Folklore Research* 26(2):123–149.

Kodish, Debora. 1981. "Never Had a Word Between Us": Pattern in the Verbal Art of a Newfoundland Woman. Ph.D. dissertation, University of Texas.

———. 1983. Fair Young Ladies and Bonny Irish Boys: Pattern in Vernacular Poetics. *Journal of American Folklore* 96(380):131–150.

Labov, William, and Joshua Waletzky. 1967. Narrative Analysis: Oral Versions of Personal Experience. In *Essays on the Verbal and Visual Arts*, ed. June Helm, pp. 12–44. Seattle: University of Washington Press for the American Ethnological Society.

Langellier, Kristen, and Eric E. Peterson. 1992. Spinstorying: An Analysis of Women Storytelling. In *Performance, Culture, and Identity*, ed. Elizabeth C. Fine and Jean Haskell Speer, pp. 157–179. Westport, CT: Praeger.

Langlois, Janet. 1991. "Hold the Mayo": Purity and Danger in an AIDS Legend. *Contemporary Legend* 1:153–172.

Lanser, Susan S. 1993. Burning Dinners: Feminist Subversions of Domesticity. In *Feminist Message: Coding in Women's Folk Culture*, ed. Joan Newlon Radner, pp. 36–53. Urbana: University of Illinois Press.

Latour, Bruno. 1993. *We Have Never Been Modern*. Cambridge: Harvard University Press.

Lawless, Elaine. 1991. Women's Life Stories and Reciprocal Ethnography as Feminist and Emergent. *Journal of Folklore Research* 28(1):35–61.

———. 1992. "I Was Afraid Someone like You . . . an Outsider . . . Would Misunderstand": Negotiating Interpretive Differences between Ethnographers and Subjects. *Journal of American Folklore* 105(417):302–314.

———. 2000. "Reciprocal Ethnography": No One Said It Was Easy. *Journal of Folklore Research* 37(2–3):197–205.

———. 2001. *Women Escaping Violence: Empowerment through Narrative*. Columbia: University of Missouri Press.

Laws, G. Malcolm. 1957. *American Balladry from British Broadsides*. Philadelphia: American Folklore Society.

———. 1964. *Native American Balladry* (rev. ed.). Philadelphia: American Folklore Society.

Lewis, I. M. 1971. *Ecstatic Religion: An Anthropological Study of Spirit Possession*. Harmondsworth, UK: Penguin.

Limón, José E. 1994. *Dancing with the Devil: Society and Cultural Poetics in Mexican-American South Texas*. Madison: University of Wisconsin Press.

Linde, Charlotte. 1993. *Life Stories: The Creation of Coherence*. New York: Oxford University Press.

Long-Wilgus, Eleanor R. 2003. *Naomi Wise: Creation, Re-creation, and Continuity in an American Ballad Tradition*. Chapel Hill, NC: Chapel Hill Press.

Lott, Eric. 1993. *Love and Theft: Blackface Minstrelsy and the American Working Class*. New York: Oxford University Press.

MacKinnon, Catharine A. 1982. Feminism, Marxism, Method, and the State: An Agenda for Theory. *Signs* 7(3):515–544.

Malone, Bill C. 1981. Booklet to accompany sound recording *The Smithsonian Collection of Classic Country Music*. RO25 P8 15640. Washington, DC: Smithsonian Institution.

———. 1985. *Country Music, U.S.A.* (rev. ed.). Austin: University of Texas Press.

Malone, Bill C., and Judith McCulloh, eds. 1975. *Stars of Country Music: Uncle Dave Macon to Johnny Rodriguez*. Urbana: University of Illinois Press.

Malone, Bill C., and David Stricklin. 2003. *Southern Music/American Music* (rev. ed.). Lexington: University Press of Kentucky.

Mannheim, Bruce, and Dennis Tedlock. 1995. Introduction. In *The Dialogic Emergence of Culture*, ed. Dennis Tedlock and Bruce Mannheim, pp. 1–32. Urbana: University of Illinois Press.

Marx, Karl. 1998 [1845]. *The German Ideology*. Amherst, NY: Prometheus Books.

Matthews, Elmora Messer. 1966. *Neighbor and Kin: Life in a Tennessee Ridge Community*. Nashville, TN: Vanderbilt University Press.

McCulloh, Judith. 1970. In the Pines: The Melodic-Textual Identity of an American Lyric Folksong Cluster. Ph.D. dissertation, Indiana University.

McLeod, Norma, and Marcia Herndon. 1975. The Bormliza: Maltese Folksong Style and Women. In *Women and Folklore: Images and Genres*, ed. Claire R. Farrer, pp. 81–100. Austin: University of Texas Press.

Mead, George Herbert. 1934. *Mind, Self, and Society*. Chicago: University of Chicago Press.

Miles, Emma Bell. 1905. *The Spirit of the Mountains*. Facsimile ed. with foreword by Roger D. Abrahams and introd. by David E. Whisnant. Knoxville: University of Tennessee Press, 1975.

Miller, Edward K. 1981. An Ethnography of Singing: The Use and Meaning of Song within a Scottish Family. Ph.D. dissertation, University of Texas.

Miller, Mary E. 1993. The Deadly Difference. *Raleigh (NC) News and Observer*, 2 May 1992.

Mills, Margaret. 1993. Feminist Theory and the Study of Folklore: A Twenty-Year Trajectory toward Theory. *Western Folklore* 52 (2,3,4):173–192.

Mitchell, Carol. 1978. Hostility and Aggression toward Males in Female Joke Telling. *Frontiers* 3(3):19–23.

———. 1985. Some Differences in Male and Female Joke Telling. In *Women's Folklore, Women's Culture*, ed. Rosan A. Jordan and Susan J. Kalčik, pp. 163–186. Philadelphia: University of Pennsylvania Press.

Newitz, Annalee, and Matt Wray. 1997. Introduction. In *White Trash: Race and Class in America*, ed. Matt Wray and Annalee Newitz, pp.1–12. New York: Routledge.

Nofsinger, Robert E. 1991. *Everyday Conversation*. Prospect Heights, IL: Waveland Press.

Ortner, Sherry B. 1995. Resistance and the Problem of Ethnographic Refusal. *Comparative Studies in Society and History* 37(1):173–193.

Paredes, Américo. 1977. On Ethnographic Work among Minority Groups: A Folklorist's Perspective. *New Scholar* 6:1–32.

Paredes, Américo, and Richard Bauman, eds. 1972. *Toward New Perspectives in Folklore*. Austin: University of Texas Press.

Patterson, Beverly B. 1988. Finding a Home in the Church: Primitive Baptist Women. In *Diversities of Gifts: Field Studies in Southern Religion*, ed. Ruel W.Tyson, Jr., James L. Peacock, and Daniel W. Patterson, pp. 61–78. Urbana: University of Illinois Press.

Patterson, Tim. 1975. Notes on the Historical Application of Marxist Cultural Theory. *Science and Society* 39(3):257–291.

Pocius, Gerald. 1976. "The First Day I Thought of It Since I Got Wed": Role Expectations and Singer Status in a Newfoundland Outport. *Western Folklore* 35(2): 109–122.

Polanyi, Livia. 1978. False Starts Can Be True. In *Proceedings of the Fourth Annual Meeting of the Berkeley Linguistics Society*, ed. Jeri J. Jaeger et al., pp. 628–637. Berkeley, CA: Berkeley Linguistics Society.

———. 1985. Conversational Storytelling. In *Handbook of Discourse Analysis*. Vol. 3, *Discourse and Dialogue*, ed. Teun A. Van Djik, pp. 183–201. London: Academic Press.

Pollock, Sheldon. 2000. Cosmopolitan and Vernacular in History. *Public Culture* 12(3): 591–625.

Porterfield, Nolan. 1979. *Jimmie Rodgers: The Life and Times of America's Blue Yodeler.* Urbana: University of Illinois Press.

Puckett, Anita. 1992. "Let the Girls Do the Spelling and Dan Will Do the Shooting": Literacy, the Division of Labor, and Identity in a Rural Appalachian Community. *Anthropological Quarterly* 65(3):137–147.

———. 2000. *Seldom Ask, Never Tell: Labor and Discourse in Appalachia.* New York: Oxford University Press.

Radner, Joan N., and Susan S. Lanser. 1993. Strategies of Coding in Women's Cultures. In *Feminist Messages: Coding in Women's Folk Culture,* ed. Joan Newlon Radner, pp. 1–29. Urbana: University of Illinois Press.

Reeves, Edward B., and Philip Kenkel. 1988. Agricultural Involution and the Sense of Place in Eastern Kentucky. In *Sense of Place in Appalachia,* ed. S. Mont Whitson, pp. 190–205. Morehead, KY: Morehead State University.

Riddle, Almeda. 1970. *A Singer and Her Songs: Almeda Riddle's Book of Ballads,* ed. Roger D. Abrahams. Baton Rouge: Louisiana State University Press.

Roberts, Leonard. 1979. *In the Pine: Selected Kentucky Folksongs,* 2nd ed. Pikeville, KY: Pikeville College Press.

Roseman, Sharon R. 2002. "Strong Women" and "Pretty Girls": Self-Provisioning, Gender, and Class Identity in Rural Galicia (Spain). *American Anthropologist* 104(1):22–37.

Rosenberg, Neil V. 1980. "It Was Kind of a Hobby": A Manuscript Song Book and Its Place in Tradition. In *Folklore Studies in Honour of Herbert Halpert: A Festschrift,* ed. Kenneth S. Goldstein and Neil V. Rosenberg, pp. 315–334. St. John's: Memorial University of Newfoundland.

Salstrom, Paul. 1994. *Appalachia's Path to Dependency: Rethinking a Region's Economic History 1730–1940.* Lexington: University Press of Kentucky.

Samuels, David. 1999. The Whole and the Sum of the Parts, or How Cookie and the Cupcakes Told the Story of Apache History in San Carlos. *Journal of American Folklore* 112(445):464–474.

Sawin, Patricia E. 1992. "Right Here Is a Good Christian Lady": Reported Speech in Personal Narratives. *Text and Performance Quarterly* 12(3):193–211.

———. 1993. Bessie Mae Eldreth: An Appalachian Woman's Performance of Self. PhD dissertation, Indiana University.

———. 1994. Bessie Eldreth: Traditional Singer and Storyteller, Brown Hudson Folklore Award Citation. *North Carolina Folklore Journal* 41(2):70–72.

———. 1999. Gender, Context, and the Narrative Construction of Identity: Rethinking Models of "Women's Narrative." In *Reinventing Identities: The Gendered Self in Discourse,* ed. Mary Bucholtz, A. C. Liang, and Laurel A. Sutton, pp. 241–258. New York: Oxford University Press.

———. 2002. Performance at the Nexus of Gender, Power, and Desire. *Journal of American Folklore* 115(455):28–61.

Scarry, Elaine. 1985. *The Body in Pain: The Making and Unmaking of the World.* New York: Oxford University Press.

Schegloff, Emanuel A., and Harvey Sacks. 1973. Opening Up Closings. *Semiotica* 7:289–327.

Schutte, Ofelia. 2000. Cultural Alterity: Cross-Cultural Communication and Feminist Theory in North-South Contexts. In *Decentering the Center: Philosophy for a Multicultural, Postcolonial, and Feminist World*, ed. Uma Narayan and Sandra Harding, pp. 47–66. Bloomington: Indiana University Press.

Scott, James C. 1985. *Weapons of the Weak: Everyday Forms of Peasant Resistance*. New Haven: Yale University Press.

Scott, Joan W. 1991. The Evidence of Experience. *Critical Inquiry* 17:773–797.

Shapiro, Henry P. 1978. *Appalachia on Our Mind*. Chapel Hill: University of North Carolina Press.

Sharp, Cecil J. 1932. *English Folk Songs from the Southern Appalachians*. London: Oxford University Press.

Shuman, Amy. 1986. *Storytelling Rights: The Uses of Oral and Written Texts by Urban Adolescents*. Cambridge: Cambridge University Press.

———. 1993. Dismantling Local Culture. *Western Folklore* 52(2,3,4):345–364.

Silber, Nina. 2001. "What Does America Need So Much as Americans?": Race and Northern Reconciliation with Southern Appalachia, 1870–1900. In *Appalachians and Race: The Mountain South from Slavery to Segregation*, ed. John C. Inscoe, pp. 243–258. Lexington: University Press of Kentucky.

Smith, Moira. 1990. Jokes and Practical Jokes. In *The Emergence of Folklore in Everyday Life*, ed. George H. Schoemaker, pp. 73–82. Bloomington, IN: Trickster Press.

———. 1995. Whipping Up a Storm: The Ethics and Consequences of Joking Around. *Journal of Folklore Research* 32(2):121–136.

Spivak, Gayatri Chakravorty. 1988. Can the Subaltern Speak? In *Marxism and the Interpretation of Culture*, ed. Cary Nelson and Lawrence Grossberg, pp. 271–313. Urbana: University of Illinois Press.

Stacey, Judith. 1988. Can There Be a Feminist Ethnography? *Women's Studies International Forum* 11(1):21–27.

Stekert, Ellen. 1965. Two Voices of Tradition: The Influence of Personality and Collecting Environment upon the Songs of Two Traditional Folksingers. Ph.D. dissertation: University of Pennsylvania.

Stewart, Kathleen Claire. 1990. Backtalking the Wilderness: "Appalachian" En-genderings. In *Uncertain Terms: Negotiating Gender in American Culture*, ed. Faye Ginsburg and Anna Lowenhaupt Tsing, pp. 43–56. Boston: Beacon Press.

———. 1996. *A Space on the Side of the Road: Cultural Poetics in an "Other" America*. Princeton, NJ: Princeton University Press.

Strauss, Claudia. 1992. What Makes Tony Run? Schemas as Motives Reconsidered. In *Human Motives and Cultural Models*, ed. Roy G. D'Andrade and Claudia Strauss, pp. 191–224. Cambridge: Cambridge University Press.

Swensen, Clifford H. 1988. Sense of Place: A Sacred Symbol. In *Sense of Place in Appalachia*, ed. S. Mont Whitson, pp. 206–224. Morehead, KY: Morehead State University.

Tallman, Richard. 1974. A Generic Approach to the Practical Joke. *Southern Folklore Quarterly* 38:259–274.

Tannen, Deborah. 1989. *Talking Voices: Repetition, Dialogue, and Imagery in Conversational Discourse*. Cambridge: Cambridge University Press.

———. 1990. *You Just Don't Understand: Men and Women in Conversation*. New York: William Morrow.

———. 1995. Waiting for the Mouse: Constructed Dialogue in Conversation. In *The Dialogic Emergence of Culture*, ed. Dennis Tedlock and Bruce Mannheim, pp. 198–217. Urbana: University of Illinois Press.

Thomas, Jeannie B., and Doug Enders. 2000. Bluegrass and "White Trash": A Case Study Concerning the Name "Folklore" and Class Bias. *Journal of Folklore Research* 37(1):23–52.

Titon, Jeff Todd. 1988. *Powerhouse for God: Speech, Chant, and Song in an Appalachian Baptist Church*. Austin: University of Texas Press.

Todorov, Tzvetan. 1984. *Mikhail Bakhtin: The Dialogical Principle*. Minneapolis: University of Minnesota Press.

Tyler, Stephen A. 1986. Post-Modern Ethnography: From Document of the Occult to Occult Document. In *Writing Culture: The Poetics and Politics of Ethnography*, ed. James Clifford and George E. Marcus, pp. 122–140. Berkeley: University of California Press.

———. 1987. On "Writing Up/Off" as "Speaking-For." *Journal of Anthropological Research* 43:338–342.

Urban, Greg. 1984. Speech about Speech in Speech about Action. *Journal of American Folklore* 97(385):310–328.

Vološinov, V.N. 1973 [1930]. *Marxism and the Philosophy of Language*, trans. Ladislav Matejka and I. R. Titunik. New York: Seminar Press.

Walkerdine, Valerie. 1990. *Schoolgirl Fictions*. London: Verso.

Wallerstein, Immanuel. 1974. *The Modern World-System I: Capitalist Agriculture and the Origins of the European World-Economy in the Sixteenth Century*. New York: Academic Press.

Weedon, Chris. 1997 [1987]. *Feminist Practice and Poststructuralist Theory*, 2nd ed. Oxford, UK: Blackwell Publishers.

Whisnant, David. 1983. *All That Is Native and Fine: The Politics of Culture in an American Region*. Chapel Hill: University of North Carolina Press.

Wilgus, D. K. 1965. An Introduction to the Study of Hillbilly Music. *Journal of American Folklore* 78(309):195–203.

———. 1981. A. J., Folk Composer: An Overview. *Lore and Language* 3(4–5):109–128.

Williams, John Alexander. 2002. *Appalachia: A History*. Chapel Hill: University of North Carolina Press.

Williams, Raymond. 1973. *The Country and the City*. New York: Oxford University Press.

———. 1977. *Marxism and Literature*. Oxford: Oxford University Press.

Willis, Paul. 2001. "Tekin' the Piss." In *History in Person: Enduring Struggles, Contentious Practice, Intimate Identities*, ed. Dorothy Holland and Jean Lave, pp. 171–216. Santa Fe: School of American Research Press.

Wolfson, Nessa. 1976. Speech Events and Natural Speech: Some Implications for Sociolinguistic Methodology. *Language in Society* 5(2):189–209.

Yocom, Margaret. 1985. Woman to Woman: Fieldwork and the Private Sphere. In *Women's Folklore, Women's Culture*, ed. Rosan A. Jordan and Susan J. Kalčik, pp. 45–53. Philadelphia: University of Pennsylvania Press.

INDEX

A

A and R men, 159, 168

adaptation. *See* narrative, adapted; song, modification of text

address, respectful form of, 94, 217n5

African Americans: contributions to mountain South of labor of, 40, 152–153; denigrating portrayal of (*see* blackface); power of impersonating, 151; songs associated with, 146, 160

agriculture. *See* work, agricultural

Anderson, Marion, 146, 163

anger, management of, 149

Anglin, Jim, 146

anthropology, concern with representation, 10–11

anxiety about performing, 199–200. *See also* insecurity

antique dealers, 60

Appalachia: as constructed concept, 2, 20–21, 61; as economic periphery, 38, 39, 65, 212; economic equality in, 57; Eldreth's attachment to romanticized images of, 4, 29, 212 (*see also* nostalgia); exceptionalism, 39, 152–153; exploitation by capitalists, 39; industrialization of, 29, 39, 41, 45, 153; less culturally isolated than supposed, 4, 26, 147, 160, 167, 209; regarded as culturally distinctive, 61; regarded as source of Anglo-Saxon stock, 38, 151; regarded as source of uncommercialized culture, 38, 159; rural character of, 29

Appalachian culture: as problematic concept, 3, 21, 209; distinctiveness an adaptation to exploitation or romantic projection, 21; Eldreth's resistance to concept, 3, 20–21, 61, 157, 204–205, 212; Eldreth's songs considered example of, 4, 212; folklorists' attachment to concept, 3; ghost stories considered an example of, 100

Appalachian historiography, revisionist, 39, 209

Appalachian singing style. *See* singing style, Appalachian

Appalachian State University (Boone, NC): Eldreth's children work at, 23; Eldreth's involvement with students from, 101, 211, 212, 218n2; Eldreth's performances at, 24, 204, 206, 218n2; scholars associated with (*see* Cornett, Judy; Conway, Cecilia; McCloud, William; McGowan, Thomas; Williams, Cratis)

Appalachian Studies, 25, 38, 43, 201

artist, Eldreth as, 156, 157

audience: appreciation of Eldreth, 202; Eldreth's sensitivity to, 207; grandchildren as, 23, 100, 131, 156 ; misunderstanding needs of, 55, 61, 114, 190; new opportunities offered by public, 3, 25, 62, 63, 71, 130–131, 185, 210, 212, 217n1. *See also* listener

aunt(s), Eldreth's relationship with, 37, 72, 107

B

babysitting, 23, 52, 182

back-talk, 20, 80, 122–123, 175, 176–178

Bakhtin, M. M.: chronotope, 42; discourse, 5–7, 12–13; fascination with novel, 6; heteroglossia, 8; Marxian perspective, 50; model of self as dialogically constituted, 5–7, 18; model of utterance as responsive, 9, 21; speech full of others' words, 8, 18. *See also* dialogism, utterance

baking: Eldreth, 51, 52, 80, 207; Grandma Milam, 33. *See also* food, preparation

ballad(s), 161, 205; American from British Broadsides, 160, 164–165; Child or English, 160, 209, 222n20 (*see also* ballads, traditional); murder, 113, 164–165, 170, 173, 175; Native American, 160, 164–165; parlor (*see* song, sentimental); sentimental (*see* song, sentimental); traditional, 4, 26, 113, 160. *See also* song

Baptist church, 43, 193, 196, 222–223n22

Bell, Ed (storyteller), 16, 55

benevolent manifestations, 103, 130. *See also* ghosts

Bicentennial (United States 1976), 23, 201, 202

biography, 2

birth. *See* childbearing

Bishop, Elva, 215n8

Black, Mary, 106, 113, 142

blackface: admiration for African American musical forms reflected in, 147; argument for studying practice distinct from condemnation of attitudes responsible, 145; as oversaturated metaphor, 155; characters frightening, 145, 147, 151; denigrating portrayal of African Americans in, 26, 144, 153, 212; Eldreth's models for, 146; Eldreth's use in practical joking, 135, 143–147, 150–155; homosexual fascination

reflected in, 147; image ubiquitous in
North American culture, 147; involves
both love and theft, 147; metaphysical,
147; political protest in, 147; power of,
155; reinforces Eldreth's membership in
white community, 151–152; reflects racial
envy, 151; Sawin's discomfort with, 21, 26,
135; seeing through the disguise, 151; use
by Al Jolson, 146; use by early country
music stars, 146
bluegrass, 163, 171, 194, 197
Blue Sky Boys, 146, 163, 165, 171
blue yodel, 161
bootlegging: Eldreth's distress over involvement with, 44, 185; granddaughter reveals
story of, 44, 184; helping father with, 35,
184
bragging, 82, 208–209
brother: Eldreth's relationship with, 22, 140;
played practical joke, 138–139

C

Carter Family, 146, 161, 162, 163, 164, 16,
222n19
character: inherent, 30, 31; develops in course
of life, 31. *See also* self, self-construction,
subjectivity
charity, 60
chickens: cross legs to be tied, 35; drown in
flood, 123; Eldreth refuses to kill, 52;
naked, 123
childbearing: assisting others, 51–52, 74–75,
86; as taboo subject, 87; Eldreth's own, 52,
76–77; learning about through experience
only, 87; vulnerability of women after,
76–77
childhood: as favored topic, 25, 28, 29, 31; as
sacred, 172; association of songs with,
171–172; disrupted by moving, 22–23, 32;
idealization of, 178; purpose of stories
about, 29; sense of security in, 172; two
versions of, 25, 32. *See also* happiness,
before marriage
childrearing, Eldreth's philosophy of, 148–149
children: Eldreth's relationship with, 83, 94,
203, 210; names of Eldreth's, 23, 217n2;
playing practical jokes on, 135, 147
choir: Eldreth's participation in, 193, 194;
leader, 194, 195; role in church service,
194; Sawin's participation in, 194
chronology: Eldreth's disinterest in, 22; ethnographer's contribution to life story, 14, 22
chronotope: idyll of agricultural labor, 42; novelistic time, 46–47
churning butter, 33
class: as dimension of difference between
Eldreth and Sawin, 4, 62, 136; contribution
of slavery to society stratified by, 153;

defined by kind and amount of work, 4; differences not recognized, 37; intertwined
with race, 151, 154; moral or social ranking
according to, 57, 104, 149; more significant
than culture in differentiating Eldreth from
new audiences, 4, 20. *See also* poverty,
wealth
clothing: accepting charitable gift of, 60; for
performance, 205; production, purchase,
and care, 51
coding, 26, 27, 99, 100, 149, 175, 213; incompetence, 150; trivialization, 131
colored child, 77, 88, 138–139
comforter, Eldreth's self-definition as, 174, 178,
211
communication, research methodologies
attempt to exceed capacities of, 3, 17
community: Eldreth uses blackface to strength-
en inclusion in white, 151; influence on
character, 25, 29, 32, 41, 48
compliance, as index of good relationship, 84.
See also obedience
complicity: folklorists' reluctance to criticize, 3,
144, 153; in oppression on basis of class,
48; in oppression on basis of gender, 3, 26,
91, 97, 112, 114, 132–133, 213; in oppression on basis of race, 3, 26, 136, 155, 213;
mixed with resistance, 8
compliment, 198
conflict: between Eldreth's hegemonic formation and life experience, 133; between
ethnographer's and subject's interpretation,
16, 30, 135, 144, 180; between two
accounts of childhood, 25, 32, 35
context: captured by ethnographer separately
from text, 17, 156; ethnographic text as for
utterances incorporated, 11; for singing,
179, 192; narratives grounded in past and
present, 18; natural, 10–11, 13, 214n1; no
single authentic, 12; read influence of prior
from dialogic utterance, 12; songbook as,
192
contradiction, containing power of, 133
conversation: Eldreth turns to own purposes,
27, 130; interview as, 14; limitations on
ethnography imposed by constraints of, 17;
supportive among women, 86, 88; with
children about their father, 94. *See also* discourse; ways of speaking
conviction, 196
Conway, Cecelia, 55–56, 63, 79–80, 88, 92,
164, 215n8, 216–217n7
cooking, men's ignorance of, 84. *See also* food,
preparation
cooperation: among women, 86; as valued
character trait, 30; by members of extended
family, 37, 41
Cornett, Judy, 101, 218n2

country music: associated with Appalachia, 4; continuities with traditional mountain music, 203; in Eldreth's repertoire, 26 (*see also* repertoire, sources); new compositions on traditional models, 161; nostalgia for past in, 43, 161, 166, 172; recording of traditional musicians and songs, 159, 161, 165

courage, 83, 99, 115, 134

courtship, 72–74, 85–86

cousin, Eldreth's relationship with, 37, 162

cowardice, 83

Cox, Joe, 77–78, 200

criticism: coded, 26, 149; implicit, 84; masked, 130; of dishonest landlord, 120; of exploitation, 29, 104; of husband, 84, 85, 120, 130; of marriage, 85; of men's abuse of power, 112

culture: as problematic concept, 21; dialogic, 4–5, 9; emerges through use of collective expressive resources, 4–5, 9; folklorists need to dismantle concept of local, 21; local generated through interaction with translocal, 43; potential for change, 5; reciprocally produced with individual identity, 5, 212

D

Dalhart, Vernon, 163, 164, 165, 166

daughter(s), Eldreth's relationship with, 78. *See also* children, Eldreth's relationship with

decontextualization, 17, 190

defensiveness, 9, 56, 61, 215n4

demonstration, 179, 201, 204, 205, 206

Depression (United States 1930s), 2, 53, 164

dialogism: anticipates receptive understanding, 1, 7, 9, 50–51; emergence of culture through, 9; emergence of ethnography through, 9–10; in Eldreth's voicing of song texts, 157; infiltration of speaker's discourse by another's style, 8; production of self through, 96; provides access to dimensions of rhetorical action beyond semantic, 7; responding to past interlocutors, 1, 7, 9, 56; shows how existing discourses may be challenged, 8; understanding ethnographic interaction in terms of, 10; utterance incorporates prior utterances, genres, speech styles, 8

dialogue: between song and speech, 176–178, 183; constructed (*see* reported speech)

disbelief, traditions of, 111

discourse(s): associated with narrative structure, 133; Bakhtin's definition of, 5–6; blocks critical consciousness, 47; conflicting, 133, 209; constitution of self through, 6, 114, 176; counter-, 178; determines experience, 46; Eldreth must respond to, 211; Eldreth situates self in opposition to other actors within, 113; Foucault's defini-

tion of, 5–6; full of prior discourses, 12; gendered positions in, 6; internalized voice of past interlocutors in, 4, 51, 178, 211; investment in, 69; involvement in continuing with prior interlocutors, 215n3; irreducible to language, 5; limitations imposed by, 6, 176–177, 211; local, 29, 56, 59, 62, 185, 210, 211; multiple intertwined, 112; positioning interlocutor in, 135–136, 155; produces permissible modes of thinking and being, 6; progressive, 69; self-construction in response to, 18, 211, 213; self-positioning in, 113, 126, 132; separability mitigates logical contradictions, 126

dissertation, Sawin's, 96, 219n1 (chap. 6), 219n2 (chap. 7)

divorce: Eldreth's condemnation of, 91, 173; loss of moral standing for those who obtain, 91, 113

doctors, 18, 51–52, 74, 93, 95, 106, 142

dream 123, 177. *See also* premonition

drowning: babies in well, 110, 119; niece, 76–77; neighbor, 117; television report about children, 174

duty: Christian, 89, 200; singing as, 200; to family takes precedence over performance, 207; to rescue child, 89; wife's, to care for husband, 78, 89, 200

dye plant (Damascus, Virginia), 23, 34, 45

dynamics, 167

E

earth tremor, 122

eavesdropping, 13

egalitarianism: as Appalachian character trait, 38; Calvinist underpinnings, 215n2; in Baptist Church, 197

Elderhostel, 24, 61, 63, 131

Eldreth, Drew. *See* grandchildren

Eldreth, Ed. *See* husband

Eldreth, Maud Killens. *See* sister(s)

Eldreth, Stacey. *See* grandchildren

Eller, Clyde Killens. *See* sister(s)

embellishment, 165

emotions: complexity of, 176–177; singing as sustenance for, 186

empiricism, radical, 12

entextualization, 16, 18

ethnographer: as listener, 2, 3, 9, 19, 27, 178, 213; attempt to efface own presence, 10–11; attempt to erase is dishonest, 13; attention sparks jealousy, 208, 227n31; conceals opinions from subject, 14, 63, 135, 139; convergence of purposes of with subject's, 18, 21, 27; dilemma over criticizing subject, 3, 144, 153; discursive positioning of by subject, 21, 26, 135–136; divergence of purposes from subject's, 3, 21; Eldreth's resistance to purposes of (*see* resistance, to being presented as example of Appalachian culture; resistance, to ethnographer's purposes); feminism of, 1, 3, 14, 63, 134, 144; influence on subject, 156, 167, 180; interpretation conflicts with subject's own, 16, 30, 135, 144, 180; presence not contamination, 12; rejects impossible disciplinary expectations, 10–11; relationship with person studied, 1, 59; responsibility to process subject's words, 11, 17, 18, 19–20, 22; role in construction of subject, 2, 29, 36; subjects evade textual domination by, 12; words of inflected by subject's, 13

ethnography: as addition to not substitute for subject's words, 16; as dialogic process, 2, 9–10, 12, 17–20; challenge of to balance coherence and preservation of subject's voice, 10, 14, 19; concern that account misrepresents encounter, 12; dialogic approach to recuperates confusing research interactions, 13; dialogic critique of, 10; dialogic perspective on resolves contextual and representational impasses, 12, 17; feminist, 2, 11, 87–88 (*see also* feminist methodology); goal of to acknowledge humanity of subject, 10; limitations imposed by focus on subject's utterances, 17; of subjectivity, 2, 4; of the particular, 21; postmodern, 19–20; reciprocal, 19–20; subjects evade textual domination in, 12

evaluation: authoritative, 25, 59, 81, 93; by men, 25, 81, 91, 93, 217n3; by mother, 59, 217n3; Eldreth contradicts men's, 89; function in narrative, 30; modeling for others, 68, 93, 97; of performance (*see* performance); of self, 68, 81, 92; positive as sign of distant relationship, 83

exceptionalism, Appalachian 39, 152–153

exemplum: clarity of moral, 101; Eldreth identifies with character in, 104; Eldreth includes in category ghost story, 100; gender unimportant in, 105; relationship with neighbors in, 101; reported speech in, 104; retold, not narrative of personal experience, 101; reward and punishment in, 105; similarity to parable, 103; temporal ordering in, 102

experience: Eldreth's narratives as definitive version of, 16; made possible by hegemonic social structures, 5

exploitation: based on class, 95, 120; based on gender, 66; created by intimacy, 85; personal criticized, 65, 95, 119–120; structural not recognized, 37, 43, 46–47, 57, 65

extract. *See* timber cutting

extractive industries, 39. *See also* timber cutting, mining

F

fabrication, 136, 150. *See also* practical joking

failure, rhetorical use of others', 83, 87

family: cooperation within, 37, 41; reunited in heaven, 92, 221n16, 222–223n22, 223–225n24

farm and forest economy, 38

father: absent or unknown of murdered babies, 113; advocates truthfulness, 33; as musician, 22, 45, 60, 181; drinking, 114; Eldreth's relationship with, 22–23, 30; made whiskey, 44, 184

fear: denial of, 115, 116; enjoyable in telling ghost stories, 142; men and women employ to negotiate power, 99, 107, 115–117, 129; of blackface character, 145, 147, 151

feminism: antiessentialist, 12; attention to marginalized, 2; critique of gender hegemony, 6; effacement of ethnographer's goals contravenes, 11; ethnographer's, 1, 3, 14, 63, 134, 144; poststructuralist, 6; tendency to valorize subjects, 3. *See also* ethnography, feminist

feminist methodology: design studies to respond to subjects' needs, 11; dilemma of writing about non-feminist subjects, 11

festival: Eldreth's involvement in, 202, 212, 228n37 (*see also* Festival for the Eno; Festival of American Folklife; Jonesboro Storytelling Festival; World Music Institute); opportunity for sociable singing, 204; participant experience, 228n37

Festival for the Eno (Durham, NC), 205

Festival of American Folklife (Washington, DC), 2, 24, 60, 178–179, 204, 205, 215n7, 217n9, 221n14, 228n37

flood, 122

folklore: attention to marginalized, 2; conceptualizes what feels real, 144; concern with natural context, 10–11, 214n1

folklorists: as resources for Eldreth's self-construction, 25; at ASU (*see* Appalachian State University); attachment to romanticized concept of Appalachia, 21, 209; collected home repertoire, 168; duty to dismantle concept of local culture, 21; Eldreth's familiarity with expectations of, 15; Eldreth's interactions with, 1, 23, 26, 179, 188, 201; influence on Eldreth, 167, 179–180, 192, 204, 210; interest in old songs, 17, 169, 209; interest in songs learned orally, 167; interest in traditional music, 159, 160, 180; Jean Reid comes to

attention of, 23, 179; needs coincide with Eldreth's, 205; needs do not coincide with Eldreth's, 205, 212; refusal to collect popular compositions, 161, 209; reluctance to criticize subjects, 3
folk revival, 168
food: preparation, 33, 51, 52, 183–184; producing own, 32, 34, 35, 51, 123, 147, 216n1. *See also* baking
framing, 62, 198, 201, 204, 205, 207, 228n37; transgression of 197, 207, 212. *See also* demonstration; performance
funeral, 77–78, 89, 174, 200, 210

G

gender: as factor in ghost stories, 111; as inevitable topic, 15, 212; as product of performance, 5; experience of influenced by class, 2; experience of influenced by region, 2; influence on benefits of performance, 157; influence on engagement with music, 180–181, 186 (*see also* music, instrumental inappropriate for women; singing, appropriate for women); influence on reaction to ghosts, 115
gender roles: challenge to posed by ghosts, 115; inflexibility of, 117. *See also* husband, traditional authority of; women's roles
genealogical landscape, 120
genre: conventions of, 112; emergent, 133; implicit expectations of, 133; mobilizes lower level expressive resources, 7; models for Eldreth's narratives and practices, 8; resource for self-construction, 4, 7–8; use of multiple constructs non-unitary subjectivity, 112
ghosts: ambiguity of, 131; benevolent are purposeful, 104; challenge hegemony, 131; conflicting models for interpreting, 126; connected to possessions of deceased, 102–103, 128; connections between experience of and changing ways of speaking, 142; connections between experience of and practical joking, 137, 142; deceased loved ones as benevolent, 111; discursive manifestation of, 211; embody hegemony, 132; empowerment by, 122; enjoyment of, 115; experience of as barometer of stress, 26, 137; fear of, 99, 107, 115, 116, 129, 134, 142; light as evidence of, 117, 126–127; lingering element of constraining past, 170; literal, psychological, and social interpretations of, 99; malevolent are purposeless, 105, 114, 132; materialize exploitation, 26, 120; men's and women's different reactions to, 116; must be reckoned with out of concern for justice, 98;

power of, 104; real in that they produce material effects, 99; reflect uncertainty in new relationship, 115; relationship to God, 125, 130, 218–219n5; represent hope and possibility, 98, 122, 133; represent injustice, 99, 102, 104, 120, 132; represent loss or something missing, 98, 111, 113, 129, 131; reveal gender inequalities, 99, 132; sense of kinship with, 115; sounds as evidence of, 116, 117, 118; troubling, 99, 105. *See also* haunting; supernatural
ghost stories: audience requests for, 98, 100, 148; compared to other personal experience narratives, 99, 100; considered a component of Appalachian culture, 4, 100; double temporal grounding of, 100; Eldreth anticipates listeners' skepticism about, 99, 131, 218n1; enjoyable, 142, 148; frightening, 142, 148; gender a factor in, 111; kinds of stories so labeled by Eldreth, 100, 101; label trivializes controversial subject matter of, 133; most welcome means for Eldreth to discuss personal experience in public, 100; motives of murder not questioned in, 112; reported speech in, 105; suspense in, 105; temporal ordering in, 105. *See also* stories
God: as listener, 200; musical talent as gift from, 180–181, 200; performance for, 200; praise for human accomplishments directed to, 198; relationship to ghosts, 125, 130, 218–219n5; singing to glorify, 195; transcends human logic, 88
good old days, 42, 46
gospel quartet, 179, 195, 196
gossip, 82
Graham, Billy, 196
Graham, Doctor, 106, 118–119, 142
grandchildren: as audience (*see* audience, grandchildren as); Eldreth's relationship with, 23, 80, 90–91, 98, 148, 184; Eldreth teaches to sing, 185, 195, 199
grandfather: Eldreth's relationship with Milam, 22, 37, 108, 119; Killens as musician, 22, 45, 181; Milam takes care of dying neighbor, 102–104
grandmother: Eldreth's relationship with, 22, 33, 37, 108, 119, 164; learning songs from (*see* learning songs, from grandmother); played practical joke, 138–139; takes care of dying neighbor, 102–104
Greene, Mary, 63, 163, 203, 204, 205, 206, 211, 220n8, 221n14, 227n30, 227n32, 227n34

H

happiness: before marriage, 48, 140, 171–172; Eldreth claims as defining trait, 24, 170;

expression of holy spirit, 193; since husband's death, 31, 129; singing promotes, 184

haunting: causes of, 111, 112, 114, 118, 128; connection between sign and event (arbitrary or logical), 117; lingering element of constraining past, 170; produced by immoral behavior, 26, 114; uninvited, 98; woman to blame for, 26, 111, 128. See also ghosts; ghost stories; house, haunted

heaven: family reunited in, 92, 221n16, 222–223n22, 223–225n24; home in, 172, 222–223n22, 223–224n24; meet Jesus in, 223n24; reward in, 172

hegemony: functioning of, 5, 114; ghosts as challenge to or embodiment of, 131–132; influence on formation of individual, 133; influence on system of social meanings, 5; partial escape from, 3

heteroglossia, 8, 18, 20, 157, 173, 178

Hiawatha, 20

Hicks family, 168

hillbilly: as racial category, 152; musicians, 161; negative stereotype, 44, 61, 205

Hinson, Glenn, 178–179, 203, 204, 211, 221n14

historiography, revisionist, 39, 209

Holland, Dorothy, 55–56, 63, 79–80, 88, 92, 216–217n7

homemade. See song, homemade

homeplace, 120

horses: racing, 37; working with, 55–56

hostess, Eldreth assumes role of, 207–208

house(s): built by sons, 120; destroyed, 23, 77, 122, 188; haunted, 107, 118, 120, 129; rented, 23, 120. See also ownership, home

housework: for pay, 23, 51, 58, 94, 104; in own home, 51, 183. See also work, women's

humor: as essential component of Eldreth's self-construction, 135; differential perceptions of, 135; in causing shock, 143; of jokes accidentally played on self, 139–140; produced by incongruity, 155. See also laughter

husband: as revenant, 128, 219n6; caring for as wife's duty, 200; domination by, 68, 84, 112, 113, 126, 131–132, 172, 176, 213; Eldreth's relationship with, 31, 64, 74, 75, 79–80, 82–84, 94, 128, 147–148; insufficient support from, 23, 65, 121; negative portrait of, 94; not included in practical joking, 147–148; punishes Eldreth through supernatural, 128; traditional authority of, 81, 117, 129, 133

hybridity, 172

hymn, 159, 160, 172, 194, 196, 205, 221n13

I

identity. See character; self; self-construction; subjectivity

implicature, 9

incompetence: as form of coded protest, 150; rhetorical use of others', 83, 87

individualism as Appalachian character trait, 38

indentured labor, 40

initiation, 143

injury suffered by Ed Eldreth, 23, 65

innocence, 212

insecurity: about changes during puberty, 86; about moral or social standing, 28, 150

interlocutor, speaker responds to present and absent, 9. See also listener

interpretation: conflict between ethnographer's and subject's, 16, 30, 135, 144, 180; conflicting models for of ghost stories, 126; narrative as model for of experience, 127, 128, 133; of silence, 89, 90; theories for of ghost stories, 99

intertextuality, 8

interview: appropriate setting for telling of oral history, 14; as conversation, 14; as performance, 206; as source of material for this study, 13; complex negotiation between ethnographer and subject, 13; Eldreth's control of, 14–15, 206; Eldreth's familiarity with conventions of, 15; Eldreth turns into singing sessions, 17; ethnographer must hold up her end of, 14, 214n2; mix of narrative genres in, 216n3; permits Eldreth to explore new facets of experience, 15; subject prompts ethnographer for questions, 14, 214n2

intuition: challengeable form of knowledge, 124; God as source of, 125

Irish: defining selves in contrast to African Americans, 152; ethnic identity of Killens family, 22

Irish Republican Army, 64

J

jealousy, 199, 208, 227n31

Jeffersonian ideal (community of yeoman farmers), 41, 43

Jenkins, Reverend Andrew, 162, 171, 220n9

Jesus Christ: answers prayer, 223–225n24; as pattern for moral behavior, 64, 89; as personal savior, 64, 197, 223–225n24; judgment by, 223n24; life of as most valuable time in history, 172

jokes women tell critical of men, 148. See also humor; practical joking

joking relationship, 148

Jonesboro Storytelling Festival, 205

K

Killens, Blanche. See cousin

Killens, Clyde. *See* sister(s)
Killens, Florence Milam. *See* mother
Killens, Joe. *See* brother
Killens, Romey. *See* father
Killens, Sidney. *See* uncle
knowledge: Eldreth's unique, 132; power of
   offered by supernatural, 132; women's, 26,
   81, 124

L

labor. *See* childbearing, housework, work
lament. *See* song, sentimental
landlord: privileges over renters, 120; with-
   holding information from renters, 119–120.
   See also renter
landscape, genealogical, 120
language does not represent external reality, 5
laughter: as healthy, 138; as relief from hard
   lives, 140; at jokes played on self, 140;
   rhetorical purposes of, 130–131, 212. *See
   also* humor
laziness, 44, 60, 120, 181. *See also* bootlegging;
   music, as leisure activity; work
Leadbelly, 146
learning songs: from aunt, 160, 162; from
   cousin, 162; from father, 160, 162; from
   grandmother, 162, 163, 164, 167, 182; from
   mother, 162; from schoolteacher, 162; from
   uncle, 43, 162, 163, 221n11; timing of, 29
leisure. *See* laziness; music, as leisure activity
life history, 2
life story, 13–15, 22. *See also* narrative, stories
listener: as co-constructor of meaning (*see*
   utterance); ethnographer as, 2, 3, 9, 19, 27,
   178, 213; God as, 200; influence of on narrative, 3; journalist as, 95–96; new opportunities presented by new, 3, 15, 25–26,
   63–64, 93–94, 95–96, 212. *See also* audience
literacy: hyper-, 19, 187; skills crucial to maintenance of song repertoire, 186, 191–192;
   women's work, 187, 192. *See also* writing
locality, sense of, 159
logging. *See* timber cutting
Longfellow, Henry Wadsworth, 20
love letters, 110, 141–142, 187
lyric. *See* song, lyric

M

marriage: a mistake, 91; as partnership, 65, 81;
   as outcome of practical joke, 143; date of,
   23; Eldreth's dedication to, 91, 143;
   Eldreth's guilt over, 176; Eldreth's reluctance to enter into, 72, 85–86, 92, 176;
   Eldreth's unhappiness in, 23, 71, 113, 135;
   ghost experiences early in, 26, 107; ghost
   experiences at end of, 129; negotiating balance of power within, 117; vows made to

God as well as spouse, 143
Mars Hill College (Mars Hill, NC), 146, 163
Marx, Karl, 50
maxims, 42
McCloud, William, 204, 205
McGowan, Thomas, 101, 170, 211, 218n2
melancholy, 178, 209. *See also* song, lonesome
memorization, 167, 168, 169
memory: Eldreth's pride in, 158; selective,
   215n1 (chap. 2)
metanarrative, 16, 127, 130, 148
metaphor, oversaturated, 155
Methodist church, 33
minstrelsy, blackface, 145–147
miscommunication between women, 25, 85,
   142–143. *See also* misunderstanding
Mississippi Sheiks, 146
misunderstanding: between ethnographer and
   subject, 9, 13, 16, 17, 49, 56, 155; of expectations of current audience, 16, 55, 61, 114,
   190, 212; of presenter's plans on stage, 205,
   212; shows narrative developed for prior
   audience, 16
modesty, 82, 89
modification of song text, 174
Monroe, Bill, 163, 171
moonshine. *See* bootlegging
moral individual produced by rural community,
   25, 41, 172
moral standing: anxiety over, 28, 60, 150; complex relationship with work, 25, 42, 48, 50,
   51, 56, 57, 60, 62, 66, 150, 181; compromised by divorce, 91, 113; connected with
   accomplishment of women's work, 150;
   determined by class, 57, 104–105, 152, 212,
   213; diminished by alcohol consumption or
   production (*see* bootlegging; father, drinking; mother, drinking; music, secular associated with alcohol consumption); established by claiming white identity, 152–153;
   established by contrast with other women,
   113, 132; precariousness of, 113, 115. *See
   also* ownership; poverty; respectability
mother: as authoritative evaluator, 59, 217n3;
   drinking, 114; Eldreth's relationship with,
   22–23, 30, 72, 83, 86, 91, 119, 142–143,
   181, 206; Eldreth's role as, 2, 28, 30, 147
moving: as disruptive, 37; frequency during
   childhood, 32; in search of work, 33, 34; to
   farm, 35
murder: as abrogation of women's role, 112; as
   cause of haunting, 109–110, 112, 218n3
music: as leisure activity, 60, 181, 184; instrumental not appropriate for a woman, 26,
   181, 210; secular associated with alcohol
   consumption, 184, 227n30. *See also* popular
   music; singing

musician: father as, 22, 181; grandfather as, 22, 181

N

naming, nonreciprocal, 217n5; of children, 217n2
narrative: adapted (or not) to current audience, 55, 58, 62, 66, 111; definitive version of Eldreth's experience, 17; dialogically constructed, 1; Eldreth repeats rather than comments on, 16; Eldreth's possession, 32; evaluation in, 30; fragmentary, 32; generalization, 42, 144, 215n3, 216n3; influence of individual experience on, 53; informs about events listener did not experience, 50, 55, 180; means of working through issues important to teller, 111; men's, 216n6; meta-, 127, 130, 148; model for interpreting experience, 127, 128, 133; models approved behaviors, 96; of ordinary personal experience rarely shared in performance, 100; reliving experience through, 66; repeatability facilitates recording of, 16; reported speech in, 68, 69–70; rhetorical goals, 53; Sawin's attempt to share own treated as interruption, 15–16, 216n5; scarcity of models for women's, 32; self-construction through, 1, 55; shapes listeners' impression of teller, 66; source of information on performance contexts, 156, 180; structure of, 121, 128, 132; tastes of prior contexts, 13; teller's inability to analyze own, 96; women's, 53, 87–88, 216n4, 216n5, 216n6, 227n29
nature. See character
neglect by husband, 64. See also husband
neighborliness: as moral trait, 48; between whites and blacks, 139, 146; mitigates economic inequality, 120; reward for, 128
neighbors: African Americans as, 139, 146, 155; Eldreth's relationship with, 29, 75, 76, 101, 144–147, 155, 208; interdependence of, 32, 37, 86; playing practical jokes on, 144–145, 147
newspaper, 96, 208
niece(s) and nephew(s), Eldreth's relationship with, 76–77, 89, 148
North Carolina Folk Heritage Award, 24
North Carolina Folklore Society, 24, 201
nostalgia: fuels popularity of country music, 43, 161, 166, 172; in sentimental songs, 172; resistance to, 52, 61

O

obedience: as valued character trait, 30, 132; to husband, 81, 84; to parents, 30
old age, 69
oppression perpetuated by oppressed, 153

oral traditions, popular music passes into, 157, 160–161, 167, 220n7
order (imperative), 73, 84, 86, 149, 218n2 (chap. 6)
ownership: home, 23, 36, 79, 81, 120, 129 (see also house); land, 22–23, 40

P

parody: ethnographic heteroglossia interpreted as, 20; in practical joking, 150
past. See nostalgia, sacred
Penfield, Sarah, 31
Pentecostal Church, 193
performance: as service, 208, 209; aesthetic considerations take precedence, 204; anxiety over, 199–200, 202; audience response to, 207, 209; avoidance of, 207; benefits of, 157, 200, 202, 206; borderline, 206; concern for quality of, 17; contribution to religious experience, 198; disclaimer of, 82, 197–198, 200, 206, 207; draws attention, 200; encouraged in church, 193; enjoyment of, 202; evaluated by effectiveness over formal excellence, 198, 209, 210, 227–228n35; everyday life presented in, 63; generates religious feeling, 227–228n35; hedged, 198, 200; influence of folklorists on, 203; informal, 194, 195; interview as, 206; liabilities of, 157; limitations based on gender, 157; other duties take precedence over, 207; preparation for, 191, 196 (see also rehearsal); problematic, 198, 206, 210; Reid's with Eldreth, 201–202, 203; Sawin's with Eldreth, 195; songbook as, 192; unhedged, 27, 200, 204, 205, 212; with presenter, 62–63, 178–179, 203, 205, 212. See also self; self-construction
phonograph, 37, 163, 164, 221n12; cylinder, 161, 162
piano, 181
poor white as racial category, 152, 154–155
popular music passes into oral tradition, 157
positioning. See discourses; ethnographer, discursive positioning of by subject; self-construction
postmodern ethnography, 19–20
poststructuralism 5–6. See also subjectivity
poverty: blamed on failings of those affected, 57, 64, 66, 152; Eldreth anticipates negative attitudes about, 56, 66, 152; Eldreth's self-description, 62; of Eldreth's family, 53; racialized, 154; undermines social standing, 57, 104, 152
practical joking: as acceptable activity for women, 141; as cruel, 135; as harmless, 135; as initiation, 143; backfires, 143, 154; benevolent, 136, 142; blackface in, 135, 143–147, 150–155; brother's, 138; connections to

changing ways of speaking, 140; connections to ghost experiences, 137, 140; dangerous, 137–138, 143, 149, 151; deception in, 137, 149; definitions of, 86, 136; denial in, 137, 139, 147, 154–155; denigrating portrayal of African-Americans in, 144, 147; distaste for seen as middle-class affectation, 136; ethnographer as victim of, 136, 148, 149, 155; ethnographer oblivious to, 155; fabrication discredited in, 150, 154; grandmother's, 138; humor in causing shock, 143; inadvertent, 136, 139–140; inherent hostility in, 137, 148; interpretation of necessarily conflicted, 136, 144; inversion in, 137–138, 150, 154; known to ethnographer through Eldreth's stories, 137; malevolent, 136; management of information in, 86, 150; models for, 137–138, 139, 140; most reportable go too far, 137; most skillful improvised and context-specific, 26, 138, 144; not motivated by enmity, 138; parody in, 150; permits escape from confining roles, 26, 136, 147, 151; permits joker to inhabit proscribed roles, 137; perpetrator must accept consequences of, 143; played on peers, 139; played on those less powerful, 139; played on those more powerful, 139; poetic justice in, 147; reciprocal, 137; release of suppressed tensions in, 137; retaliation for, 148; Sawin's dislike of, 21, 135, 148; self as victim of, 139–140; strengthens friendship, 137, 155; toughens victim, 149; traditional, 138, 143; unconscious revelation of core beliefs in, 137, 152; veiled criticism through, 4, 147–149, 154–155; victim of required to be good sport, 137, 148; victimization of children in, 135, 144, 147–148
praise. *See* evaluation
pregnancy, warning against, 113, 119
prejudice. *See* racism
premonition: ambiguity of sign, 100, 124; as empowering, 124, 126–127; as frightening, 124; benefits of acting upon, 124; Eldreth as authoritative interpreter of, 127; God as source of, 125; husband's skepticism of, 123, 124, 132, 217n1; models for experience of, 121, 125; mother's of danger to children, 121, 122, 124; supports Eldreth's challenge to husband, 26, 126, 217n1; treated as irrational, 124
Presley, Elvis, 162
Presnell family, 168, 188
Profitt family, 188
pronunciation. *See* singing, pronunciation in; speaking, proper
prostitution, 110, 112, 119, 185
protest, coded, 99, 100, 175, 213

proud, 208, 217n4
public work. *See* work, public
purification: of ethnographic relationship, 11; futility of attempts at social, 154

R

race: as issue in Eldreth's stories, 77, 88–89, 139; difference used to obfuscate class difference, 152; intertwined with class, 151, 154. *See also* blackface
racism: attributed to poor whites, 154; debate over extent of in mountain South, 153; denial of, 154–155; evidence of, 144
radio, 164, 167, 186
railroad: extended into Ashe County 1914, 36, 39; travel by, 34, 35
reciprocal ethnography, 19–20
recontextualization, 17, 20
recording(s): as source of Eldreth's repertoire, 186 (*see also* phonograph); commercial, 159, 164, 167; cylinder, 173; Eldreth's of own singing, 158, 185, 189; ethnographer's of Eldreth singing, 158, 182; of traditional mountain musicians, 159, 164; unselfconscious, 226n28. *See also* repertoire, Eldreth's desire to have recorded
regularize situation, 114
rehearsal: church choir, 194; divergence of performance from, 207; Jean Reid insists upon, 207; writing song texts as, 191, 207
Reid, Jean Woodring: anxiety about performing, 199; borrows Eldreth's songbooks, 188, 189; criticism of hillbilly stereotype, 205, 217n9; Eldreth brought to public attention through, 201; insists upon rehearsal, 207; involvement with folklorists, 201; nursing school, 201; performing with Eldreth, 201, 202, 217n9; preference for traditional repertoire, 167, 203; reveals Eldreth's involvement in bootlegging, 44, 184; singing career, 23, 201–202; source of information on Eldreth, 185. *See also* grandchildren, Eldreth's relationship with
renters: blame for injuries suffered by, 120; status of, 57, 120. *See also* landlord
renting: house, 36, 37, 57, 79, 120; land, 23, 35, 36, 39
repeatability: does not guarantee origin of narrative, 17; facilitates recording of narratives, 16
repertoire: accumulation of, 156, 171, 187 (*see also* learning songs); breadth, 203; challenges image of Appalachian isolation, 209; consists of historically traceable artifacts, 156; constantly maintained, 192; early acquisitions guide subsequent, 171; Eldreth's desire to have recorded, 17, 156, 158; hybrid, 172; influence of folklorists on

Eldreth's, 203; literacy crucial to maintenance of, 186; men's, 167–168, 227n31;
old, 171; preservation of quirky songs in,
168; reasons for inclusion of song in, 157,
167, 171–172; reflects beliefs and values,
157, 169, 173, 178, 198, 222n20; retention
of early pieces, 171; selection, 158, 169,
173; size, 156, 158, 186, 190; sources,
157–169, 222n20; stability, 211; women's,
167–168, 227n31
reported speech: better conceptualized as constructed dialogue, 70; depicts knowledge as
negotiated, 125; depicts self as authoritative knower, 125; evaluation through, 70;
in exempla, 103; in ghost stories, 105, 117;
functions of in narrative, 18, 70, 93, 103,
105, 125; maximizing distinction between
own and other's, 8; means of repeating
praise, 82; portrays agreement, 103; portrays negotiation of power, 117; recirculates
utterances from previous interactions, 4;
represents typical ways of speaking, 25, 96
representation, ethical dilemmas involved in,
3, 10
resistance: ethnographer's to subject's positioning of, 135–136, 155; everyday forms of,
114; mixed with complicity, 8; to being
told what to do, 148; to being presented as
example of Appalachian culture, 3, 20, 61,
204–205, 209, 210, 212; to class limitations, 3; to critique of exploitation, 43, 57;
to demonstration frame, 206; to gender
limitations, 3; to husband's domination, 68,
84, 112, 113, 126, 131–132, 176, 213; to
ethnographer's purposes, 16; to marriage,
72, 92; to nostalgia for past, 52, 61; to privileging husband in narrative, 32, 82,
214n3; to role as mother, 48, 138, 149, 151;
to role as wife, 31, 48, 92
resource(s), expressive: employed in self-construction, 2, 7–8; employment of all available, 136; ethnographer's interactions and
products become, 96; include discourses,
genres, ways of speaking, 4; incorporated
into dialogic utterances, 7–8; paradoxical
power of denigrated as, 154
respectability: anxiety over, 45; conferred by
behavior, 175; conferred by class, 57,
104–105, 152, 175. See also moral standing
responsiveness, book as form of, 21. See also
dialogism, utterance
revenant, 128. See also ghost
revenge, 129
Reynolds, Aunt Polly, 102–103, 218n2
Riddle, Almeda, 14, 222n20
rights, 83, 89
Robison, Carson, 165

Robison, Doctor, 74, 87, 93, 95, 211, 212
Rodgers, Jimmie, 146, 161, 162, 163, 164, 166,
171, 175, 203, 220n6, 222n19, 226n25
routines of victimization, 137. See also practical joking

S

sacred: boundary of with secular negotiable in
song repertoire, 197; childhood as, 172;
past as, 159 (see also nostalgia)
Sawin, Patricia: attention to Eldreth sparks
jealousy, 208; borrowing Eldreth's songbooks, 189; dissertation, 96; Eldreth's
impressions of, 59, 61–62, 214n6. See also
ethnographer, folklorists
Schoolcraft, Henry Rowe, 20
selection: as ethnographer's responsibility,
19–20; Eldreth's among available discourses, 211; Eldreth's of songs from available
sources, 158, 169; ethnographer's from
materials collected, 158
self: as performance, 4, 7–8, 17, 151; as product
of social interaction, 4; not remade from
scratch, 7–8; performed is only form others
can know, 17; reproduced through thought
and talk, 6; transformation of, 73. See also
self-construction, subjectivity
self-censorship, 84
self-construction: audience as resource, 4; book
contributes to Eldreth's, 21; change over
time, 71, 73, 211; complexity of, 3, 150,
211; consistency, 211; contradictory, 213;
dialogic, 1, 5, 18, 70, 93, 213; each chapter
explores one facet of Eldreth's, 24; emergent, 5; ethnographer's access to subject's,
4; impossibility of complete transformation
in, 134; in relation to prior interlocutors, 4;
interactive, 4; of those who do not explicitly resist hegemonic discourses, 8; ongoing,
97; racial, 150, 152; recursive, 1, 134; tension within, 180, 211; through conversational interaction, 2, 50; through positioning in discourse, 4, 6, 25, 114, 132, 211,
213; through narrative, 1, 93, 97; through
practical joking, 137; through singing, 179;
through use of expressive resources, 2, 4;
through work, 50; transformation in, 133;
variability, 211, 212; women's experience
promotes conflicted, 6
self-sufficiency: as moral trait, 37–38; as
Appalachian cultural trait, 52; born of
necessity, 52; rhetoric of, 37
settlement school workers, 159, 160
sexuality, women's, 86, 110, 113, 142–143
Shea, George Beverly, 196, 227n34
sharecropping, 40
sheet music, 164

sign language interpreter, 204

silence: about husband's abuse of wife, 94; correctly interpreted by women, 89, 90; ethnographer's, 135, 139; expresses modesty, 77–78, 89; husband's depicts his lack of concern, 25, 75–76, 83; husband's when proved wrong, 124; indicates disapproval, 89–90, 139; reflects powerlessness, 72, 90, 91, 94; speaker not first to break eternal, 6; suggests unspoken challenge, 115

singer: Eldreth's self-definition as, 156, 179, 195; Eldreth's role as constructed by women, 89, 200; interaction with song in performance, 173; traditional, 179

singing: appropriate for woman, 4, 26, 181, 200; as accompaniment to work, 26, 180–184, 210; as contribution to religious experience, 26, 197, 199, 210; as form of women's work, 4, 182–183, 210; associated with prostitution, 185; at home, 168, 179, 180–186, 210; centrality in Baptist worship, 193; expresses coded resistance, 175; for self, 168, 180; husband's intolerance for, 179, 185, 227n31; interruptible, 183; in church, 173, 179, 193–200, 210, 227n33; in public, 173, 179, 200–209, 210; pronunciation in, 166, 173; sacred as hedged performance, 193; secular morally suspect, 185, 210; sessions, 158; sociable rare with adults, 185, 188, 210; socially valuable, 156; solo, 194, 195, 203; stories about, 45, 78, 180–185; teaching to grandchildren, 185, 195, 199; to glorify God, 195, 199, 200; style (*see* singing style); with grandchildren, 185 (*see also* Reid, Jean Woodring)

singing style: Appalachian, 166; *bel canto*, 165; Eldreth's, 165–167, 173, 182–183, 195, 221n13; influence of folklorists on, 203–204; of church choir, 194–195; vibrato, 166; yodeling, 162

sister(s): Eldreth's relationship with, 22–23, 30, 35, 73–74, 76–77, 85, 141–143, 147, 208; experience with ghosts, 109–110; playing practical jokes on, 141–143, 147

slave: Eldreth called, 64, 151; ownership of associated with business diversification, 153; protagonist of song, 146

slavery: institution crucial to class-stratified society, 153; prevalence in mountain South, 40, 153

Smithsonian Festival of American Folklife. *See* Festival of American Folklife

song: associated with childhood, 171–172; Civil War, 146; composition (*see* song, homemade); homemade, 159, 176–178, 184, 223n24, 226n26; homiletic, 173; identification with character in, 175; inspiration for, 184; learning (*see* learning songs); lonesome, 170, 171, 174; lyric, 160, 170; modification of text, 174; obligation to share, 158; old, 169, 192, 209; sacred, 159, 160, 197, 223–225n24 (*see also* hymns, spirituals); sentimental, 160, 170, 172, 174, 220n7, 221n16; soldier, 170, 174; special, 227n33; talking back to, 176–178; texts, 17, 187; traditional, 157, 159, 172; valued for personal associations, 167, 171–172

song service, 193

songbooks, 186–192; as context for performance, 192; as reference, 189, 205; constantly recreated, 200; Eldreth's interest in Hattie Presnell's, 188; lending, 188, 189; little concern for physical preservation of, 189; means of preserving song texts, 189; modeled after hymnals, 188; opportunity for sociable interaction, 188; record memorized texts, 189; recopying and disposing of worn, 190; use of literacy skills to create, 26, 186

songs (in Eldreth's repertoire): "Amazing Grace," 160; "Banks of the Ohio," 160, 165, 171; "Barbara Allen," 159, 160; "Blind Child's Prayer," 170, 174; "Blue Christmas," 162, 171; "Blue Moon of Kentucky," 171; "Bonnie Blue Eyes," 160, 220n4; "Bury Me Beneath the Willow," 164; "Can I Sleep in Your Barn Tonight, Mister?" 171; "Dream of the Miner's Child," 171; "Drunkard's Prayer," 171, 173; "Dust on the Bible," 172, 199; "The Eastbound Train," 160, 170, 171; "East Virginia Blues," 160, 164; "The Fair Maiden," 207; "Floyd Collins," 161–162, 163, 171, 221n11; "Handsome Molly," 160, 165; "He Touched Me," 166, 182, 196; "I Won't Have to Worry Any More," 222n21; "If We Never Meet Again This Side of Heaven," 172; "If You Love Your Mother, Meet Her in the Skies,"172; "I'm Just Here to Get My Baby out of Jail," 171, 182, 183; "I'm Sitting on Top of the World," 146, 176; "I'm So Lonesome I Could Cry," 170; "In the Pines," 160, 164, 220n5; "I've Got a Home in Glory Land," 222n21; "Jealous in the Bible," 199; "John Henry," 153, 160; "Just Another Broken Heart," 163; "Just Break This News to Mother," 164, 170; "Keep on the Sunny Side of Life," 222n19; "Knoxville Girl," 160, 165, 171, 203, 221n16; "The Last Letter," 170; "The Lawson Family Murder," 160; "Letter Edged in Black," 164, 170, 221n16; "Little Birdie," 164, 176; "The

Little Girl and the Dreadful Snake," 163; "Little Girl's Prayer," 173, 175, 207; "Little Maggie," 160, 164, 167, 170, 182, 203; "Little Orphan Girl," 161, 170, 173; "Little Rosewood Casket," 160, 161, 220n7, 221n16; "Live and Let Live," 170, 171; "London City"/"Butcher Boy," 160, 165, 189; "Lonely Mound of Clay," 170; "Long Black Veil," 171, 189, 203; "Making Believe," 176, 177; "Mansions Over the Hilltop," 172, 222n21; "The Maple on the Hill," 28, 43, 172; "Mary, Mary, What You Gonna Call That Baby?" 146, 160, 163; "Mississippi River Blues," 162; "Mother's Not Dead She's Only A-Sleeping," 170; "My Lord, What a Morning," 146, 160; "My Mother Was a Lady," 164, 175, 182, 183, 220n6, 226n25; "My Name Is Written There," 222n21; "Neoma Wise," 160, 165, 170, 203; "No Hiding Place Down Here," 146; "No More the Moon Shines on Lorena," 146; "No, Not a Word From Home Any More," 170; "Old Cotton Fields Back Home," 146; "The Old Crossroad," 196, 227n32; "Our Home Is So Lonesome Tonight," 176, 226n26; "The Pale Horse and His Rider," 196; "Peach Picking Time in Georgia," 162, 222n19; "Philadelphia Lawyer," 164, 170, 203, 222n18; "The Picture from Life's Other Side," 173; "Pins and Needles in My Heart," 170; "Poor Wayfaring Stranger," 160, 197, 221n16; "Precious Jewel," 170; "Pretty Polly," 160, 165, 203; "Pretty Polly"/"Wagoner Boy," 160, 164, 171, 222n19; "Put My Little Shoes Away," 170; "Rank Stranger," 172; "Red River Valley," 161; "The Red, White, and Blue," 163, 171; "Rock of Ages," 160; "Sailor on the Deep Blue Sea," 164; "Satisfied Mind," 173; "Searching for a Soldier's Grave," 171; "Short Life of Trouble," 164; "Silver Haired Daddy," 170, 171, 174, 197; "Singing Waterfalls," 163, 170, 171; "Single Girl/Married Girl," 164; "Six O'Clock," 28, 45–46; "Snoops the Lawyer," 162, 164, 203, 205, 220n10; "The Soldier's Last Letter," 171; "The Soldier's Sweetheart," 171; "Someday I'm Going to Heaven," 174, 223–224n24; "Someone's Last Day," 174, 176, 184, 203, 223–224n24; "Springtime in Alaska," 171; "The Storms Are on the Ocean," 160; "Supper Time," 172; "Sweet Fern," 164, 171; "Sweeter Than the Flowers," 227n32; "T for Texas," 162, 182; "TB Blues," 162, 171; "Teardrops Falling in the Snow," 171;

"Tennessee Waltz," 170; "That Glad Reunion Day," 172; "There Are Times When I am Lonesome," 174, 223–225n24; "There's a Light," 218–219n5; "There's No Depression in Heaven," 162; "There's No Hiding Place Down Here," 160; "They're All Going Home But Me," 171; "This World Can't Stand Long," 146; "Those Wedding Bells Will Never Ring for Me," 176; "Ticklish Reuben," 162, 203, 205, 220n10; "Treasures Untold," 170, 222n17; "Victory in Jesus," 222n21; "Voice from the Tombs," 163, 206, 227n32; "Wait a Little Longer, Please, Jesus," 170; "Were You There When They Crucified My Lord," 146, 160; "What Am I Living For?" 205; "When I Have Gone the Last Mile of the Way," 222n21; "Where Is My Wandering Boy Tonight?" 170; "Where Parting Comes No More," 172; "Where the Soul Never Dies," 222n21; "Where We'll Never Grow Old," 222n21; "White Dove," 170; "Wild Bill Jones," 160, 165, 170, 171; "Wildwood Flower," 162, 170; "Will You Miss Me When I'm Gone?" 77–78, 160, 162; "Wreck on the Highway," 173

son(s), Eldreth's relationship with, 90, 94–95. *See also* children, Eldreth's relationship with

sorry (inept), 136

Southern Folklife Collection (University of North Carolina, Chapel Hill), 219n1 (chap. 7), 220–221n10

speaking: as practical consciousness, 50; back to husband, 80, 122–123, 175; back to song text, 176–178, 183; demonstrates ineptitude, 82–83, 87; empowerment in, 69; pragmatics of, 69; proper, 37, 166, 173; self-construction through, 50. *See also* dialogism, discourse, ways of speaking

speech, authoritative, 8. *See also* evaluation

speech, reported. *See* reported speech

speech act, 69, 96

speech behaviors. *See* ways of speaking

speech community, 71

speech roles. *See* ways of speaking

spirit possession, women's, 125

Spiritual Heirs, 166, 194

Spiritualism, American, 125

spirituals, 160

Spitzer, Katie, 101, 218n2

Stevens, Stella, 24, 202

stories: Aunt Polly Reynolds, 102–103, 218n2; babies drowned in well, 109–110; baby cases, 74–75; bad girls, 109–110, 218n2; bear skin in bed, 141–142; biscuit, 79–80,

85; Bob Barr house, 106–107, 218n2; brakes fail, 122; bringing Ed water to wash in, 84; building pigpen, 54; building porch for mother, 54; burrs under oxen's tails, 139–140; cat in molasses, 139; chickens cross legs to be tied, 35; children in blackface hidden under bed scare boy, 145, 147; churning butter, 33; cutting timber with Clyde, 55–56; decision not to remarry, 92; decision to marry, 72; dish pan, 63–64; Doctor Graham house, 106, 218n2; dye plant, 34, 47; drowning child, 76–77, 89; earth tremor, 122; Eldreth delivers baby, doctor accepts fee, 95; false teeth in cup of coffee, 138; father advocates telling the truth, 33; first married, 107–108, 218n2; first song, 45; flood, 122–123, 218n2; flu epidemic, children die in, 121; flu epidemic, protection from, 46; funeral, 77–78, 89, 200; giving Ex-Lax instead of candy, 144; Grandma Milam gives spoiled bee bread to colored girls, 138–139; grandmother's "Only lazy people sit down to churn," 33; helping father make whiskey, 44; helping father skin groundhog, 30; helping neighbors, 32; hiding love letters, 141; hoeing corn as child, 33; hoeing corn for stingy brother-in-law, 95; husband urges her to sell house, 79; Joe Cox's funeral, 77–78, 89, 200; Joe got Dad in the bees' nest, 138–139; learning songs from grandmother, 33; left alone as child, 30; light in the bedroom, 126–127, 131; little slave, 64; looking for land to build house, 78–79, 89; marrying Ed, 72; Mary Black killed her twins, 106; mean horse, 75–76; mother's "You're different," 30; mother whips snake off Eldreth's legs, 46; moving to Pennsylvania, 34; neighbor, "You work just like a man," 54; pinch, 122, 218n2; pointing hand, 102, 218n2; premonition of children's death, 121; prunes, 140; raising own food, 32; repairing house, 54; scaring neighbors with blackface, 144–145; sound of baby walking, 106; sound of door slamming open, 107–108; sound of knife on clothesline, 107–108; stealing Ed from Clyde, 73–74, 143; suitcase full of ham biscuits, 35, 41; three little pigs (told by Cratis Williams), 206; throwing steel trap under bed, 141; trading shoes for pig, 54; train conductor's "The mother of seven children," 34, 47; uncle bitten by rattlesnake, 46; watching over older sisters as child, 30
story. *See* narrative
structuralism, 5
structure. *See* narrative, structure of

structure of feeling, 169, 171, 172, 178, 209
subject formation. *See* self-construction
subjectivity: as product of performance, 4–5; constructed through discourse, 18; contrasted with humanistic concept of essential identity, 5; dialogic construction of, 7; gendered, 6, 8; investment in subject positions and, 6; neither consistent nor static, 6; non-unitary, 5–6, 112, 133, 137; produced reciprocally with culture, 5; understanding of through ethnographic analysis, 17. *See also* self, self-construction
suffering, conspicuous, 174
suicide, 104
supernatural: challenge to conventional gender roles, 117, 122; encounters with, 98, 100; experience of coincides with marriage, 110, 111, 115; experience with empowers Eldreth to challenge husband, 122–123; husband punishes Eldreth through, 128; knowledge offered by, 132; reflects imbalance in human relationships, 124. *See also* ghosts, haunting
suspense, 102, 105, 121

T

Tabernacle Baptist Church, 193 *See also* singing, in church
taboo subjects, 87
talent as God-given, 158, 180–181, 200
talk. *See* speaking
teaching, joint performance with granddaughter represents, 204. *See also* song, teaching to grandchildren
television, 174, 183
temporal grounding of ghost stories, 100
temporal ordering: in exempla, 102; in ghost stories, 105; in stories of premonitions, 121
testimony, 197, 207, 213
text(s): Eldreth's collections of written song, 186–192; do not preexist discursive encounter, 13; documented separately from typical contexts, 17, 156; modification of song, 174; retain traces of previous contexts, 214n1
timber cutting, 22, 35, 51, 55, 59, 63–64
Tin Pan Alley, 43. *See also* song, sentimental
trivialization, 131, 133
truthfulness: advocated by father, 33; as moral trait, 42, 215n4

U

Uncle, Eldreth's relationship with, 37, 43, 163, 221n11
utterance: anticipates response, 7; as rejoinder in dialogue, 4–7; completed by responsive understanding, 7; language enters life

through, 5; multiaccentuality of, 7; pragmatic communicative capacity of, 7; primacy over system of language, 6

V

vibrato, 166, 196
video about Eldreth, 215n8
virtue. See moral standing

W

warning: danger of pregnancy to unmarried woman, 113, 119; supernatural experience as, 100. See also premonition
Watson, Doc, 24, 168
ways of speaking: Appalachian, 206, 215n1 (chap. 3); changes in, 80; class difference in, 88; generational difference in, 71, 91; indicate respect, 94; local, 49, 53; men's, 71, 81, 83, 84, 90; represented in reported speech, 96; resource for self-construction, 4, 215n1 (chap. 3); taking on new, 70, 73, 217n3; women's, 71, 85, 86, 88, 217n3
wealth: of public audiences, 24, 59, 61, 62; of family and neighbors, 37, 53, 95; grandparents commended for sharing, 105
Weavers (folk singers), 146
"What's up? Not much" pair, 49
whiskey. See bootlegging
white privilege, 143, 213. See also race
white trash as racial category, 152
widow, 226n27; Eldreth as, 31, 129; freedom of, 68, 129, 202–203
wife, Eldreth's role as, 2, 28, 30, 31
Williams, Cratis, 201, 203, 206, 211, 228n38
Wills, Bob, 146
women, unruly, 113, 132
women's roles: challenge to supported by super-

natural agents, 117; conflicting discourses on, 132; double standard in, 218n4; Eldreth's investment in conventional, 133, 147, 150; literacy, 187; practical joking as acceptable, 141; preparing dead for burial, 146; resistance to in practical joking, 138, 144, 149–151, 154; stresses of, 134; violation of in ghost stories, 111, 112. See also work, women's
work: agricultural, 22, 36; combining agricultural and wage, 22–23, 41, 47; constitutes relationships, 50; Eldreth's desire to communicate extent of her, 25; ethnographer's, 61–62, 66–67; excessive, 51, 65; gender appropriateness of, 55, 58; husband's minimal, 65; industrial, 23, 48; in fields for pay, 23, 51, 59, 95, 104; men's, 54, 58–59; morality associated with, 25, 42, 48, 50, 51, 56, 57, 60, 62, 66, 181; of African Americans, 39, 152–154; practical joking as respite from, 140; public, 35, 59; rewards of, 81; shame attendant on woman accepting public, 59–60; singing as (see singing, as form of women's work); singing compatible with (see singing, as accompaniment to work); wage, 36, 37; with horses, 55–56; women's, 51, 53, 149, 181, 184. See also housework
World Music Institute (New York, NY), 204, 207
writing: as form of rehearsal for singing, 191–192; as leisure activity, 187. See also composition; literacy; love letters; songs, homemade

Y

yodeling, 162